Radical Ecopsychology

SUNY Series in Radical Social and Political Theory
Roger S. Gottlieb, editor

Radical Ecopsychology

Psychology in the Service of Life

Andy Fisher

foreword by David Abram

State University of New York Press

Cover illustration, *Moon Howl,* compotina print by Martina Field
Courtesy of Martina Field

Published by
State University of New York Press, Albany

© 2002 State University of New York

For information, address State University of New York Press,
90 State Street, Suite 700, Albany, NY 12207

Production by Dana Foote
Marketing by Michael Campochiaro

Library of Congress Cataloging-in-Publication Data

Fisher, Andy, 1963–
Radical ecopsychology : psychology in the service of life / Andy Fisher ;
foreword by David Abram.
p. cm.—(SUNY series in radical social and political theory)
Includes bibliographical references and index.
ISBN 0-7914-5303-0 (alk. paper)—ISBN 0-7914-5304-9 (pbk. : alk. paper)
1. Environmental psychology. 2. Nature—Psychological aspects.
3. Environmentalism—Psychological aspects. I. Title. II. Series.

BF353.5.N37 F57 2002
155.9′1—dc21
2001059888

10 9 8 7 6 5 4 3 2 1

For the long haul

CONTENTS

FOREWORD

Ever since the Enlightenment, technological civilization has assumed a clear divide between the presumably "exterior" world of material nature and the presumably "interior" world of the mind and emotions. In Europe and North America we have lived with this division for several long centuries, and it has taken a tremendous toll—on ourselves, on our relationships, and on the animate earth around us. Nevertheless, the bifurcation persists: today, for instance, the science of *ecology* studies the external realm of earthly interactions, while *psychology* ponders and ministers to the internal realm of our mental life.

As its name implies, *ecopsychology* (or ecological psychology) neatly explodes this age-old divide between mind and matter, between the psyche "in here" and nature "out there." Ecopsychology suggests that the psyche cannot really be understood as a distinct dimension isolated from the sensuous world that materially enfolds us, and indeed that earthly nature can no longer be genuinely understood as a conglomeration of objects and objective processes independent of subjectivity and sentience.

The book you now hold is the most important work yet written on ecopsychology from a clinical perspective. As a practicing psychotherapist, Andy Fisher is well aquainted with the manifold stresses and sadnesses that beset contemporary persons, and he has come to believe that a genuine comprehension and amelioration of these ills cannot proceed without a radical metamorphosis in our understanding of the psyche, and a new recognition of the psyche's entanglement with the more-than-human natural world.

Dr. Fisher has read widely and deeply, and he gathers insights from a rich diversity of sources, greatly expanding our awareness of the manifold springs from which ecopsychology can drink and draw sustenance. Yet he tests the reflections of others against his own experience, synthesizing the disparate strands into a uniquely coherent and compassionate vision. His voice is at once poetic and precise, and thus implicitly opens the way for a style of speech unencumbered by obsolete distinctions between subjective and objective modes of discourse.

Among the divergent springs that feed these pages, the most consistent philosophical source is that of *phenomenology*—the study of direct experience. Developed in the first half of the twentieth century, phenomenology sought to ground its investigations neither in an ostensibly rock-solid external world, nor in the pure and precise ideas of an interior self, but rather in *experience*—in the ongoing, lived encounter between oneself and the world. As a result of phenomenology's careful attention to direct experience, and its attunement to the deeply *embodied* nature of such experience, the practice of phenomenology gave birth to existentialism, and to the various streams of existential psychology that grew out of this movement. Gradually, as they pursued their investigations, the more brilliant phenomenologists began to discern that the earth, and the elemental powers of nature, exert a much more profound influence on our human experience than is commonly assumed within the modern era.

Yet in the latter half of the twentieth century this philosophy of experience was eclipsed by a new fascination with language, texts, and the social construction of knowledge. The intellectual discoveries spurred by this new attention to the determinative power of language and of societal structures are many, and they have helped to destabilize, and fluidify, our very modern belief in the unshakable solidity of objective, "external" reality. Yet they have also perpetuated a kind of human arrogance already endemic to the modern era, by implying that human language, and the dynamics of human society, are the real powers that structure the world we experience. It is true, of course, that our particular cultures and languages greatly influence our experience. But it is increasingly evident that our societies and even our languages have themselves been profoundly informed (and dynamically structured) by the diverse terrains, climatic cycles, and biological rhythms of the animate earth—by this more-than-human world with its thunderstorms and forests, its ravens and malarial mosquitos, its deserts and tumbling rivers and bison-stomped prairies.

In recent years the science of ecology has disclosed the radical interdependence of the manifold organisms that populate, and constitute, this earthly world—including, of course, the *human* organism. The new awareness of our coevolved embeddedness within the terrestrial web of life inevitably raises the question of whether the human intellect can really spring itself free from our carnal embedment in order to attain to a genuinely objective, or spectatorlike, understanding of nature—or whether, in truth, all our thoughts and our theories are secretly dependent on, and constrained by, our immersion in this earthly world, with its specific gravity and atmosphere, its particular landscapes, its myriad plants and animals, so many of whom are now threatened with extinction.

The latter intuition is that which motivates the emerging field of ecopsychology. Yet if ecopsychology is to pursue this intuition, it is in need of a much more humble way of speaking than that which prevails in the conventional sciences—a new style of speech and of thought that honors the dependence not only of our bodies *but our minds* on the more-than-human natural world. Such, in fact, is the poetic language that was gradually being developed by various phenomenologists at midcentury—and so it is only natural that the new field of ecopsychology would begin to rescusitate and carry forward the rich work done by some of those thinkers. Indeed, Andy Fisher makes careful use of such phenomenologists as Martin Heidegger, J. H. Van Den Berg, and especially the brilliant French phenomenologist Maurice Merleau-Ponty, as well as a number of their more recent followers.

Fisher has also learned from hermeneutics, from psychoanalysis and Gestalt psychotherapy, and from some of our best wilderness writers, as well as from the unique and prescient reflections of Paul Shepard—the maverick "human ecologist" whose audacious writings, so little known, have nevertheless influenced so many environmental theorists. Yet Fisher brings to these various thinkers a keen social and political awareness rarely present among those who write on behalf of the natural world. His own turn toward the animate earth is not at all a turn away from the social and economic relations that so influence our psychological life; rather, his work suggests that our widespread social injustices can no longer be understood without taking into account the unnecessary violence inflicted on the rest of nature by a society impervious to all that stands in the way of "progress." Fisher implies that the many-voiced earth is the ultimate context of our social as well as our pychological experience. His *Radical Ecopsychology* calls us toward active engagement in a transformation of society no less profound than the transformation of personal life that he invokes, and makes clear that these two projects cannot genuinely be separated.

Both political and deeply personal, stirring us both ethically and aesthetically, Andy Fisher's vision enlivens the young field of ecopsychology. With any luck, his book will infect the wider (and all-too-complacent) discipline of psychology, inducing more than a few therapists to throw open the windows of their consulting room, letting a wild wind rush in to jostle their papers and to join in the conversation.

—David Abram

PREFACE

This book is both an introduction to ecopsychology and an attempt to encourage the field to become more comprehensive and critical. Ecopsychologists argue that genuine sanity is grounded in the reality of the natural world; that the ecological crisis signifies a pathological break from this reality; and that the route out of our crisis must therefore involve, among other things, a psychological reconciliation with the living earth. This, to be sure, is a compelling starting point. What ecopsychology has yet to do, however, is organize itself as a coherent project, its efforts to date remaining largely unconnected to one another. It has, furthermore, yet to demonstrate an adequate grasp of the intellectually complex and politically charged territory that ecopsychologists have entered into. The main goals of this book are accordingly twofold. I aim, first of all, to map out the field of ecopsychology in a way that shows how its various elements hang together as a radical whole. By this exercise I hope both to make the field more intelligible and to provide a means for ecopsychologists to better locate and coordinate their activities. My second aim is to offer one version of what a comprehensive and radical ecopsychology might look like. I do this by methodically building my own nature-centered psychology and by indicating how it can be used as a strong foundation for both ecopsychological practice and critical social theorizing. Above all, I want this book to appeal to a wide range of people—to other ecopsychologists, to students, psychologists, ecologists, environmental educators, philosophers, critical theorists, activists, and general readers—who may find it of relevance in naming and advancing their own pressing concerns.

For all my desire to complexify the field of ecopsychology, I also want to present its basic message in simple, human terms. What motivates me as an ecopsychologist is simply a concern for life. I became an ecological thinker because of my disquiet over the violation of nonhuman life, because of the tearing in my heart over the wasting of the earth. I later became a psychotherapist for a similar reason, as a response to the routine violation or wasting of human life. Daily existence within our economized and technologized reality has been described by some as a process of low-grade, chronic traumatization. The field of psychotherapy is itself undergoing something of a paradigm shift now that the role of abuse and trauma in the generation of "mental disorder" is increasingly being recognized. I have nonetheless wondered at the absurdity of lining up the wounded at the psychotherapist's office, and of researching the minutiae of the therapeutic process, while the everyday social forces that violate our nature, and guarantee a steady supply of crippled souls, go for the most part unquestioned—and while these same general forces continue to go about their business of tearing down the biosphere. In a critical sense, then, ecopsychology is for me an effort to understand the social links between these two areas of violence, between the violation we recognize as the ecological crisis and the violation we recognize in human suffering. The more popular or familiar sense of ecopsychology, by contrast, is what I call its therapeutic and recollective sense. Here ecopsychology is an effort at recovery, at recalling just how—in psychological terms—we humans are part of the big life process. Its vision is that of humans healing and flourishing in concert with the healing and flourishing of the larger natural world, in one great celebration of life. I argue that ecopsychology needs *both* of these aspects. An ecopsychology with both critical and therapeutic-recollective moments, in other words, will truly be a psychology in the service of life.

To be radical means to go to the roots. I chose the title *Radical Ecopsychology* because ecopsychology is a radical undertaking in both of the two senses just mentioned. Critically, it takes us to the root cultural, social, and historical arrangements that authorize, legitimate, or give rise to the simultaneous injury of human and nonhuman nature. While therapeutically and recollectively, ecopsychology takes us to the roots of who we are as human beings in a more-than-human world. If ecopsychology is an inherently radical project, as I am claiming here, then my title is of course redundant. The title does, however, play the strategic role of emphasizing that as ecopsychologists we need to catch up with the full radicalness of our own field. A more self-consciously radical ecopsychology would also be in a better position to make a deliberate place for itself. It is a radical fact that we are limited in our ability to study the psychology of the human-nature relationship because this relationship is so attenuated within modern society. Indeed, the phrase "human-nature relationship" designates a kind of forgotten land, a zone of reality that is relatively hidden for most modern people. We also lack ready intellectual environments for articulating this reality. The human or social sciences (such as psychology) depict a world largely devoid of nature, while the natural sciences (such as ecology) depict a world largely devoid of humans. Where, then, does a field that unabashedly straddles the dreaded human/nature divide (such as ecopsychology) fit in? How might it find its conceptual legs? My own answer is that as ecopsychologists we need to discover a voice that is true to our territory; must invent or dream up our own terms so that we can then argue our positions on them. For it is only with new intellectual frameworks and new kinds of practice that we will get a handle on our own unique sphere of conceptual and political struggle. By "radical," then, I do not mean extremism and heavy-handed moralizing, but only a certain insistence that we get to the bottom of things, and that we remake our world as we do so.

I ultimately conceive of ecopsychology as a psychologically based ecological politics. I call my own psychological approach "naturalistic" because it takes seriously that we too are nature. It asserts that we belong to the natural order, and so that we are claimed by it, are limited by it, and feel its demands within our bodily experience. I also call my approach "experiential" because it uses felt experience as its touchstone, and focuses on the natural ordering of our experience. Indeed, I think of ecopsychology as a field in which the human and the natural are joined in experience. The advantage of such a naturalistic and experiential approach is that it can speak relatively directly to how each of us experiences the ecological crisis, how we carry the pervasive mistreatment of nature (both human and nonhuman) in our bodies. In this way it can then also help identify the life-denying aspects of our society (as we experience them) and awaken our genuine hungers for a more life-centered world. It thus gives us a more qualitative way to go at the social challenges of our times. Consider, in this regard, Tom Athanasiou's remark: "To win, greens, workers movements, and human-rights activists must go global, just as the corporations have done."[1] This is a good point. Yet the thought of having to "go global" puts my body into spasms. I do not say that we should therefore neglect global issues, but only that it is important to pay attention to body spasms. My conviction, in other words, is that our attempts to come to grips with the ecological crisis will only benefit if we incorporate into them a good, embodied understanding of what kind of creature we are, what our own nature is like. For a different starting point I therefore turn to Audre Lorde's statement that "poetry is not a luxury"—I seek an approach in which critical analysis is allowed to coexist with talk of deer tracks, sunshine on tree trunks, and heartfelt hugs. I have chosen to approach the social question in my own naturalistic and experiential way.

I need to admit, finally, that this book is itself not radical enough. Given the usual constraints of time and energy, I was not able to follow the implications of my own ideas to the radical lengths they would ultimately have me go. Although I talk in these pages about what ecopsychology is and how it might go, I am thus aware of having done so from my own limited perspective and social location. Despite inevitable limitation, what I hope to have made clear is that the project of ecopsychology is the main thing. It is still early times for this project. Indeed, much of my own labor has so far gone into just getting my approach right. Let this book stand, then, as a kind of preface in itself.

Outline of the Book

The book is divided into two parts, with part one laying the ground for part two. In part one, "Groundwork," I introduce the reader to the terrain of ecopsychology; reflect on the overall ecopsychological project; and situate my own work within this larger project. The two chapters that comprise this part of the book are the most heavy-going and academic in tone. The reader who is put off by such weightiness, or who prefers to go straight to the main event, may therefore wish to either skip or skim them. I do, however, encourage such readers to consider circling around to pick these chapters up after having reached the end.

Chapter one, "Approaching the Field of Ecopsychology," begins with a brief discussion of currently used definitions of ecopsychology, as well as some of its historical antecedents. The bulk of the chapter consists of a discussion of the four main tasks that in my view comprise the essential work of ecopsychology. I call these the psychological task, the philosophical task, the practical task, and the critical task. The best way to define the project of ecopsychology, I suggest, is to trace the interrelationships among these four historical tasks. Given that all of these tasks rely on each other, I argue that they ought to be pursued more or less in unison, whether through a coordination of separate efforts or through an inclusion of all of them within individual undertakings. For the purposes of demonstrating the interdependencies among the four tasks, I have opted in this book for the latter strategy. I address the psychological task by proposing a "naturalistic" psychology—one that aims to link the claims and limits of human nature to the claims and limits of the larger natural world. I address the philosophical task by adopting an approach to theory-building that is grounded in the experiential or phenomenological traditions in both philosophy and psychology. I address the practical task by providing an experiential framework for undertaking a wide range of practices that go counter to the life-negating tendencies of our society. I address the critical task, finally, by locating my project within what I regard as the deeper and more critical currents within both psychology and ecology, and by demonstrating how a naturalistic and experiential psychology may be used as a basis for developing a critical theory of modern society.

In chapter two, "The Problem with Normal," I reflect on what kind of discourse the terrain of ecopsychology is calling for, that is, on what sort of method is most adequate for approaching the subject matter of ecopsychology. The problem with normal, mainstream psychology—including "environmental psychology"—is that it is committed exactly to those philosophical dualities (inner/outer, human/nature, subjective/objective) that ecopsychology must overcome. For my own project I therefore adopt an interpretive or "hermeneutical" method—one that can work in the difficult space *between* the "human" and the "natural," and that can disclose aspects of the human-nature relationship that normal science simply cannot. Because I wish to set up ecopsychology as a project that raises radical doubts about the course of modern society, I also adopt a rhetorical method. As an art, rhetoric has historically employed language as a symbolic means to create specific experiential effects in the psyche or soul, so as to inform, please, and move the listener. As James Hillman has suggested, this makes a rhetorical approach particularly appropriate for psychological discourse. For a radical project such as ecopsychology, moreover, I suggest that an openly rhetorical approach is imperative. The hermeneutic and rhetorical traditions both recognize the primarily symbolic or metaphorical nature of reality and make room for discussion that can both touch us where we live and advance viewpoints that go counter to the social and cultural status quo. An interpretive and rhetorical discourse, in short, can speak to the felt reality of our alienated relationship with the life process and then say something critical that might help move our society forward from that estranged starting place.

In part two, "Nature and Experience," my goal is primarily to demonstrate the feasibility of the project—to show that the leap from a human- to a nature-centered psychology may draw strength from much that is already agreed on or familiar within psychological and ecological thought, and that many practical and critical implications can immediately be drawn. I call this part of the book "Nature and Experience" because these are my two central terms. *Nature* refers to ecology, *experience* to psychology. We discover the claims of nature precisely by interpreting our bodily felt experience of them. I thus argue that if we are to better understand our own nature, as well as our place within the larger natural order, it is crucial that we work experientially. Learning to do so, moreover, has the character of a therapeutic and historical task, in that those of us living within the repressing structures of the modern world tend to lose touch with our own bodily experience. As a consequence, we become limited in our ability to take guidance from our own feeling process and vulnerable to ideological manipulation of all sorts. It is for this reason that I conceive of ecopsychology as a kind of naturalistic and experiential politics that struggles against the nature-dominating and reifying aspects of this society as it correspondingly works to relocate the human psyche within the wider natural world.

In the tradition of the existentialists, I suggest in chapter three, "Beginning With Experience," that we need to ground ecopsychological inquiry in lived experience. The aim of the chapter is thus to provide some introductory concepts, descriptions, and exercises that will get the reader on speaking terms about "experience." More specifically, I want the reader to appreciate that our experiencing is always an organismic or bodily phenomenon, and that it is also always an interacting with an environment. Once this basic appreciation is gained, it is a short step into ecopsychology. I additionally introduce the key notion of the "life process." Both epidemic human psychopathology and the ecological crisis can, I suggest, be fruitfully understood in terms of a general violation of the life process under capitalist social relations. This understanding makes for a helpful critical strategy for linking psyche and ecology. It also offers a way to conceptually unify our psychological and ecological crises under the umbrella of our nihilistic cultural condition, wherein the violation of life is tied to a frustrating absence of meaning or widespread impoverishment of our experience.

Chapter four, "From Humanistic to Naturalistic Psychology," is a bridge between chapter three, which still draws primarily on "humanistic" sources, and chapter five, which proposes a specifically "naturalistic" approach. The bridge itself is an inquiry into nature and human nature, wherein I describe what I mean by these hugely contested terms. Although this seems a foolish exercise, it is nonetheless a necessary one, for the plain reason that so much rides on our understanding of nature, including how (and if) we understand ourselves as spiritual beings. I discuss a number of conceptualizations of nature within three general categories: the natural world; the essential quality, way, order, or character of a being; and the life force (desire, spirit, etc.). While it is right to allow for a plurality of interpretations within these categories, I also believe that it is fair to argue for *better* interpretations—one's arrived at through a deepening and broadening of one's experience. It is only by undertaking hermeneutical inquiries into the meaning of nature (even if such inquiries have no final endpoint) that we may make persuasive arguments for just what is being violated and what needs to be recovered. Showing my realist colors, I assert that the place of humans in the natural order is not some insoluble puzzle, but is to be found in the given order of our own bodily, world-bound nature; and that the demands of nature, inside and out, can therefore simply not be intellectualized, marketplaced, or bulldozed away.

Chapter five, "Naturalistic Psychology: A Sketch," is my outline of a kind of psychology that would serve the life process or hold out the human-nature relationship as an ultimate concern. Naturalistic psychology advocates fidelity to nature, being in the service of nature, and seeing humans as part of a larger natural order. I want to develop a psychology that reinterprets our current situation in ever-more primordial terms, even as it acknowledges the historical and culturally mediated nature of human reality. At the core of this psychology are three hermeneutical (or "sense-making") principles that I suggest will be helpful, at this early stage of inquiry, for getting our bearings. The first holds that we are ordered by nature to participate ever-more widely in the world; the second that our language is always a "singing" of this world; and the third that all phenomena intertwine or mirror one another as a common "flesh." I finish this chapter by illustrating these principles through an examination of the human life cycle in the context of a more-than-human world. I discuss the infantile need for loving, responsive human relations and for exploratory contact with wild nature; the childhood need for playful immersion in the natural world; and the adolescent need for rites of passage into a sacred adult cosmos, wherein the natural world is understood not as a fallen realm to be transcended but as the everyday ground of our limited and mysterious human existence. Attending to the human life cycle is a key concern of my approach.

In my sixth and concluding chapter, "Making Sense of Suffering in a Technological World," I emphasize the need to create a psychology that is not just for those who like the outdoors (or whatever), but which can be used as a basis for social criticism. This chapter is thus my most concentrated attempt to tie my psychological efforts into a critical framework. Given my own approach, I take the ideology of technological and economic progress as the theme of my criticism. My arguments turn on the conviction that humans will never find happiness through the "progressive" immiseration of the rest of the natural world. In truth, our economic and technological system has made a perverse necessity of suffering. A society that is organized primarily to serve the expansion of capital—rather than to serve life—must increasingly exploit both humans and the natural world, and so generate a state of psychospiritual ruin and ecological crisis. While I am not out to tell anyone precisely what to do, I am thus at least certain that the practice of ecopsychology needs to be a countering of this system. I suggest in this chapter that the most crucial element of such "counterpractice" is that it give authority to our (naturally organized) experience, all the more so as we learn to listen to and focus it. Experiential politics is not about violent revolution or abstract master plans, but about taking life-forwarding steps that emerge from making honest contact with presently felt reality. Such politics may, then, help people to live ecologically radical lives in whatever ways make sense from within the context of their own life experience and interests. I see two main requirements for ecopsychological practice: that it offer support for resisting or opposing the life-denying tendencies within modern society and for building an ecological society instead; and that it revive those essentially human forms of practice, largely forgotten, that involve meaningful and reciprocal engagement with the natural world. I finish the chapter with a reply to Freud, arguing that the "fateful question" for our time is not whether the instinct for life can win out over the instinct for death, but whether or not we will choose to find collective ways to bear our pain and suffering, to strengthen ourselves, so that we can then stop negating life and instead get back to it.

ACKNOWLEDGMENTS

I am pleased to make my grateful bows to some of those who have helped me along the way.

This book started out as a doctoral dissertation at York University, Toronto. For financial support throughout my student years, I am thankful to the taxpayers of Canada and to the Social Sciences and Humanities Research Council of Canada. Thank you, next, to Mora Campbell, for encouraging me to write what was in me and for being so available, collegial, and warmhearted in all your advising. To the rest of my committee members, who came and went over the years, I also give thanks: Peter Timmerman, Stephen Levine, Reg Lang, Neil Evernden, Jay Tropianskaia, Ray Rogers, and Leesa Fawcett. I want to thank Stephen and Jay, in particular, for numerous fruitful disagreements and insightful suggestions. I also wish to thank two other figures who played an important role in my university education: Sam Mallin, whose kind philosophical mentorship during my early years as a graduate student helped me to understand so much; and John Livingston, whose impassioned rhetoric still rings in my ears. To Anita McBride and the Student Programs Office staff, I am most thankful for a smooth and friendly trip through my years at the Faculty of Environmental Studies.

I have benefited, beyond words, from many other skillful teachers. From the Gestalt Institute of Toronto, a place of a different sort of learning, I give my big thanks to JoAnne Greenham, Jay Tropianskaia (again), and to all the members of my training group. From the Center for Focusing in Toronto, I am grateful to Mary Armstrong, Jan Winhall, and my fellow trainers for all that cleared space. For her lessons in radical humanism, I am forever indebted to my first teacher of Re-evaluation Counseling, Shirley Russ. I am deeply grateful to my Dhamma teacher, S. N. Goenka, for bringing Vipassana meditation and the Buddha's teachings to a place where I could then get on the path myself. For their many gifts to me, and for the kind of people that they are, I am also thankful to my guides in the wilderness quest, James Wright and Hannah Maris.

Books, says Gary Snyder, have become our teaching elders. What I have learned from my many elders—the writings of Snyder, Paul Shepard, Eugene Gendlin, Joel Kovel, James Hillman, Fritz Perls, Paul Goodman, David Levin, Martin Heidegger, Maurice Merleau-Ponty, Albert Borgmann, and others who fill my bibliography—is so beyond reckoning that I cannot imagine my life without them. I give my gratitude to them all. Thanks, also, to Joanna Macy for (among other things) inspiring the dedication to this book.

Friends and family have been universally supportive. For warm, musical, and thought-provoking friendship, I am particularly thankful to my class (and canoe) mates Jean-Marc Daigle, Donna Havinga, Joanne Nonnekes, Lionel Normand, Adrian Ivakhiv, mark meisner, Ian Attridge, Stephen Horton, David Berger, Dieter Brock, Julie Palmer, Randee Holmes, Anne Bell, and Connie Russell. The generous love of my parents, David and Marnie Fisher, is a constant source of good feeling; as is the presence in my life of sister Lynne, brother Richard, sister-in-law Shelley, and niece Gwyneth. Closest to heart and home is my wife, Jill Dunkley, who throughout our time together has graced me with her humor, patience, emotional support, and gut-felt criticism. I also wish to acknowledge here my grandfather, George Gilmour, who died some months before I was born, but whose religious and scholarly spirit has become a welcome force in my life.

Since "coming out" as an ecopsychologist, I have been encouraged-on by a number of good people. Robert Greenway was the first to suggest that I look for a publisher and has been a generous supporter of my work. I am honored to know this wise and spirited man. David Abram's enthusiasm for the manuscript really got me going on the book, and a number of his suggestions have helped me to improve it. He is a wonderful ally and mentor. Joel Kovel took time out of his own busy writing schedule to carefully read my work and offer some tough and thoughtful advice. I look forward to carrying-through on many of his suggestions in future efforts. An encouraging letter from Steven Foster, who also found the time to read the manuscript, did much to warm my heart. Jed Swift and Laura Sewall invited me to an ecopsychology workshop in Boulder, Colorado, in the summer of 2000. It was in preparation for that event that I did much of my final thinking about the project of ecopsychology itself. The reception that my views received from the participants at that event emboldened me to put them into print. Laura, who has since become a collaborator in thinking about ecopsychology, kindly helped me to hone my vision. My deepest thanks to all these people.

For making available a copy of her beautiful print, *Moon Howl,* for the cover of this book, I am grateful to Martina Field. Thanks, also, to a number of anonymous reviewers, who made a number of helpful comments; and to my editor at SUNY Press, Michael Rinella, for taking this on. And thanks to my mother, Marnie Fisher, for her last-minute commentary on the entire book.

Finally, I want to mention the many other-than-human beings, from icicles to cormorants, who keep me writing. I am especially thankful to the powers of the Leslie Street Spit, and to my neighborhood crows (for their constant reminders).

PART I
GROUNDWORK

It is in country unfamiliar emotionally or topographically that one needs poems and roadmaps.

—Clifford Geertz

1

THE PROJECT OF ECOPSYCHOLOGY

The Terrain of Ecopsychology

Human sanity requires some less-than-obvious connections to nature as well as the necessities of food, water, energy, and air. We have hardly begun to discover what those connections may be. . . .

—Paul Shepard,[1] 1969

Around the time that Rachel Carson's *Silent Spring* was igniting the modern environmental movement, the psychoanalyst Harold F. Searles published a book that received a much quieter reception, a thick volume entitled *The Nonhuman Environment: In Normal Development and in Schizophrenia.* His guiding idea was that, whether we are aware of it or not, the "nonhuman environment"—the trees, clouds, raccoons, rivers, skyscrapers, and manifold other nonhuman phenomena that weave together as the larger matrix for the affairs of humans—has great significance for human psychological life, a significance we ignore at peril to our own psychological well-being. In introducing his subject matter, Searles paused to comment that it "may be likened to a vast continent, as yet largely unexplored and uncharted."[2] Sensing this large territory before him, he wrote: "During the past approximately sixty years, the focus of psychiatry's attention has gradually become enlarged, from an early preoccupation with intrapsychic [interior] processes . . . to include interpersonal and broad sociological-anthropological factors. It would seem then that a natural next phase would consist in our broadening our focus still further, to include man's [*sic*[3]] relationship with his nonhuman environment."[4] Four decades later, this next phase in the broadening of psychology's[5] focus—call it "ecopsychology"—is finally beginning to take shape.

In offering definitions of ecopsychology, most of the people presently developing this field do indeed say something along the lines of Searles. They talk about synthesizing ecology and psychology, placing human psychology in an ecological context, and mending the divisions between mind and nature, humans

3

and earth. Many have simply adopted the position that, as human ecologist Paul Shepard put it in 1973: "If [the] environmental crisis signifies a crippled state of consciousness as much as it does damaged habitat, then that is perhaps where we should begin."[6] In the words of one of its most visible representatives, cultural historian Theodore Roszak, ecopsychology does not want to "stop at the city limits," as if "the soul might be saved while the biosphere crumbles,"[7] but rather illuminate the innate emotional bonds between "person and planet." Such characterizations are appropriately in harmony with the root meanings of "ecopsychology." Psychology is the *logos*—the study, order, meaning, or speech—of the *psyche* or soul. "*Eco*" derives from the Greek *oikos* which means "home." Ecopsychology, then, would approach the psyche in relation to its earthly or natural home, its native abode, and explore "the basic shifts in our patterns of identity and relationship that occur when we include our connection to the web of life around us as essential to human well-being."[8]

Ecologists study nature, while psychologists study human nature. Assuming these natures overlap, psychology already has obvious potential links to ecology. Indeed, before ecopsychology even became a word a small number of psychologists and ecologists were already crossing the boundaries. Any thorough reading of the works of depth psychologist Carl Jung, for example, will demonstrate that ecopsychologists are by no means starting from scratch. Among many other noteworthy remarks, Jung wrote that as:

> scientific understanding has grown, so our world has become dehumanized. Man feels himself isolated in the cosmos, because he is no longer involved in nature and has lost his emotional "unconscious identity" with natural phenomena. These have slowly lost their symbolic implications. . . . No voices now speak to man from stones, plants, and animals, nor does he speak to them believing they can hear. His contact with nature has gone, and with it has gone the profound emotional energy that this symbolic connection supplied.[9]

To be sure, among their various sources ecopsychologists have drawn heavily on Jungian or archetypal thought, the clearest example of which is Roszak's positing of an "ecological unconscious."[10] Noting that in Jung's hands the so-called collective unconscious[11] took on an increasingly "incorporeal and strictly cultural" flavor, removed from more bodily and earthly contents, Roszak proposes that the "collective unconscious, at its deepest level, shelters the compacted ecological intelligence of our species."[12] Although the notion of the ecological unconscious remains undeveloped by Roszak, he writes that we are repressing this "ecological level of the unconscious," leaving unawakened our "inherent sense of environmental reciprocity"—and suffering the ecological crisis as a consequence.

From the reverse starting point of ecology, we may recall Aldo Leopold's remark (from his 1949 classic *A Sand County Almanac*) that the basic concept of ecology is that "land is a community," of which humans ought to be regarded as "plain members."[13] "We abuse land," he said, "because we regard it as a commodity belonging to us. When we see land as a community to which we belong, we may begin to use it with love and respect." In this vein, ecopsychologists argue that if we accept the ecological view that we are members of the biotic community, rather than its mere exploiters, then we may learn to recognize the natural world as a social and psychological field, just as we do the human community. In his work on cybernetics, for instance, especially from the late 1960s onward, Gregory Bateson (a protoecopsychologist) sought to explain how our personal minds are part of a larger "eco-mental system" or Mind. The titles of his two best-known books, *Steps to an Ecology of Mind* and *Mind and Nature,* suggest the territory he was walking. Although his work (and cybernetics in general) has been criticized for its ironically disembodied and purely formal portrayal of human consciousness,[14] his claim that polluting Lake Erie is to drive it insane is certainly one way to identify a suffering in the soul of the natural world. Leopold spoke, in this respect, of his living "alone in a world of wounds." Ecologists, he suggested, are trained to see the "marks of death in community that believes itself well and does not want to be told otherwise."[15]

I have intended these introductory remarks and brief background samples to provide the reader with an initial sense for what comprises the terrain of ecopsychology. It remains to acknowledge, however, that ecopsychology is a product of the modern or Western mind. Those indigenous or aboriginal peoples whose lifeways are still dedicated to the maintenance of reciprocal relations with the natural world are, by contrast, said to have no need for an ecopsychology. In fact, the direct engagement of many indigenous peoples with plants and animals, earth and sky, make the confinement of modern psychology to a strictly human bubble seem odd in the extreme. One of the few contributors to the ecopsychology literature of Native American heritage, Leslie Gray, thus claims that we "have only to look at the cross-cultural practices of perennial shamanism to find effective models of applied ecopsychology."[16] The archetypal psychologist James Hillman similarly contends that we must reimagine what it means to "make soul" by, among other things, getting "out of Western history to tribal animistic psychologies that are always mainly concerned, not with individualities, but with the soul of things . . . and propitiatory acts that keep the world on its course."[17] As still others have remarked, however, ecopsychologists must guard against becoming part of the historical process of colonizing and appropriating indigenous cultures that today includes the plundering of traditional spiritualities by Euroamerican seekers or new age "wannabes."[18] They must also be careful not to blindly assume that all aspects of all indigenous societies are unquestionably good. Given their obvious relevance, it is inevitable that ecopsychologists be familiar with some indigenous beliefs and practices—and this may remain a source of tension for some time. I believe, however, that most nonindigenous ecopsychologists are committed to keeping themselves based primarily in the contexts of their own traditions, with which they are most familiar.

Getting a Handle on the Project: Four Tasks

Broad definitions of ecopsychology, such as I have just introduced, are easy enough to come by. Many people are still left wondering, however, just what ecopsychology is or what exactly an ecopsychologist does. I think there are two main reasons for this. First of all, the combining of psychology and ecology opens up such a vast terrain that it can seem limitless at times. Psychotherapy with "nature," contemplative practice, wilderness practice, vision quests, earth poetics, ecological restoration, ecological design, building sustainable communities, shamanic counseling, Jungian dream analysis, deep ecology, environmental education: all have been associated with ecopsychology. How can a field that includes so much be considered a field at all? The second reason why ecopsychology is hard to define is because there is actually not a lot of strictly ecopsychological work that one can define it by. The literature of ecopsychology is still small, and much of it consists of explorations directed "toward" an ecopsychology rather than attempts to actually build one. The challenge I want to take up in this section, then, is that of getting a handle on a field that seems to have so much possibility yet so little actuality.

I suggest, to begin, that ecopsychology is best thought of as a *project,* in the sense of a large, multifaceted undertaking. This makes room for a great number of perspectives and interests and rules out the idea that ecopsychology will ever resemble a traditional discipline. I suggest, next, that ecopsychology be considered a *historical* undertaking—which is to say that it has arisen in response to specific historical conditions. More exactly, I believe there are four general tasks that ecopsychologists are in fact engaged in, each of which aims at resolving a corresponding historical need. I call these the psychological task, the philosophical task, the practical task, and the critical task. These tasks identify the common burdens that befall ecopsychologists, regardless of our particular orientations or vocabularies, for they derive from a historical moment we all share. Nature and history demand that we undertake these tasks. Hence, our work as ecopsychologists is to feel this demand in our bodies and to be true or faithful to it in our own particular ways. When the examples of ecopsychological work that do exist are organized into these four tasks, the overall project comes into view. Thus, I propose that it is these four tasks—or, more precisely, the interrelations among them—that define ecopsychology. In other words, the four tasks weave together to form the whole endeavor that I am calling the project of ecopsychology.

In what follows I walk through the four tasks in turn, describing the historical situations from which they arise and offering brief examples of ecopsychological works that are addressed to each of them. The section concludes with a discussion of some of the interrelations among the four tasks, so that my definition of ecopsychology as an intricately woven general project can be further elaborated. I wish to say, finally, that my goal with this exercise is not to nail down ecopsychology for good, so that it can never move again. Certainly, there are other formulations of the tasks and other examples that could be given. My goal, rather, is to provide a scheme that can bring into better focus what we are doing as ecopsychologists, or at least provide a basis for some good discussion, while nonetheless leaving lots of room to maneuver.

The Psychological Task: To Acknowledge and Better Understand the Human-Nature Relationship as a Relationship

> *It may seem absurd to those unfamiliar with psychoanalytic thought to suppose that man treats Nature in terms of dominance and submission as he might treat another human being with whom he has not been able to establish a one-to-one relationship, but I believe these attitudes can not only be demonstrated, but are actually important for our understanding of what has gone wrong in our relationship with the natural world.*
> —Anthony Storr,[19] 1974

Ecopsychology is a psychological undertaking that essentially says "we too are nature." Its first task is therefore to describe the human psyche in a way that makes it *internal* to the natural world or that makes it a phenomenon of nature. Stated otherwise, the task is to build a psychology that expands the field of significant relationships to include other-than-human beings; a psychology that that views all psychological and spiritual matters in the light of our participation within the larger natural order. Ecopsychology is still concerned with our suffering and happiness, our dreaming, our search for meaning, our responsibilities to others, our states of consciousness, and so on; it just frames these concerns within the fuller, more-than-human scope of human existence.

The historical situation from which this task arises is obvious enough. Modern society is in an extreme, pathological state of rupture from the reality of the natural world, as is indicated on a daily basis by the ecological crisis. There is, moreover, little public recognition that this crisis is indeed a psychological one. This lack of recognition extends most crucially to the arena of psychology itself, as has been discussed by David Kidner in his recent exploration of why psychology is so conspicuously mute about the ecological crisis. Kidner notes that most psychologists are unwilling to regard our ecological troubles as evidence of "pathology in the relationship between humanity and the natural world." Ecological problems are effectively "dichotomized into individual and environmental problems, and any possible relation between the two is repressed." The result is that "environmental destruction is invisible to psychology."[20] Searles likewise commented on psychology's indifference toward the world of nature, stating in 1960 that in the writings of developmental psychologists "the nonhuman environment is . . . considered as irrelevant to human personality development, . . . as though the human race were alone in the universe, pursuing individual and collective destinies in a homogeneous matrix of nothingness."[21] Perhaps one day it will seem strange that psychologists were ever so deaf and blind to the natural world—at which point ecopsychology will simply be psychology itself.

The initial challenge for ecopsychologists is thus to counter this deeply ingrained habit of ignoring the psychological significance of the human-nature relationship. This amounts, first of all, to *acknowledging* the human-nature relationship *as* a relationship. In other words, it means granting the natural world psychological status; regarding other-than-human beings as true interactants in life, as ensouled "others" in their own right, as fellow beings or kin. The requirement, in short, is to conceptualize the natural world in a way that is more satisfying for the purposes of psychological understanding than are the more usual representations of nature as a realm of mere scientific objects, resources, or scenic vistas. The demand here is also to find ways to talk about the human-nature relationship that do not set humans outside of nature, that is, that clarify how it is that we relate to "nature" while also being an embodied part of nature, involved in its processes ourselves.

As an example of one person's efforts to undertake this first task, perhaps no one has done more to reconceive other-than-human beings as psychological *counterplayers* (Erik Erikson's term) than the human ecologist Paul Shepard. Shepard claims that our psychological development inherently calls for a childhood immersion in wild nature and for a subsequent adolescent tutoring into mature, reciprocal, and harmonious relations with the larger natural world. Given this unconventional view, he then interprets our society's persistent degradation of its own habitat in terms of a widespread arrestment of this "normal" process of psychogenesis. General, "culturally-ratified distortions of childhood" and "mutilations of personal maturity," argues Shepard, are at the root of our "irrational and self-destructive attitudes toward the natural environment." He writes:

> The archetypal role of nature—the mineral, plant, and animal world found most complete in wilderness—is in the development of the individual human personality, for it embodies the poetic expression of ways of being and relating to others. Urban civilization creates the illusion of a shortcut to individual maturity by attempting to omit the eight to ten years of immersion in nonhuman nature. Maturity so achieved is spurious because the individual, though he may be precociously articulate and sensitive to subtle human interplay, is without a grounding in the given structure that is nature. . . . Indeed, the real bitterness of modern social relations has its roots in that vacuum where a beautiful and awesome otherness should have been encountered.

Westerners, suggests Shepard, "may now be the possessors of the world's flimsiest identity structure." "The West is a vast testimonial to childhood botched to serve its own purposes, where history, masquerading as myth, authorizes men of action and men of thought to alter the world to match their regressive moods of omnipotence and insecurity." In short, we are "childish adults" who keep our society going only at the private cost of "massive therapy, escapism, intoxicants, narcotics, fits of destructive rage, enormous grief, subordination to hierarchies, . . . and, perhaps worst of all, a readiness to strike back at a natural world we dimly perceive as having failed us."[22]

The Philosophical Task: To Place Psyche (Soul, Anima, Mind) Back into the (Natural) World

> *Psychology without ecology is lonely and vice versa. The salmon is not merely a projection, a symbol of some inner process, it is rather the embodiment of the soul that nourishes us all.*
>
> —Tom Jay,[23]
> commenting on the view of Northwest Coast Indians, 1986

The thought of ecopsychology shakes us to our modern foundations. Most obviously, ecopsychologists reject the presumed dichotomies that underlie the modern enterprise, especially the human/nature and inner/outer splits. Indeed, the dualistic cleavage of our "inner" lives from an "outer" world may well be the core problem of ecopsychology, for it divorces mind from nature. As a project, ecopsychology therefore has no choice but to undertake philosophical efforts that will give it a more adequate intellectual home. This is a genre or concept-making task, as there are few existing theoretical frameworks that do not suffer from dualistic biases. To be sure, the split between humans and nature—as well as a near endless stream of related ones—runs through most of modern philosophy, science, and art.[24] Such a bifurcation of reality, however, is *historical;* it reflects a withdrawal of reality into the head of the modern Western individual and a corresponding estrangement of that individual from the "external" social and ecological world.[25] Modern psychology, like most things modern, has nonetheless taken this dichotomized reality as its starting point. "Having divided psychic reality from hard or external reality, psychology elaborates various theories to connect the two orders together, since the division is worrisome indeed. It means that psychic reality is conceived to be neither public, objective nor physical, while external reality, the sum of existing material objects and conditions, is conceived to be utterly devoid of soul. As the soul is without world, so the world is without soul."[26] In other words, if mind is all "inside" and nature all "outside," then psychology and ecology have nothing in common. The broad historical requirement of ecopsychology, then, is to "turn the psyche inside out," locating mind in the world itself—healing our dualism by returning soul to nature and nature to soul. In a statement definitive of ecopsychology's terrain as any, Jung once said: "Our psyche is part of nature, and its enigma is as limitless. Thus we cannot define either the psyche or nature."[27] The alchemical healer Sendivogius likewise said, "The greater part of the soul lies outside the body."[28] In more recent times, there are two main figures in ecopsychological circles who have explicitly argued such positions: the post-Jungian James Hillman and the ecophilosopher David Abram.

Hillman's strategy is to revive the Latin term *anima mundi* (anima = soul), which gets translated as the "soul of the world." The way to counter dualism is not to deny that there are inner and outer *poles* of reality.[29] That worldly things have their own inwardness is the very condition for their appearing as meaningful, having their own depth, mystery, and intentions; and for their being able to invite us into some kind of relation, to elicit our imagination. The soul of the world is this inner sense that runs horizontally through all things, showing itself as that implicit reality that shines forth from the world. "Each particular event, including individual humans with our invisible thoughts, feelings, and intentions, reveals a soul in its imaginative display."[30] Or as George Steiner wrote: "It is hidden Being that gives the rock its dense 'thereness,' that makes the heart pause when a kingfisher alights, that makes our own existence inseparable from that of others."[31] An intangible inner presence lends the world the richness of its outer visibility, gives it personality, and unites all phenomena beneath the surface of reality. In this case, it makes more sense to say that "we are *in* the psyche" than that our psyches are in *us*.[32] Hillman argues, however, that a kind of mass soul loss defines the modern epoch; and the world correspondingly robbed of soul has therefore taken on a relatively flat, disconnected, uninviting, depersonalized, and literal appearance for most of us. By pressing all of the soul into the human being, we have *deanimated* the world and simultaneously inflated the significance of the human person. Hence, "I must be desirable, attractive, a sex object, or win importance and power. For without these investments in my particular person, coming either from your subjectivity or my own, I too am but a dead thing among dead things, potentially forever lonely. . . . What stress, what effort it takes to live in a cemetery."[33] Because a dead, soulless world offers no intimacy, an enormous weight now rests on human relations, which have become "overcharged with archetypal significance": "our mothers fail, for they must always be Great, . . . having to supplant the dead depersonified world and be the seasons of the earth, the moon and the cows, the trees and the leaves on the trees. All this we expect from [human] persons."[34]

While arriving at similar conclusions, David Abram makes his arguments from out of a different tradition, namely, the philosophical movement known as *phenomenology*.[35] Because the method of phenomenology is unfamiliar to most people, I will attempt a brief explication before turning to Abram's thought itself. (The "transcendental" phenomenology of Edmund Husserl is usually distinguished from the "hermeneutic" phenomenology first articulated by Husserl's student, Martin Heidegger. I refer primarily to the latter.) Phenomenology, most importantly, begins with *phenomena,* the reality given in lived experience prior to reflection. Eschewing statements that cannot somehow be related to our everyday experience of things, phenomenologists adopt as their method the *description* of the world as it is actually lived. In the words of the great French phenomenologist Maurice Merleau-Ponty, phenomenologists wish to re-achieve a "direct and primitive contact with the world." They point out how poorly the various theoretical notions we habitually use to explain reality actually conform to our pretheoretical experiencing of it. The goal is therefore not to produce one more causal model to predict and control the world, but rather to find those words that are true to our experience—and so which, like good poetry, effect a shift in that experience, bringing us a new awareness or understanding of things.

Phenomenology's experiential focus and "demand for awareness" make it a kind of therapy for healing the splits of modern thought. Many phenomenologists suggest that the delinking of inner self and outer world is an illusion, and describe instead how inside and outside intertwine as a single interactive structure they call "being-in-the-world." One of the basic arguments of phenomenology is that no so-called inner experience can ever really be had. If we were to take the metaphor of "inside" literally and cut into our bodies, perhaps our brains, we would of course not find there any thoughts, images, emotions, percepts, or behavior, for all these things arise only in relation to or contact with a world. If I see something, this mug of tea before my eyes, I see it not as a representation on some mental screen in my head, but as that thing *in front of me,* out in the world, where I meet it or am with it. Similarly, my anger, although inwardly felt, is not something I can identify as an isolated content in an inner psychic container, for it is indivisible from the entire situation in which I am feeling angry. This is true even in my dreamworld, where I still live in relation to the sights and sounds around me. It was in this sense that Merleau-Ponty said that we live "out there among things,"[36] in a kind of communion with the world: "there is no inner man, man is in the world, and only in the world does he know himself."[37] Through their descriptions of prereflective experience, then, phenomenologists disclose human existence as a network of *relations;* our being is not locked up inside us, but is in fact spread throughout this web of worldly interactions in which our existence continually unfolds. Or to turn to Merleau-Ponty one more time: the world is the "natural setting of, and field for, all my thoughts and all my explicit perceptions."[38]

Abram's project is to draw out the ecological implications of phenomenology's quest for the primordial and its relational emphasis, especially as these are expressed in Merleau-Ponty's philosophy. The "hidden thrust of the phenomenological movement," says Abram, "is the reflective discovery of our inherence in the body of the Earth"—for "the 'world' to which [Merleau-Ponty] so often refers is none other than the Earth."[39] Merleau-Ponty's philosophy was itself gradually revealing the earth as the original field for all human experience, the ultimate source of, or necessary ground for, all psychological life. He called perception a "mutual embrace" or conversation between body and world, such that the sensible world solicits our bodily responses and our bodies in turn interrogate the sensible.[40] Claiming, as did Merleau-Ponty, that we can have no experience, perception, or self-knowledge without a world in which to bodily interact, to touch and be touched by, Abram argues that the earth—the soil, wind, birds, insects—is the given world that our sensory life opens on to, anticipates, and is fed by. Turning to Abram's evocative words themselves:

> The human mind is not some otherworldly essence that comes to house itself inside our physiology. Rather it is instilled and provoked by the sensorial field itself, induced by the tensions and participations between the human body and the animate earth. The invisible shapes of smells, rhythms of cricketsong, and the movement of shadows all, in a sense, provide the subtle body of our thoughts. . . .
>
> By acknowledging such links between the inner, psychological world and the perceptual terrain that surrounds us, we begin to turn inside-out, loosening the psyche from its confinement within a strictly human sphere, freeing sentience to return to the visible world that contains us. Intelligence is no longer ours alone but is a property of the earth; we are in it, of it, immersed in its depths. And indeed each terrain, each ecology, seems to have its own particular intelligence, its own unique vernacular of soil and leaf and sky.
>
> Each place its own mind, its own psyche. Oak, madrone, Douglas fir, red-tailed hawk, serpentine in the sandstone, a certain scale to the topography, drenching rains in the winter, fog off-shore in the summer, salmon surging in the streams—all these together make up a particular state of mind, a place-specific intelligence shared by all the humans that dwell therein, but also by the coyotes yapping in those valleys, by the bobcats and the ferns and the spiders, by all beings who live and make their way in that zone. Each place its own psyche. Each sky its own blue.[41]

The Practical Task: To Develop Therapeutic and Recollective Practices Toward an Ecological Society

> *Of course I am in mourning for the land and water and my fellow beings. If this were not felt, I would be so defended and so in denial, so anesthetized, I would be insane. Yet this condition of mourning and grieving going on in my soul, this level of continuous sadness is a reflection of what is going on in the world and becomes internalized and called "depression," a state altogether in me—my serotonin levels, my personal history, my problem. And the drug industry . . . and insurance companies are in general agreement. You must become even more anesthetized. Take Prozac: Depression is a disease and weakens the economy.*
>
> —James Hillman,[42] 1996

The practical sphere of ecopsychology is the most difficult to delimit. Almost any existing "psychological" activity (e.g., psychotherapy) can be placed in an ecological context, and almost any "ecological" activity (e.g., ecological restoration) can be approached in terms of its psychological effects or benefits.[43] As I mentioned above, this makes for a great deal of potential "ecopsychological" activity. Although people will no doubt draw their own lines around the *content* of ecopsychology practice, if we are to get a better handle on the project of ecopsychology we do at least need to specify what *characterizes* its practical dimension. As with the other three areas of ecopsychology, I believe the best way to do this is to ask ourselves what general task we are undertaking and what historical need we are thereby attempting to fill. To answer this question, furthermore, I suggest that it is helpful to regard ecopsychology as a psychologically based ecological politics. Viewed this way, the broad practical task is to develop psychologically informed practices or interventions aimed at creating a life-celebrating society. This task, in turn, has two overlapping aspects: practices that play a supportive or therapeutic role and practices that play a recollective role.

Therapeutic ecopsychological practices are those aimed at addressing the emotional and spiritual conditions underlying the ecological crisis. We live in a world where very little seems secure; where many people feel isolated, worn down, beleaguered, disempowered; and where the future can look even more unjust and hopeless. The ecopsychological task, in this respect, is to design practices that provide supportive or therapeutic contexts for people to find their footings in life and turn their attention to the real work of creating a life-centered society, whether this work be private actions or more public forms of political involvement. What makes such practice "ecopsychological" is its emphasis on the psychospiritual side of building an ecological society. For example, psychotherapy or spiritual training with ecological activists is in my view a form of ecopsychological practice, whereas the activism itself is not (unless undertaken precisely as such practice[44]).

Recollective practices, on the other hand, are those activities that aim more directly at recalling how our human psyches are embedded in and nurtured by the larger psyche of nature and at relearning the essentially human art of revering, giving back to, and maintaining reciprocal relations with an animate natural world. Recollective practices, as the name suggests, invite us into zones of reality that may be quite unfamiliar, where a bird or a stone just might have something important to say to us. One such practice that is growing in popularity (at least in the United States) is the "vision quest," in which a solo quester typically spends a number of days fasting in the wilderness in order to seek guidance and spiritual renewal through openly encountering the forces of nature (a practice that, while being recollective, also has a therapeutic dimension).

What I propose, then, is that ecopsychological practice can presently be grouped into these two general areas, even if there may at times be considerable overlap between them; and that what characterizes the practice is both a psychological intention or emphasis and an alignment with the historical goal of building a society in which human and nonhuman nature can flourish together.

Although therapeutic and recollective practices are not mutually exclusive, I wish to offer some further examples below that relate primarily to the former. I have chosen this focus not because I think that the one area of practice is more important than the other (far from it), but simply because this seems the right place to talk about therapeutic practices and because the theme of recollection will appear throughout much of the second part of this book.

The work of the ecological, peace, and social justice activist Joanna Macy and her colleagues probably offers the most extensive answer to the need for therapeutic practices. Macy offers an illustrative story. "Once, when I told a psychotherapist of my outrage over the destruction of old-growth forests, she informed me that the bulldozers represented my libido and that my distress sprang from fear of my own sexuality."[45] Macy's experience, she says, is not untypical; therapists often interpret feelings of despair "as manifestations of some private neurosis." In her own work, she has therefore made a point of validating, as healthy and real, what she calls our "pain for the world": "the distress we feel in connection with the larger whole of which we are a part." Refusing both dualism and individualism, she says that we suffer *for* old-growth forests and *for* other people in pain because we and these others are so interdependent. The immeasurable losses we are experiencing—including the loss of the biosphere as a viable habitat for countless life forms—comprise "the pivotal psychological reality of our time." Our emotional responses are appropriately complex: fear, dread, or terror before the forces presently threatening life on earth; anger and rage at having to live under such threat; guilt for being "implicated in this catastrophe"; and, above all, sorrow—a "sadness beyond telling" that arises from confronting "so vast and final a loss as this."[46]

Macy says that she has yet to meet anyone "immune" from this pain for the world. Yet, precisely because this suffering is so collective and great we face an additional difficulty: the tendency to *deny* or *repress* this pain. The notion of "psychic numbing"—coined by psychologist Robert J. Lifton to describe the lack of feeling capacity among Hiroshima survivors—is often used to make sense of this denial. Immersed in an emotionally overwhelming reality, we anaesthetize ourselves and blot out or dissociate the unwanted truth. As therapist-activist Elissa Melamed wrote: "We may know intellectually that we are in desperate straights, but emotionally we are unconnected to this knowledge. An aura of unreality hangs over the whole thing. . . . We are dealing with a vast psychological problem, a planetary clinical picture of flattened affect, if you will, yet psychology offers little in the way of assistance."[47] Although it is understandable that we cut ourselves off from our painful feelings, people like Melamed and Macy point out that by doing so we deprive ourselves of the energy and direction our emotions might lend us toward taking creative political action. By staying numb, we stay stuck.

Against this emotional background, some ecopsychologists are now exploring how the ecology movement may in fact be "organizing, educating, and agitating with little regard for the fragile psychological complexities of the public whose hearts and minds it [seeks] to win."[48] Roszak, for example, goes right to the point: "Environmentalists are among the most psychologically illiterate people you will ever meet. They work from a narrow range of motivations: the statistics of impending disaster, the coercive emotional force of fear and guilt . . . they overlook the unreason, the perversity, the sick desire that lie at the core of the psyche. Their strategy is shock and shame."[49] In this light, many environmental groups may actually be *exploiting* our emotional condition—our fear, guilt, and so forth. Macy herself says that the grim information held up by activists "*by itself* can increase resistance, deepening the sense of apathy and powerlessness."[50] Amongst its goals, ecopsychology thus "seeks to acquaint the environmental movement with a subtler, more sensitive psychological approach to the public it seeks to win over to its cause."[51] Educator Mitchell Thomashow similarly claims that environmentalists have a responsibility "to provide support for the anxiety that accompanies the perception of cultural upheaval and wounded ecosystems." They must learn to facilitate the inner changes in the public that will help bring about the policy and behavioral changes they desire. "In this way, the environmental profession becomes a healing profession."[52]

Macy comments that "unless you have some roots in a spiritual practice that holds life sacred and encourages joyful communion with all your fellow beings, facing the enormous challenges ahead becomes nearly impossible."[53] The role of psychological and spiritual practice in ecopsychology is currently being developed in a number of ways. Organizations such as the *Center for Psychology and Social Change* (with its Institute of Ecopsychology, Psychotherapy and Health) in Cambridge, Massachusetts, and the *Shavano Institute* in Boulder, Colorado, for instance, hold workshops where health professionals, activists, and others are introduced to ecopsychological theory and a range of psychological and spiritual practices to assist them in their work and lives. Macy and others have also responded to the need for healing on a more collective level by developing community workshops aimed at facilitating the so-called inner work of social change. One of the purposes of these workshops is to help participants overcome the oppressive taboos against expressing their pain for the world. As Sarah Conn notes, to become responsible for the current state of the world one must regain the ability to "feel and to engage rather than to become numbed and dulled."[54] The workshops typically take place over a number of days, and proceed through three typical stages which spontaneously flow one into the other. The first stage involves using exercises to evoke the dreadful social and ecological realities of our times. People are supported to feel their pain for the world in a group setting and to cathartically express formerly blocked emotions. This expressive process sets the ground for the second stage, in which participants come to realize that just as there is pain in being interconnected with others, so too is there synergy and power. The "collective nature of our pain for the world is recognized as evidence of our interexistence, revealing the larger transpersonal matrix of our lives."[55] The third and final stage is called "empowerment," in which participants experience their personal power, broaden their vision of what is possible, and acquire skills for social change work. Because of the intense sharing of emotion and transpersonal sense of this work, it carries a distinctly spiritual charge.

The basic principles of despair and empowerment work have also been focused by Macy and others into another, more exclusively ecopsychological or deep ecological practice called "The Council of All Beings."[56] This Council is a ritual meant to help people "think like a mountain" (as Aldo Leopold phrased it). Through exercises aimed both at freeing up painful emotions over our society's destructive relation to the natural world and at deepening a sense of identity or connection with other-than-human beings, participants are supported to become more "ecologically conscious" and are allowed to "express their awareness of the ecological trouble we are in, and to deepen their motivation to act."[57]

The Critical Task: To Engage in Ecopsychologically Based Criticism

> There is a blind spot in ecopsychology because the field is limited by its Eurocentric perspective, in the same way that the environmental movement as a whole has been blind to environmental racism. . . . I've been saying to my friends for a long time, "Why is it so easy for these people to think like mountains and not be able to think like people of color?"
> —Carl Anthony,[58] 1995

When Searles proposed a broadening of psychology's focus to include the human relation to the nonhuman environment he probably did not foresee how deeply such a move would cut. For when revealed *as* a relationship the human mistreatment of nature—the bulldozing, blasting, eliminating, slaughtering, polluting, and so on—comes glaringly into view. The rising exploitation of the natural world by our society has been justified only through a historical process of despiritualizing and depersonifying other-than-human beings so as to rule out any sort of ethical or sensitive relations with them.[59] Ecopsychologists propose an undoing of this human-centered—or "anthropocentric"—reduction of the being of nature to raw, moldable, inferior stuff that exists as if only to be on-call for human use.[60] They would reconceive nature along less narcissistic lines, as a sacred realm of intrinsic worth and as a world full of vital "others" for the articulation of the human psyche. (This, to say the least, changes everything.) This challenging of anthropocentrism is an example of the critical work of ecopsychology: to engage in ecopsychologically based criticism. Such criticism is called for because the world ultimately envisioned by ecopsychology is simply not the world of today.

As I conceive it, the critical task consists (at least initially) of bringing together the sorts of social and cultural criticism found among the more radical voices within both ecological and psychological circles. I believe it is fair to say, however, that most of the criticism currently encountered within ecopsychology is of the "cultural" variety (such as the critique of anthropocentrism) rather than the "social." Indeed, the more socially critical elements of the radical ecology movement have yet to really make an appearance in ecopsychology. Ecopsychologists have made little use, moreover, of the socially radical views found within the literature of *psychology*, many of which are critical of the "psy" practices (psychiatry, psychology, psychotherapy, etc.) themselves. Of the four tasks or historical demands I have identified, I therefore suggest that the demand for criticism has so far received the least satisfying response from ecopsychologists. Hence my emphasis in what follows is on the vital need for ecopsychologists to become more thoroughly engaged in social analysis. Because my treatment of this task will involve detailing the points I have just introduced, the discussion here will be lengthier than each of the previous three.

Roughly speaking, mainstream environmentalists aim for reforms "within the system," while the radicals want to reconstruct or change the system itself. On the whole, radical ecologists argue that without challenging the cultural backgrounds (beliefs, values, attitudes) and social arrangements (institutions, material conditions) that have historically sanctioned ecological degradation, nothing much will change. Among radical ecologists themselves, however, there is much disagreement about the best way to go, as is indicated by the numerous different schools or movements to which they variously belong, and by the vigorous debates that often occur between them.[61] Of these schools, it is "deep ecology" and "ecofeminism" that have had the greatest influence on ecopsychology, primarily the former. Indeed, some say that ecopsychology is simply an outgrowth or instance of deep ecology. The result of this situation, however, is that the tension between deep ecology and the rest of the radical ecology movement has effectively carried over into ecopsychology. Plainly put, ecopsychology is currently vulnerable to the same criticism that is often made against the deep ecology movement itself: that its social and political thought lacks depth. To understand this point, we first need to take a look at deep ecology itself.

As with ecopsychology, deep ecology defies easy definition. I would briefly characterize it, however, as a movement to bring our personal lives and our culture into alignment with an ecological view of reality. It is usually defined by a broad eight-point platform written by philosophers Arne Naess and George Sessions, the main planks of which involve making an "eco-centric" commitment to the well being and flourishing of all "Life on earth," to ensuring that a richness and diversity of life forms exist.[62] What deep ecology is perhaps most well-known for, however, is the attention that its supporters have paid to the relationship between ecology and self-identity. If everything is connected to everything else, if everything internally relates,[63] then what am I? The Buddhist-poet Gary Snyder remarks: "If people can acknowledge their membership in the fabric of the whole, acknowledge that they are part of the habitat, part of the network, part of the web, and feel that the welfare of the web is their welfare, and their welfare is the welfare of the web—in other words, not be mindlessly but mindfully one with the whole—that is an extraordinary spiritual and political step right there, and it dumps the cartridges out of the weapons."[64] Indeed, much of the deep ecology literature is about experiencing the interrelatedness of all things in wilderness settings—as when the nineteenth-century wilderness advocate John Muir sensed trees and mountains shining with a kind of psychic aura, everything being luminously present as an interdependent whole. The shift to such an "ecological" mode of consciousness, in which one's sense of reality lines up with the ecological givens, is held out by many deep ecology supporters as a necessary step toward an "ecologically mature" society. The deep ecology scholar Warwick Fox has in fact argued that what distinguishes deep ecology is precisely this psychological dimension. Because ecological consciousness (or *Self-realization,* as it is also called) involves transcending the more narrow, biographic, egoic, or personal sense of self, he suggests that deep ecology has much in common with transpersonal psychology, which takes spiritual (beyond-the-personal) experience as its subject matter. He even proposes replacing the term deep ecology with *transpersonal ecology*—the idea being that as one develops a sense of self that is both transpersonal and ecological, one will care for the earth without being morally persuaded to do so because one will identify with it as Self.[65] It is thus through a process of psychospiritual growth that one will become motivated to develop an ecocentric lifestyle and participate in actions such as the direct defence of threatened wilderness areas.

While having great appeal for its placing of humanity back within the web of earthly life, deep ecology has not escaped criticism from the other schools of radical ecology; its criticisms have themselves been criticized.[66] Deep ecology supporters generally view the ecological crisis as a crisis of "character and culture."[67] Their criticisms therefore tend to be along characterological and cultural lines. They denounce our modern culture (worldview, paradigm) for its anti-ecological qualities—for its anthropocentrism, its disenchanted and mechanistic science, its fixation on progress, its technocratic ways, and so on. They also criticize our culture for the shape it lends to our modern character. The modern, Western self is individualistic, egoistic, consumersitic; in a word: ecologically immature. The critics of deep ecology point out, however, that our character and culture themselves have a *social* context—a context that the deep ecology movement has to a large extent ignored. For example, while deep ecology supporters wish to support a revolution in worldviews (from Newtonian-Cartesian to holistic-ecological), they tend not to consider how our worldview is itself anchored in particular social structures and everyday relations within a racist, sexist, classist society. At times they therefore give the impression that worldviews change merely through revolutions in thought or through the introduction of a new science.[68] Such criticism will not of course apply to all of those who think of their work as being deeply ecological. It is worth taking note, however, when one of the defenders of deep ecology, Kirkpatrick Sale, defines it by the fact that it thinks primarily "in biotic rather than social terms."[69] For it is precisely over this point that the other areas of radical ecology have taken deep ecology to task.

Much of the criticism of deep ecology has come from ecofeminism. Ecofeminists bring attention to the historical fact that under patriarchal rule the repressing and exploiting of women has gone hand-in-hand with the repressing and exploiting of the natural world. The domination of nature, say ecofeminists, cannot be satisfactorily understood unless viewed as a feminist issue, so close is the connection between the man-centered or "androcentric" exploitation of nature (regarded as feminine) and of women (regarded as natural).[70] Many ecofeminists suggest that as a movement deep ecology is insufficiently sensitive to the complex ways in which naturism (domination of nature), sexism, racism, and classism interlock, and to the strategically central role that gender analysis could play in dismantling all of them.[71] In reference to Fox, for example, Ariel Salleh charges that the attraction to transpersonal psychology "hangs on the self-actualizing logic of middle-class individualism," and betrays comfortable doses of "illusion and self-indulgence."[72] (The kind of psychology advanced by many ecofeminists, by contrast, is a version of the feminist "self-in-relation" model—one in which the self is defined by its concrete and caring relations to particular others, human and otherwise, and by an openness to a plurality of other voices.[73]) It is exactly deep ecology's preoccupation with psychological and metaphysical themes, and the relative weakness of its social analysis that concerns her. Although the ecofeminist literature is widely held to be an important source for the development of ecopsychology (ecofeminism anthologies appear on all the ecopsychology bibliographies), the more demanding political claims made by ecofeminists such as Salleh have simply not been taken up by ecopsychologists.[74]

The relative lack of social radicalism in ecopsychology is also indicated by its near complete neglect, so far as I am aware, of the social ecology and ecosocialist literatures. Broadly stated, social ecology is an anarchist movement based on the notion that social conflict is of a piece with our ecological troubles, that is, that oppressive social relations and the domination of the natural world share a single hierarchical mind-set; while ecosocialism goes beyond the classical Marxist analysis to emphasize how the contradiction between expanding economic production and finite ecological limits (i.e., between the forces/relations of production and the conditions of production) will also play a role in the transition toward a postcapitalist society.[75] The one notable person to contribute views to ecopsychology in this social area is the environmental justice activist Carl Anthony.[76] One of Anthony's main points is that the so-called ecological self has to date not been a "multicultural self," and that deep ecology's embrace of diversity and interdependence has not in practice extended to an embrace of *human* diversity and interdependence. "An ecopsychology that has no place for people of color, that doesn't set out to correct the distortions of racism," he says, "is an oxymoron." Deep ecology, he says, tends to construe the ecological crisis in terms of a "white" identity, neglecting the experiences and history of people of color, including the estrangement of blacks from the land under slavery. He also speaks of "the sense of loss suffered by many people living in the city, who are traumatized by the fact that they don't have a functional relationship to nature." Suggesting a possible area for ecopsychological investigation, he notes, finally, that the "environmental justice movement . . . needs a greater understanding of the psychological dimensions of environmental racism."[77]

Whether any given ecopsychologist aligns him- or herself with environmental justice, ecofeminism, or some other socially critical brand of radical ecology is not my main concern. My intention in these paragraphs has simply been to identify (in an admittedly limited way) a general area of radicalism that is at present not well-enough occupied by ecopsychologists.

The other general area relatively unoccupied by ecopsychologists is that of socially radical *psychology*. Psychological knowledge, insofar as it exposes the unlovely shadow side of a society, is dangerous knowledge.[78] As psychology unmasks, it has the potential to threaten—a fact well known by those, such as feminist psychiatrist Judith Herman, who have fought to disclose the widespread occurrence, and devastating effects, of domestic abuse and political terror. As witnesses to the psychic injuries wrought by our society, psychotherapists are uniquely positioned to be social critics. Indeed, there is a sort of latent affinity between social radicals and psychotherapists in that they both have an interest in identifying our self-deceptions and mystifications, in piercing our illusions and making better contact with reality. From a psychological angle, I therefore believe that what Joel Kovel has said about psychoanalysis also needs to be said about ecopsychology: that it "*necessarily* has to adopt a deeply critical attitude toward society" and that it "cannot be itself unless it is linkable—at least in principle—to a radical political attitude."[79]

The number of radical thinkers in psychology is relatively small, these including, in my reading, Herman, Kovel, David Ingleby, Russell Jacoby, Christopher Lasch, Peter Breggin, Philip Cushman, and Isaac Prilelltensky. What these radicals lack in numbers they nonetheless make up for in polemical bite. They accuse the psychological mainstream of being an instrument of social conformity and depoliticization; of propping up an oppressive ideological status quo; of obscuring the sociocultural and political origins of psychological distress by adopting medical, natural scientific, individualistic, and male-centered models; and of repressing Freud's scandalous insights into the socially generated sickness, the "demonic terror," hidden in the depths of the modern mind behind the "facade of consciousness." Freud, some of them say, amply demonstrated that "individual neurosis is a response to brutal social conditions,"[80] that the Western tradition has a "seamy side;"[81] and yet—to update Marx—"psychotherapy has in some respects been even more successful than religion in deflecting energy away from the need for radical social change."[82] "Indeed, an opacity to the actual social basis of psy practice is one of the defining features of these professions."[83] Dreyer Kruger writes, finally, that "it is one of the ironies of contemporary psychology that it fails to demonstrate a concern with the problem of man, that it allows its views of reality to be dictated to it by technology and its concomitant social structures, that it has hardly any historical dimension, that it is oblivious to the problematic past and blind to the possible agonies of the future."[84]

While a thorough examination of the "morals and politics of psychology" is beyond the scope of this book, I suggest that if ecopsychology is to be a radical project then it must seek out the critical currents within psychology itself, not just ecology. As I read it, the central message of critical psychology is that (1) the organization of society affects the organization of psyche; and (2) psychologists uncritically participate in, and so reinforce, many oppressive aspects of our society which themselves contribute to psychic suffering. My concern with the development of *eco*psychology is correspondingly that it not (1) reductively cast social and ecological issues in purely psychological terms; and (2) itself maintain oppressive social relations.

Regarding my first concern, there is growing awareness within ecological politics (as I discussed above) that we are now facing a "social-ecological crisis;" that the earth will not be saved while issues of justice, power, and emancipation go ignored.[85] Translated into the domain of ecopsychology: if we are, in good faith, to understand the psychopathology in the human-nature relationship, we cannot avoid an examination of the social mediation *of* this relationship. If the psyche exists beyond the boundaries of the skin, then this makes it a social as well as an ecological phenomenon, and ties our alienation from nature to our alienation within human society. I repeatedly come back to Kovel's work in this book because (among other reasons) he has been carrying on a discourse that parallels ecopsychology's, but on a sociological plane. He turns psyche inside-out to land it not in a forest, but in an unjust, fragmenting society.[86] Kovel convincingly argues, then, that "the social" is a category with which psychologists—and I would add ecopsychologists—must reckon.[87]

Ecopsychologists have approached the psyche-society connection in several ways. Some are simply quiet on the matter; as is Fox, for example, in his elaboration of transpersonal ecology.[88] (To be clear: I take no issue with talking about the transpersonal self, but only insist that we discuss *at the same time* the violent social conditions that make a *de*personalized self the more likely reality for most of us.) Among those who do speak directly to social issues, there is nonetheless a tendency to reduce these to the outward "manifestations" of our inner state of consciousness, rather than to consider how socioeconomic and political forces *themselves* contribute to that inner condition.[89] Finally, there are a small number of ecopsychologists who go so far as to examine the effect of social forces on our psychic lives, such as the role played by the advertising industry in fostering consumerism.

Allen Kanner and Mary Gomes speak, for example, of the "outright abuse of psychological expertise" in the advertising field.[90] On the whole, however, there is still a minimum of critical social theory within ecopsychology. This is no small matter, for if our goal is ecological consciousness, and if our society produces a devitalized, narcissistic consciousness instead, then it is imperative that we give critical attention to the social order. Indeed, for ecopsychologists to overlook social analysis in favor of a more narrowly psychological approach is no less than to bypass one of the main factors in our ecopsychological situation.[91] I cannot myself claim to have adequately achieved a socially radical ecopsychological stance (one that thoroughly incorporates, rather than bypasses, the social sphere), as the interdisciplinary demands and personal commitments necessary to get there are great. I do, however, hold this task out as a challenge to myself, and hold the same challenge out to the rest of the field.

Regarding my second concern, that ecopsychology not involve itself in oppressive social forms, I suggest that some conservative tendencies within ecopsychology act to undermine its own radical implications. Roszak, for instance, has put forward the idea that it "might generate a new, legally actionable, environmentally based criterion of mental health that could take on prodigious legal and policy-making implications."[92] Sarah Conn has similarly offered that the American Psychiatric Association's *Diagnostic and Statistic Manual* (DSM) be revised to include such diagnoses as "materialistic disorder," the need to consume.[93] My own wish, by contrast, is that ecopsychology stay well away from any numerically coded catalogues of "mental illnesses." The danger is that the DSM is a highly contested document that has been criticized for both its metaphysical dubiousness and its use as a tool for oppressing and mystifying people by medicalizing them and labeling them deviant, thereby serving the dominant power-interests of our society.[94] Speaking of the sheer massiveness of the DSM, Kovel writes that the "age-old dream of science, that of total control by man over nature, embodied here in the endless proliferation of categories, lists and 'decision trees,' becomes thereby an instrument of domination."[95] Roszak and Conn genuinely want to challenge psychology's lack of consideration for our relationship to the earth, and Conn is herself a critic of the DSM.[96] My concern, though, is that proposals to institutionalize ecopsychology may wind up further legitimizing the authority of an oppressive, nature-dominating mental health establishment.[97]

In his *The Voice of the Earth,* Roszak does give brief mention to "Radical Therapy." He comments, however, that his "impression has been that those who commit to Radical Therapy may never get beyond heroic opposition to the psychiatric establishment."[98] I think this remark too easily passes over the need to reflect on the position of (eco)psychology within society. One of the stated functions of the Ecopsychology Institute at California State University, of which Roszak was formerly Director, is to develop ecopsychology as a mainstream academic discipline and profession. With such mainstreaming, however, I fear that ecopsychology would indeed become "disciplined," its radical implications fading from view. I do not want ecopsychology to become a marginal movement made up of a handful of "beautiful losers," nor do I wish to create unnecessary rifts within the field. I only ask that we keep the question of social radicalism open before us.

As a final note, I think it is important to recognize that the critical task also includes taking social actions that are specifically inspired by ecopsychological criticism. I am not aware of any examples of such actions at this time. I can, however, easily imagine ecopsychologists rising up in protest on account of what they know *as* ecopsychologists. One example would be for ecologically minded psychotherapists to organize against the nature-dominating and repressing aspects of this society because of what they understand as both healers and radical ecologists (a possibility that interests me, as I mention in chapter six). Because actions of this sort are so closely connected with the work of criticism, I decided to mention them here rather than under the practical task (which I have conceived as being more strictly psychological in focus).

Defining Ecopsychology: Interrelations Among the Tasks

Having looked at the four tasks of ecopsychology (psychological, philosophical, practical, and critical), I now want to say that what defines ecopsychology as a unique undertaking is not only these four tasks but also the interdependencies among them. Considered as a project in which all four tasks explicitly feed into one another, I believe that ecopsychology has tremendous promise. An advancement in any one of the four areas would then more or less directly support advances in the others, each step helping to open up a comprehensive ecopsychological space. The power and complexity of ecopsychology lies exactly within the connections between the four tasks. The whole is indeed greater than the sum of the parts. To conclude this section I therefore want to evoke a sense of this whole project by briefly tracing some of the interrelationships among the tasks that stand out for me—an exercise that might also help the reader to digest the large volume of material I have already introduced.

Part of the *psychological task,* first of all, is to utterly dispel the illusion that we are somehow exempt from membership in the natural world and to overcome the delusion that we could ever be sane while alienated from our own earthiness, from the bodily ground we share with the twigs and mice. In this respect, the psychological task clearly feeds the critical task, in that it provides a good base from which to criticize our earth-punishing society. The *philosophical task,* next, feeds the other three tasks by supplying the conceptual-linguistic or ontological environment in which to articulate and unfold them. The *practical task,* in turn, feeds the psychological and philosophical tasks by providing a body of experience from which to then build psychological and philosophical theory. It also feeds the critical task, in that ecopsychological practices not only provide support for radical actions, but also show us what kind of shape our psyche's are in; by showing us the emotional and spiritual toll exacted by the modern world, they provide material for indicting modern society. The *critical task,* finally, feeds all the other tasks by making room for them. While it is ecopsychology's goal to foster a sense of connection with nature, including our own, the major structures of our society generally function by rubbing out that connection (a claim I will expand on later). The critical work of ecopsychology thus makes room for the other tasks in the sense that it demonstrates the very need for an ecopsychology. The critical task also feeds the philosophical task, in that our dualistic thought has emerged within a particular historical and social context. In order to ultimately overcome dualism we must become different people, must overcome the mode of existence in which our dualistic thought is rooted, and for this our repressing and fragmenting society must itself fundamentally change. Lastly, the critical task feeds the practical task as well, in that it offers up ecopsychological critiques that may then provide further ground for social action.

The project of ecopsychology, as I have just described it, is a big one. It will take a great number of committed people, working together, to keep it rolling. Some will want to concentrate on or go deep with one particular task. Others, like me, will want to keep all four on the go, working from a sense for the project as a whole. Indeed, my intention in this book is to promote the project of ecopsychology by illustrating it with an approach of my own.

A Naturalistic and Experiential Approach

I call my own approach to ecopsychology naturalistic and experiential, as these two dimensions run through my handling of each of the four tasks. In this section, I want to introduce my approach only enough to briefly situate myself within the field and to set up the discussion on ecopsychological discourse that I present in the next chapter.

Naturalistic

> *We need to see ourselves as part of a larger order that can make claims on us.*
> —Charles Taylor[99]

The discourse of the ecology movement focuses on the *claims* and *limits* of the natural world. Stan Rowe, for example, writes: "we belong to the encompassing world and sooner or later it claims us."[100] Much psychological discourse *also* addresses the claims and limits of nature, as when Konrad Stettbacher says that: "Child neglect runs counter to all the dictates of Nature."[101] Not only external nature, the biotic community, but our own human nature makes demands on us and sets limits. The work of ecopsychology, naturalistically conceived, is to relate or unify these claims and limits. Naturalistic psychology advocates fidelity to nature, being in service of nature, and seeing the human as part of a larger natural order. The ecological and psychological crises of our time may then *both* be traced to the violation of nature. The destruction of rain forests and the neglect or abuse of children are equally transgressions of the natural world, for children are nature too. Ecopsychology, in this sense, is the ecology movement not only psychologized, but *expanded* to include the domination of *human* nature. When we include human nature within ecological discourse—is it not odd that it is usually left out?[102]—that discourse necessarily turns psychological.

Despite the dangers of doing so, I thus propose that *nature* be adopted as a radical concept. In this, I fortunately have an ally in Kovel, who in his own writings has attempted to "rescue the notion of human nature . . . for radical discourse."[103] Only something that has a nature can be violated; thus, as we recognize violation so do we recognize nature. Precisely how we are to understand this nature remains for me to elaborate in the chapters to come. I have said, however, that the society that violates nonhuman nature is the same society that violates human nature. A naturalistic psychology that keeps both of these abuses in sight will not abandon human society for the wilderness, nor will it deny the deep need we all have to be initiated into mature, personal relations with the natural world. As critical thinkers such as Kovel tell us, modernity's infamous domination of nature faces in two directions: in one it diminishes the earth (ecological crisis), in the other it diminishes the human (social and psychological crisis). A naturalistic approach carried through to its proper conclusions will therefore itself face in these two directions—as did John Rodman when he made the following remarks: "I strongly suspect that the same basic principles are manifested in quite diverse forms—e.g. in damming a wild river and repressing an animal instinct (whether human or nonhuman), in clear-cutting a forest and bombing a city, in Dachau and a university research laboratory, in censoring an idea, liquidating a religious or racial group, and exterminating a species of flora or fauna."[104] An important implication of the kind of naturalism I propose is thus the need, in some fashion, to comprehend the complex nexus of psychological, social, and ecological factors at play in our field. Throughout part two I touch on the need for such understanding (focusing especially on our economized and technologized reality) and indicate some of the points from which it might be further pursued.

Experiential

> *The only "drive" or instinct of which one can usefully speak, in human behavior, is the drive to interact with the environment itself.*
> —Gordon Wheeler, commenting on the view of Kurt Goldstein[105]

The kind of naturalism I am proposing requires an experiential approach, for the demands of nature are discovered precisely via our experience of them. Fidelity to nature is gained, that is, only through fidelity to experience—through paying attention not only to our experience *of* nature, but to the nature *in* our experience. (That "we too are nature" is an idea in which ecopsychology must keep itself soaked.) Our experience is grounded in our bodily nature, in felt intentions that arise of their own (and yet which are "ours") and demand of us some kind of satisfaction. An experiential approach is based on a faith in the organismic wisdom at work in such bodily felt experience, and relies on what John Dewey called "the directive powers" that inhere in it.[106] It means therapeutically resensitizing ourselves to and taking practical guidance from our experience, the only ground we ultimately have. Working experientially also offers a way to formulate alternative interpretations of reality, one's drawn from our own felt contact with the world, and so to challenge the existing reality principle. Indeed, an experiential approach is indispensable for the difficult philosophical task of articulating a nondualistic psychology, as well as for the critical task of articulating a socially radical psychology. In introducing a number of experiential concepts—taken mostly from humanistic psychology and the overlapping philosophical traditions of phenomenology, existentialism, and hermeneutics—I am thus intending to add some theoretical support to the field.

While experience is had through bodily feelings, it is also an *interactive* process. Our experience is always directing us toward some sort of contact with the world and the world itself calls forth our experience. John Welwood writes simply that "psychological events must be understood as forms of interaction."[107] Insofar as psychology takes an interactive view of reality, it may then also join ecology along the common axis of "interaction." Psychology deals with interactions as they are meaningfully felt from the inside, whereas scientific ecology has traditionally dealt with them as external events. If, however, we give our relationship to nature psychological status, then we may study the inner sense of our interactions with, and participation in, the natural world. Part of my strategy toward this end is to build up in the reader an *experiential sense* for the interactive or dialogical nature of reality. For having a sense for how all phenomena mirror each other, intertwine, and arise only in contact with one another, radically undoes our more usual dualistic, isolated-in-the-head, feel for the world.

Perhaps what is most radical about an experiential approach is that it gives authority to our experience, all the more so as we learn to listen to and focus it. As discussed above, social movements do not always attend well to what people are experiencing, and it is not uncommon to hear of activist organizations that are themselves oppressively run. An experiential approach to politics makes the open sharing of experience and the active supporting of personal healing central to its agenda. At a time when many of us are struggling just to make it through the day, such an approach may have much to contribute to resolving the kind of problems identified above. Experiential approaches avoid being dogmatic about what people must or ought to do. They do, however, maintain that our bodily experience of the world implies certain social changes, and encourage us to take actions that move in the direction of those changes.[108] This is not to say that experiential politics takes no guidance from social theories, as these are certainly important for helping us to interpret our situations. It concentrates as much, though, on taking life-forwarding steps that emerge from making honest contact with presently felt reality. Experiential approaches take advantage of the creativity of the life process, of the arising of new meanings and possibilities with the unfolding of experience itself. To the extent that it adopts this kind of approach, ecopsychology may avoid fitting itself into ready-made forms, and seek new ones instead. (The despair and empowerment work of Macy and her colleagues is an excellent example of how a radical new form of practice may develop through paying attention to what our experience is calling for.) Most generally, by acknowledging the uniqueness or particularity of people's life situations, an experiential approach allows for a high degree of flexibility and a wide variety of options. It may, then, help us to live radical lives in whatever ways make sense from within the context of our own life experience and interests.

2

THE PROBLEM WITH NORMAL

Discursive Problems

There are few experiences quite so cruel as, when after having made a well-argued, even elegant and moving case to someone, you lean back expecting the warm sparkle of shared insight and understanding, only to encounter the flat opaqueness of complete and utter incomprehension.

—John Livingston[1]

Philosopher Albert Borgmann writes that the discourse of modernity, narrowly focused on the prediction and control of events, is simply not capable of lending us a human "voice in which to articulate our misgivings and aspirations."[2]

> We predict the weather and try to control inflation because we are not the weather and not inflation. . . . the dominant discourse about the future of our society is composed of the vocables of prognoses, projections, extrapolations, scenarios, models, programs, simulations, and incentives. It is as though we have taken ourselves out of reality and have left only objectified and disavowed versions of ourselves in the universe we are trying to understand and shape. We vacate our first-person place and presence in the world just when we mean to take responsibility for its destiny.[3]

Nowhere are the inadequacies of modern discourse more apparent than in what Owen Barfield once called "the virtual breakdown of communication between the devotees of technocracy on one side and the habitual lovers of nature and life on the other."[4]

It is a source of some dismay for ecological advocates that the things they are moved to talk about often find no home within the official views of reality that dominate our public language. Robert Socolow, for example, writes: "conservationists have separate languages for talking to one another, to politicians, and to

29

their avowed opponents. Except when they talk to one another (and perhaps not even then) they refrain all too often from articulating *what really matters to them.*[5] John Rodman similarly writes of his impression that when legal and moral philosophers use "logical gymnastics" to advocate for the "rights" of natural entities—whether laboratory animals or trees—"they sound as if they want to say something less reasonable, less moralistic, more expressive of their total sensibility, but are afraid of seeming subjective, sentimental, or something that's not quite respectable."[6] Putting his finger on this dilemma, Neil Evernden notes that: "not everyone feels compelled to defend a mountain. But those who do . . . find it an awkward compulsion, for they must reconcile the conflicting tasks of being faithful to their subject and maintaining their credibility."[7] Because ecopsychologists share the basic concerns of the ecology movement, they are to a large extent in the same boat: they are burdened with the task of finding a language capable of honestly illuminating their ecologically and psychologically informed accounts of what truly and finally matters, while at the same time being respectable or legitimate before a public audience.

And so we must talk about discourse. A discourse (as I use the term in this chapter) is a way of making sense with words; as such, it is from the start an interpretation of the world. When our interpretations are just too far off the norm, however, our audiences—as John Livingston says regarding wildlife ethics— "literally do not know what we are talking about."[8] The danger is that the reality we care for and feel compelled to talk about may be so poorly recognized by others that it is simply "leaving the realm of discussibility."[9] In this respect, historian Michel Foucault claimed that an era's reigning discursive practices act to police which beliefs, values, and attitudes get to be included within a society and which get excluded, setting the boundaries on what is understandable or acceptable. In a related vein, the communist Antonio Gramsci believed that changing the structure of society is no longer a matter of military revolution but of rhetorical struggle. He spoke of the need for "new popular beliefs, that is to say a new common sense and with it a new culture and a new philosophy which will be rooted in the popular consciousness with the same solidity and imperative quality as traditional beliefs."[10] Insofar as ecopsychology seeks to help reverse, at the level of psyche, one of the cardinal features of modernity—the domination of nature[11]—it may be thought of as an effort to move beyond the modern era. And like other holders of nonmainstream perspectives, ecopsychologists want their radical notions to one day be part of the common sense which governs our everyday existing.[12]

The purpose of this chapter is to offer a reflection on the discursive possibilities—and pitfalls—open to ecopsychology in pursuing this end. I am framing the discussion as "the problem with normal" in order to highlight, first of all, that normal psychological discourse is incapable of making good sense of the terrain of ecopsychology because of the dualism entrenched into it. Quite simply, in contesting the strict division between inner, subjective, human reality and outer, objective, natural reality, ecopsychology implicitly puts the whole research tradition that is based on this division into question. Whereas conventional modern science holds that the best way to disclose the natural world is to eliminate any personal or subjective relations with it, ecopsychology seeks a nature that is known precisely through *enhancing* this relationship. There are, of course, certain kinds of truth that only a scientific method can reveal, and there are many varieties of science. However, because ecopsychologists wish to grant the natural world its own subjectivity, agency, or personhood, they, of all people, need to protest the rigidly scientific viewpoint that denies nature these properties, and must embrace other, less divisive and more qualitative methods of inquiry. While the supremacy of the modern scientific method is increasingly questioned among qualitative researchers in the human disciplines, Norman Denzin and Yvonna Lincoln note that the challenges are still many: such "researchers are called journalists, or soft scientists. Their work is termed unscientific, or only exploratory, or entirely personal and full of bias."[13] These are the same barbs that will undoubtedly be used against ecopsychology (and which, incidentally, have already been tossed at some of my own work by a peer-reviewer). I believe that foregrounding this issue will better allow ecopsychology to deal with such criticism and make the case for privileging a "not-so-normal"[14] discourse. More specifically, I suggest that ecopsychology needs to wrestle with finding interpretive, experiential, or "hermeneutic" forms of discourse which, being demanded by the subject matter itself, have their own validity and necessity.

A second bit of trouble facing ecopsychology is the privilege normally granted to our technocratic and economic discourses. As Tom Athanasiou notes, it is doubtful whether "greening" is even possible so long as "economics is taken as the sole source of sound judgment and virtue," and while economists themselves grope "even to locate the ecological crisis on their charts."[15] Within such a climate, how can ecopsychology win an audience for its own discourse? How can it gain any recognition for its own radical set of priorities and ultimate concerns? My suggestion on this matter is that ecopsychology adopt an openly rhetorical style of speaking. As I discuss below, there is a strong affinity between the hermeneutical and rhetorical modes, and both are well-suited for navigating through psychological terrain. I propose, in short, that a hermeneutical and rhetorical method is well-suited for the purpose of establishing a radical ecopsychological discourse.

Between the Human and the Natural

We shall . . . have to rediscover the natural world . . . , and its mode of existence, which is not to be confused with that of the scientific object.
—Maurice Merleau-Ponty[16]

The subject matter of ecopsychology is neither the human nor the natural, but the lived experience of interrelationship between the two, whether the "nature" in question be human or nonhuman. In their quest for scientific respectability, however, modern psychologists have thoroughly adopted an objectivist outlook, which to a large extent excludes this subject matter from consideration. Natural scientific empiricism and rationalism continue to exercise a "dual hegemony" over academic psychology, providing the bulk of its taken-for-granted background assumptions.[17] In other words, mainstream psychology is organized around the very dualism that ecopsychology would overcome. Rationalists, such as cognitive psychologists, focus on such things as the internal processing of "information," while empiricists, such as behavioural psychologists, focus on data gathered from the external world (e.g., human behavior). Within this mainstream, questions concerning "the environment" are dealt with by the existing field of "environmental psychology," a field from which ecopsychologists generally distinguish their own efforts.[18] In what follows, I suggest that—precisely because of its continuity with a dualistic research tradition—environmental psychology is simply not capable of disclosing those meanings that concern the more radical field of ecopsychology. Ecopsychology tends to attract the more experientially oriented and less mainstream psychologies, while environmental psychology tends to hold that scientific line.[19] The challenge for ecopsychology is thus to give up psychology's attachment to the various forms of objectivism, and, accordingly, to find a mode of discourse that can walk in the challenging space *between* the human and the natural.

The goal of environmental psychology is to use traditional scientific methods to study the impact of certain environmental factors—atmospheric conditions, pollution, stress, noise, urbanization, crowding, and so forth—on individual human well-being. The research in this field is dominated by the behavioral and cognitive traditions, neither of which has much of a presence in ecopsychology. Although I do not intend to discuss in any great detail the kind of findings produced by these two approaches, I will venture here to say that ecopsychology reaches beyond them to a more qualitative or poetic consideration of the interweaving of humanity and nature, one that reveals aspects of the world and modes of experience that are not visible to the modern scientific persona. One leading pair of cognitive researchers, Rachel and Stephen Kaplan, who clearly bring much sensitivity to their work, admit in this regard that "it is hard to justify the role that nature plays in rational terms." Their findings are largely limited, then, to how nature can provide a "restorative environment" that supports humans in recovering from "mental fatigue," and so in regaining the ability to effectively "manage information."[20]

In addition to making for narrow findings, the scientific worldview adopted by environmental psychology quite simply preserves the human/nature split. As David Kidner remarks, "scientific and technological 'objectivity' serve to stabilize a style of personality functioning in which the relation of humanity to the natural world is one of comfortable domination." Hence, "the anthropocentric viewpoint is overwhelmingly predominant" within environmental psychology.[21] Two implications are that environmental psychologists attend primarily to human built environments and that they designate an environment as "healthy" simply if it promotes human health. They also take a managerial and resourcist outlook. In one of the more well-known studies to involve "the natural environment," Kaplan and Kaplan conclude, for instance, that "it is rare to find an opportunity [i.e., as is provided by nature] for such diverse and substantial benefits available at so modest a cost. Perhaps this resource for enhancing health, happiness, and wholeness has been neglected long enough." They further ask: "Is there a way to design, to manage, to interpret natural environments so as to enhance these beneficial influences?"[22] Again, the language here is hardly that of a psychology that would ponder our membership and earthly responsibilities within the community of all beings.

This last point leads to a final one: the political goals of environmental psychology are unambiguously those of mainstream or reformist environmentalism.[23] In their recent text on environmental psychology, Russell Veitch and Daniel Arkkelin write of the need

> to produce changes in human behavior to preserve the environment and quality of life. This social technology entails knowledge of individual human behavior (e.g., techniques to promote the use of public transportation or to encourage energy conservation in the home). The science of psychology has been devoted to understanding human behavior and developing technologies for changing behavior.[24]

The ethos of environmental psychology is frankly technocratic. Among the goals of one behavioral psychologist, for example, are the manipulation of citizens (e.g., through altering rewards and costs) toward "global change-producing behaviors," the elimination of "barriers to adoption of technologies and practices to mitigate global change," and the "identification of cost-effective interventions by government and other actors."[25] In other words, environmental psychology *medicalizes* the ecological crisis (as does much of the environmental movement), treating it as a kind of clinical problem to be technologically solved. Through its research we therefore discover little as to what this crisis is all about, who we are, or what it means to be a human being on a living earth. While I am not able to speak for all ecopsychologists, I think it is fair to say that there is less interest among them in manipulating behavior, and more in allowing people to imagine, and practically seek, a more mature, satisfying relation to the world of nature.

Ecopsychology is an effort not just to apply modern, objectivist psychology to environmental problems, but to consider more fully how nature figures in the human life-world. I have already noted ecopsychology's refusal to see the natural world only as it is revealed by conventional natural science, that is, in that severely restricted way that makes it amenable to prediction and control. Indeed, it especially behooves ecopsychologists to criticize the idea that modern natural science gives us the only solid way to know reality.[26] But what of *human* nature? To reduce people, as is common in psychiatry, to genetic, biochemical, or neurophysiological explanation, is surely to see humans in an equally restricted way. The science of psychiatry, to pursue this authoritative field, has grown particularly "hard" since the 1980s, when—spurred on by the development of psychiatric medications—it was overtaken "with a fervor for biological explanation."[27] The experiential critique of biological psychiatry begins with the assertion that human *existence* is a totality, simultaneously psychic and somatic, and so is prior, and irreducible, to either of these two aspects.[28] No physiological condition is ever just a "natural" phenomenon, but is *lived*. Lived, moreover, within a political, economic, and sociocultural field. Whatever is the "organic" contribution to, say, schizophrenia (and there is no unanimity of opinion on this[29]), to attend mostly to manipulating the physicochemical structure of schizophrenic people is to refuse to give their hellish existence a hearing, to listen to the meaningful voice—the logos—of their suffering souls.[30] The medical strategy that would bring schizophrenia "under the sway of medical technics," says Kovel, and so reduce this horrific "collapse of being" to a biochemical abnormality in the brain, has

> obvious cultural power, since it combines in one conception the mystique of the machine and the managerial ethos. In its system the doctor-expert is the manager of the soul, regarded now as a mechanism like any other, capable of tuning up or overhauling. . . . The notion also has a political power, . . . disease is something going on within a person; it is to be looked for in the malfunctioning of the 'parts' of his personality and not in the entire relationship between the self and the world; and it is to be remedied by individual or particularistic action. . . . It should not [, however,] be thought that social problems are beyond the scope of the medical model. Quite the contrary: it exists to gobble them up and medicalize them.[31]

I have cited this passage to indicate how the modern project of splitting off and mastering nature has made its way into the psychiatric establishment, as it has with academic psychology more generally. By keeping madness primarily on the far (nature) side of the human/nature divide, in the realm of broken machinery, it helps obscure the role that social disintegration, poverty, family stress, child abuse, sexism, racism, class discrimination, dehumanizing institutions, ecological collapse, and other stressing social factors also play in the genesis of suffering[32] (even if these are not entirely ignored by psychiatrists[33] and even if medical knowledge and psychiatric medication are indeed sometimes called for[34]). More generally, however, my intention in this paragraph has been to highlight the need to develop better conceptions not only of nonhuman nature, but of human nature too.

The challenge posed by "human nature" is that it is the one notion in which humans and nature undeniably cross. Although this phrase puts the words "human" and "nature" next to one another, the normal scientific reduction of nature to matter-in-motion renders the question of human nature paradoxical.[35] We have to either slide humans into "nature" and so imagine ourselves as mechanical animals, or come up with a nature for ourselves that has only sociocultural or psychological, that is, "human," dimensions—neither of which option keeps the tension between the two terms alive. It is noteworthy, for this reason, that the founder of twentieth-century psychotherapy, Sigmund Freud, did not entirely avoid this dilemma. On the one hand, Freud recognized a natural moment to human existence—that of instinct, appetite, energy, force—to which he applied a natural scientific approach in his more abstract ("metapsychological") writings. He called the mind a "mental apparatus," and drew numerous analogies from hydrodynamics, mechanics, optics, and other areas of natural science. On the other hand, for his more concrete, clinical findings he posited a human moment—that of language, symbols, representation, meaning—to which he brought a discourse that demonstrated much artistry and interpretive virtuosity. In so doing, Freud introduced a method explicitly attuned to *meaning*, and thereby made a historic break from normal psychology. Nonetheless, his attachment to the idea of being a natural scientist prevented him from ever finding any intermediate terms to comprehend the act of translation between our instinctual "nature" and our "human" experience. (To return to the medical model, there is just no way to conceptually demonstrate how anybody's brain chemistry, considered to have only external or objective reality, can eventuate in inward, subjective experiences, such as delusions of grandeur.) In the end his was therefore what Paul Ricoeur called a "mixed discourse": an "objective discourse of force uneasily combined with [a] subjective discourse of meaning."[36]

Because Freud's discourse acknowledges that human being is subtended by nature, and yet also preserves an experiential or "meaning" component, it may be thought of as transitional toward a form more adequate to ecopsychology. Whereas Freud treats natural force and human experience within separate domains, ecopsychology requires a *singular* discourse in which the human and the natural may be held together in more unitary terms. The limitations of the natural scientific disclosure of the world become apparent when we apply it to ourselves and then, realizing that there is more to us than blind matter, we create a dualism in order to save ourselves. The attempt to find a discourse free of such dualistic trouble puts ecopsychology right in the middle of those difficult philosophical problems, still very much in play, that have preoccupied Western thought. I introduced some of these in the previous chapter, and in the next four consider further some of the philosophical and psychological options available to ecopsychology for its own efforts at resolving them. Suffice to say for now that our discourse will come to walk between the human and the natural, and so escape the trouble discussed above, only as we learn to describe how we *experience* them together: the move away from dualism is the move toward experience.

In Praise of the Not-So-Normal: The Hermeneutic Dimension

Making your unknown known is the important thing—and keeping the unknown always beyond you. Catching, crystallizing your simpler clearer vision of life—only to see it turn stale compared to what you vaguely feel ahead—that you must always keep working to grasp.

　　　　　　　　　　　　　　　　　　　　　　—Georgia O'Keeffe[37]

A good research method is one that allows some interesting phenomenon to reveal itself as truthfully as possible; the method must be suited or adequate to the phenomenon or the phenomenon itself gets missed. If ecopsychology is to be a discourse of the human-nature dialectic that is "liberated from the spurious narrowing imposed by the model of the natural sciences,"[38] then what exactly are the methodological options available to it for rejecting a normal scientific approach and developing a not-so-normal one? The general route out of objectivism is to participate more intimately or concretely in one's subject matter and thereby discover meanings, develop understandings, or make interpretations not accessible to the remote observer. Ecopsychology would thus do well to enter the field concerned precisely with how we understand and interpret the world: *hermeneutics*. Richard Rorty writes that hermeneutical discourse is "*supposed* to be abnormal, to take us out of our old selves by the power of strangeness, to aid us in becoming new beings." It plays the cultural role of (in John Dewey's words) "breaking the crust of convention," guarding us from the self-deception "that we know ourselves by knowing a set of objective facts."[39] Such inquiry is also based on the view that the "keys to understanding are not manipulation and control but participation and openness, not [data] but experience, not methodology but dialectic."[40] Conflict or debate is not ruled out, but rather turned to advantage— to revealing prejudices, overcoming misunderstandings, and finding more common ground. Understood as a kind of open conversation with few hard and fast rules, hermeneutical discourse is thus more truly a *discursus,* "a running to and fro" toward better understandings. Its course is not straight, but is a dis-course. I will myself be leaning heavily on hermeneutic principles throughout this book. In this section I therefore want to introduce three aspects of hermeneutical inquiry that are relevant to ecopsychology, and to which I am myself committed. My points are made here in a rather cursory or compact way, but should gain strength as I revisit and flesh them out in the remaining chapters.

Overcoming Alienation. J. H. van den Berg once called child psychology the "result of a state of emergency," its "scientifically-phrased understanding" being "the *smallest compensation* for the lost natural understanding between old and young."[41] Anthropologist Stanley Diamond likewise commented that his own discipline has grown popular precisely because civilization has exacted such an acute loss in our understanding of ourselves *as human beings*. Yet, anthropology is in the main a "narrow discipline with mechanical techniques and trivial goals" that represses its own urgent and central question, namely, "what part of our humanity have we lost and how and in what form we may regain it."[42] I take these blunt statements from van den Berg and Diamond as suggesting that our scientific "ologies" not only restrict our vision, but largely *define our estrangements*. As the scope of our historical alienation widens, and as the losses are felt, disciplines or fields such as child psychology and anthropology—and now ecopsychology—are born.

The ecophilosopher George Sessions has traced ecopsychology's beginnings to Jean-Jacques Rousseau, one of the first Europeans to articulate the "psychological importance of relating to wild Nature."[43] Van den Berg claimed, though, that the "sense of nature" Rousseau would have us believe was "a valuable matter which people for some inexplicable reason had never seen before" was in fact "the discovery of a loss."[44] Does it not seem fitting to suggest that the "vast continent" to be mapped by ecopsychologists is, in truth, a terrain born of alienation? Richard Nelson writes: "Probably no society has been so deeply alienated from the community of nature, has viewed the natural world from a greater distance of mind, has lapsed into a murkier comprehension of its connection with the sustaining environment."[45] I imagine van den Berg and Diamond, then, cautioning ecopsychologists not to forget the "state of emergency" that has initiated our own field; to beware the danger of attempting "to find in science a substitute for lost orientation."[46] As ecopsychologists, we need to keep our own broad and urgent questions of alienation, of loss and recovery, before us.[47]

This is where hermeneutics comes in; for a hermeneutical inquiry is one that studies something strange, unfamiliar, or alien that must be made comprehensible, familiar, or near through a process of interpretation.[48] One of the key figures in hermeneutics, Hans-Georg Gadamer, described it as letting "what is alienated by the character of the written word or by the character of being distantiated by cultural or historical distances speak again."[49] And alienation takes place "when we have withdrawn ourselves and are no longer open to the immediate claim of that which grasps us."[50] To hear Gadamer's words with the idea that it is *nature's* claims that have been made distant is, I suggest, to reveal ecopsychology as a hermeneutical form of inquiry. It seeks to listen to or interpret the voice of nature in a way that normal science simply cannot. What Gadamer tells us—that estrangement is overcome "only through a dialogical encounter with what is at once alien to us, makes a claim upon us, and has an affinity with what we are"[51]— thus applies equally, and especially, to our current relationship with nature, including our own.

Hermeneutic investigations have previously granted a voice to historical texts, traditions, works of art, foreign cultures, and so on, but not so much to nature. Borgmann notes, for example, that Rorty, one of the main advocates for conversation and solidarity with others, believes nature to be "utterly silent."[52] Rorty himself says that "nature has no preferred way of being represented."[53] This is no incidental omission, but a highly limiting prejudice *within* hermeneutics— and grounds for a strong critique of much hermeneutical practice itself. For, aside from presuming that the birds, lakes, and trees make no claims on us, it leaves little room for how *nature enters into our experience through the body*. While Gadamerian hermeneutics does hold that interpretations are always drawn from experience, in practice it has little to say about the bodily nature lying right at the heart of the human situation. According to Kovel, hermeneutics thus drifts "toward an ulti- mately repressive and flattened view of human beings," one in which desire and unconsciousness have no place—as if experience had no negativity or depths, but consisted primarily of writing and interpreting texts.[54]

Gadamer's philosophical hermeneutics, because so influential, may come in for particular criticism here, for it tends toward a kind of linguistic idealism, in which reality is felt to be constituted by language alone (the poststructuralist view).[55] There are, however, a handful of philosophers—including Merleau- Ponty, Eugene Gendlin, and David Levin—for whom our bodily nature *is* a central thematic, and to whom Kovel's comments do *not* therefore apply. Against much current scholarship, Gendlin writes, for instance, that "it is nonsense to say that only [human] language and culture create meaning."[56] "Language and cul- ture," that is, "do not abolish the animal."[57] Even these authors, however, while willing to give nature its due, have ventured little into the realm of *nonhuman* nature. To borrow a phrase from Abram, their thought "never quite leaves the city."[58] A hermeneutics of nature proper, such as ecopsychology might become, must turn that much more sharply back on hermeneutics itself, because—as I try to show in chapter five—it makes *both* human and nonhuman nature central to the genesis of meaning or understanding, that is, hermeneutics' very subject matter. As Abram noted in the previous chapter, this is exactly the direction in which Merleau-Ponty's own hermeneutic phenomenology was headed.[59]

Risking Being Changed. A basic tenet of hermeneutics is that all experience takes place within an implicitly sensed context or "horizon" of background understand- ing, which for the most part remains obscure or concealed. Most of what we understand was never given to us in the form of an explicit belief system or theory, but is simply embodied in shared daily activities or cultural practices we have meshed ourselves into. We do not teach children, for instance, how far to stand from other people; instead, they catch on to our subtle distance-standing practices by imitating adults, with little awareness that they are doing so.[60] In like fashion, we also pick up or come to grasp specific points of view and ways of conceiving things—all of which adds up to a pervasively felt "preunderstanding" that "fore- structures" our perception of the world. Thus, no matter how clear and distinct our knowledge, it will always trail off into an unclear background sense whose origins will forever remain mostly in the dark.

There can therefore be no presuppositionless understanding, no coming to some topic without any biases or tacit expectations.[61] Otherwise, we could not make any contact with our subject matter to begin with; it could not even show up as something interesting or worthy of study. The process of interpretation, accordingly, must proceed from whatever understanding we already have; it has no absolute beginning or end, but takes place within the so-called hermeneutic circle. In reading this chapter, for instance, you, the reader, are grasping the meaning of my words under the condition of whatever prior understanding of things you bring to them. Certain passages, if quite unfamiliar to you or foreign to your background, may be opaque; while others will be more readily gathered. In any event, if after finishing this chapter you read it again, my words will inevitably make more sense. This is because the first reading will have granted you a feel for the chapter-as-a-whole, however tentative, which will then act as a new horizon within which to continue puzzling out its various details. You will, in short, be interpreting what I am saying by cycling back and forth between the various pieces or particulars of the chapter and the chapter considered more globally; by reading the ending into the beginning, and vice versa. This interpretive dialectic, in which "a partial understanding is used to understand still further,"[62] and in which one's felt sense of the "text" is explicated by shuffling between parts and whole, is the hermeneutic circle.

Notice that in the process just described the reader's own horizon of understanding must somehow meet the implicit horizon of the text, such that there is what Gadamer called a "fusion of horizons."[63] In other words, as we make genuine contact with something novel or alien, our own horizons are broadened and enriched. What is more, the alien context provides a contrasting ground against which buried prejudices hidden within our own preunderstanding are made more visible. A central tenet of hermeneutics is therefore that we gain self-understanding only through our interaction with others. Gadamer was insistent, however, that we not merely explicate our own prejudices, but be willing to *risk* them. Readers of this chapter who are committed to a traditional scientific view, for example, might become more aware of their own prescientific assumptions and perhaps willing to examine and/or modify some of them. Or they might disagree with what I have said, but still find that this helps them sense, clarify, or advance their own understanding of things. This kind of hermeneutics asks, then, that we risk, as one anthropological title puts it, *Being Changed* by our encounter with the other.[64] The kind of reality we discover depends on the kind of people we are. If we wish to uncover new realities we must therefore be willing to become new people. In short, the "hermeneutical task is to find the resources in our language and experience to understand . . . initially alien phenomena without imposing blind or distortive prejudices on them";[65] and this is accomplished only as we reveal and risk our own prejudices, and dialectically bend ourselves toward the phenomenon's own governing demands; let it grasp us as much as we grasp it— *serve* it, in a sense.

Being Creative. Considerable scholarship has been devoted to demonstrating that, in a qualified way, *all* inquiry is hermeneutical. Every researcher, including the natural scientist, participates in an interpretive community, with its own shared, implicitly grasped practices, points of view, and fore-conceptions.[66] Hermeneutics, then, is *universal.* What makes a science normal is simply that this preunderstanding is taken for granted. Normal scientists get on with studying the "facts" (now read: interpretations) revealed within the horizons of their chosen paradigm, being inclined to leave all the philosophical discomfort to their less normal colleagues.[67] What concerned Gadamer was that research *not* become blind to its hermeneutical dimension, that it not get trapped in an unreflective methodology that "flattens experience and inevitably leads to a betrayal of what is specifically other."[68] Gadamer was imploring, then, that thinking remain creative, dialectical, responsive. Always located in that zone between the familiar and the not-yet-clear, hermeneutic researchers must work with a taste or feeling for that which has yet to be formulated, letting their intuition for the subject matter guide their engagement with its particulars. They do not work solely in the "well-lit world of observables,"[69] but rather face the arduous task of bringing new truths to light. Indeed, as was declared by the Eskimo shaman, Baleen, just before being swept away into ritual ecstasy: *"It is a hard thing to speak the truth. It is difficult to make hidden forces appear."*[70]

I am suggesting that ecopsychology itself adopt such a creative hermeneutic spirit. Ecopsychology is not about lying on the couch; it is a unique undertaking which will have to struggle to find its own particular praxis. Allen Kanner says that "we have no words in our psychological parlance to describe the deep disturbance people experience when the urge to be in contact with the natural world is repressed, or where we are routinely isolated from the patterns and rhythms of the rest of the Earth."[71] Robert Greenway likewise speaks of the frustrating dearth of terminology available for lighting up the human-nature relationship, calling ecopsychology, as much as anything else, "a search for a language."[72] In view of this linguistic poverty, I find Christine Downing's comments on the hermeneutic efforts of Freud and Jung to be instructive.

> Both really invent their own language to communicate their own vision; *there is no given mode of discourse,* no recognized literary genre, no established philosophical option, which is wholly adequate. Their fusions of the language of myth and of science are not confusions but conscious and deliberate undertakings. Because they are *writing out of their unique and overwhelming experiences*—Freud out of the

discovery, "I am Oedipus," precipitated by his father's death; Jung out of his six-year-long deliberately chosen "confrontation with the unconscious"—they could not borrow another's language to render them. To them their own speech was alive, pregnant, *avowedly metaphorical.*[73]

When in the grips of an experience, we interpret it by formulating *whatever* language helps elucidate that experience—that "saves the appearances." Does it not make sense, then, that the most exciting discourses in ecopsychology will be born by those who can find original terms to symbolize their own "unique and overwhelming experiences"? As Freud and Jung made much use of the arts to develop their theories, so Greenway and others have insisted that poets, nature writers, novelists, musicians, visual artists—those most gifted at truth disclosure—will hold an important place within ecopsychology. While I agree with this, I also emphasize the importance of finding our *own* voice. In other words, I suggest that we each get a handle on the kind of experiences that have led us to ecopsychology—that are defining the field—and to then let *these* serve as the determining grounds for our own creative theorizing, including how we appropriate the arts.

I suggested above that ecopsychology was born of alienation. While alienation may not be every ecopsychologist's defining experience, I do suggest that ecopsychology has emerged largely from a sense of loss. We have little positive to go on, have few words, because our experience is of absence, of lack, of relationships that aren't. We are grasping at a painful hole, at nonbeing. Peter Mathiessen writes: "The sun glints through the pines, and the heart is pierced in a moment of beauty and strange pain, like a memory of paradise. After that day, at the bottom of each breath, there is a hollow place that is filled with longing."[74] Richard Nelson watches a Raven fly off, and says: "As I watch him grow smaller in the distance, I feel a deep longing, pangs of uncertainty, and a sense of aching, overpowering loss."[75] Nelson is among the most articulate of nature writers, yet here is an inchoate longing that admits of little explication—like a rage, unsure of its target, that can only scream. That we have no existing framework or mythology for making sense of these experiences is in itself a sign of the magnitude of our loss. It is precisely this sense of loss, moreover, "present in eco-radicalism and absent from reform minded strategies," that the critical environmental thinker Ray Rogers suggests is one of the "most significant contrasts that separates the radical and moderate perspective."[76] I am aiming, then, to adopt a genre of discourse based on the experience of loss. Of course, many have sat in sweat lodges with animal spirits lighting up the darkness, cried for visions and received them, felt the immanent power of the Goddess, surrendered in yoga or meditation into profound body awakenings, made a living in the outdoors, delighted in newts and salamanders, or found other ways to personally acquaint themselves with the psyche of nature, and this is all to the good. My own interest, though, is to develop a discourse more centred on speaking to and illuminating our estrangement, for that is where I believe our common experience most lies.[77] Although I have found my own ways to converse with nature, my experience, too, is still overwhelmingly that of loss—of grief and longing—and so it is here, in all honesty, that I must begin my inquiry. My experiential approach to nature (or naturalistic approach to experience) grew precisely out of my efforts to better understand the nature of our shared loss and to trace some of the conditions that contribute to it. (Because I am concentrating on the experience of loss, some will fault me for being nostalgic and for ignoring what has in fact been gained in modern times. I think it is wrong, however, to automatically slot any discussion about loss into the nostalgia category, as I discuss in the following endnote.[78])

All experiential approaches require first contacting whatever one is actually experiencing, in the faith that this will lead to the next step forward. Abram writes that the "pain, the sadness of [our] exile" from nature "is precisely the trace of what has been lost, the intimation of a forgotten intimacy."[79] As Macy might have it, this pain and sadness will be our guide. Hence, ecopsychology, as I see it, will take the course of a gradual process of healing, of slowly allowing ourselves to be changed and reclaimed by nature, and of charting or interpreting this process one little bit at a time. This means that the practical side of ecopsychology will play a particularly key role in the development of its theoretical side. While ecopsychologists may have defined a new field of study, this does not mean they yet know much about it. In my view, then, the leading edge of our theory will be the leading edge of our experience.[80]

To adopt a genre based on loss is to set a tone or mood that may disclose some of the painful reality lying behind the manic mask of modernity. Following Borgmann, I regard this effort of mine as a experiment in questioning and finding a way beyond the modern frame. I am working from a felt sense of incompleteness, from a feeling for what is needed, even if not entirely known.[81] My style is to begin with this felt sense and to slowly fill in some of the pieces, to place a few broad, initial strokes on an admittedly large canvas. While this may make for many gaps and some fuzziness in the picture, I do not see this as a problem; for it reflects the actual nascent state of ecopsychological inquiry, and it demonstrates the process to which I subscribe, namely, entering the hermeneutic circle from wherever one is. The struggle to make meaning, to lend form to experience, is like the struggle to recall something forgotten; we feel an immediate satisfaction when words finally come for the recollected thing. So it is for any moment when we recognize a pattern, contact some truth, or bring into symbolic focus a feeling that has been haunting us from the deep. I thus have in mind a style of inquiry with lots of ragged edges, unanswered questions, and loose ends; and yet with an atmosphere and an impelling force that can be felt; where points, even if surrounded by ignorance, nonetheless get made and are able to dialogically elicit fruitful responses from the reader.

The Symbolic or Metaphorical Nature of Reality and the Discursive Primacy of Rhetoric

Metaphoric usage is appropriate to [philosophy] because reality is itself metaphoric.

—Erazim Kohák[82]

. . . to assert our concepts of reality . . . or to offer our imaginative pictures of man or nature is necessarily to immerse ourselves in rhetoric.

—Paul Campbell[83]

In the previous section, I characterized my approach as hermeneutical, in that it operates on the basic level of how we experience, interpret, or understand the world and highlights how all inquiry has a hermeneutical dimension. I now wish to further designate my approach as *rhetorical*, in that rhetoric is the persuasive use of language on this same primordial plane and because I wish to highlight how all discourse also has a *rhetorical dimension*. To make the link between hermeneutics and rhetoric, I introduce below the idea that these two fields are simply more deliberate instances of two interrelated symbolic or metaphorical activities we are always *already* involved in: interpreting reality and speaking to one another. As an art, rhetoric has historically employed language as a symbolic means to create specific experiential effects in the psyche or soul, so as to inform, please, and move the listener.[84] James Hillman has thus called rhetoric the "speech form" of the soul, the soul being "precisely that mode which recognizes all realities as primarily symbolic or metaphorical."[85] To the extent that ecopsychology openly positions itself within this rhetorical dimension, I believe that it will enjoy greater freedom to both criticize and create. Indeed, for ecopsychology to eloquently argue its radical positions, for it to disclose or make figural the ultimate matter which concerns it (namely, the human-nature relationship), an explicitly rhetorical discourse is most appropriate.[86] In this section I outline a form of discourse which, because it aims to be rhetorical precisely by being hermeneutical, I am adopting for my own ecopsychological efforts. *Deictic discourse* was first named as such by Aristotle. For my purposes, however, I am staying closer to the way in which it has been characterized by Albert Borgmann in his philosophical works on technology, even if I take a more psychological route than he. The significance of a deictic discourse, according to Borgmann, is that it lets us "be true to our deepest experiences and aspirations and to make these prevail against technology."[87] It is a style of rhetoric that uses a language of personal resonance,[88] addressing itself to those aspects of our lives for which smooth and efficient functioning is not the main issue. It does so, finally, in order to recall something that is endangered in our technological age, yet which, being "other and greater than ourselves," needs once again to be brought to the fore so that we may reorient or focus our lives in relation to it. One such something, of course, is nature.

Owen Barfield once observed that there is a "figurative relation between man and his environment, out of which the words he is using were born."[89] Even the most literal or nonfigurative of words contain within themselves the traces of their metaphorical origins. The word *metaphor,* for starters, is itself a metaphor, one that means "to carry" (*pherein*) "beyond" (*meta*). Thus may a given word like *tongue* (in Latin: *lingua*) serve as the carrier for a meaning that goes beyond an initial sense to form a new one: "language." In like fashion, it can be demonstrated that all words ultimately draw their significance from the deep pool of metaphorical possibilities latent within our experience of the world itself. There would be no word *language* unless there was a tongue in our mouths that we can experience shaping the words we speak, and so use as a metaphor for the whole field of word-use itself. Hence the conclusion that "every modern language, with its thousands of abstract terms and its nuances of meaning and association, is . . . nothing, from beginning to end, but an unconscionable tissue of dead, or petrified, metaphors."[90] More radically still, we may suggest that every metaphor is a *poetic* creation, in that it uses words in some novel way to reveal fresh meanings—and then say, along with Ralph Waldo Emerson, that our everyday language is "fossil poetry."[91] Poetry, in this sense, is not an adornment of the prosaic world, but its origin. Literalness is a quality some words acquire as they become sedimented into habitual usage, but only as they lose their metaphorical or poetic ring, which may yet survive as the hidden "soul" of the word.[92]

If words are symbols or metaphors, then our speaking is never neutral. Whenever we speak, we *select* linguistic symbols in order to evoke those *particular meanings* that will communicate *our own view or sense of reality.* This nonneutrality of speech is what in a broad sense characterizes its rhetorical quality. As Kenneth Burke succinctly remarked, "wherever there is 'meaning,' there is 'persuasion.'"[93] While *persuasion* may seem too strong a term to apply to *every* speech act, I use the term only to indicate that all speaking calls forth meaning, bears an interpretation, has a directionality, or, indeed, issues from a certain *persuasion*—and so aims to "sway" or affect us somehow, no matter the intent. "Every utterance is intended by the utterer to be heard, accepted, acted on, judged valid, or deemed meaningful."[94] Mikhail Bakhtin held, along these lines, that every utterance is a response *to* others and is itself molded in anticipation of a response *from* others. It is "filled with dialogic overtones." To my mind, this supports the idea that our speaking will always have a rhetorical dimension, whatever the level of discourse may be: "our thought itself—philosophical, scientific, and artistic—is born and shaped in the process of interaction and struggle with others' thought, and this cannot but be reflected in the forms that verbally express our thought as well."[95] The poetic-rhetorical, in short, is the "single inevitable dimension of language."[96] Before anything else, we are every one of us poet-rhetoricians—symbolic and dialogical beings.

What, then, is the relationship between rhetoric and hermeneutics? The fields of rhetoric and hermeneutics can both be said to work in the symbolic or metaphorical mode, as speaking and interpreting are both acts of symbolization or metaphor use. The difference lies in their emphases, the former on the communicative arts, the latter on the event of understanding or meaning creation. Given that both communication and understanding are involved in any sort of inquiry, however, it is safe to say that these two fields have a close relation. Says Gadamer, "Convincing and persuading, without being able to prove—these are obviously as much the aim and measure of understanding and interpretation as they are the aim and measure of the art of oration and persuasion." We would not be seeking to persuade others unless shared understanding were at issue, and there would be no hermeneutical task unless, in the pursuit of better understanding, we were engaged in dialogue. Hence, "rhetorical and hermeneutical aspects of human linguisticality completely interpenetrate each other."[97]

In this book, I am myself attempting to maintain a balance between rhetorical and hermeneutical goals by speaking "deictically." "The word *deictic* comes from Greek *deiknynai*, which means to show, to point out, to bring to light, to set before one, and then also to explain and teach. Speakers of deictic discourse never finally warrant the validity of what they tell but point away from themselves to what finally matters; they speak essentially as witnesses."[98] The challenge for a deictical speaker is to make an ultimate concern tangible to others, to articulate a world that has this concern at its centre. As Borgmann says, modern scientific laws are unable to elucidate "the crucial and remarkable features of the modern world" and so by themselves cannot provide us with the orientation we so need. Scientists begin their explanatory work only *after* some subject matter has emerged as worthy of investigation; they cannot explain the emergence of this significance itself. For significance resides in-the-world, not in decontextualized or "deworlded" data.[99] Deictic discourses, then, are *experiential;* they play the role of offering the orientation, the larger context of meaning, that is missing from our more narrow scientific or "apo-deictic" discourses.[100] Of course, blank opposition to all scientific investigation is an untenable position, for there are certain kinds of regularity within the natural world that only the scientific mode can detect. Indeed, we would be much the poorer without such undertakings as attachment theory and conservation biology. The experiential critique, in general, insists only that scientific knowledge be placed within the context of, and so take its sense or bearing from, our whole lived existence.[101] Erazim Kohák writes in this vein that there is "something wrong when we use medicine to deaden our sensitivity, when we . . . blind ourselves with the very lights we devised to help us see."[102] Providing a sensitive vision of what truly matters, and which may bring some sense to our science, is, by contrast, precisely the task of deictical rhetoric.

In place of our more usual technical rhetoric, then, deictical rhetoric is *disclosive.* It requires of us not scientific exactitude, but a sharpness of another sort: for symbolizing and appealing to experience, for bringing to light what is going on. It throws us back onto our shaky selves, onto our interpretive abilities. Part of the therapeutic work of ecopsychology is exactly to resensitize ourselves to what we might perceive *without* the aid of science or other forms of explanation, by consulting our experience. As Joanna Macy suggests: "Our capacity to reach each other stems less from our command of statistics than from our existential confrontation with the dangers of our time. . . . In all such conversation, we need to believe . . . that there is that in the other person that can hear us at the level of these deep concerns. To the extent that we can address the human being— somewhere there inside—we become effective communicators."[103] Or as Wendell Berry writes: "It is not necessary to have recourse to statistics to see that the human estate is declining with the estate of nature."[104]

I am calling my own work deictical because it is part of a larger effort to establish or open up the human-nature relationship (*as* a relationship) as a domain of concern, to make it discussible. Borgmann says that to get out of the modern era we must let "the things that are beyond the control of modernity . . . speak in their own right."[105] This statement could well serve as a motto for my own naturalistic approach. In pointing toward wilderness as the most obvious realm that stands in its own right outside the rule of modern technology, however, Borgmann is typical of writers who effectively locate wild nature in the woods, not in the body, and so avoid confronting more psychological themes. I wish, rather, to demonstrate that not only field and forest, but our own bodily nature lies essentially outside the control of modernity, is wild; and to reject mainstream psychology's alliance with the prevailing technological-economic order, allying my psychology instead with the order of primordial nature, inside and out.

The way I am doing this is by building an approach: a set of concepts and working principles by which the human-nature relationship may be understood and practical actions encouraged. My intention is not so much to announce a system as to disclose a matter of deep concern. Inasmuch as we are all poetic-rhetorical beings, and that I want to address the reader at the level of our essential humanity, I would like to use a poetic-rhetorical language in my efforts. Indeed, Borgmann asserts that "poetical speech is the purest kind of deictical discourse since it is the most adequate medium of ultimate significance."[106] His is not an uncommon sentiment. Great poetry is language at its most hermeneutical, for truth "is always in poetic form; not literal but symbolic."[107] Ecopsychology, in particular, must embrace the poetic principle exactly because a gross imbalance toward the rational principle has been so pivotal in the historical divorce of human consciousness from nature.[108] Lamenting this divorce, Calvin Martin comments that: "If anyone is going to reinvent humanity, surely it will be the poets."[109] The problem, of course, is that the darkness of poetic meanings often makes them inaccessible. When it comes to deciding on official matters, moreover, it is not the poets and prophets to whom we generally lend our ears. Gary Snyder comments, in this regard, that "poetry has been a long and not very successful defending action."[110] What, then, to do? I have myself felt sustained over the years by the rich smell of wet earth and the generous sound of wind through trees; have experienced the natural world beyond any doubt as the "horizon of all horizons"; and have begun a painful and rewarding journey of recalling my own embodiment. Yet, my intention is not to write poetry. Here, I again follow Borgmann, who positions his own work in the gap that has opened up *between* art and science, calling his "para-deictic" writings a historically necessary intermediate form of discourse.[111] A paradeictic discourse uses a combination of conceptual precision and poetic sensitivity in order to draw out broader concerns and patterns than does a more concrete deictic discourse.[112] Its quality of light is thus neither that of the scientist's spotlight nor the artist's studio. As a former applied scientist on his way to becoming I'm-not-quite-sure-what, such a discourse suits my own in-between perceptions and abilities.

In matters of ultimate concern there can be no knock-down arguments.[113] The form of deictic discourse I am seeking, however, "reaches out to its listeners, takes account of their situation, and searches out the strongest existing bonds between the audience and the matter of concern. Thus it is most likely to create conditions of collective assent and the basis of common action."[114] Continuing on with what I have said above, my rhetorical strategy is to try to find the words that may touch that part of you, the reader, that feels the same general loss that I do. I ask that you measure my words against your own experience, seeing if they stir anything inside you, make any sense, or speak to whatever your own version of loss may be. Indeed, it is this very sense of loss that forms the basis for my social criticism. Because I am talking from my own perspective, my own felt experience, the discussions I present will not reach every reader in the same way. Nonetheless, the human-nature relation includes all of us; I am not just talking about myself. In other words, I am locating my inquiry within, and speaking to the life process, which in one way or another is common to all of us. At bottom, then, my appeal is to the reader's sense of life itself, however she or he may uniquely sense it.

PART II
NATURE AND EXPERIENCE

If, indeed, science cannot be expected to "save" nature, then it is important to resurrect the tradition of experiencing the loss of nature as the loss of human identity.

—Raymond Rogers

3

BEGINNING WITH EXPERIENCE

"Returning to Experience"[1]

In order to understand ourselves and heal ourselves in this age of abstract horror, we must regain the sense of the totality and the immediacy of human experience.

—Stanley Diamond[2]

On the way to becoming an ecopsychologist, my imagination was decisively sparked by two environmental thinkers who each argue for a "return to experience": John Livingston and Neil Evernden. Livingston, first, claims that reasoning alone will never really serve the cause of wildlife, for those persons who would save a wetland or defend a river are not really motivated *by* such reasoning. They simply inhabit an experiential universe, a world, in which actions of this sort make sense; they are motivated by their felt relation to things, by what they care for, not by principles of logic. Livingston thus concludes that, at bottom, "wildlife preservation is entirely dependent upon *individual human experience.*"[3] Evernden addresses the same problem, saying that for activists to adopt a technocratic language and method is actually to betray their own cause; for it converts nature into voiceless objects to be managed for human utility, nothing more. He urges the environmentalist, then, not to accept "beliefs that trivialize the experience of living and assert the reality of a valueless world," but to "attest to his own experience of a meaningful, valuable, colourful world."[4] Evernden and Livingston deliberately leave their works suggestive, being openly cautious about offering any "solutions" that would undermine their own noninstrumentalist views. I believe, however, that their writings *do* point toward a particular kind of project—a project they each repeatedly mention, but refrain from pursuing in any depth.

For Livingston, we might call this project one of "recovery." Such would entail a "compliant acceptance" of our human membership "in the beauty that is life process," as against the life-alienating tendencies of our modern culture. To illustrate what he means by this, Livingston invites the reader to take a moment to "look at the cock pigeon strutting on the eavestrough [*sic*]. . . . See the bird; really *see* him, and *feel* the urgency and the perfection and the beauty of his hot being. . . . Know that you and he pulse as one, and that you always did."[5] For the vast majority of modern folk, however, I suggest that such an exercise, to borrow one of Livingston's own phrases, is going exactly nowhere. It's just not that easy. Most of us simply do not have the *capacity* to feel what Livingston is attempting to evoke in us. And the reason we do not is contained in the very notion of "recovery." To recover a sense *of* unity with all life is to also recover *from* the trauma of having been so utterly divorced from it. I thus contend that what Livingston's work essentially invites is the development of a more *concretely detailed* understanding of the nature of this trauma and of the *specific processes* necessary for some sort of genuine recovery.

We might, in similar fashion, call Evernden's project "listening for a new story." Evernden describes humans as "natural aliens" in that as a species we are born into the natural world problematically, as a kind of niche-less exotic that must always mediate a relationship to nature through culture, must adopt some story about how we fit into the scheme of things. Because our current story dictates that we ravage the planet like some global locust, his hope lies with the possibility of choosing a *new* cultural self-interpretation, one in which we might recognize the natural world as a community of fellow subjects rather than a collection of meaningless objects to be humanly exploited. In order to facilitate the arrival of a new story, Evernden counsels a surrender of common sense, a letting go of existing categories, so that we may recover a sense of wonder, experience the world afresh, and so hear the notes of a new song, should one be in the offing. As with Livingston, however, I believe there is more to consider here than Evernden allows. While I certainly agree that the place of humans in the natural world is a troublesome question, it is also important to recognize that our current state of extreme alienation is "achieved only by outrageous violence perpetrated by human beings on human beings."[6] Indeed, our current story is so thoroughly geared against the life process that stepping away from it will require a great deal of social struggle and healing along the way.

What is common to these two projects is their orientation toward some kind of experiential renewal. Both prescribe a suspension of the belief system of our culture in order to allow for a more direct contact with wild others and so for a more authentic self-understanding and cultural script to emerge. What they both lack, moreover, is any kind of practical or detailed insight as to just what this might involve. It is perhaps unfair to expect of these two thinkers something that neither professes to offer. However, without an understanding of the violence inherent in our present manner of existing and of the nitty-gritty of recovery work, that is, without taking a closer look at what is presently going on with our experiencing, the kind of renewal they propose can only remain an idea. It is this "closer look" that I want to start undertaking in the next four chapters. Need it be said, my intention in doing so is to honour the efforts of Livingston and Evernden—for we most respect other people's work when we try to pick up some of its strands and weave them a little further. My work has effectively become a response to theirs, a conversation with theirs. I like to frame it as such, in any case, as a strategy for bringing some focus to my own critical and recollective project.

Talking About Experience

The concept of experience seems to me one of the most obscure we have.
—Hans-Georg Gadamer[7]

The purpose of this section is to lay down some concepts, introduce some notions, that will get us on better speaking terms about "experience." It is an endless topic. In what follows, I have therefore restricted myself to four subject areas, all of which will figure prominently in the remaining chapters: the primacy of experience or *felt meaning* in human existence; the *embodied nature* of our experiencing; the power of a relational or *interactive* framework (so different from the individualistic and dualistic framework of our Western tradition) to open up satisfying new avenues of understanding; and the *suffering* we experience when our human nature is violated. Each of these, in turn, have an important connection to the *life process*, which for this chapter is my bridge into ecopsychology. The section roughly progresses in order through these four areas, building on earlier terms as it goes, and always aiming to bring along the reader's own experience.

Experience Comes First

Somehow, the individual's "own" experience . . . must become a trustworthy ground. . . . if we do not have any faith in the truthfulness of the individual's experience, then we have succumbed to the self-destructiveness of nihilism.
—David Levin[8]

Beginning with experience is what existentialists do. Not just those French ones who feel that human existence is absurd and nauseating but, more broadly,[9] anyone who feels that, as Wilhem Dilthey put it: "Life cannot be brought before the bar of reason." To get close to the things that matter we have no recourse but to our bodily experience. The philosopher and psychotherapist Eugene Gendlin writes:

> Within experiencing lie the mysteries of all that we are. For the sake of our experiential sense of what we observe, we react as we do. From out of it we create what we

create. And, because of its puzzles, and for the desperation of some of its puzzles, we overthrow good sense, obviousness, and reality, if need be.[10]

I consider this statement to be a kind of experientialist's equivalent to the Freudian dictum that human behavior has unconscious motivations. Whether scientist or poet, we all move through life on the basis of meanings that are implicit in our experience; and yet very little of these are ever consciously known to us, even as they color our world and direct our actions. The Western tradition has proceeded to ignore all this and to instead make human existence walk "on its head."[11] To make the mysterious reality we actually live the primary ground is thus the first step in adopting an experiential approach. We can (as others have noted) attempt to explain our psychology in terms of our biology, our biology in terms of impersonal chemistry and physics, and these in terms of quantum mechanics, but abstract theories about subatomic whirly-gigs do not really help us much when it comes to choosing our lives, making sense of our deaths, understanding our fears and desires, or bearing our suffering, all of which are irreducible, experiential tasks.[12]

What makes the deliberate adoption of an experiential approach necessary is that our age has so marginalized and mystified our experience. As Gendlin remarks, "Nothing is as debilitating as a confused and distant functioning of experiencing. And the chief malaise of our society is perhaps that it allows so little pause and gives so little specifying response and interpersonal communion to our experiencing."[13] This malaise has everything to do with the entire tradition surrounding the division of the world into subjective experience and objective reality. To confine truth to the latter is to trivialize and derealize the former, is to "dissolve it into nothingness."[14] Thus, the success of science has brought about the surrender of our own experience, including the claims it makes on the "outer" world. This has also given rise to the "expert," whose authority has replaced the wisdom of our own feeling process. When Theodore Roszak dreams of a body of expert ecopsychologists who could bring "the full weight of professional psychological authority" to the assertion "that people are bonded emotionally to the Earth,"[15] I believe, therefore, that he is playing an old game. The same goes for his remark: "If human conduct were governed by *reason alone,* what science has taught us about the great ecological patterns and cycles of the planet might be enough to reform our bad environmental habits."[16] Reason alone, as Max Horkheimer once observed, attaches little importance to whether the purposes to which it is put "are themselves reasonable."[17] It only wants to serve some master in efficiently achieving some given ends; beyond that it is rudderless. Reforming "bad environmental habits," putting a man on the moon, or producing nerve gas are all the same to it. What is lacking in our response to the ecological crisis, then, is *not* expert advice. In 1973 Paul Shepard wrote that: "Sufficient ecological data to guide the redirection of society toward environmental harmony has existed for more than thirty years."[18] A quarter of a century later what is still apparently missing is not the scientific data, but the existential sensitivity, the felt orientation.[19] A story from my own life may help to make this point.

When I was a child I had a compelling love affair with all things rocky: bedrock outcroppings, cliffs, mountains, sandy beaches, stones. I would sit for great lengths of time among limestone boulders on the shores of the Bruce Peninsula, just sensing their timeless presence, their heavy being. As a student geologist later in life, I undertook a research project on what is known as the "Kingston limestone," a lovely rock with a warm glow. From a local quarry I obtained a section of rock core and then diamond-sawed it into cylinders two inches in diameter and five inches tall. These were placed one at a time between the plattons of a servo control compression testing machine, and then slowly squeezed to the breaking point, so as to measure their strength. As I watched that rock crumble, I felt a voice inside me scream; yet the mood of the laboratory overrode it. It was not until some time later that I let myself feel the shame for what I had done.

Ecopsychology, as I discuss throughout, is fundamentally a response to violence (for to violate something is precisely to insult its *nature*). From this view, the goal of the ecopsychologist is to work toward the recovery of our ability to *perceive* and *answer back* to this violence, and to engage in nonviolent modes of relating. The story I just told was meant, in this respect, to illustrate the principle that violence "cannot be seen through the sights of positivism."[20] ("The objects weep, but the researcher sees no tears."[21]) Despite my repeated criticisms, I mean no disrespect to modern scientists. In a scientific age, we are all more or less naive positivists. What is so transgressive about smashing rock samples, anyway? What matters *to me* is that in order to participate in the rock-breaking incident I had to deflect my own felt recognition of violence. The promise of an experiential approach for ecopsychology is that it may give such feelings a place, accord them their proper truth and weight. While a psychology based on the model of externalized nature aims to produce positive knowledge, a psychology based on *relationships* has no choice but to be experiential. For the "data" of relationships are the feelings, realities, or meanings born of interaction. That is, an interactional perspective resignifies experience; it brings—to use the familiar terms—*objectivity* to the subject and *subjectivity* to the object. Thus, to study the human-nature relationship is to pursue the essence of experience itself. While, conversely, to revivify our experience is to find nature at its heart.

Experiencing: Interaction Between Bodily Felt Meaning and Symbols[22]

Experiencing is essentially an interaction between feelings and "symbols" (attention, words, events), just as body life is an interaction between body and environment.

—Eugene Gendlin[23]

Any explication of the process of experiencing will reflect the degree of the author's own awareness and understanding, and is best be read in that light. I think it is helpful, for instance, to say that Cartesian dualism truly describes only self-estranged, disembodied, narcissistic experience; and that with a deepening of experience, mind, body, and world increasingly unify. My tutors in the deepening of my own experience have been humanistic psychologists, existential-phenomenological and hermeneutic thinkers, and Gautama the Buddha. In what follows, my aim is to introduce some general concepts that come from the traditions of these teachers (leaving Buddhism mostly for the next chapter), so that we may get an initial sense of what is meant by the notion of "experiencing."

An experiential approach is one that takes "experience" as its root metaphor or main guide. The basic scheme I use for describing the process of experiencing comes from Gendlin. In its simplest formulation, *experiencing is the interaction between feelings and symbols.* To understand this better we need to say more about "feelings," "symbols," and the nature of their interaction. Before doing that, however, I must make two notes about word usage. First, *experiencing* carries a double meaning, referring both to the flow of feelings which interacts with symbols and to this process of interaction itself. Given the internal relationship between feelings and symbols, however, this ambiguity is fitting, and in my experience causes no confusion. Second, although generally referred to as a noun—as experi*ence*—the phenomenon of experienc*ing* is a process, and so needs to be heard as a verb—as in What are you experiencing?

Any piece of experiencing, then, whatever it might be, will always have two basic aspects or orders. The *symbol* is the direct *form* of the experience. It is some figure of awareness: a thought, a behavior, a sight or sound, an emotion (which, as I clarify below, is not the same as a feeling), an image, a rite, an event, some words. The *feeling* is the ongoing, concrete, underlying "inward sentience" or bodily sensitivity that accompanies and interacts with these symbols: the felt background that lends meaning or sense to the figure. Because they comprise the *sense* we bodily-have in relation to any content we may be experiencing, feelings are also called *felt meaning.* As Gendlin says, without having a "feel" for a concept it is only some verbal noise, lacking in meaning; it is in the dimension of feeling that the meaning of the concept is *experienced.* Note that felt meaning is *explicitly* known only when given some symbolic form that houses and so *completes* the meaning. From the reverse direction, note also that felt meaning is "called forth" when we interact with something whose symbolic character arouses in us a feeling. Symbols and feelings are thus mutually formative or determining: the traffic between them moves in both directions. The *difference* between feelings and symbols is most noticeable, perhaps, when we have a feeling but can find no words to express it. We must then stay with the feeling and wait for the right word-symbols to come. Or we may say something, but not *mean* it. Here, we have some word-symbols, but they are hollow because lacking in feeling—which we must then sense if we are to speak more authentically. It is, then, the interaction between these two basic orders that makes up experiencing. While not all of these terms may be clear at this stage, I do want the reader to eventually develop a good feel for them, to get a solid experiential sense for what *these* word-symbols *mean*. The descriptions and examples I offer in this section, along with a couple of exercises, are intended to help with that process. For now, I wish to make a number of points only toward some initial clarification.

"Feeling is the very state . . . in which our being human hovers."[24] This remark of Heidegger's makes my first point. An experiential approach does not advocate swimming around in emotions and eschewing all intellection. It instead acknowledges that there is a felt or experiential dimension to *everything;* that the world is intelligible only on account of the feeling tone that pervades, usually unnoticed, all our thinking, speaking, and doing (including our emoting). Thinking does not therefore escape feeling, but is rather "the process of successively 'selecting' symbols for present felt meaning, finding that the symbols 'call forth' more meaning than one anticipated, then 'selecting' more symbols from some of this excess."[25] Feelings are our bodily grasping of all that is nonfocal at the moment; they are our sensing, all at once, the many background meanings that are in play or relevant to us in any given situation. Feelings are thus more diffuse or fuzzy than emotions, less distinct or clear, because they contain all of these meanings as a prereflective mass. It is, however, exactly *because* feeling is a constant and pervasive factor in human existence that Heidegger called it the "basic mode" of human being. When asked what I am experiencing, or how I am, or what I mean, I turn to my feelings. They are the primary way I know, and may hermeneutically inquire into, my own being-in-the-world. (A brief aside: while the question always looms about the relationship between Heidegger's thought and his unsavory politics, I have chosen to selectively employ his thinking throughout this book.[26])

My second point of clarification is that the term *symbol* is meant here in a wide sense. We are used to thinking of symbols as a special class of entities, such as those we find in churches or dreams. By saying in the previous chapter, however, that all of reality is symbolic I was using the word *symbol* in a wider-than-normal sense. *Symbol* is a compound of two Greek words, "*sum-ballein,*" which may be translated as "to draw or throw together." In other words, a symbol gathers, brings together, or calls forth a confluence of meanings that are felt when we interact with it. The richest symbols are those with great disclosive power. It is the case, though, that *anything* we meaningfully encounter may be thought of as a symbol. In other words, whatever we experience—a dinner party, a bird in the forest, a fantasy, a summer breeze—symbolizes that experience immediately.[27] We may then find *further* ways to symbolize the experience, to bring out some more of its hidden meaning—perhaps by doing a dance about the breeze. Or we may find no more symbols for the experience at all. Much "nature experience" is like this; we feel much meaning in our contact with a landscape, but are at a loss for words to describe it. The experience is ineffable, but the landscape symbolized it right on the spot. Similarly, ordinary sense perception involves what Gendlin calls "recognition feelings." I see something familiar, say a table, and understand what it is without having to think about it as such. Or as you gesture at me I pick up your meaning; not through some intellectual analogy, but directly, because I am myself a gesturing body that resonates to your actions, feels their meaning. All learning is to an extent like this, wherein we "get" some meaning. (This comes out in the word *comprehend*, the Latin *prehendere* meaning "seize" or "take hold.") Learning a new word, for example, is a matter of grasping how it is used, "much as one imitates a gesture."[28] All of which is to say that the world we experience is always already symbolically meaningful to us, most of the time.

My third point, finally, concerns the figure/ground structure of experiencing. Cézanne tells a story about wanting to paint a still life he found described in a book. The setting includes bread rolls that appear to "crown" the napkins on which they are sitting. Cézanne remarks, though, that it is impossible to paint "crowned." He must faithfully paint only the tangible details of the napkins and rolls, and then wait for the intangible "crowned" quality to shine through the dabs of paint.[29] This illustrates the principle that, as Merleau-Ponty put it: "Meaning is invisible."[30] The visible is "pregnant" with the invisible; while the invisible is the "secret counterpart" of the visible, is its "inner framework"—or as we said in chapter one, its soul. The meaning we experience is not itself tangible, but must be symbolically mediated. The symbol is the line in the drawing, the voice in the singing, the image in the dreaming. The sense these have, by contrast, "is always a production of absent things."[31] In other words, what is tangibly present is always pervaded by what is absent, by an intangible atmosphere we implicitly feel. (Intuitions come exactly from having a sense for this felt absence.) Or in our earlier terms, the meaning of the figure, our interpretation of it, is itself mediated by the felt ground. This figure/ground (theme/horizon, explicit/implicit, focus/field) relationship is the basic structure of experience. I stress the importance of this relation especially because, as I discuss next, the body is itself a kind of ground.

The Bodily Ground of Experience

> *Only human beings have come to a point where they no longer know why they exist . . . they have forgotten the secret knowledge of their bodies, their senses, their dreams.*
>
> —John (Fire) Lame Deer[32]

We have access to nature, said Merleau-Ponty, through that "vital relation" we have "with a privileged part of nature: namely, our body."[33] Our divorce from nature, whatever else it may involve, has surely been a progressive cutting of this vital relation. Any hermeneutical effort to overcome our alienation must therefore also be a retrieval of our embodiment. This comes as no surprise, for the somato-phobia of the Western tradition is a matter of historical record and present-day experience. My own first deliberate efforts to become more inwardly aware of my body were like trying to force a large balloon under the surface of a lake. Toward the end of this section I will discuss some of the social factors that motivates us to take such fearful flight from our bodies, so that we might better understand this most central of issues for ecopsychology. For the discussion here, however, my focus is principally on a positive reappraisal of the being of the body, specifically on how it orders (organizes, commands) our experience, and on the intimate, felt relationship that exists between body and world.

Historical prejudices against the body are by now well-known. Nietzsche wrote of how Western thinkers before him "despised the body: they left it out of the account: more, they treated it as an enemy."[34] Plato dumped the body for suprasensuous Ideas. Later, the erotic body was seen as the Devil itself, the very site of corruption. During the witch trials, the witch "had her sensualism burned out of her."[35] The body, in general, was resented and feared because it linked us to a fallen, beastly nature; imprisoned us in flesh. The Cartesian mechanizing of the body and disembodying of the soul can in retrospect be understood as an attempt to resolve this terrible dilemma. Today, the dominant model of the body is still a scientific one: a physiological system with no significant relations to the world; a material container for the mind (the latter of which can potentially be made immortal, some claim, by being "downloaded" into machines[36]); a corpse even.[37] The history of our abandonment of the body has perhaps reached its extreme in the appearance of what Robert Romanyshyn describes, in a frankly upsetting essay, as two complementary bodies: that of the astronaut, the "masculine spirit taking leave of a despoiled earth," and that of the anorexic, "the dying, starving body, the discarded feminine, left behind."[38]

From out of this disturbing history our task is to reclaim a body that walks on, and is nourished by, the living earth. Given that we are making of this a psychological exercise, it makes sense to begin with Freud. The part of our person-ality that corresponds to nature Freud called the "id" (better translated from the German "es" as "it"). Of the id, he wrote: "we call it a chaos, a cauldron full of seething excitations. . . . It is filled with energy reaching it from the instincts, *but it has no organization,* produces no collective will, but only a striving to bring about the satisfaction of instinctual needs."[39] Freud thus feared that unless we repress our instinctual id-body it will, as Alan Watts wryly put it, "turn out to be a wild animal rutting and snarling in the squalor of its own excrement."[40] Civiliza-tion may be a mess, but without it what "would then remain would be a state of nature, and that would be far harder to bear."[41] Freud's opinion is consistent with a long tradition that equates our nature with irrational tendencies that must be either controlled or broken.[42] Indeed, by the time of the Age of Reason it was our very animality that was considered to be at the root of madness; the insane person was robbed of humanity and thereby returned to a chaotic, autistic, animal state, the "zero degree of his own nature."[43]

A model of nature that identifies it with madness obviously makes a poor, if not ironic, starting place for ecopsychology. Indeed, a great deal turns on this point. For if our nature is chaotic then our experience has no intrinsic order. The id, said Freud, is asocial.[44] The part of us that deals with reality, the ego, is thus wholly a product of whatever order a society imposes on top of, or molds out of, our unruly id-nature. The assumption here, that the precivil body has no organization of its own, that rational order must be pressed on it, is however a bias that not all accept.[45] Specifically, I believe that a better interpretation of human nature— one more phenomenologically true—is to be found within the general camp of humanistic psychology. What Freud did not recognize, humanistic psychologists say, is the ongoing creativity of the human organism, its inherent wisdom, its holistic knowing, its self-organization. This organism, then, is not to be confused with the literal, material body of natural science, nor the Freudian body of chaotic drives, but understood as an *intelligent* body which has a precisely attuned intentional relationship with the "external" world, as we experience it from within.

That the body is self-organizing is obvious in the experience of hunger. For hunger is the physical *implying* of feeding; it is a feeling that points to, intends, calls for, or means eating. Eating, in turn, symbolizes and resolves the hunger. Similarly, when feeling dull-headed in a stuffy room our bodies are telling us to go outside for some air. Such cases of meaningful somatic direction, although quite simple, are no different in principle from instances of more complex living. In general, that is, our bodies are always sensing our whole life-situation and urging us toward the next action that will, as Gendlin phrases it, *carry our lives forward.* Every feeling is a holistic implying, a steering of our lives in some direction, a stirring of the life force toward the unfolding of our existence, often in unpredictable ways. The body is thus more truly a finely ordered *living responsiveness,* always seeking some sort of symbolic completion for its needs or intentions, whether the "hunger" be physical, social, emotional, developmental, intellectual, sexual, spiritual, aesthetic, or whatever.

Gendlin has developed an experiential practice called "focusing" which works with this natural ordering or demanding of the body, and illustrates it well. (I should add, however, that it is only *one* possible mode of experiencing or felt interacting—an inward directed conversation with "ourselves" that Gendlin calls "self-responding.") In the process of "focusing," we turn our attention to our bodies in order to get a single, diffuse feel for the whole mass of meanings that are implicitly functioning in relation to some situation in our lives, the ground of our experience. By attending to this feeling, by listening for the direction that is coming from our bodies, we may then come to live more awarely. As Gendlin says: "Your body enacts your situations and constitutes them largely before you can think how. When your attention *joins this living,* you can pursue many more possibilities and choices than when you merely drive your body as if it were a machine like the car."[46] I invite you, the reader, to now let me lead you through an exercise in such "joining" with your own bodily living.[47]

In one sense, there is nothing special about focusing. It is simply a more deliberate way of letting our bodies guide us than is our normal custom. On the other hand, most people are so unused to working in this way that it can be difficult, strange, or even scary at first. To learn focusing, therefore, people generally need to have someone teach it to them over a number of get togethers. (It is the more rare, bodily attuned person who catches on straightaway, already being a "natural" focuser.) With these comments in mind, the point of the following exercise is not so much to teach you to focus, but only to give you a rudimentary sense of what it involves. I suggest you undertake it only if, after having read through the instructions, it feels right to do so. If you do not feel comfortable about doing the exercise, however, you might choose to notice what that feeling is like.

The first part of the exercise is only to explicitly experience a "felt sense" or feeling. Focusing works best if you are relaxed and undistracted, yet not so relaxed that you cannot sense your physical body. Begin by bringing your attention into the center of your body, to the zone that includes your throat, chest, stomach, and abdomen. Just pay attention, in a curious way, to whatever you notice there: your breathing, some tense spots, a warm sensation, whatever. A felt sense is a murky, unclear, subtle feeling about some aspect of your life that forms in this sensitive zone of your body. It is physically felt, but is also more than just a sensation, being meaningful in some way. You may in fact already have a felt sense about something going on in your life: some quarrel with a friend, event you are planning, issue you are concerned about. Or, as is not uncommon, you may not feel much at all.

As a way to now deliberately engender a specific felt sense, pick two people in your life, one of whom you get along with well, the other not so well. With your attention still in your body, imagine that the second person enters the room—and notice any felt difference this makes. You might now feel some "butterflies" in your belly or tension in your throat. Whatever your response, stay with the implicitly complex, globally felt quality this person calls forth in your body: this is your experiencing of the person, your feeling of what she or he means to you. Now imagine this person leaving; notice again whether this brings any change in your body; and then bring the other person into the room. How does this person feel to you? You may sense some easing of tension; some warm, happy feelings perhaps. Again, the exercise is only to notice your experience— what you feel in this interaction.

Once you have a hold on a felt sense, the process of focusing involves "sitting" with this feeling. When making direct reference to a felt sense we are sensing much more than what we already consciously know: those innumerable facets of background meaning we have yet to put into words or move into some other kind of symbolization. For either of the two people you chose to get a sense of, then, you might inquire into this deeper knowing. Open ended questions are best. What is this feeling all about? What is so terrible/wonderful about this person? What does this feeling need from me? What

*action would help it? The important thing is that you direct these questions toward,
and let any answers come from, the bodily felt sense, not your head. You may suddenly
realize who the person reminds you of, or what you appreciate about her or him, or
what you need to say to her or him. Such moments of awareness are signaled by a* felt
shift *in the body, a relaxing or resolving of the feeling, which signals a disclosure of
meaning, a moment of forward living. These shifts are the body's way of saying "Yes,
that feels right" to whatever came. You may not have experienced such a shift here—
which because I am talking to you from this page and not in person is even more likely
than is usually the case. You may, however, be able to recall a time when some insight
just "came" to you that felt right—which is the same thing.*

Following this excursion into the felt body, I wish to touch on several points
that the practice of focusing brings out.

First of all, many people are *surprised* to discover on learning to focus that
their feelings are so intricate, that they mean something, that their bodies are
ordered to spontaneously carry their lives forward (as just described in the above
exercise). Focusing is a deliberate way of "dipping down" into that bodily felt place
whence life-forwarding steps of change may come, where our organismic wisdom
resides. Even without being a "focuser," however, most people can recall being in
some situation that "just didn't feel right," or by contrast that "just felt right." This
feeling of *rightness* is an important touchstone for anyone who works experientially. As Gendlin notes: "Every bad feeling is potential energy toward a more right
way of being if you give it space to move toward its rightness. The very existence of
bad feelings within you is evidence that your body knows what is wrong and what
is right."[48] Hence: "The life process in us has its *own* direction *and this is not
relative*."[49] In other words, the life process has a certain autonomy.

We cannot impose whatever meaning we like on our experience, some story
we want to have as our own, for then we could be just whatever we choose. This is
why being authentic, being what we *are,* is not simply a matter of nonconformity,
but also of bringing ourselves before our experience and pursuing only those
possibilities that arise from this felt starting place, the ones that are genuinely
"ours." Similarly, we do not become free of our life difficulties by wishing them
away, but often must complete very precise, sensitive, and difficult experiential
steps that satisfy what our bodies are calling for. The felt sense, in other words,
adjudicates our responses to it. Feelings cannot be fooled or bypassed; they shift
only when rightly symbolized. When an expression is on the tip of our tongue, our
felt sense will keep *rejecting* the phrases we "try on" until the right words at last
appear and bring us that wonderful sigh of relief or outflow of energy. This
example also shows that our bodies *understand language.* While language use is in
important respects different from a behavior such as eating, it is also the same
inasmuch as they both carry life forward. Thus, the conversation or book that is
boring or senseless is the one that does nothing for our lives. By contrast, when a
person says something that is deeply meaningful or relevant to us, it touches us

right at the center of our living or opens up some sense that helps move our lives along. Or as Susan Griffin observes, "when a lie is told the body is cast into a state of profound disturbance."[50] Language, then, is *of* the order of experiencing, and not simply a stamp *on* it.[51]

The commitment I am introducing here—to the notion that all meaning is grounded in the life process and that we feel in our bodies what is for or against this process—is not currently in favor. The ruling assumption is "that there is no nature, no human nature, no truth, and no rightness, other than whatever variant has been programmed into us by culture."[52] Hence, relativism[53] is widespread in academia, as well as in much of our postmodern culture. Relativists must assume, tacitly or otherwise, that human life has no significant organic basis, that nature makes no felt claims on us. If we have no nature, no organic ties, then the meaning of life is arbitrary, which is to say that it has no meaning at all (the nihilistic view). Just so, the "postmodern body" has been described as a "de-natured" body or a "dis-embodied" body.[54] To the extent that postmodernists "resist incarnation," however, they are still very much *in line* with modern thought. They continue to side against nature, in favor of a free-floating language and all-ruling culture; they still seek "to obtain release from the world by transforming it and themselves into a text."[55] Many recent thinkers, such as Michel Foucault, view the body simply as a surface on which history imprints itself, a docile receptacle or material substratum on which political power is inscribed. Thus, in the terms I have introduced here, what these thinkers assume is that our experiencing is wholly determined by the symbolic order, which is itself limited to cultural-historical-linguistic forms. *What they do not recognize is an organic, bodily felt, responding moment within this experiencing.* In other words, they do not allow for how symbolic forms and experiencing *interact in a life process.* One of the consequences of this is a tendency to locate meaning only in language, rather than in a broader process of bodily living-in-the-world that *includes* language. Or it leads to the deconstructionist conclusion that even language does not ultimately refer to anything, that it only consists of formal distinctions that always break down under scrutiny, that all meaning is merely an "effect" issuing from the play of signifiers.[56]

While the life process never stops making its demands, the shape our experiencing actually takes obviously *does* have much to do with the specific social practices and cultural forms—ideological, philosophical, religious, aesthetic, scientific, historical, linguistic—that wind up "occurring into" these demands. Our feelings, to be sure, are "always already culturally patterned."[57] In opposing relativism, I am not therefore making an appeal for some "pure" realm of experiencing entirely unaffected by the symbol systems we publicly share. As Gendlin remarks, "experience is always organized by the evolutionary history of the body, and also by culture and situations partly organized by language."[58] There are many experiences that are obviously nonlinguistic (at least in a narrowly verbal sense), such as meeting the eyes of a raccoon. It does not follow, however, that language is not *implicit* in these experiences. For no matter the situation, we simply could not understand the world as we do without all those background meanings that have been formed in words. I have come to make sense of the world through a history with language that leads all the way up to that wild encounter with the raccoon. *On the other hand,* our experience is also *thicker,* more "intricate," than any words, concepts, theories, or existing forms; these do not, in other words, wholly *encompass* our experience.[59] With the raccoon, I am drawn into a unique event of contact. The meaning disclosed in that moment is not only a matter of prior social learning, but also of how available I am to the claim of the raccoon's otherness. The raccoon, too, is a symbol or form capable of stirring up feelings in me—as am I for her or him.

I am dwelling on the topic of language because it is so crucial for ecopsychology. Without an extralinguistic space within our experiencing, without an *opening* beyond our previous symbolizations, the meanings we find in relation to nature can never be other than what our existing language-forms already say. When a person like John Livingston remarks that his feelings "cannot be force-fitted into convenient categories of common . . . experience,"[60] he is communicating that he feels something *more* or *other* than what these existing categories mean, even if a better language has yet to arrive. The latter may well come, however, if we are able to locate what Merleau-Ponty referred to as that "primordial silence" or "mute presence" which exists "beneath the chatter of words"[61]— the Gendlin-ian bodily felt sense from which original intentions and creative expressions arise. Conversely, to "tell people that any saying must inevitably fail, that it cannot help but fall into the old dead forms, is just another mode of silencing that [which] in them . . . needs to speak."[62]

A final point that the practice of focusing demonstrates is the unity of body and world. "In the body," says Hans Jonas, "the knot of being is tied which dualism does not unravel but cut[s]."[63] The body is the site of intersection of inside and outside, self and world; it belongs to both realms and mediates their relations. As I noted above, the felt sense has "a life of its own." It is precisely via our bodies' implicit dialogue with the world, gathered in the felt sense, that we feel the quality of our relationships with others, orient ourselves, and take the actions we do. We sense our situations, say a social function, as a global flavor, texture, energy, or mood. This felt sense is our tacit bodily grasp of what is going on, what is relevant, what might happen, and so on. Most of the time we just have our feelings "in-action" as they implicitly govern our lives, without paying much attention to them. If I walk into a room and my stomach lurches, however, I must consult my bodily felt sense if I am ever to discover what I am so scared about and what course of action might be the right one. Without doing so, I will just cringe in the corner, unaware of what the situation really means to me.

Whether I focus this feeling or not, it is not just an inner event, but a prereflective sensing of my whole "outer" situation as I feel it from the "inside."

The felt sense is thus a bodily knowing of how I am in-the-world that is *prior* to any cleavage between inside and out (which are only metaphors for zones of awareness or aspects of reality).[64] In the language of Gestalt therapy, our "feelings are not isolated impulses but structured evidence of reality, namely of the interaction of the organism/environment field, for which there is no other direct evidence except feeling."[65] Recall from chapter one that it is of our cultural pathology to *interiorize experience*. The idea of an "organism/environment field" is meant to suggest instead the intimacy or inseparability of the body-world relation—as in the inhaling and exhaling of air. Our bodily felt intentions (as Merleau-Ponty wrote) are the threads that connect us to the world. Assigning intentionality to the body itself thus incarnates and enworlds the mind, so that it is no longer tucked away up in the skull.[66] Hence, body and world are *originally* together, and are only isolated—turned into cadaver and object—in an act of reflective abstraction. As we *live* them, in short, what differentiates body and world "is not a frontier, but a contact surface."[67]

Contact: The Process of Interacting

> As human beings, our primarily dwelling is "outside" in the space of action constituted by relations to things, plants, animals, other human beings, ourselves, to heaven or earth in their totality.
>
> —Medard Boss[68]

The unfolding of our lives is not just the flowering of some inner potential—as if the only role of the outer world were to water our seed—but a process of interacting with others in which we seek the best fit we can between our bodily intentions, needs, or desires and what our environments have to offer. As Medard Boss remarks, we *are* "at any given time nothing but *in* and *as* this or that perceiving, instinctual, impulsive, emotional, imaginative, dreaming, thinking, acting, willing, or wishing *relationship toward* the things which [we] encounter."[69] In my relationships with others I invent and discover the meanings by which I both grow and adjust to the world in which I find myself. Aside from this interacting, there is no "me." *Contact*, then, denotes the activity of ex-change, transaction, meeting, fusion-across-difference, transmission, encounter, or engagement with the world—without which no life or experiencing would be possible.

Contact is the opposite of in-difference. It is our being changed by interacting with that which is *different*. The word "contact" therefore applies principally to those events in which we come in touch with the world and acquire a new meaning—when the ground of our existence is altered (if only a little). We may be affected by others on an implicit level, but only when we symbolize how we have been touched—perhaps by realizing years later how somebody cared for us, and how much that meant to us—do we make *explicit* contact with this touch. *Reality* is most fully given or revealed under ongoing conditions of good, organismically satisfying contact; while we suffer a diminished and decaying reality under conditions of weakened or distorted contact. Contact is itself one of the great mysteries of the universe, as the variety of metaphors used to describe it suggests. In what follows, I discuss a number of these metaphors, each of which has its own merits and limitations.

The first metaphor is that of *dialogue* (conversation, verbal interaction). This metaphor acknowledges the power of language (even if, primordially considered, not all language need be verbal); it indicates the very real importance of having an expressive "voice" for the making of contact. It also suggests the back-and-forth or dialectical motion wherein we feel our impact on one another as we are "played" by the subject matter of our dialogue. Dialogue does not, however, consist only of words bumping into each other. Good contact insists that my words be truthful. For example, when I recently told my wife, Jill, that "our marriage bond feels a bit wobbly of late," it named something we had both been sensing and opened up an exchange of feelings which then deepened our bond. My bodily felt sense implied some sort of contact, the saying of some words that belonged to the situation we shared, that would restructure or carry forward our lives together. Where life lacks contactful communication such as this it becomes overly routine, dull, and thin.

The second metaphor for contact is that of *touching*. Indeed, tactility inheres in the very word *con-tact:* touching together, touch-touching. We talk of "being touched" by someone or "getting in touch" with some part of ourselves. A pure, disembodied consciousness could never experience anything because it is not capable of touching and being touched, has no flesh. Contacting always occurs at a boundary, in this metaphor the skin surface. Our skin, as Gestaltists observe, is less a part of ourselves than it is an "organ" of the relationship between organism and environment, delimiting (containing and protecting) the former and joining it to the latter.[70] It binds the organism both *from* and *to* the environment. Touch is the paradigm for contact because it is a "close" sense, as opposed to "distant" ones such as seeing or hearing, which more easily become bodiless or remote. In the act of being touched we are *vulnerable*. As a metaphor for contact, touching thus suggests the danger or *peril* that resides in the middle of ex-per-ience.[71] Every contacting is to some extent a *risk*, for it involves being changed and its outcome is never quite certain. We are, accordingly, always balancing the need to grow and change with the need to resist the intentions of others and maintain or conserve our existing ground. In a hostile or unnourishing situation, the latter need takes precedence; whereas in a friendly and giving one it is the former. I discuss this topic below, so will only note here a major psychological issue of our time: that for many people today the peril of contact feels too great, the fear of touching one another too large, for them to take "the reasonable risks which are part and parcel of growing and living."[72]

Eating metaphors, next, pervade discussions of experience. Hunger, appetite, tasting, chewing, swallowing, vomiting, digesting, assimilating, eliminating—all apply to how we relate to the "material" or "food" of our experience. We speak of "soul food" and "toxic" experiences. The cyclical nature of hunger/eating makes it a good model for the whole organismic rhythm of experiencing, as will come out in the discussion of the final metaphor below, that is, a cycle or wave. Here I want to focus on how the eating metaphor is a particularly apt one for ecopsychology—for it connects experience to food: to plants and animals. As Paul Shepard remarks: "Being human has always meant perceiving ourselves in a circle of animals. The crucial event in this encounter has been ingestion. We have attended passionately to this consuming force until the idea of assimilation has permeated the nature of experience itself."[73] Gordon Wheeler criticizes the food metaphor—at least as it was developed by the founder of Gestalt therapy, Fritz Perls—arguing that it turns others into mere objects of oral aggression.[74] I think it better, however, to recognize that if we are to live, we have *no choice* but to eat others. As Perls himself noted, it "is as impossible to feed off oneself psychologically as it is to feed off oneself physically."[75] The real issue, then, is what kind of *attitude* we take toward our food. A Cheyenne Indian saying—"let us all be meat, to nourish one another, that we may grow"[76]—indicates how, rather than seeing the world only in its object-being, it is possible to see the animals and plants we put on our table as kin, and to therefore adopt a fiercely moral, celebratory, and nonviolent attitude toward our food.[77] With factory farms, supermarkets, and fast food, there is of course little of this left, and it becomes progressively harder to sense that eating might be a form of nature communion.

A last group of metaphors—a cycle, wave, or behavioral sequence—characterizes the whole process by which an experience begins in a feeling, excitedly builds toward symbolic completion or resolution, and dissolves back into the ground of our ongoing experiencing. In addition to hunger, the sexual cycle is often used as a model for this, illustrating as it does how an experience moves from an awareness of felt need through the orderly stages of rising excitement, taking action to satisfy or extinguish the need (orgasm), and integrating and withdrawing from the experience. Each such experiential cycle, passing through a sequence of phases or behaviors in self-organizing waves, forms an experiential whole or *gestalt*, which is *the basic unit of experience*. Depending on the experience, these cycles can last anywhere from a brief instant to the whole of one's life (one's life-gestalt). The movement through waves of experience—and through waves within waves—is the rhythm of life itself. Every cycle of experience is a step of living. I therefore want to describe the different phases of these cycles in some detail, as we move through them in complete or undistorted experiences.

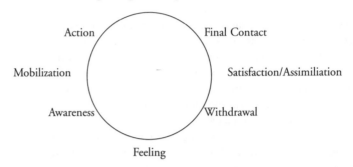

An experience begins as a *feeling* or *meaningful sensation* (e.g., hunger) arising out of the relationship between body and world (the organism/environment field), the ground of our experience. This ground consists of the *past learnings* or meanings we have incorporated, the *unfinished experiences* (whether old or freshly emerging) still pushing for completion, and the *currently encountered environment,* with various figures flowing in and out of our focal awareness. Experiencing is an interacting, so it is hard to say at any one time whether we or the world is leading. From the side of the organism, an experience starts as a bodily felt need that implies or prefigures some sort of future contacting in an environment that will consummate this need, be it eating, dancing, love-making, playing outdoors, or praying to a deity.[78] We do not just bodily anticipate our environments, however, but our environments also arouse or call forth our intentions, offer us opportunities, place demands on us, and make our lives difficult. What we implicitly feel at any given moment takes all of this into account, so that the need contained in our felt sense is the one that is most urgent or highest in priority for coping with our environment and carrying our lives forward at that point.

The next phase in an experiential cycle is our coming into *awareness* of the bodily need of the moment, that is, of what has arisen in the first phase. Our need becomes figural ("I am hungry"). This phase is thus an initial symbolizing or contacting of what our bodies are implying or intending in some situation. It is followed by a phase of *mobilization,* in which we prepare to take some action that will put our bodily intention into motion. This involves readying ourselves (imagining what we might eat, developing necessary skills, getting physically prepared, etc.) and letting our energy build toward the coming action.[79] An important theoretical point is that we have the most vivid awareness and mobilize the most excitement (life force) only for those actions that are organismically important. Any other will suffer from a lack of motivation, interest, and vitality. Hence, whenever we force ourselves to pay attention to something uninteresting (like a dull school lesson), we feel bored and tired, our bodies refusing to lend their energy to the situation.

In the *action* phase we undertake deliberate efforts (e.g., walking to the fridge) toward the fulfilment of our needs or intentions. What comes out clearly in this phase is how the primary orientation of our lives is *outward,* toward the world. The "ex" of the words we use to describe our living marks this point: ex-perience, ex-istence, ex-pression, e-motion (*ex-movere*). In Boss's words, we *body-forth* our existence. We bodily reach toward the contacts or relationships that will complete our felt meanings (prefigurations, anticipations, expectations, purposes, aims, desires, needs, intentions) and thus carry our lives forward. I live *through* my body, not as an object inside of which I am stuck, but as a power for inhabiting and disclosing a world, for engaging in the "forward-looking, problem-solving, meaning-making activity"[80] of working out the best resolution possible between my needs, urges, dreams, hopes, and so on, and the actual conditions of my life, with all of its contingencies, limitations, and dangers. Action-taking, moreover, is necessarily *aggressive,* in the sense that it requires the taking of *initiative.* As its etymology suggests, aggression is simply the "stepping toward" whatever is needed or else in the way of our lives (whether frustrating or threatening). In its nonmalignant form, aggression is thus not an evil but an essential aspect of any vital existence. Without it we would never engage the world or get on in life; we would lack any assertiveness, inquisitiveness, critical ability, self-confidence, or creativity.[81] (*Pathological* aggression, as I discuss below, derives from the *frustration* of this intrinsic aggression, which then turns hateful and violent.[82]) It is the action phase, finally, that most involves our free will. In it we make *choices* about what kind of contact we will actually pursue and how we might get there.

Final contact, to use a biological metaphor, is the exchanging of material across an osmotic membrane. To make good contact we must relax our boundaries enough to allow something new "in" (eat the food) but not so much as to lose our integrity.[83] Thus do we surrender into an orgasm, dissolve into our grief, acquire a skill, learn something, flow into an expressive movement, recognize ourselves in another, receive some message, let some reality come home. In final contact our experience takes meaningful form, our need is met, our question answered, our tension released. This is the phase where we feel a shift in or restructuring of our ground, where our experience comes to a symbolic point, where we are changed. We may experience an "aha!" when a gestalt coheres vividly, but most contact occurs more subtly, in everyday ways.

The postcontact phase of the cycle is *satisfaction-assimilation,* wherein we enjoy an "afterglow" and "digest" the meaning of our experience. The meaningfulness of an event is a matter of whether and in what respects it carries our lives forward or satisfies our bodily demands.[84] (Hence, Perls's simple formula that "the meaning of life is that it is to be lived."[85]) It is exactly this understanding that overcomes the Freudian dualism between *natural* organismic force and *human* meaning. For the organism *itself* seeks meaning, and it is our own most important business in life to *identify* with this organism and find completion for its intentions (overcoming dualism, recall, means giving mind back to nature). Every completed gestalt is a finished meaning, which is then integrated into our ongoing ground of experiencing—on the basis of which ground we are always imagining or interpreting the world as we do.

The last phase in an experiential cycle is *withdrawal.* The experience has come to a close; it no longer holds our interest or our energy; it is finished. Having gone through all the previous stages, we spontaneously pull back from contact into the fertile void, where our sense of self diminishes, where we rest. It is in this phase, having let the previous experience die, that our next experience is waiting to be born.

The psychotherapist Carl Rogers said that one of the qualities of mature persons is that they are willing to be a process.[86] Gestaltists similarly say that what we call the 'self' is simply the experiential cycle in motion, the contact process itself (the functioning of the boundary in the organism/environment field). Or as Gendlin puts it: "We are our felt experiencing." We only know ourselves (*are* ourselves) in our movements in and out of interaction with the world. I want to close, then, with an exercise in noticing just this.

As with the previous exercise, the most important thing in this one is simply to notice what you are experiencing (even if it is only your resisting of my suggestions). The purpose of the exercise is for you to "try on" my description of the cycle of experience by attending to how you are experiencing this chapter. *Recall the phases of this cycle: feeling, awareness, mobilization, action, final contact, satisfaction/assimilation, withdrawal. Now pay attention to what you are sensing in your body, and ask yourself what you are aware of. Is this chapter holding your interest (is it appetizing) or is there something else you need or want to be doing? How actively or energetically are you engaging it? Do you drift off? What sort of contact are you making with it? Do you feel touched in any way? Does it seem relevant or meaningful to you? Do you feel any satisfaction? Do you pause to chew on and digest some piece of what I am saying? What do you find objectionable, that is, what do you not want to take in? Do you withdraw from the text when you have had enough? In short: How is this chapter interacting with your living? What kind of experience are you having?*

Psychopathology: Disturbed Contacting, Constricted Existing, Blocked Living

> Anyone caught in self-defeating patterns, malfunctioning character
> structures, pathological repetitions, and so forth, feels these as
> painful. . . . it is the very living of the organism not able to proceed.
> Right in the middle of how pathological patterns are experienced . . . are
> the felt life-forces tending toward resolution.
>
> —Eugene Gendlin[87]

"Psychopathology" refers to the suffering (*pathos*) of the soul, and to the kind of voice (*logos*) we allow it. That suffering is part of the human condition is contained in the First Noble Truth of Buddhism, and is an obvious enough fact to anyone who reflects on the matter. Suffering, in other words, seems intrinsic to experiencing itself. To be experienced, it is said, is to have suffered through; to have had the vessel of one's self repeatedly broken and reformed over countless experiences. To change is to *suffer* a change. Gadamer, for instance, says that every "experience worthy of the name *thwarts an expectation*,"[88] is some kind of negation. Otherwise we just remain the same old person we already are, with our same old understanding of things. I believe, however, that he is partly wrong in this—and for telling reasons. He is right inasmuch as he has identified those experiences that force us to relinquish the security of our former beliefs or ways, disturb the sedimented meanings to which we have grown attached, or touch us with some painful truth. We will never grow or learn unless we are open to such experiences. But he is wrong not to further identify in what way experiences also *fulfill* our expectations. Our interactions do not just displace *old* meanings, but may also satisfy *prefigured* ones. Here, again, a lack of appreciation of the organismic nature of experiencing has lead to a misconception. In Gadamer's view, for an event to count as a genuine experience we must not expect it, we must be surprised and disillusioned by it.[89] What I have been suggesting in this chapter instead is that our bodily felt needs are precisely the expectations or intentions that reach toward the world to be specified and completed, so that our lives may both continue and unfold. A child finding all kinds of new things in a pond is hardly a convincing image of suffering. The theme I pursue under this heading, in fact, is that of how much *unnecessary* suffering is engendered exactly from the violent disregard of our *inherent* expectations (which are *wrongfully* thwarted) and in the struggle to get these life needs met.

The line I wish to develop is as follows. I am persuaded (by the Buddha and my own experience) that suffering is indigenous to an Egoic mode of existence (the capital *E* differentiating a pathological sense of Ego from a basic sense of ego, the latter simply being the agent of the organism). As I discuss in the next chapter, the Ego isolates itself from the ground of being, attempts to exist for itself outside the flux of life, to become a permanent island in the swirling ocean of nature— and suffers from the impossibility of the project. While the tendency toward this suffering mode is given in the human situation, the attitude a society adopts toward it is *not*. A society, that is, can develop ways to understand, find meaning in, minimize, and move through suffering; or—at the other end of the spectrum—it can choose to mystify, institutionalize, exacerbate, and exploit it. I put our own society in the latter camp. (The emergence of a "socially engaged" Buddhism indicates a recognition of this social factor.) In the account I offer below, then, I discuss our suffering specifically as it originates in social antagonism toward the life process. According to the view of this chapter, that is, pathology is generated in the hurtful conflict between the demands of our own nature and those of the life-denying and life-threatening social forces we encounter in the world—as well as in the subsequent chronic interrupting of our own life processes that we ourselves perform as a means of survival.[90] Ego grows, in fact, precisely in response to hostile conditions, as a defensive structure that aims "to obtain love by way of mastery in an unloving world."[91] While this may not yet be an adequate account of the deeper spiritual nature of our suffering, it is nonetheless congruent with one. For any route out of suffering will surely point the way back into life. And any ecopsychology must surely do the same.

I have chosen five features of psychopathology specifically for how they illustrate the relationship between suffering and the life process. Given the grossly pathological state of our normalcy,[92] I presume that readers will to at least some extent recognize themselves in my discussion of them. My aim is to introduce an interpretation of psychopathological phenomena that will serve the needs of the rest of the book (even if it is by no means a complete account of these phenomena). I need say that although the material to be covered here is not pleasant, I do not want an immobilizing heaviness to descend on the discussion. Please bear in mind, then, that I am venturing into these challenging places only because we are already in them, and because we find more satisfying life options only to the extent that we are willing to recognize this.

Creative Adjustment and the Destruction of Experience. As living organisms, we are not just cogs in the machine of the world, but are naturally ordered to grow and expand our boundaries through contacting an environment. The willingness or ability of our environments to satisfy our needs or support our lives, however, is highly variable and we must also accommodate ourselves to the demands that others place upon us. To find the best ways forward in life, then, we always have to creatively work them out in concert with the actual situations or environments in which we find ourselves. The cycle of experience I described above is itself this creative process, wherein through interacting with or contacting the world we find novel solutions to the ever-renewed problem of maintaining and unfolding our lives. Whether facing a math problem or a marital problem we must feel our way toward just those answers—the new gestalts, learnings, structures, ways, or understandings—that will dissolve the tensions in the field of our experience.[93]

What I am suggesting here (and elaborate further in the final section of this chapter) is that the general hostility of our current social environment forces us to make the most drastic of "creative adjustments."[94] I assume the reader already has at least some sense for the assorted ways in which we get wounded in this society, as these make up so much of the fabric of everyday life. They include, at a minimum, the pervasive violations we pass on through the generations, often unaware—abuses of a sexual, physical, psychological, or emotional nature, as well as those resulting from drug- and/or alcohol addicted parents, neglectful parents, and so on. Children are particularly vulnerable to being hurt, for they are "all need."[95] Much violation of our nature occurs, as it happens, via parents using their children in a misguided attempt to gratify their *own* unmet, and so now "frozen," childhood needs. We are also widely hurt via social oppression—the systematic mistreatment of particular groups or communities. Racism, classism, and sexism are the most recognized of these institutionalized abuses, although people are discriminated against on an astonishing variety of bases. While it would be possible to elaborate *ad nauseum* the manifold ways in which we hurt one another in this society, my aim at this stage is only to introduce the *idea* of these violations and to make mention that they themselves can all be understood as instances of "naturism": the global mistreatment of nature by our society.[96]

Good contacting occurs at an optimal experiential "distance." Hurtful contacts, by contrast, are either "too close" (dangerous, invasive) or "too distant" (neglectful, absent). In other words, in situations antagonistic to our living, our boundaries are either overwhelmed through direct intrusion or become unbearably tense through starvation (or both).[97] In such a setting, to openly express (or even know) our needs or make life-forwarding contact with others becomes difficult, anxiety-filled, or unsafe. The creative adjustments we are then motivated to adopt take the form of coping strategies that both distort our contact with others and block our own life urges. A person, for example, may develop very subtle and ingenious ways to manipulate others as a way to maintain some sense of control in an otherwise chaotic or ungiving situation. Or a person who has learned to fear open, face-to-face love, may adjust by becoming a fetishist who contacts others via, say, their shoes, thereby preserving an experience of intimacy. Despite that they are our best efforts at living, these kinds of creative strategies are nonetheless all interruptions of our full experiencing, such that much of our common experience is incomplete, distorted, or deficient in satisfaction.

In order to further demonstrate this last point, I want to consider the general creative adjustment known as *desensitization*. All self-interruptions can be located somewhere along the experiential cycle (for our living consists precisely of this cycle). Desensitization occurs at the beginning. It is the manipulating of ourselves (e.g., tightening the surficial muscles of our bodies) in such a way that we lose bodily feeling and blot out our perception of a hurtful world. When, for instance, we feel unloved as a child or that our caregivers are rejecting our needs, our bodies become a source of terrible pain and anxiety. We then adjust exactly by renouncing these needs and fleeing our bodies—abandoning reality in order to survive. Such desensitization reaches the point of "depersonalization" when it penetrates to our very sense of self, and "dissociation" when our felt disconnection from the world or divorce from inner reality becomes severe—two linked phenomena routinely experienced by trauma survivors.[98] Desensitization is, however, only one of many possible ways to habitually interrupt our experience, as will become clear in my further discussions.

Self-interrupting creative adjustments have one further aspect worth noting. When met with abuse or neglect children simply cannot *understand* it because it so contradicts their inborn expectation that they will be lovingly welcomed, held, comforted, and attended to; it betrays an ancient pact that their caregivers will nurture their growth. That is why it is so painful. The child, however, has to *make sense* somehow. Why am I being punished and prevented from crying and screaming? At an early age, the reality that our caregivers might not love us is too painful and incomprehensible to let in. The meaning that children almost invariably make out of their abuse is therefore that *they* must be bad, inadequate, wrong, useless, unimportant, and so on for others to be so mistreating them. Their creative adjustment is to blame themselves. That children do this again and again shows that we will do almost anything to preserve our relationships with others, so central is our need for them. (Victims, in general, often identify with and find ways to love those who perpetrate violence against them.) We create whatever meanings we need in order to carry on.

Summarizing this unhappy discussion, R. D. Laing once said that only by "the most outrageous violation of ourselves have we achieved our capacity to live in relative adjustment to a civilization driven to its own destruction."[99] The squashing of our own vitality, the distorting of our contact with the world, and the adopting of a pained meaning system are our general solutions for adjusting to a soul-punishing environment, to the "chronic low grade emergency"[100] of modern life. These are the strategies, said Laing, by which we destroy our experience.

Fear-Laden Rigidity: The Frozen Ground. The vision of a vital existence within an experiential framework is that of persons who move flexibly and awarely from experience to experience, making satisfying contact with the world, responding openly and creatively to new life situations. Their figure-ground relationship is elastic and reversible, such that they experience their lives hermeneutically: as a forward moving dialectic between symbols and felt meaning, forever changing their understanding of things as they continually enrich the basis of their experiencing. In a pathogenic environment, however, this original mode of experiencing must be sacrificed because it is too dangerous a way to live. If our world is not a place in which our trust and faith can flourish, then the need for security and control wins out over the need for open contact and growth. Our adjustments then include finding patterns of living that seem to work best, all things considered, and sticking to them for the relative safety or comfort they provide. We stop being a process and instead "take refuge in stasis,"[101] insist on a familiar world, cling to the status quo. The fear is that to change or step out of our habitual patterns will only stir up distress we would rather not feel or else make matters worse. From a ground of hurtful experience we imagine that the same injuries we experienced in the past will be repeated in the future (even if we sense these only as a general dread or aversion), and interpret the world in this unchanging light. Thus does Konrad Stettbacher call suffering "the fear-laden, painful anticipation of the past"[102] and do Gestaltists call neurosis a "fixation on the unchanging past."[103]

To the extent that we live in these fear-based patterns, our lives become rigid, each pattern corresponding to a frozen ground or unchanging horizon of experiencing. In those areas of our lives where we are so-patterned we are not really experiencing because we are just repeating the same old stereotyped routines based on *past* experiences. Our feelings do not change because we have made them unavailable for interaction, bound them off in a background that is not modified, because not contacted, by present situations. That is, our inaccessible feelings are not actively functioning in a life process; all we have instead are the symbolic patterns we keep enacting. When our experiencing is rigidly symbolized or "structure-bound" in this way we do not freshly interpret our situations, but keep having the same old automatic meanings—the same old thoughts, emotions, reactions, behaviors, and so on—over and over again. As Gendlin says, we perceive only a "bare outline" of the present. Famously, for example, we react to people just as we did to our parents, seeing only authority figures rather than unique persons, and remaining in patterns of submission, anger, panic, or whatever our particular obsolete responses may be. As this also shows, each such pattern contains within itself the "unfinished business" that led us to adopt it in the first place.

Psychopathology, then, tends toward a constricted, unfree, contact-impoverished existence. In pathology, *the symbolic moment of experiencing dominates,* that is, our lives become feelingless and form-ulaic—the form or shape of our existence becomes fixed. (To repeat, a feelingless life is not necessarily one lacking in strong emotion. What is frozen, rather, is the underlying, subtle, bodily felt sentience needed to understand and shift—rather than stay stuck in—these emotions.) Any life will involve making contact with the world in routine, day-to-day ways, wherein we ride our already-acquired structures or habits. The more severe our pathology, however, the more do these routines become all. When our very survival seems at stake, making contact with that which is novel or different (i.e., contact in the principle sense) becomes rare or alarming. We are resistant to change because who we are, our interpretation of the world, is fearfully "locked in" on a feeling level to which we have little conscious access.

Because pathology involves a restricted ground of available feeling and a limited contact style it also involves a *loss of self.* The self exists to the extent that we respond to and maintain our own process of felt interaction with the world. Where our lives are frozen this process of experiencing is *missing*—and thus so are we. We feel alien to ourselves, disorganized, out of it; the center does not hold.[104] Some degree of depersonalization or soul loss is therefore a component of all suffering. In "psychosis" the functioning of feeling is so distant and interaction so curtailed that the contents of experience are overwhelmingly alien: hallucinated voices, foreign invasions, and so on. Psychic disturbance, then, is a narrowing of our manner of experiencing, a constricting of our openness. In depression, for example, our sense of temporality shrinks to a meaningless present: the past does not nourish, the future does not invite. Our spatial world, meanwhile, narrows down to the chair we are sitting in and the wall we are staring at. Our contact is constricted and distorted in such a way that the world may reveal itself as only so many disapproving faces, critical voices, and other confirmations of our own worthlessness.

Alienation From and Conflict With Our Organismic Self. One of the main consequences of adjusting to environments that are at odds with our nature is that we come to live according to certain meanings—beliefs, concepts, rules, moral injunctions—that *replace* our own organismic, implicitly felt meanings. Rather than our bodily felt intentions we follow "introjected" social conventions. As Carl Rogers understood this, the "experiencing organism senses one meaning in experience, but the conscious self clings rigidly to another, since that is the way it has found love and acceptance from others."[105] The feeling of being unloved, as I noted above, is unbearably anxiety-provoking, leaving us all alone in the cosmic void. We thus agree to obey or adopt meanings opposed to our organismic self— what Rogers called "conditions of worth"—as a way to minimize any threatening difference between ourselves and others and so to secure some measure of love and social belonging. Men, for example, are often alienated from their experience at such an early age that they are guided almost wholly by introjected beliefs about masculinity, duty, responsibility, and so on. Or as Alice Miller notes: "The more successfully a person was denied access to his or her feelings in childhood, the larger the arsenal of intellectual weapons and supply of moral prostheses has to be, because morality and a sense of duty are not sources of strength or fruitful soil for affection. Blood does not flow in artificial limbs."[106] The result of such bloodless living is that "consciously we are moving one way, while organismically we are moving in another."[107]

What characterizes the process of introjection, in general, is the taking "in" of experiences or meanings without having yet made adequate contact with them. We take on another's values, ideas, or modes of being without going through the sequence of chewing on these, assimilating those aspects that feel organismically right (in that moment), and then spitting out the rest.[108] This happens in abusive situations when our boundaries are violated and the abuser gets right "inside" us. So long as the traumatic experience is unfinished we are then haunted by the internalized presence of the abusive other. The meanings we adopt in abuse are thus imposed, forced in; they do not come from a life-forwarding process, but an overwhelming one. As Perls et al. write of childhood introjection: "Whatever the child gets from his *loving* parents he assimilates, for it is fitting and appropriate to his own needs as he grows. It is the *hateful* parents who have to be introjected, taken down whole, although they are contrary to the needs of the organism. Accompanying this is the starving of the child's proper needs and his repressing of rebellion and disgust."[109]

As this last line indicates, alienation from our organismic self also means being in active *conflict* with it. The part of the personality most opposed to organismic life is what Freud called the "superego" and what is popularly called the "inner critic." It is generated in a complex way, from our introjected "bad parents," from negative beliefs about ourselves we have inferred from our environment, and from aggression (hatred) we have repressed or disowned. It takes the form of a hostile and critical voice that haunts us, squashes us, comes at us (and yet which is "ours"), usually operating outside of explicit awareness. It is constantly telling us how we are screwing things up, how we are bad, and what we *should* be doing. Under the influence of the superego, we go to war with ourselves, diverting our energy away from the process of growing, bending it back so as to "jail" our rejected bodily impulses. Our own genuine needing or wanting then becomes a source of anxiety, as we squeeze ourselves against our own spontaneous bodily urges out of the terror that to really express ourselves or make any demands on the world will lead only to further rejection and loss of love. We live not for ourselves, but for the pseudolove of others; and then become increasingly guilty both under the admonitions of our superegos and out of indebtedness to our own unlived existence. The words of Ellen West, one of existential psychiatry's most famous cases, and who was later to commit suicide, portray vividly the nature of these dynamic inner conflicts: "I feel myself, quite passively, the stage on which two hostile forces are mangling each other."[110]

The price we pay for alienating ourselves from the life of our own bodies is great. First of all, we lose the vitality, spontaneity, and creativity that comes only from being in touch with our organismic being. Our actions become repetitive, feelingless, unconnected to organismic need. Like Ellen West's, our lives become—as Perls called it—a "self-torture game," in which alien introjects battle it out with now-alien organismic hungers (Freud's id). We become unsure of ourselves, confused about what we need or want, because we are without inner guidance. Unable to make discriminations based on anything other than what we have been socially programmed to believe or what other people tell us, we chase after one thing, then another. Fighting against our bodies rather than letting them organize our experience, our gestalt formation is weakened. Few of our interactions actually satisfy our needs, and so we come to trail a growing bag of unfinished experiences behind us, especially those involving the grief and anger our superegos chide us against expressing. Lacking appetite, direction, bodily satisfaction, self-esteem, outgoing energy, and a willingness or ability to express forbidden emotion, we become prone to depression.

What replaces a bodily based existence is a verbal, intellectual, fantasy-based one. In a hostile environment, divided against ourselves rather than directed toward the world, we retreat into an inflated inner life. Dreams and fantasies become the primary safe realm and are maximized accordingly.[111] Our frustrated or unwelcomed intentions are gratified or entertained only in fantasy—those of sex, adoration, fame, revenge, disaster, destruction, wealth, paradise, adventure, the past, the future, and on and on—all of which become part of the ground by which, in the absence of better contact, we distortedly interpret the world and maintain our illusions. Identifying ourselves largely with this fantasy realm, much of our energy goes only there, withdrawn from the senses and muscles we might otherwise use for contacting the outer world. The other safe zone for us is the verbal intellect. Perls was right to say that most moderns live in a "verbal trance." The intellectual, in particular, is often a person for whom only cognitive feelings have survived, and who has adjusted by making a career out of this state. As Bakhtin long ago lamented, however, intellectuals tend not to put their theories into life, into the *action* phase of an experience, and thereby avoid becoming more answerable to them. The "living, compellent, and inescapable uniqueness of our actual life is diluted with the water of merely thinkable empty possibility."[112]

According to Jeannette Armstrong, the Okanagan word for "insane" describes, in part, the activity of being "in a state of talking talking inside the head."[113] If and when we do manage to come down from our heads into our bodies, what re-jects (or vomits out) our introjects is exactly a "thick organic living process."[114] Those things that are toxic to the organism—inner abusers, false beliefs about ourselves, hurtful social codes, empty ideas—are ejected as we rei-dentify with our bodies, rediscover the world, and reown our existence.

Shame, Isolation, and the Loss of Sociality. An interactive framework puts a radical stress on our inherent togetherness, interdependence, or *sociality.* Merleau-Ponty called the subject a "project of the world" as a way to make this point (while also granting to subjects their own unique perspectives on and intentions toward this world). This also means, however, as I have been discussing above, that psycho-pathology is not just an individual matter, but involves disturbances in the whole social field.[115] As J. H. van den Berg noted, psychopathology is at bottom the "science of loneliness."[116] Only a being who essentially belongs *with* others can suffer from isolation. When hurt by others, our basic social sense is damaged. Our trust in relationships, our faith in the nature of things, and our belief in the safety and goodness of the world—all are weakened.[117] In what follows, what I want to discuss, in particular, is how *all* chronic interruptions or absences of contact are isolating, and how the emotion that goes with this feeling of aloneness is *shame.*[118]

Shame is the experience of having some part (or the whole) of ourselves, some need or urge, some action or movement of ours toward contact with others, disapproved of, ridiculed, refused, unsupported, violated, or unacknowledged by our environment. Our natural desires are bad. We are exposed as "dirty," defective, unworthy, despicable, not enough, not part of the human family or of this earth. The feeling of shame is about as awful as anything we are likely to experience. When feeling shame we avoid eye contact, hang our heads, shrink. Other, less obvious signs that we are experiencing or trying to relieve our shame include irritation, rage, competitiveness, addictions, attacking, blaming, power-seeking, showing-off, perfectionism, gossiping, making excuses, lying, and so on. While in an adaptive or functional sense shame does serve to limit socially undesirable behavior, a society that is itself undesirable—that makes nature the adversary and uses humiliation as an everyday child-rearing method—will *universalize* shame. When our needs are unmet or refused they become "shame-linked," that is, the shame attached to our bodily intentions will stop us from bringing them forth into the (now tabooed) contacts they imply.[119] We disown or repress these unreceived, rebuked, or nonaccepted parts, make them "not me"—this act then creating "holes" in us where specific voices and capacities, certain zones of feeling or meaning, used to be or never came to be. Having introjected the shaming messages of our social surroundings, moreover, the scolding and put-downs of our superegos becomes our own private source of bad feelings. Thus do we come to make contact with others from a sense of isolation, inadequacy (finding ourselves wanting in comparison to others), and dread of further rejection or unacknowledgment.

Since it is of the very nature of shame to hide, it has until recently been little studied by psychologists, who have in this area concentrated rather on guilt.[120] As Gordon Wheeler suggests, the historical neglect of shame is also due to the fact that it can be truly grasped only within an interactive scheme, as opposed to the dualistic one that has dominated our psychological theorizing.[121] Shame arises from out of a break in the "natural connectedness between me and my surround," where others "refuse to receive me."[122] Wherever there is disharmony in a social environment we may therefore expect the presence of shame and wherever there is a sense of unity we may expect its absence. On this understanding, an individualistic ideology will be *intrinsically* shaming. As Wheeler suggests, under the reign of this unhealthy ideology "the hallmark of health and 'maturity' becomes the ability to *manage, deny, and compensate for* a constant background level of shame."[123] Prior psychological theorists, themselves "mature" in this sense, have thus only been able to see shame as an emotion tied to an infantile, feminine, or regressive dependency on others. Made sense of, rather, in relational or social terms, shame is revealed as a ubiquitous, if not foundational, emotion in our culture—even if many or most of us refuse to explicitly feel it.

The dynamics of shame are particularly evident in the creation of gender, which is largely a product of shaming interactions. For both males and females some ways of being are accepted, and so accentuated, while others are rejected, and so disowned. In this way, shame holds our oppressive gender patterns and social structures in place. Gender is thus itself "a codification or vehicle for shame in our culture."[124] Boys are socialized precisely to be disconnected, which means the way they are raised is *unavoidably* shaming of them. By an early age, most boys have learned that they must be independent, which sets in motion a life-long, shame-bound vicious cycle of not getting the support they need from others and fearing that they may not measure up to the male stereotype. Many men will sacrifice their inner lives, even go to war and die, rather than face their shame (so shameful is it to be ashamed). Females are shamed, in turn, by a society that pervasively devalues their very femaleness. Noteworthy here are the societal introjects concerning women's bodies and their perceived imperfections—for which they must (apply) "makeup," and so feed a multibillion dollar a year cosmetic industry.[125] Only in a society that has made it shameful to be "fat," moreover, does anorexia and bulimia become epidemic. Gender patterns, finally, are further enforced by the oppression of gays, lesbians, bisexuals, and transexuals, groups with whom it has historically been made shameful to in any way be identified.

The Repressed Unconscious: Frustration of the Life Process. Ernest Becker writes that psychopathology "is always fundamentally a problem of organisms which are crippled, cramped, or blocked in their experience."[126] From my perspective, the most essential feature of pathology is that it involves a frustrating of the life process. Repression is the chronic nonliving, blocking, or reversing of our world-bound energies or intentions; the contracting of ourselves against our own internally directed expansion into the world; the nonrealizing or stopping of certain kinds of implied relationships or contacts with others—such that we do not body-forth our lives. As Boss notes, "relationships which are not openly admitted do not flow through the bodily realm of existence in their movement toward the perceived things. They come forth and *remain within the sphere of the body,* so that there is a 'jam' instead of vibration."[127] We learn to deliberately intercept our bodily intentions until this becomes habitual, falling out of explicit awareness. Our urges then persist only in a cramped or dammed-up form—as bodily blocked sexuality, anger, grief, fear, terror, love, joy, and so forth—which color our perception as they relentlessly push in the background toward some final contact and closure.[128] They are felt only as a *ground of pain,* as an aura of frustration, agitation, dissatisfaction, fear, lack, incompleteness, and so on, which permeates our world.

What I am introducing here is an experiential theory of the repressed unconscious. Gendlin writes simply that "the unconscious consists of the body's stopped processes, the muscular and physiological blockage."[129] What is unconscious are the world-relations that are interrupted, unexpressed, not mirrored, unconsummated, or concealed between us; yet which, as I just suggested, are present in a jammed manner, as our implicit and unfocused bodily sensing of them. The unconscious is thus a *relational* or interactive phenomenon.

"The unconscious" . . . is all those parts of experience that remained inchoate and unarticulated, parts for which we never developed a full voice, for want of that *receptive intersubjective field* that is requisite . . . for the full development/articulation of the self. . . . experience that is felt but cannot be shared, represented, articulated, echoed, [symbolized,] and thus integrated into the whole social field thus tends to become stunted and arrested at best, if it doesn't disappear from felt reality altogether.[130]

The zones of existence we block, shamefully disown, or never come to understand are the ones our social environments are unwilling or failing to occupy, the kinds of relationship they do not allow (which we then learn not to allow *ourselves*).[131] These have traditionally included the sexual and aggressive regions of existence, but as ecopsychologists we need, of course, to add the ecological (as I discuss in chapter five when I revisit the notion of the "ecological unconscious"). The rationalist attack on the unconscious may in these terms be criticized as a war on the life process itself, as an opposition to uncontrollable organismic intentions that want to move us toward those kinds of relationships regarded as threatening to the existing social order.

The repressing of life is not, however, only the blocking of our original intentions toward the world, but also the further interrupting of our *healing* intentions. When hurt, we experience distressful emotions. We heal and make sense of such hurts by then expressing these emotions and making the kind of contact with others that they imply. When the child of some friends of mine got stuck under a couch, for example, he screamed and hollered until rescued. My friends then stayed with him in a relaxed and attentive way while he "cried out" the hurt. As they acknowledged and mirrored the scary incident with him, his tears gradually dried, his experience came to a close, and he happily turned his attention to other things.[132] If he had been taught, however, that "boys don't cry" or was told to "shut up or I'll give you something to cry about," then he would not have been able make sense of or assimilate the distressful experience because he would have been denied a healing life process.[133] (We are often unwilling to welcome strong emotions in others, including children, because they symbolically call forth our own unhealed pain, our own shame-bound and unfinished experiences that we would rather not feel.) Hurtful contacts thus always open up an emotional experience which *also* persists bodily until allowed to finish, and which likewise may become unconscious through habitual interruption. Resentment and hatred, for example, are forms that anger takes when we prevent it from unfolding into the kind of confrontational contact that would actually let it go.[134] The incomplete anger festers, grows corrosive or hostile, has a simmering and old quality. It then gets unawarely channeled into all the crimes of which we *are* so aware, as well as into acts of violence—both covert and overt—we commit against ourselves.

Experiential conceptualizations of the repressed unconscious differ significantly from the traditional one, which depicts it as a container for unwanted psychic contents. The initial problem with such a conception is that it unintelligibly splits our experience, makes the unconscious a kind of separate mind within the mind.[135] For an experiential approach, the unconscious is an intrinsic aspect of bodily existence; it is our unaware sensing of the blocked and background living that wants to come forth. In other words, when the unconscious is understood in the mode of a remote repository full of discrete mental contents (ideas, images, emotions), we come to think of mental phenomena as belonging in some disembodied head-space. Understood rather in the mode of our world-entangled bodies, psychological life becomes intensely somatic. What is unconscious to us are our body's relations to the world that we are not explicitly taking up and acting on— living as we are, instead, in our narrow and automatic patterns.[136]

An experiential approach further criticizes the traditional model of the unconscious for reifying experience by focusing on isolated *contents* rather than seeing these as aspects of a felt *process*.[137] When some content of experience—an emotion, idea, memory, dream image—passes out of focal awareness (for whatever reason) it does not stay all neatly formed as it is. It does not get filed away as a discrete entity, but instead melts back into the flow of our bodily experiencing, goes into solution, as it were, to become "part" of the complex and holistic felt ground of our ongoing interacting with the world. Contents may of course be reformed (as in a memory) when some relevant situation or supportive context draws them out, for they are still implicit in our experience. But the unconscious, experientially conceived, does not strictly *consist* of such contents. Merleau-Ponty thus called it "a retrospective illusion" to assume that what we become aware of in a moment of insight exists ahead of time as unconscious psychic material.[138] The practice of focusing, for example, does not involve unearthing buried contents, but rather allows some unfinished feeling to be symbolized—in that very moment—into consciousness. I want to associate the unconscious, then, not primarily with images (as do Jungians), but rather with the life process, in which images play the crucial role of life-forwarding symbols. Even the most dreadful dream contents come to us as an invitation to some further living—for which our bodily felt sense is always the touchstone.

Experiential Destruction and Ecological Crisis

The impoverishment of our experience is enormous. . . . Lacking . . . sensory experience of ourselves, devaluing and perpetually in conflict with many of the quiet, wordless, simple sensations that inform us at every moment of the complexity and wholeness of our being, we hide in our thoughts, our images, our self-images. We fear our sensations, paradoxically, as threatening to our being. . . . if we arrogantly ignore the sensory messages that clearly are instructing us that we need to cry, we may easily ignore with similar arrogance the sensory messages and requirements of the earth.

—Deborah Rinzler[139]

Testimonials galore give witness to the "destruction," "impoverishment," "attenuation," and "extinction" of our experience in modern times, as well as a chilling "waning of affect."[140] We have entered the age of the "neurotically split personality" say the psychotherapists[141]—an age of "bland numbness,"[142] in which many people's "inner selves become silent and almost disappear";[143] an era pervaded by a "sense of loss, of longing for something [we] cannot name, a feeling of being off-center, of missing something."[144] In my view, a big part of the work of ecopsychology has to go toward clarifying the connection—or as Chellis Glendinning calls it, "the screaming link"[145]—between this morbid state of our experiencing and our ecological troubles. The search for such illumination, in turn, means inquiring into the general mistreatment of nature under current sociocultural arrangements.

Paul Goodman wrote that if we are going to recognize the existence of an "anti-social personality" then we ought to be willing to conversely identify an "anti-personal society"—a kind of social field which in order to maintain itself must destroy persons.[146] Such a society as ours, to be sure, is a threat to personhood in general, both human and nonhuman. This is not to suggest that the person is without agency, to blame it all on "society" or "the system," but rather to recognize that the person always exists within a social reality that greatly influences how that agency gets exercised, including in the service of repression. The very existence of the repressed unconscious, suggests Joel Kovel, "reflects the split between the human and natural world."[147] Hence, "to comprehend the unconscious . . . the actual structure of the [human social] world must be given conceptual weight." As Kovel himself remarks, however, no adequate theoretical framework presently exists to bring to light the complex relationships between our social institutions and culture and our psyches.[148] He offers, for example, that the most viable way to synthesize Marxism and psychoanalysis is to recover from each of them their hidden spiritual motivations, and then to marry them within this common spiritual dimension (a not insignificant point for some of my own efforts below and in the chapters ahead, even if Freud and Marx enter only marginally into them).[149] A greater challenge still for ecopsychologists is to also bring the *ecological* dimension into our understanding of psyche and society. How, then, to proceed?

My own strategy is to always stay close to nature and experience. In this section, I therefore attempt to open up this topic by continuing to ask about our society's relation to the life process. My intention is not to entirely solve the theoretical difficulty just posed, but rather to briefly see what this one conceptual thread—the life process—might at this stage begin to show us, that is, how it might start to help us tie our various crises together. I begin by focusing on the place of nature within our economic system and finish by looking at the ecological crisis as a problem of lost meaning or feeling, of our cultural nihilism. In doing so, I am also using this section to introduce themes that will reappear in later discussions.

The Economization of Reality. A recent newspaper ad by Fortune Financial reads: "Garth Turner believes the world is about to fall apart. Find out why that might be good for your investments."[150] An alarmingly frank statement, it embodies the principle of the *economization of reality:* "the reduction of everything to relations of exchange, . . . the ever-expanding power of money and the corresponding decline in the spiritual and the sacred."[151] The aim of an economized reality, as Wendell Berry comments, "is to separate us as far as possible from the sources of life."[152] From an experiential perspective, what is most striking here is the increasing extent to which economic forces structure our day-to-day living or social relations, including the form that our families, work, and relations to the natural world must take.[153] In the efficient factory or rationalized office, for example, "every manifestation of what is informal, spontaneous, or emotional is ruthlessly suppressed"[154] in the interest of keeping our nature-exploiting economy on the roll.[155] (Dilbert cartoons are funny only pathetically.) As Ray Rogers comments, "The structures of everyday life and the structures that cause environmental problems are one and the same."[156] In short, the relationship between humans and nature, including the way we act toward our own nature, is almost wholly "absorbed by modern economic realities."[157]

Karl Marx used the notion of "commodity fetishism" to describe the capitalist condition wherein commodities are worshiped while human relations are equivalently devalued or deprioritized. In more ecological terms: "Through the massive inversion of reality that drives capital, we increasingly grant social standing to dead things (commodities) and deny it to living things (humans and nature)."[158] Capital, in brief, is "a set of processes and relationships which, through its necessity to expand, draws life out of humans and nature." As Rogers puts it simply, ours is "a world in which living things die to make a dead thing grow."[159] It is hard to imagine stating our society's opposition to the life process in bleaker terms. Our social relationships fall more and more under the influence of marketplace competitiveness as a given sensuous reality is progressively replaced by an abstract, rationalized, and administered one that silences nature's claims and replaces the living with the dead (including a living humanity with a deadened one).

The notion of commodity fetishism reveals capitalism as a perverse system of social organization, a single system of violence directed at both human and nonhuman nature. As Vandana Shiva writes: "More commodities and more cash means less life—in nature through ecological destruction and in society through the denial of basic needs."[160] The viciousness of this double violation of nature was explored many years ago by Max Horkheimer: "Domination of Nature involves domination of man. Each subject not only has to take part in the subjugation of external nature, human and nonhuman, but in order to do so must subjugate nature in himself. Since the subjugation of nature, in and outside of man, goes on without meaningful motive, nature is not really transcended or reconciled but merely *repressed*."[161] What Horkheimer and other critical theorists described was a social order whose essential trajectory is precisely to become *increasingly* incompatible with or repressing of nature.[162] The lone phone operator in a fluorescent-lit cubicle whose performance is being monitored by computer is hardly unfolding her or his existence as nature intended. Horkheimer observed that when we dominate nature we inevitably get pulled into the arena of violence as we ourselves are converted into instruments and resources (this is not to posit a homogenous humanity lacking in social distinction, but to assert that no one escapes some kind of mistreatment[163]). I call this vicious dialectic "the double violation of nature" in order to emphasize this rebounding or mirroring effect. As Kovel describes it:

> Our society is an immense machine constructed to extract wealth from the earth through unlimited economic penetration. Its raw materials extend to nature (viewed as "resources"), other societies, culture, and critically, the selves of individual persons.[164]

Hence:

> The great menace of capitalism, the one to which the entire ecology movement is responsive, is that all of nature itself will come under the sway of the commodity and be violated. . . . as the forest becomes a field which becomes a lawn which becomes Astroturf, so is the human organism converted into a zone of commodification. . . . In the emergence of the narcissistic character as the central figure of late capitalism, we see this movement appear in the self.[165]

Because the capitalist order insists on economic growth, and because profits are made by taking it out of the earth, (human) nature must be exploited on a perpetually escalating scale. Trade agreements (GATT, NAFTA, etc.) are simply the latest developments in this history of economic expansion, in which "ecological rapine and human slavery are both means of lowering prices on merciless global markets."[166] The workings of capital, that is, violate the nature of things *in general*. And as Kovel here suggests, this process now shows up in humans as the universalizing of pathological narcissism.

The permeation of our culture by narcissistic features[167] signals one of the central psychological outcomes (and engines) of our historical mode of relating to nature. While narcissism is usually discussed in terms of grandiosity and self-absorption, I want to emphasize that at the core of the classic narcissist is an utterly shame-bound person whose early needs were severely violated and who consequently has only an abysmal sense of self. Narcissists are wounded to such an extent that they have almost no sense of their own insides, their own bodily felt living. They identify instead with grand self-images that act in fantasy to compensate for their terrible sense of inadequacy. They spend their entire lives propping up these images and insisting brittlely that others be their loving mirrors. The cult of celebrity—in which we adore and identify with images of the rich, the powerful, and the beautiful, found in those glossy magazines at the supermarket checkout—likewise betrays a pervasive sense of worthlessness in our society. On the whole, however, this condition is not a problem for the running of a capitalist society, for feelingless, hungry narcissists are in many ways perfectly adapted, if not tailor-made, for it.[168] Having had their own nature violated, and lacking much grasp of their inner motivations, narcissists consume endlessly in a quest for lost selfhood, and, seeking self-esteem through productivity, performance, ladder-climbing, and hollow expressions of brute power, are all too prepared to participate in the technological ruination of nature.

My depiction here of the ecopsychological implications of our economized reality has been but a rough sketch. My purpose was simply to evoke a sense for the all-around irrational mistreatment of nature under the dominance of our economic system and, in the face of it, to draw attention to the importance of reprioritizing the life process. John Rodman took up this point when he argued that the motivations of radical ecologists are based *in* this life process, whose felt authority they put above any economic calculus:

> Acts of ecological resistance do not stem so much from calculation of enlightened self-interest . . . as from a *felt need* to resist the repression, censorship, or liquidation of potentialities that lie within both human and nonhuman nature. . . . the river struggles against the dam like an instinct struggles against an inhibition or a social movement struggles against a restrictive institution. The threat perceived by the human 'Friends of the River' who try to prevent the dam's being built in the first place . . . is the threat of wildness being tamed, of a *natural process interrupted and distorted,* of the 'individuality' of a natural being made to conform to an artificial pattern imposed upon it, of *repression in the most general sense.*[169]

The legitimacy enjoyed by different kinds of argument is a matter of what ultimately concerns us. If, like Livingston, we care for "the phenomenon of living" more than we do for "the contorted belief system" of our culture,[170] then arguments *from* felt need, and *against* repression, will persuade us. If, moreover, the narcissist is to Astroturf as the vital human being is to an undiminished forest, then whatever we say in defence of nonhuman nature we may also say in defence of human nature. If, on the other extreme, what most concerns us as a society is the financial bottom line—a concern symbolized in that dominant monument of our age, the banking tower[171]—then only economic and resourcist arguments will do.

Finally, I need note that we are not committed to a violent economic system without reason. Environmentalists have long been frustrated by how easily "fear for the economy" displaces "fear for the ecology."[172] I believe this fear is key. We are born into a social world in which our need for personal viability or security gets "met" by being twisted down along narrow economic pathways which then become difficult to leave, for both emotional and structural reasons. We are just too existentially vulnerable for it to be otherwise, at least for most of us. These pathways, however, fail to bring us the release from fear we desire. For it is the very pattern of relationships within the system of capital that generates our deep and desperate insecurity in the first place. Thus, the whole historical dialectic of double violating nature is essentially a compulsive and doomed search for an ever-more-elusive sense of security, in which the repression and degradation of human and nonhuman nature has become a strange and viciously spiraling end in itself.[173] To understand all this better I suggest we need a concrete mapping of the connections between the form of our society, the nature of our experience, and our relation to more-than-human reality. Chapters four through six are exercises toward this end.

Nihilism: A Unifying Experiential Theme. Philosopher David Levin calls nihilism a "collective and archetypal madness . . . that defines the spirit of our epoch."[174] I suggest that our psychological and ecological crises are each manifestations of this nihilism and so are essentially unified in it. Nihilism is a condition in which we experience little meaning, depth, dimensionality, or transcendent bearing in the world, and where we ourselves feel empty, cut-off, homeless, soulless; many of us frantically trying to "be" somebody. As Jules Henry writes: "Life in our culture is a flight from nothingness."[175] How might we relate our nihilistic pathology to the life process and so to the ecological crisis?

First, Evernden claims that "although they seldom recognize it, [environmentalists] are protesting not the stripping of natural resources but the stripping of *earthly meaning.* . . . Ironically, the very entity they defend—environment—is itself an offspring of the nihilistic behemoth they challenge."[176] Meaning, born of interaction, is both found and made, is coconstituted, in the opening out of a life process. That our society senses little meaning in the natural world is because our concrete interactions with it are so restricted, because we do not make it relevant or include it in our daily living. "The environment" exists, remarks Evernden, precisely "because we have excised it from the context of our lives."[177] Where there is no contact, participation, or experience, there is no meaning. And that which has no meaning simply does not matter. By contrast, for many of those who have indeed spent a life in open contact with nonhuman beings, the natural world is peopled with beautiful and mysterious others deserving of respect and solidarity. In this case, even arguing for the "intrinsic value" of nature seems a clumsy or not-quite-right affair, a strategy that betrays our nihilistic times. For as Romand Coles suggests, value is not some quanta, but "emerges like breath exhaled under water from encounters between self and other."[178]

Perhaps the connection I am exploring here is most simply made in R. D.

Laing's oft-cited line that: "If our experience is destroyed our behaviour will be destructive."[179] Nihilism is a *frustrating* cultural condition; it engenders rage and (self-)destruction (i.e., an-nihil-ation). The more our living and feelings are blocked, the more we are estranged from our own bodily-felt nature, the more does the aggression within the life force press up against this repression; hence "adjustment in our time involves an element of resentment and suppressed fury."[180] As many have noted, violence often originates in repressed aggression combined with an inner sense of shame or impotence. That is, acts of rageful violence can be seen, in part, as desperate attempts to assert one's existence or personhood, so as to defend oneself against the painful feeling that one is a nothing or a nobody. There is, furthermore, no shortage of literature describing much of the male-driven mistreatment of the earth as an act of blind hostility, in which nature, denuded of meaning to the status of brute matter, becomes the target for guilt-free or morally sanctioned acts of violence. Barry Lopez, for example, writes that the historical slaughter of wolves in North America is rooted in "theriophobia," a fear of the beast (within). All that has become violent, irrational, insatiable, and disinhibited within humans is disowned from awareness and then projected onto animals who do not themselves "rape, murder, and pillage." This projection, notes Lopez, has stuck particularly well to wolves, who when targeted for annihilation are therefore asked to pay the price (as are all dogs who get kicked) for the distortion and repression of life among men.[181]

Konrad Stettbacher calls our feelings "the guardians of life." Rinzler likewise remarks that "the only safety and protection we can ever know is in our profound connectedness with our sensory selves, as part of the living earth, warning us of our danger."[182] As Audre Lorde has noted, however: "Within structures defined by profit, by linear power, by institutional de-humanization, our feelings were not meant to survive."[183] And as Heidegger suggested, this means that our time is "no longer able to experience its own destitution."[184] One final way to view the domination of nature, then, is simply as a "cruelty sanctioned by tradition,"[185] wherein we do not feel the impact of our violent actions. The narcissist is just unable to recognize the self or personhood of others, and thus to value and care for life.[186]

In "beginning with experience" in this chapter I have also begun my efforts to demonstrate the centrality of the human-nature relationship in all psychological, social, and ecological matters. In my view, thinkers who wish to oppose the destructive aspects of our society need to acknowledge the primary authority of self-organizing nature—so that they may both more adequately gather the essential nature of our crises and, just as importantly, find this nature in their own experience as a source of guidance. Such privileging of nature is certainly not unique to me, but is common to all radical ecologists. In its linking of the hatred of nature to the hatred of women and in its opposition to panmechanism, for example, ecofeminism has largely defined itself exactly by its life-orientation.[187] Ynestra King writes: "In ecofeminism, nature is the central category of analysis. An analysis of the interrelated dominations of nature—psyche and sexuality, human oppression, and nonhuman nature—and the historic position of women in relation to these forms of domination is the starting point of ecofeminist theory."[188] What has yet to be developed, however, is what in the next two chapters I call a "naturalistic psychology."

4

FROM HUMANISTIC TO NATURALISTIC PSYCHOLOGY

The Irony of Humanistic Psychology

Fidelity to human order, . . . if it is to be responsible, implies fidelity also to natural order.

—Wendell Berry[1]

In the previous chapter, my main psychological sources were humanistic. What makes this camp of psychology valuable to ecopsychology is its experiential, interactive focus and the sensitive attention it gives to human nature. The irony of humanistic psychology, however, is that it has come to cherish human nature largely by distinguishing it sharply *from* the rest of nature, the latter eclipsed by the human marvel into near irrelevancy. This situation is consistent with the general tradition of humanism: "a style of thought or an attitude which makes the human central, important, valuable, crucial, pivotal, wonderful, powerful—even miraculous."[2] The original raison d'être of humanistic psychology was in fact to "resist the reduction of humanness to Nature" by emphasizing such special human properties as will, freedom, and consciousness—and so, for at least some,[3] to establish a "radical break" with nature (seen as mechanically determined matter-in-motion).[4] One of the first humanistic psychologists, Erich Fromm, wrote in 1941 that man's remaining ties with nature actually *block* "his full human development."[5] While not all humanists would today agree with him, what can be safely said is that few have taken the position that our humanity is most nobly realized exactly *through* those natural ties that Fromm so regretted.[6]

This chapter and the next together make up a kind of hermeneutical exercise aimed at such a vision. In them, I make the turn from humanistic to "naturalistic" psychology. I have set myself the task, that is, of carrying forward some of the biases within humanistic psychology that are enabling or fruitful for ecopsychology (e.g., its organismic focus and its interactive view of reality), while leaving behind some of those that are blinding or false. Ecological thinkers have brought much criticism down on humanism, calling it, among other things, an "ideological fixation" on humans.[7] When it comes to humanistic *psychology*, however, I would rather put it in dialogue *with* radical ecology in order to create something that benefits from and filters out weaknesses in both of them. The basic image of human nature that unites the humanistic psychologies is that of a continual state of becoming, emerging, or unfolding.[8] We are most human, in other words, when perpetually transcending or growing beyond our current mode of being. The problem from an ecological perspective is that this process is largely disarticulated or disembedded from the natural world, and so lacks any restraint or necessary commitment to an earthly place. Humanists often proclaim our *unlimited* potential, sometimes even fantasizing of planetary omnipotence.[9] To put it plainly, then, the ecologizing of humanistic psychology will require a certain amount of deflation. Hans Peter Duerr writes, in this regard, that to be able to "speak" with nonhuman entities "a person needs what the [Native Americans] call 'reverence.' Humans must become *unimportant* before the other things of nature."[10]

I have already voiced my concerns about the natural scientific disclosure of nature. The exercise in this chapter is thus to begin inquiring into the meaning of nature in more psychological, primordial, and openly dialogical terms. I do so by defining nature under three headings, namely, the natural world, the essential qualities or character of some phenomenon, and the life force. This will then set the stage for me to outline a naturalistic or nature-centered psychology in the chapter to follow. In sum, I would note that the word "human" comes from the Latin *humus,* meaning soil or earth. The naturalistic psychology I propose in the chapters ahead attempts to stay attuned to what is indeed distinctive about being human, while nonetheless keeping us grounded in the earth of which we consist.

On Nature and Human Nature

Many of the proposed solutions to the current ecological crisis are taken in by traditional interpretations, ignore questions of hermeneutics, and so overlook the underlying fantasies and prejudices that condition . . . our perception of the natural world—and thereby also our interaction with the environment.
—Graham Parkes[11]

Hermeneutic inquiry arises out of some sort of alienation from meaning. Our nihilistic era, however, suffers from a general loss of meaning *across the board,* a condition both born and perpetuating of violence. My own interpretive and rhetorical strategy is to counter this nihilism by taking nature as my theme, for it is in this direction that I feel the sources of meaning are to be found or rediscovered, and our violence is to be understood. To do this, however, is to walk into tricky territory, so ideologically misused is the notion of nature (e.g., capitalism is natural) and so blunt a tool is it for justifying any kind of status quo ("that's just human nature"). The muddying of the whole idea of nature—to the point where nature is said not to exist at all—is nonetheless exactly the point. The notion of nature has been ideologically perverted precisely because it is so powerful, so very much at the heart of it all, so decisive in how we understand and behave in the world. Stronger still, it is because our society so poorly acknowledges and understands the nature of things that we continue to grossly mistreat them, as I began to argue in the previous chapter. Rather than give up on or renounce the concept of nature as irremediably or unavoidably a product only of human discourse, I therefore say that ecopsychologists need to make deliberate efforts to reclaim and defend this "nature" against reactionary, conservative, or naive usage.[12]

We can all agree, I presume, that nature is a matter of interpretation. My general ontological outlook—which I call *plural realism*[13]—is that there are innumerable ways of disclosing or interpreting reality. This position does not naively suggest, however, that all perspectives are equally valid; it does not rule out criticism and debate. What it does do is seek a "middle way" between the extremes. Most notably, it is neither objectivism nor relativism. That *different* interpretations are possible, that many truths can coexist, refutes objectivism. That *better* interpretations are possible, that our experience can always adjudicate the truth or falsity of an assertion, or lead us into more satisfying contact with reality, refutes relativism. Hence, to think of truth in plural terms is not say that anything goes. In other words, as a plural realist I hold that many different interpretations of a phenomenon are possible, but also that these will not all be equal in their truthfulness or openness to the phenomenon in question (as Simone Weil writes: "Every being cries out to be read differently"[14]). How we understand nature, then, depends on the quality of our relation to it, our mode of existence, the ground of interpretation, the historical and personal prejudices we bring to it. One way I see naturalistic psychology is therefore as a dialogue concerning different symbolizations of nature, in which the participants must be willing to be changed, to work experientially, in order to better hear and more faithfully respond to the phenomena of nature. While, for example, I have learned a great deal about nature from Buddhism, the practice of Buddhism is still largely human-centered.[15] As Gary Snyder remarks, there is little in the traditions of any of the major world religions, including Buddhism, that addresses the question: "Well, what do you say to Magpie? What do you say to Rattlesnake when you meet him?"[16] Although different approaches or schemes reveal nature in their own ways, my faith is that our comprehension will benefit from an open dialogue among them—so long, that is, as we take our concepts experientially, making an effort to practically embody them or see what felt differences they make, rather than just bandying them about in the air.

In an exercise such as this, where we are feeling out a large terrain, we must speak broadly. For this section, I have chosen three broad categories within which to discuss a number of meanings of nature, and thereby to establish a basis for advancing a naturalistic psychology.[17] (The boundaries between the categories, however, are utterly permeable, and I have made no attempt to stop the flow of terms across them.) The exercise is intended as a "first pass" or introductory treatment, on the understanding that much of what I talk about will gain from the discussion in the remaining chapters. I am not, moreover, aiming at a final or definitive account of this subject, but merely a *sufficient* one to give credence to a naturalistic approach. Despite having read about it, for instance, I have only the meagerest sense of what it is like to live as do oral, myth-telling people, with all the things they know about the nature of the world.[18] My argument, however, is that this lack of experience need not stop me or anyone else from engaging in a recollective process. For my own rhetorical purposes, it would in fact do no good to spend my whole time quoting Black Elk. That said, I do include a number of indigenous and anthropological voices in my dialogue on nature, both because they so clearly give form or support to points I want to make and also because they help evoke a sense, however vaguely, for what has been lost.[19]

Nature as the Natural World

> The knife of separation is cruel. I not only remember in a factual sense but I can feel to this day the anguished frustration, the knowledge that I could never—not ever—be more than a boy on the grass, excluded from [the world of toads and frogs and newts] wholly and eternally.
>
> —John Livingston[20]

This first category is what we simply call the natural world, sometimes including ourselves in it, sometimes not. How are we to understand this ambiguity?

Creatures of Distance: The Gap. Speaking of his intimate relationship with an Alaskan island, Richard Nelson writes: "There is nothing in me that is not of the earth, no split instance of separateness, no particle that disunites me from my surroundings. I am no less than the earth itself. The rivers run through my veins, the winds blow in and out with my breath, the soil makes my flesh, the sun's heat smolders inside me." While in a less ecstatic mood, however, he elsewhere admits that "as much as I love it [the island], I feel distant and disconnected, still struggle with questions about belonging here. . . . Perhaps I want more closeness than could ever exist for me."[21] Nelson's struggle demonstrates what psychologists recognize as the tension between our wish for fusion with the universe and the inescapable fact that we are "creatures of distance."[22]

To overcome alienation and dualism is not necessarily to adopt a monism, for we are never entirely coincident or "one" with others.[23] As a means to understand the human relation to nature I propose instead a *kinship continuum*.[24] On one end of this continuum I place the world according to Jean-Paul Sartre, in which humans and nature are utterly void of common ground. The relation between them, in Sartre's view, is that of a totally free, hyper-Cartesian human consciousness (Nothingness) standing in hostile opposition to a "massive, inert, repulsive and nauseating 'mother' nature" (Being).[25] At the far end of this continuum, by contrast, I place the world of the mystic in a state of nirvana. Reportedly, in this blissful experience of total unity a person's sense doors are closed, such that from the outside she or he looks dead. Scattered between these two end points lie the rest of us. Although, "end point" is perhaps not the right term; for kinship denotes the experience of unity-within-separation, likeness-within-difference, continuity-within-discontinuity, or identity-within-differentiation. Sartre senses no continuity between his own being and that of others, while the blissed-out mystic experiences no difference (I presume). Thus neither the Sartrean nor nirvanic state count as one of kinship; they are better understood as asymptotes.[26]

Sartre and the mystic are not what I am primarily interested in, even as they help me define nature as a world of others with whom we feel varying degrees of kinship. (In fact, the likely Indo-European root for *nature* is *gen,* which among its other derivatives—such as *generate*—gives us the words *kin* and *kind*.[27]) What I wish to stress, rather, is that alienation is a state poor in kinship feelings, and so that our estranged and divided society lies closer to the Sartrean end of things (although I do not suggest nirvana as a necessarily ideal state either). We may perhaps feel our kinship with the rest of the natural world only as a certain attraction or draw toward it; as a desire to sit our bones down on a piece of bedrock, where we then experience a sort of inner soaring as we watch the gulls fly by. Experientially, the route out of alienation is marked by an increase in such kinship feeling: by a growing sense of commonality, solidarity, or belonging with others of all kinds. What we yearn for, then, is to be on more familiar terms with other beings, to be a part of it all—not so much for a feeling of pure undifferentiated unity, but for a sense of comm-unity; not union, but comm-union.[28] It is the common ground we *do* sense with animals (human or nonhuman), plants, rocks, water, and so on, that lets us say that "we too are nature," while it is the feeling of difference and distance that forces us to call nature a world of "others." Nature in this sense is "the whole ground of Otherness"[29] and human nature the otherness "we experience about ourselves."[30]

The etymological meaning of distance is "stand apart" (*di-stance*). As I aim to show in what remains of this book, it is of our human nature to wrestle with or learn the art of distance. As an experiential concept, distance refers to nearness or farness of contact, regardless of literal distance. To be aware of reality as such, to get perspective on things, requires that we withdraw from our ontological medium or step back from being (or as Heidegger would say, that being itself withdraw from us). Humans are able to feel awe and wonder because as creatures of distance we can differentiate and contact the world in its sheer and inexhaustible otherness, grasp it in its unfathomable mystery. Under the best conditions, we are creatures of *right* or *optimal* distance: the distance where we make meaningful contact,[31] where good gestalts are formed.[32] The crisis in our current relationship with nature is not, then, one of distance per se, but of *over*distance. Joel Kovel is accordingly critical of deep ecology supporters who seek to abolish *any* sense of difference between humans and nature, for this ironically "deprives humans of what is in fact our peculiar nature. The dialectic, to be both part of and [experientially] separate from nature, is in fact human nature."[33] The step back from being opens up an experiential gap—the moment of separation—which is our human lot to negotiate, with all the beautiful and tragic possibilities it entails. Shepard claims, in this regard, that it is "an attitude of *accepted separateness* . . . which characterizes both the great naturalists and primal peoples."[34] As Nelson reports, offering one example of this, for Koyukon Indians "humans and animals are clearly and qualitatively separated." Despite that the "natural and human communities originated together in the Distant Time and have never become completely separate," there is still a "narrow gap . . . between the worlds of humanity and nature."[35]

In the human-nature relation, then, one sense of "human" is that of a community of human beings bounded by shared language, myth, custom, and so on, as it collectively interacts with nonhuman others. As Sean Kane observes, in archaic human societies this boundary is often physically marked by, for example, the edge of the forest or the surface of the sea, where worlds meet and exchanges take place.[36] I leave it for Kane and others to detail what such primal life at the edge of mystery is like. What I would emphasize is that kinship with the rest of nature has traditionally been won by admitting of boundaries and then *dialoguing* with the nonhuman presences on the other side of them, through ritual, dream, myth, nonordinary states of consciousness, skillful everyday interaction, and so forth. This involves the working out of covenants, and the maintenance of a complex balance between the worlds, governed by taboos and rules of exchange that guard against overexploitation. As Barry Lopez notes, "our relationships with animals were once contractual—principled agreements, founded in a spirit of reciprocity, mythic in persuasiveness. Among hunting peoples in general they consisted of mutual obligations and courtesies."[37] More generally still, in such conversation humans relate not to some homogeneous or undifferentiated Nature but to particular beings, to elk or beaver people, even as these others themselves interrelate as an ecological whole. Experienced as kin, such persons are approached with respect and confidence, for they are not seen as adversaries.[38] For us, on the other hand, the disappearance of this kind of intense and respectful interaction has turned a narrow gap into a spiritual chasm, into which we are now forever falling.

Nature and Spirit. Cultural narratives around the globe signal the gap between humans and nature in their stories of a human fall from grace, of a departure from purity or harmonious unity, or of an introduction of separation and self-conscious struggle between humans and the rest of nature.[39] Our original sin, the mark of shame on all humanity,[40] comes from this essential sense of isolation or of being cut off from the world of nature. Nature for us is that which we have lost; and we experience this separation as a sense of lack, deficiency, or incompleteness on our part. Hence the basic shame inherent in the human condition. In asking about the human/nature relation we thus come to the "problem of man"; or as I prefer to say: the question of nature raises the question of spirit. I use the word *spirit,* in this instance, to refer to a mode of experience that tends in the direction of reunion with nature or that works to overcome splits between realms of being.[41] With the exception of our own largely despiritualized society, spiritual practice has been a prime, if not all-encompassing, concern throughout the record of human existence. I do not hesitate therefore to call the spiritual an essential form of experience for humans. Or as Kovel puts it: "human beings are configured spiritually."[42] A being who was already at one with nature would have no need of spiritual lessons (or of "nature"). On account of how we stand in relation to the rest of nature, then, it is of our own human nature to be spiritual.

The spiritual urge is so strong in us humans because in our incompleteness we are bound to ask about the meaning of life and the ground of our existence. But what is this ground? As a network of relationships the natural world is not a thing at all, but a constant flux of interweaving processes, lacking in any permanence or ultimate solidity. In standing apart from nature, this nonsolidity, groundlessness, or "emptiness" to reality is revealed to humans as such—which makes us *anxious.* In the face of the so-called void, the separated self or Ego then seeks security through creating the illusion that it is an immortal substance exempt from the law of change or impermanence.[43] As an illusory structure, however, the Ego is haunted by the void—by a sense of lack, emptiness, insecurity, or tenuousness; by the agitated prospect of its own annihilation. As the word suggests, what we ultimately a-void with our fearful and rigid life-patterns is *the* void. The fear of our future death derives in fact from this implicit dread or more basic anxiety of being suspended over the abyss at every present moment.

As David Loy has suggested, drawing on Buddhist and existential psychology, "the most fundamental dualism of all" is that between the separated or isolated self and the no-thing-ness or void that perpetually threatens its existence.[44] From this view, we see that the Ego is caught in an endless struggle between the desire to exist for itself as a separate being and the desire to not exist, to be fused back into the whole, so as to extinguish the pain of separation. The story of a schizophrenic man who spends much of his time bowing illustrates this dynamic. Asked why he bows, the man says he is balancing his emotions; when feeling isolated and lonely he leans forward to be close to others, whereupon he immediately feels afraid and straightens back up, pulling away from contact— only to once again feel lonely and to commence another bow.[45] What this man describes is an oscillation between those two well-known poles of life that I call our "twin terrors."[46] One terror is that of being all alone in the cosmos, wherein the void looms large to the extent of our Egoic isolation. The other is that of the death of our Egos, or of being engulfed or overwhelmed by others—what has been called "annihilation panic." While few today actually contemplate the void, the twin terrors are the stuff of everyday interpersonal relations. They are seen, in particular, in the lives of trauma survivors, which often swing dramatically between states of intense attachment and terrified withdrawal.[47] It takes little effort, however, to see such dynamics in almost anybody's life: the anxious isolate (fearful of intimacy), the needy "codependent" (fearful of independence), the addict (fused with her or his "drug"), and so on. We may also experience the void whenever our lives are in transition or limbo—when we switch careers, get divorced, lose a loved one, develop an illness, or leave home for the first time—when we can no longer hold onto our old identities and relationships and must instead confront a distressing gap in the continuity of our existence.[48] While I can only demonstrate it in this limited way, my point here is that the spiritual conditions of human existence, based in our distanced relation to nature, while they may be a-voided, can never be escaped.

One of the nature-violating hallmarks of our own society, then, is that it does not adequately attend to the spiritual region of existence. Significantly, our repressed fear of the void, our hidden ontological insecurity, then gets translated into (among other things) a fear of nature: a million tentacles, creepy-crawlies, microorganisms, or hidden beasts—alien and fearsome others—threatening our vulnerable and precarious Egos. Indeed, Horkheimer wrote that the "history of Western civilization could be written in terms of the growth of the [E]go,"[49] its rational functions being employed to dominate and control nature (whether id or wilderness) in an endless and self-defeating search for security. As Kovel notes: "Egoic experience gravitates toward paranoia, and does so precisely because of the splitting and domination conjugated into it. . . . The concrete effects . . . are the repression of the body and the inevitable return of the repressed. Ecologically, nature turns into wilderness which must be 'tamed,' that is, paved, converted into Disneyworlds or simple raw materials. . . . Ego is thus the specific antagonist of any emancipatory project. It is what an ecologically sensitive practice must overcome."[50] In short, because the Egoic mode is so antagonistic to and split from nature, ecopsychology is called toward a spiritual mode, one that would overcome Ego.

To finish this discussion I wish to speak briefly about three aspects of spiritual life that will be relevant to discussions ahead. First, as Loy suggests, the antidote for fear of the void is to *become* the void. In other words, spiritual practice is the dissolving of Ego and the realizing of ourselves in relation to others. I imagine all "nature lovers" know the experience of at least temporarily releasing their Egos outward, so as to spontaneously flow with birds, trees, wind, sky, water, rock, moss, flowers, insects—in which they feel a relative loss of self-density, noticeable for its peacefulness, spaciousness, vividness, or at least its freedom from a more confined Egoic mode of existence. Sartre's world, by contrast, is imbued with the dread and unreality of existential isolation. Thus, while there are many ways of being spiritual, all of which involve discipline and work, it is not difficult to gather that the more we identify with the greater rhythms of life, the more community, common ground or kinship we sense, the less anxious we will be, because less attached to our own individual atom. Second, spiritual life confronts death. The question of nature brings the topic of our death aversion, our impoverished comprehension of the interplay between birth and death in the larger stream of life, right to the fore. As Gary Snyder teaches, to "acknowledge that each of us at the table will eventually be part of the meal," rather than being a source of disgust with self, humanity, and life, can be a way into the sacred, celebratory, and sacramental side of existence. The fact that life unavoidably involves death-dealing can be taken, that is, as a spiritual challenge: as an invitation to understand "the play of the real world, with all its suffering," to realize that all "of nature is a gift-exchange, a pot-luck banquet" at which we ourselves are both gift and guest.[51] Third, spiritual life is the development of our capacity to love. As Fromm wrote: "The awareness of human separation, without reunion by love—is the source of shame. It is at the same time the source of guilt and anxiety. The deepest need of man, then, is to overcome his separateness, to leave the prison of his aloneness."[52] To be loved is to have our being affirmed, to feel connected to and embraced by others; love is thus the source of our ontological security, of feeling grounded in our own being.[53] To love others is to identify their interests with our own, while nonetheless maintaining our distance from them, so that they (and we) may unfold their own particular natures, or be.

Nature as Mysterious Birth, Genesis, Growth, Unfolding. "Nature" comes from the Latin word *natura*, which means *birth*. Hence the widespread (though apparently not universal) association of nature with "mother" and the feminine; and its relation to such words as *natal* and *pregnant*. (The Latin for *mother*—mater—is in turn the source for such words as *matter* and *matrix*.) The Greek word is *physis* or *phusis*, which similarly means the process of genesis, growing, a-rising, e-merging, opening up, unfolding—as in the blossoming of a flower.[54] Such words make the link between nature and *life*. Note also how nature in its primordial sense is a *process*, is a verb. Nature as a noun, as physical matter, is thus (as Heidegger observed) nature in a "restricted sense." The natural world is fundamentally, therefore, a field of arising-and-passing phenomena or appearances, a myriad of unfolding-and-dying interactional events.

How are we to grasp this primordial sense of nature? We might begin by noticing the countless cyclic phenomena in the world, such as breathing, the rising and setting of the sun, the turning of the seasons, or the life cycle of a plant, animal, river, or mountain. The character of the bear, in particular, has through much of human cultural experience been a "mentor in birthing and dying in the endless cycle of becoming," a "master of renewal and the wheel of the seasons"[55]—as she rotates across the northern sky in the constellation of the Great Bear or goes "underground" to den for the winter, emerging once again in the spring (perhaps with the new life of cubs). Indeed, the verb *to bear* means to bring forth or give birth. We may also return here to much of what I discussed in the previous chapter. All complete experiences are an arising from out of the felt ground and a passing away back into it, a forming and dissolving of a gestalt, a contacting and a withdrawing. Our human experiencing, as I took pains to say, is but a cyclic process within the vaster natural world. "The naturalist," says John Livingston, "sees a wild animal as one among uncountable ephemeral corporeal emergences, one minor miracle to remind us of the ineffable whole."[56] So might we see ourselves.[57]

All phenomena arise from out of a larger field or ground, as plants perhaps teach best. They all, therefore, have a hidden dimension: they are *mysterious.* The natural world, as a play of appearances in which the things that are disclosed to us are rooted in what still remains closed, is intrinsically mysterious. Think about the origin of things. Dream images are *given,* emotions just *come up.* We may say something and then ask ourselves Where did *that* come from? Symbols, in other words, emerge spontaneously into the space our existence helps to hold open; they float to the surface, according to an order of things that is beyond our reckoning. The much talked about "Dreamtime" of Australian aborigines, while difficult for us to understand conceptually, is apparently something like a time out of time that lies *within* evident reality; it refers to a perpetual emerging of the world from out of a mysterious depth or earthly dreaming.[58] To speak of mystery is to say that the world contains invisible grounds, unseen forces. In fact, the early Greek thinker, Heraclitus, claimed that nature itself "loves to hide." Or as Kane writes, the minds or intentions of the ecological complexities of nature "prefer to be kept hidden."[59] Archaic myths, he says, do not explain the why of it all, but are rather stories about the links or relationships among things, the general patterns of the natural world (as in, to use a minor example, "red sky at night, sailor's delight"). More to the point, myth-telling peoples have injunctions against attempting to eliminate mystery, against bringing everything out into the open, for such acts encourage a destructive or meddling hubris.

It is the business of Ego, however, to break "itself off from the mystery."[60] The rise of the Ego through Western history has accordingly been paralleled by a shift in the way the natural world has displayed itself to us, becoming increasingly distant, hard, literal, mute, static, passive: unmysterious. While, for example, modern people perceive the world as a kind of picture that stands in front of them and recedes away from view,[61] the experience of Medieval people was more like that of being *in* the picture, as is indicated by the (to us, odd looking) absence of linear perspective in their art. Although it is hard to imagine, people felt themselves mysteriously immersed with other beings and with their language "in something like a clear lake of . . . 'meaning.'"[62] Today's scientific project of total unconcealment is an offense against the things of nature (including ourselves) because it attacks the mystery that is essential to them and only invokes them to further withdraw from us, thereby taking us all that much more out of the picture.[63] The idea of nature as otherness, then, implies an opacity, polydimensionality, or wildness that asks to be respected. Barry Lopez writes of wolves, for instance, that: "No one—not biologists, not Eskimos, not backwoods hunters, not naturalist writers—knows why wolves do what they do."[64]

Nature as Any *(Personified) "Other."* Although the historical Buddha spoke a language known as Pali, the word used for nature within Buddhist thought is most often the Sanskrit term *dharma* (spelled *dhamma* in Pali). Dharma is a multifaceted word denoting an all-pervasive reality. What I would draw out here is that among its usages the term signifies *any* phenomenon: any kind of being that arises, stays awhile, and passes away. Hence, we may speak of "a" dharma, or "a" nature, to refer to whatever is borne by the mind,[65] that is, to whatever appears in our awareness as some "other." Buddhism adopts, then, what is called a phenomenological ontology, the view that *whatever* we experience (phenomena) has some manner of reality. In our own time the predominant understanding of nature, of the real, is that of matter. The many nonmaterial phenomena that stubbornly persist in our experience are then given a derivative or secondary status, degraded to epi-phenomena. Hence, for a recollective project such as this I suggest that a phenomenological ontology is imperative. We might do our best to adopt a kind of mythological consciousness, wherein "*anything* of existential significance or displaying affective power is important and hence real. For example, dreams are considered real events, and the emotional impact of dreams about deceased persons accounts for the absence of a strict separation between the living and the dead. . . . The world is not measured by consistency but by existential import."[66] We need also admit that: "In a multiple world I too am multiple. Otherness is inside and out, a part of myself and a part of the outside world."[67]

What this all means is a loosening up of our grip on the real. To say that nature is "other" means that we exist both in and as our felt relations to whatever symbolic otherness we encounter, in whatever realms or modes of experience we may be open to—whether private or public, ordinary or nonordinary. Thus, any so-called spirit-being—whether a critical superego, bear-spirit, angel, bad introject, malevolent possession, dream figure, ancestor, transpersonal guide, or hallucinated sound—may be taken simply as a hidden presence or spectral force in our lives, one that visits us, helps us, possesses us, haunts us: claims us somehow.[68] Eugene Gendlin writes that the bodily felt sense "comes between the conscious person and the deep universal reaches of human nature where we are no longer ourselves."[69] The otherness that Jung attributes to the unconscious may also be read, then, as the autonomy that Gendlin attributes to the body (in its relation to the world). This autonomy of the body-unconscious leads, moreover, to a paradox that is well known to anyone who does inner work: that our experience is not exactly "ours."[70] "Like the fox in the forest which is not mine just because I see it, so the fox in the dream is not mine just because I dream it."[71] In inner work, we are asked to "own" our experience, feel our feelings, while nonetheless *dis-identifying* from what we experience, creating an aware or detached distance from it, imagining it as *another person*. Doing so opens up the needed space to then converse with it, make *contact* with it, and—paradoxically—achieve greater close-ness or intimacy with it. In the practice of focusing, for example, we often symbolize a feeling by allowing an inner image to emerge from it, whether this image be a block of ice, a scared little boy, or a prowling wolf. We then enter into a relationship with this imagined and personified other—as it is still felt in our bodies—getting to know it, seeing what it wants, getting close to it, working out conflicts with it, and so on.[72]

One of the additional things focusing demonstrates, then, is that the *person-ification* of otherness is indigenous to the psyche.[73] We *do* recognize the living quality of nonhuman beings, their inwardness, whether these others be an inner image, a cat, or an old pair of hiking boots. It is a great irony that so many psychologists have described personification as "primitive" or childish animism; for no good therapist (it seems to me) can ignore it. This shows how easily one of the most obvious and significant tendencies of the psyche can be pushed aside by an objectivist view. We may love others, and feel loved by them, only if we understand them as persons.[74] As I discussed in chapter one, moreover, there are efforts afoot to revive an animistic sense of things, which has always been the common sense among indigenous peoples. A traditional Hopi belief, for instance, is reportedly that "humans emerged into the world as corn does," and so, con-versely, that corn ought to be treated as newborn persons.[75] If this seems too outlandish an idea, we may simply recall that one of the goals of hermeneutics is to grant others their own voices and intentions.

In a well-known reflection on a path through a field he walked as a boy, Heidegger wrote that "the message of the Fieldpath speaks only as long as there are human beings who, born in its air, are able to hear it. . . . The danger threatens that men of today remain hard of hearing to its language."[76] Following Heidegger, we may understand or imagine the natural world as a communicative and person-ified body, even if we have trouble hearing its speech. In my own experiences of conversing with nonhuman others, the moment of contact arrives like a window opening: I feel a sudden resonance, where a message unmistakably comes through, as when a Raven flew onto a nearby branch of a hemlock to tell me who is boss and whose world I should be paying attention to. Such experiences need no justifica-tion beyond themselves—for meaning is transmitted in them, and I feel a clear change in my existence, in the way I sense things following them. The more I am able to attune myself to the natural world the more I discover that it is correspondingly attuned to me. Like being in a great big dream, relevant messages are being spoken everywhere, telling me things I need to hear, and to which I need respond. I offer this modest testimonial only to suggest both the very ordinariness of such earthly communication and its utter mystery.[77]

As a final note, I wish to clarify how I will hereafter use the term *natural world.* Although I call any "other" a natural event, I still wish to employ the "natural world" as a shorthand for that realm of wild and diverse processes found most fully, though not exclusively, in relatively unhumanized places, where a richer community of beings is present. To make this relative distinction I will therefore at times refer to the "wider" or "larger" natural world. At other times, however, I will use "natural world" and "nature" without qualification, unbothered by the ambiguity. What matters most, from my perspective, is the *quality of our experiencing* among the various realms of otherness, a point I hope to make evident enough regardless of terminological difficulties.[78]

Nature as Essential Quality, Way, Character, or Order

> *Bears and tigers . . . [are] revelations of bearness, of tigerness, of wildness.*
> —John Livingston[79]

I have already spoken of certain qualities of the natural world, such as its inherent mystery. Given that all phenomena interrelate to comprise a single whole, people everywhere have intuited that there is a *general way* to this mysterious world of changing appearances. Big words like *Phusis, Tao, Being, Great Mystery, Logos, Dharma, God,* and so on get used for it. This sense of nature will come out further below when I discuss the next category of nature, a general organizing force in the world. We may quickly get a feel for it, however, simply by pointing to the principle of *karma,* some version of which is recognized across cultures. Karma means action. Roughly speaking,[80] to harm others is to harm or bring down misfortune and suffering on oneself. Good karma, on the other hand, bears the fruit of good luck, grace, or release from suffering. Buddhists, Christians, and primal peoples (among others) all say something like this, although the last group is more likely to talk about proper or nonviolating actions in relation to *nonhuman* persons as well, or at least to do so in more local detail. Plainly put: "The natural world responds to us in a universal language. If we're behaving badly, the world will tell us."[81] That is its nature.

　　Moving from the character of the natural world, to that of particular entities within that world, nature here refers to the essential qualities, calling, virtues, excellences, or life of a being. *Dharma* means "that which bears its own nature . . .

The blazing of the sun is its characteristic."[82] All dharmas are said to sustain one another by keeping to their own unique modes of being. In its primordial sense, *phusis* denotes the unfolding of entities as a whole whereby they can emerge "of their own accord from out of themselves—coming forth *uncompelled* from concealment."[83] That is, the essential nature of an entity is the way it organizes itself, implies its own further living, even if it is externally compelled to deviate from this nature. James Hillman remarks that each animal has its own kind of self-display, and that "the animal's urge to self-revelation is reason enough for its creation. . . . the animal continually reminds that the play of creation is revelation."[84] All beings also have their own characteristic *liveliness*. The things we experience as being most alive are those that self-emerge most intensely, with the greatest energy, motion, brilliance, or power (this idea coming from the Greek word for life, *zoe*, which is a characteristic of, or equivalent term for, *phusis*[85]). What we normally regard as a living being, say a squirrel, is simply a self-emergence that stands out for the captivating or striking way in which it exhibits itself—in contrast, say, to the less lively sidewalk on which it hops.

What the essential nature of some entity may be is obviously debatable or subject to different interpretations. I would only repeat here my commitment to the notion that we can know the nature of things more or less authentically. Indeed, another meaning of *dharma* is that which it is "right" for something to be.[86] We will not always agree on what makes for the nature of a little brown bat or a silver maple, but there will be better or worse readings of these, depending on the conditions of our relations to them. In the stories of indigenous peoples, animals and other nonhuman beings are often portrayed with distinct personalities that convey their essential characters. Such narratives vary from place to place, but the attempt to understand and respect the nature of local beings does not. In any case, what I would hope we can agree on is that different beings *must* have their own natures because we draw on them metaphorically to understand *ourselves* (e.g., "I am a rock") and because they have lessons to teach us—a topic I consider at some length in the next chapter, and so leave aside for the time being.

What, next, are we to make of *human* nature? I suggest we can deviate from, or be ignorant of, our essential nature, but that it will ultimately call us back or be rediscovered as we deepen our experience. I showed this in the previous chapter when I discussed the inherent life-forwarding orderliness of our bodily nature, and under the heading above when I talked about our spiritual nature. What follows is a discussion of three aspects of human nature that builds on or adds to these earlier discussions.

Our Hermeneutic (Poetic, Life-Forwarding, Symbolic, Metaphorical, Sense-Making, Relational, Dialogical, Playful, World-Disclosing, Caring) Nature. Hermeneutics refers to the very motion of human existence, the process of experiencing itself. The long list of parenthetical adjectives in my title here shows how rich or multifaceted I feel this idea to be. I will not go over what I have already said about hermeneutics. What I do want to get at, however, is a sense for how it is of our nature to understand, or to grasp the meaning of things; to create symbols or metaphors from out of our dwelling in or experiencing of the human/nature gap; to sing, dance, and play in the mystery; to care for being, the process of living; and to celebrate and converse with the cosmos, helping to keep all the world in shape or in balance. There is no positive way to prove all this, for the truth of our hermeneutic nature lies in our felt sensing of it, in our experience of "rightness" as we come home to it or feel it near.[87] As with so much of what I discuss here, these are among the most obvious of things to most indigenous societies.

As hermeneutic beings we are poets by nature. In order to best make this point I need to back up and note that this is so only because the natural world *as a whole* is poetic. The early Greek word for poetry, *poiesis,* refers to the bringing forth, making, or creative revealing of beings from out of the hidden or earthy depths of reality. As a continually changing emergence of the myriad forms of being, *physis,* primordial nature, is a mode of *poiesis;* it is poetic in its sheer beauty, suchness, or presencing—radiating forth, just now, in the swaying of *these* branches or the graceful breaking of *this* wave. "*Physis* is indeed," said Heidegger, "*poiesis* in the highest sense."[88] Prior to any human speaking, notes Sean Kane, "a world of poetry . . . already fully exists, in the darting red streak of a sapsucker or in the rainclouds gathering ominously over Hecate Strait."[89] This is a crucial message for ecopsychology, as previous psychologies have so far "refused to see that the animal kingdom is first of all an aesthetic ostentation, a fantasy on show, of colors and songs, of gaits and flights, and that this aesthetic display is a primordial instinctual force laid down in the plasma."[90] Hillman rightly says that psychologists have instead degraded animals to mere symbols for our own "lower" instincts, denying to them *their* own self-displaying natures. According to Owen Barfield, the hallmark of poetry is *movement,* the unfurling of meaning or stretching out toward life.[91] Thus, the cloud "poetizes" because it goes "beyond itself to what is no longer itself."[92] We recognize poetry, moreover, by the experiencing of aesthetic pleasure, which, as etymology suggests, is a "breathing in" of the beauty of the cosmos.[93]

If nature is essentially poetic, and if we too are nature, then humans have a place in nature's creativity, in its motions, in its birthing of new forms. As Robert Avens notes: "*Physis,* in her *psychic aspect,* is . . . the ultimate source of thought, language, poetry."[94] If nature were not ordered poetically, then metaphor-ing— the carrying forward of meaning and life—would not be possible.[95] Human nature is the felt process of completing needs, meanings, or intentions as they "phusically" arise in the interplay between body and world, creatively giving them some symbolic form.[96] Thus, the artist who is "pregnant with things needing form"[97] describes all of us. We must agree with Freud, then, when he said that "a human being in the spirit of all times [is] an artist."[98] Or as Paul Goodman put it, the self is the "artist of life"; it plays the "role of finding and making the meanings we live by," of creatively responding to the demands of existence—even if the "verbalizing personality" of our times now uses a most unpoetic speech.[99]

The early Greek word for art is *techne,* from which we get our word "technology." Although our modern technology obscures this point, techne was originally also considered to be a mode of poiesis, that is, of poetic deliverance. It referred to the unique way that humans, as participants in phusis, bring into appearance forms that are already latent within nature and that we are called on to assist into being—artworks, poetry, myths, rituals, craftworks, clothes, tools, and so on.[100] Techne in this sense is thus a secondary kind of poiesis, for what comes into being does not arise solely from out of itself, but also with the assistance of, or dependence on, humans. It is a working in concert with or serving of nature, and so in early Greek times had a life-giving and life-enhancing meaning.[101] As a skillful know-how, techne was thus not only a *making* but also a *finding* and *allowing* into being of hidden entities that are ready to emerge—as when a sculptor imagines the prefigured shape, lying within a piece of wood, that wishes to reveal itself. These notions give some sense for what the poet Hölderlin meant when he said that: "poetically, man/Dwells on this earth."[102] Heidegger cited this line when he claimed that humans are essentially *dwellers* on the earth, poetically caring for being and so "safeguarding . . . each thing in its nature."[103] Thus, while it is indeed human nature to be involved in the transfiguration of the natural world, our making of things is most originally an artful response to a call that originates from within this world itself.

Calvin Martin suggests that hunter-gatherers understand themselves to be "cosmic artificers." Keepers of "formulaic stories, the narrators and symbolizers of the blueprints of creation," they "believe themselves responsible for repeating these tales in order to keep them alive and, further, to regenerate the system."[104] That is, it is our nature, our deepest calling, to articulate and tend to the cosmos, to call forth or lay open the world by means of ceremony and ritual, storytelling and myth.[105] Heidegger came to this theme by saying that through our poetic attending to things we mortals participate, along with the earth, the sky, and the gods, in the gathering and illuminating of the world. This world-disclosing process is at the same time a playful celebration, an expression of the "simple, flexible characteristic of our human be-ing to care for others, to laugh, dance, and sing in otherness."[106] This point comes across in an instructive story in which all the beings of the world gather for the purpose of clarifying their natures or ways of serving Creation. The beavers' job is to look after the wetlands and streams, the worms burrow through the earth so as to keep the soil in shape, the deer slide through the woods, always keeping a watchful eye on what is happening. The humans, however, are perplexed about their role. It falls on all the other creatures, therefore, speaking in chorus, to remind the confused humans that their purpose is to "glory in it all," to praise and give thanks for Creation itself.[107]

General Species Characteristics or Needs: Our Transhistorical Human Nature. This is the "nature" that has come in both for so much misuse and abuse. I need to state right away, then, that I am attempting in this book to walk a middle path between the modern emphasis on the general (or universals) and the postmodern stress on the particular (or differences). Here, I would speak to what can be said in general about human nature, without in any way denying to people their particular natures. Indeed, it is shaming and wounding not to have our unique qualities or differences acknowledged and affirmed. I would assert, however, that it is in a similar way hurtful not to have our *general* nature, our common species needs, also recognized and honored. (Please note that I am using the word *general* in the sense of "*approximately* universal." We come into the world with all sorts of things already going on, and do not always experience the world quite the way that humans do in general. I will have more to say about this in the last section below, but will make the obvious remark here that knowledge of the general need not obscure that of the particular.) Those who deny the existence of a human nature— either strongly (we have no nature) or weakly (we have a multipotential nature)[108]—say that the variability of culture makes it impossible to assert anything about humans in general. To anticipate a discussion in the next chapter, my response to this denial is that it misconceives culture, for a reason I have already indicated: the organization of our experiencing runs deeper than any particular culture.[109] Cultural practices, symbols, forms, beliefs, rites, and so on are essentially ways of cultivating, completing, or carrying forward our nature; they are not "imposed on nothing,"[110] but rather interact with or "enter into" our needs, our natural intentions or felt expectations. It is the forgetfulness of transhistorical needs, in fact, that permits a culture to so violate them, for that which is unremembered or unheard becomes either neglected or transgressed. As I use the term, needs are not closed instincts. They are always situational, felt in concrete instances of body-world dialogue. Insofar as we share a *human situation,* though, certain needs *will* arise in general. These are the nonnegotiable, unremitting demands that govern our unfolding.

Calling this sense of nature "transhistorical" suggests that it is *prior* to any particular historical situation, traceable to the prehistory or past of our species.[111] Experientially, the past is not a receding time line but is rather incorporated into our ongoing living. Merleau-Ponty writes that his personal existence is "the resumption of a *pre*personal tradition. There is therefore another subject beneath me, for whom a world exists before I am here, and who marks out my place in it. This captive or natural spirit is my body."[112] This body is an "anonymous and general existence" that is involved in a "communication with the world more ancient than thought." Our bodies, in other words, bear the past within them and so anticipate or are prestructured for the world. For Gestaltists, "the body is full of inherited wisdom—it is roughly adjusted to its environment from the beginning. . . . in its emotions it has a kind of knowledge of the environment as well as motivations of action; the body expresses itself in well-constructed purposive series and complexes of wishes."[113] We have an inborn sense or preunderstanding of how, in general, things are supposed to go. Or as Gendlin notes: "What is planned for in the organism is as real as the organs of the body."[114] The body implies "a whole vast maze of behaviors and the *environmental circumstances* in which the behaviors would occur."[115] We arrive already unfolding "very highly organized interaction patterns,"[116] expecting that suitable responses will be forthcoming from others or that certain kinds of presences will be on hand. Medard Boss spoke of the "inherent world-relations," "pre-given world patterns," or "inborn poten-tialities for relating"[117] that organize our emergence or arising as human beings. To deny these relational patterns is to posit a strict discontinuity with our past and an extreme historicism. On the contrary, nature is precisely that which "resists history."[118] This is especially noticeable in infants, whose enormous dependency needs originate outside of history, even as these infants are entering into history.[119] In general, infants need love, safety, good mirroring, empathy, freedom for self-expression, approval, close physical contact, respect, comfort, and so forth. Unless these "early universal patterns" (Gendlin's phrase) are satisfied, we inevitably suffer narcissistic injury.

Perhaps, as this last sentence implies, the best way to gather that we have species needs is to witness the suffering that ensues when they are not met. Indeed, my discussion in the previous chapter about the violation of our nature would have been senseless if we did not have such needs as can be either satisfied or frustrated. The champions of cultural difference do not tend to ask about what sorts of wounding may be occurring within all of this cultural diversity. While, for example, Balinese reportedly do not weep at funerals, this does not mean that they can just do away with the need to mourn after experiencing a loss. As Thomas Scheff observes: "The absence or curtailment of mourning in a society would show that mourning was unnecessary only if it were also shown that no deleterious effects followed. None of the studies of cultural variation even address this prob-lem, much less conduct research on it."[120] My own sense is that the more we come to recognize the general ways in which people get hurt, the more we will discover the common human being hidden inside the diversity of cultural forms. One of the main ways we today become aware of general needs is by tracing lines of suffering back to those events where these needs were negated. We know, for example, that we need to be loved because it hurts so deeply to be unloved. "Hospitalism" among infants taught us that babies need to be touched and interacted with. Meanwhile, it was only a matter of time before someone like Victor Frankl came along to say that we need meaning in our lives, for we have entered the painful age of nihilism.[121] As a final example, the worldwide epidemic of traumatic stress has made a whole host of developmental needs readily appar-ent, such as those for trustworthy social relations and support in developing basic human powers such as boundary setting and handling one's emotional life.[122] Indeed, if we had no nature then trauma would have no meaning.

My conviction, in short, is that the more we do come to recognize our wounds and feel our suffering, the more will we come to understand our nature.[123] Our society, though, is often motivated *not* to recognize suffering (and so not to understand human nature) since to do so is both hard to bear and generally not "good for the economy." It is worth noting, in this respect, that although child sexual abuse has been widespread since at least the turn of the century, it was considered rare by psychiatrists and psychologists right until recent decades, and is still viewed as a hoax by many people.[124] It is a sad paradox, furthermore, that our needs often become unclear precisely to the extent that they are unmet. We are not quite sure what we are looking for until we see it or find it; our intentions are vague until symbolized by the arrival of the needed things. When these things are unavailable, all we have is an unspecified, achy feeling. How very hard must it be, then, to know our needs in relation to other-than-human beings. Shepard writes: "Modern life conceals our inherent need for diverse, wild, natural communities, but it does not alter that need. Evidence for this deprivation is so omnipresent that we cannot see it directly, since much of it is expressed as psychic distress and social disorder. Masking the effects of deviating from the world to which we are adapted is the universal act of modern denial."[125] As a society, we have learned to adjust to certain developmental deprivations for so long that we simply do not recognize these as such.[126] When it comes to our needs for contact with the natural world, then, we are born as if into an ecological and cultural vacuum, feeling only an inarticulate anguish. The meeting of these needs is so wholly muffed that it is difficult to identify them; and our society's human-centered prejudices eternally point us elsewhere.

There are many general, transhistorical needs we *can* and do know about, some of which I mention throughout these pages. Our bodies, moreover, still carry the knowledge of our buried needs, of our unactivated interactional patterns. The ecopsychological task is to put some symbols to our "eco-suffering" and thereby to gradually name some of these vital demands. As a project of critical hermeneutic retrieval, this cannot but be a process of working from felt hunches and intuitions. It also means finding ways to re-create conditions under which these needs may be more readily recognized and met. I return to all of these matters in the discussions ahead.

Basic Goodness: Our Original Nature. The Buddhist teacher Chogyam Trungpa wrote that every "human being has a basic nature of goodness which is undiluted and unconfused." Thus, when "we hear a beautiful sound, we are hearing our own basic goodness."[127] This so-called original nature may not be obvious to all, especially today, but it is nonetheless *discoverable*. Buddhist practice is exactly about awakening to this our "true" nature. Beneath "all the busyness of thought," writes the Buddhist teacher Jack Kornfield, there lies "a sweet, healing silence, an inherent peacefulness in each of us, a goodness of heart, strength, and wholeness that is our birthright."[128] Without recourse to Buddhist literature and practice, however, we find similar conclusions among humanistic psychologists, who commonly believe that it is of our deepest nature to be creative and loving.[129] Experience shows over and over again that as people heal from old wounds they inevitably recover more and more of this basic nature—they find their "inborn sanity," their love and compassion, waiting for them, as it were, under all the old hurt. I have myself regularly experienced that when shame-bound people (i.e., most of us) allow themselves to be touched by an affirmation of their goodness, their grief instantly emerges. Their pain spontaneously comes out of the background to be healed once they experience a respectful enough context in which their innate beauty can finally shine forth. Indeed, I regard humanism's generous view of human nature as a valuable balm for our wounded times.[130] It is also in line with the notion, stressed by deep ecology, that all of nature is intrinsically worthy. The beauty of nature is our own. To say otherwise is to tacitly accept the idea that human nature cannot be trusted and must be repressed.[131] In light of the decidedly unlovely human behavior enveloping this planet, I thus suggest that it is helpful to adopt the view that: "human beings are marvelous creatures with a tremendous capacity for harmonious relationship with the environment. We just happen to be wildly off the track right now."[132]

Our original nature contrasts with what is referred to as our second or historical nature. So much of what gets attributed to human nature is in fact this derivative nature. "Original" and "second" nature are used, roughly speaking, to refer to our nature before and after it has been affected by socialization or history. Second nature is an important critical theoretical notion, as it draws attention to how our nature is deformed through social domination.[133] Negatively, it signifies the automatic habitual patterns, the blind and rigid behaviors, the life-denying meanings, that have become sedimented into our bodies, forming our surface character, as a crust over our more spontaneous and lively selves. In a nonnegative sense, however, it simply refers to the fact that nobody lives outside of history and so our nature is always elaborated in the terms of our own time and place, for better or worse. Some degree of "character" is inevitable in any life, as we all suffer a more or less distant relation to our own Buddhahood and must struggle with the essential precariousness of being human. Our original nature, however, *can* be felt. It serves as the deep ground for all healing work, for overcoming the distortions of our second nature. I believe that it, along with the goodness of others, is in fact what makes healing *possible*.

Nature as Life Force or Sacred Power

> *Everything, including us, has . . . life force in it. We're the same as
> everything else. Only our form changes, because everything has to reveal itself
> in a different form so that this wonderful creation can be.*
> —Jeannette Armstrong[134]

This final category is the aspect of nature having to do with force or power. When we talk about nature, we normally mean the first two categories, namely, "the natural world" and "the nature of things." Nature conservation documents are not known to talk about the life force. In discussing it, therefore, ecopsychology may bring in a sense of nature normally overlooked, one that is especially experiential. Many different terms are used for it, and as always there are no final interpretations. We can be sure, though, about the category itself.

The Powers of Nature. As expressed in Native American traditions, nature is the Great Mystery, an intangible creative power or life force, of which all beings are said to be manifest.[135] *Physis* also originally meant the power that emerges or that permeates all beings.[136] We speak of the creative or fruitful powers of the land. Or we might say, as did the Lakota medicine man Lame Deer: "There is power in a buffalo—spiritual, magical power—but there is no power in an Angus, in a Hereford"[137] (domestication, in other words, has knocked much of the life essence out of the animal). Humans themselves resist oppression due to "forces *within* the person that are mysterious and out of reach of society."[138] That all beings—from stones to caterpillars—exhibit life force is a basis for feeling our kinship with them, in the sense that we "don't own life, we just take its shape and then pass it on."[139] We all share in the life force, as a common breath that circulates via the interactions among us. Life force, moreover, is not a substance separate from or added to the events of nature, but is intrinsic to them. That is why it is the process of contact itself that energizes, enlivens, or gives rise to each of us.

For indigenous peoples generally, the natural world is populated by spiritual powers. As Nelson comments of the Koyukon view, the "more potent these powers are, the more demanding they become of human deference and respect, and the more numerous are the ways of showing it."[140] The blessings of these spiritual powers, furthermore, are "given only to the reverent." These are, of course, matters from which our Western society is enormously removed, and my own grip on them is that of a novice. What I understand is that our life among others is one of "constant spiritual interchange," where through various kinds of contact-making the powers or meanings of nature are transmitted. Thus, a person may acquire the powers of a plant or animal by eating it; or a shaman may contact a "power animal" for the purposes of healing; or a vision quester may sit at a "power spot" and cry out in the hope that a spirit-being will respond to her or him in some way. Calvin Martin notes that a common Native American belief is that our "humanity remains incomplete and unhinged" until we have received such empowerment from other-than-human beings.[141] On this view, nature is itself "the primordial religion," wherein everyday life involves humans in sacred processes and exchanges with other-than-human beings.[142] Thus did the ecologist Stan Rowe say that: "The scalpel-wielding hands might tremble were scientists to entertain the belief that spirit is inherent in all things."[143]

A Healing Force. If nothing else, ecopsychology is an effort to understand the
healing powers of nature. As Peter Mathiessen writes: "By seeking to dominate
[the natural world], the white men set themselves in opposition to a vital, healing
force of which they were a part and thereby mislaid a whole dimension of existence."[144] Among primal peoples generally, health is an omnipresent concern, for
it is believed to be a function of one's relations with the natural world. Illness arises
out of some imbalance or improper state of interaction with the powers of nature,
while health and healing follow from being in right relation.[145] While the
"developed" world has had little use for such ideas, David Abram suggests that
their truth is glaringly obvious:

> With thousands of acres of nonregenerating forest disappearing every hour, and
> hundreds of our fellow species becoming extinct each month as a result of our
> civilization's excesses, we can hardly be surprised by the amount of epidemic illness
> in our culture, from increasingly severe immune dysfunctions and cancers, to wide-
> spread psychological distress, depression, and ever more frequent suicides, to the
> accelerating number of household killings and mass murders committed for no
> apparent reason by otherwise coherent individuals. From an animistic perspective,
> the clearest source of all this distress, both physical and psychological, lies in the
> aforementioned violence needlessly perpetrated by our civilization on the ecology of
> the planet; only by alleviating the latter will we heal the former.[146]

I take Abram's remarks about our bad karma very seriously. As I discussed in
chapter three, the life force wants to move events in certain directions; we know
the way of this life force by the feeling of rightness; and it is by following this way
that we are lead to health. These broad principles certainly apply to the situation
outlined by Abram, as being in right relation to the world involves listening to
what is called for in our interactions with others. The life force can also be felt,
however, in practices that are less directly or concretely involved with the goings-
on in the wilderness; where this force is channeled within or limited to a space that
is more narrowly focused on human interactions and interests. For the purposes of
illustrating the *very presence* of this spirit force I wish to discuss my own general
experience with some of these practices, all the while recognizing the very real
ecopsychological need to expand the focus of them.

In all four of the experiential trainings I have undertaken, a similar optimal
attitude is required, namely: being aware of or concentrating on what one is
experiencing; finding the right distance from this experience; and keeping a
curious, allowing, welcoming, kind, and caring state of mind toward it.[147] It is this
attitude that frees up the life force. Each of these practices, moreover, takes place
under particular conditions that affect how the life force is experienced. In
Vipassana meditation, for example, one adopts a posture that includes closed eyes,
a straight back, and a relaxed body.[148] With an equanimous attitude one then
moves one's awareness throughout one's body, observing whatever sensations are

arising (whether pleasant, unpleasant, or in-between), and making efforts not to develop cravings for, or aversions to, any of them. The openness or yielding provided by this nonreactive and aware attitude allows the life force to then go to work on burning up old negativities in the mind, releasing energy that is locked up behind rigidities and compulsions, untangling knots in one's body, and gradually dissolving one's Egoic solidity and illusions of separateness. Because I go through this kind of subtle process on a daily basis, the autonomous reality of the life force is simply incontestable to me. This is the same autonomy I mentioned in the previous chapter, albeit in a different context, when I discussed how our bodies urge us in a prolife direction. As my teacher says, the job of the meditator is not to fix anything, but rather to "leave it to dharma." The word dharma directly translates as "the bearer." Dharma is the life force that sustains or supports us, carries us forward, gives us strength, bears us onward, liberates us. As a meditator, one gradually comes to feel borne along by this force, like being buoyed up by that wonderful oceanic sound made by grasshoppers and crickets in late summer. Said Heidegger, those who are existentially daring, who hold themselves face-on into the abyss, are "*sustained* by that on which they expend themselves"[149] (a notion found in all sorts of spiritual traditions). By meditatively going into one's suffering one is supported by nature in going *through* that suffering, in widening out a ground of inner peacefulness and strength, or opening up a clear and loving space within which a continual stream of new phenomena may then enter, arise, or show themselves.

Although Vipassana meditation is a way of getting to know the life force by means of an exploration of the interaction of mind and matter within one's own body, Buddhist practice is not confined to the meditation hall. The idea is to take what one learns there out into the world, where the task of life becomes to meditatively work toward the happiness of all beings. Historically, this has not always converted into an active pursuit of reciprocal relations with the natural world, which is why an eco-Buddhism is now emerging along with ecopsychology. My point, however, is that I believe the life force, the Dharma, the Great Mystery, all to be the same, even if some traditions or practices feel this spirit force within a relatively restricted field of otherness. What is more, the fact that the responsive and respectful attitude one adopts within these various experiential practices seems to be roughly the same suggests that this attitude, the one that serves the life force, that allows things to heal and flourish, is the one that is *called for by nature,* whatever the sphere of otherness happens to be. Even the more narrowly focused experiential practices, then, teach an attitude that I think readily translates into a more-than-human realm: a posture of patient listening to the voices one finds both inside and out, of aligning oneself with what needs to happen or will do no/ least harm, and of opening oneself to the claims of others.[150]

An Erotic Force: Desire. In the formation of our selves, a residual reality is created outside ourselves, a reality we have lost, feel as a lack, and so *desire*.[151] This reality is "nature," which, as Joel Kovel notes, is "the generic object of desire."[152] Charles Bergman writes: "We are drawn to nature, impelled by some desire, like body moving to body. And if, for Western culture now, in the late twentieth century, desire is experienced primarily as an absence, . . . even a wound, it must be that the longing for nature is more intense, more poignant, more cut with a sense of its own inevitable impossibilities, than ever before."[153] The life force, as desire, thus has a basis in separation itself, is "a pull or polarization between things that have been separated."[154] Such an understanding of desire puts it on a spiritual or ontological footing. As against a purely biological conception of desire, Kovel thus calls it "the roiling of indwelling nature striving toward spirit." Spirituality is then "the desire for being," for a melting of Ego and an opening of the self toward all reality (Jung's "thirst for wholeness"). We do not normally think about desire in such spiritual terms, for the very reason that our natural desires have become so repressed and problematic in our despiritualized society. Indeed, the "sphere of the political economy as a whole . . . may be seen as a gigantic and self-contradictory negation of desire." That is, "the extreme degree of binding imposed by the culture necessary for the accumulation of capital has alienated desire itself, has twisted it about, and made it spectral and monstrous."[155]

We need to make a distinction, therefore, between what Kornfield calls skillful and unskillful desire. The former "is directed by love, vitality, compassion, creativity, and wisdom" and includes "desire for the well-being of others, the desire of awakening, the creative desires that express the positive aspects of passion and beauty."[156] Pathological desires, on the other hand, include those of "addiction, greed, blind ambition, or unending inner hunger." These find no true satisfaction, do not tend toward spirit, but only multiply or carve themselves deeper with each round of desiring; they do not aim to care for, but rather to possess, control, or suck dry the other. Significantly, however, underneath our unskillful desire we will always find "a deep spiritual longing for beauty, for abundance and completeness." This "underneath" is the felt place where we touch down into the true needs of the soul which underlie all of our surficial and painful desires. What the experience of desire tells us, then, is both that felt-separation from nature is definitive of our psychology and that the less our desiring is supported the more will it lead us into trouble or manifest itself as an ever-deepening longing. Longing is exactly "the heightening of appetite confronted with a distant object, in order to overcome distance or other obstacles."[157] Our society's desperate search for spiritual understanding—for which the popular psychology or New Age section of any bookstore may stand—speaks to just how great this longing has become.

We are led, finally, to the notion of *Eros*, which reveals itself precisely as our bodily desires. David Levin refers to Eros as "an immortal aspect of *Physis:* the sheer energy and ecstasy of Being."[158] Freud called it the love instinct, its aim being "to establish ever greater unities and to preserve them thus—in short, to bind together"[159] or reunite what has been separated. For Gestaltists, Eros is the excitement of vividly felt creative living, transpiring right at the contact boundary between organism and environment. Our bodily intentions all imply some desired *relationship,* and so are *essentially* erotic[160]—the erotic life is life itself. (Hence the connection between Eros and Psyche in Greek myth.) Terry Tempest Williams calls the erotic life a "making love to the world that I think comes very naturally." Both she and Audre Lorde distinguish the erotic from the pornographic by the absence of feeling in the latter, by a "denial of the *power* of the erotic."[161] Hence, even our daily "intercourse" becomes pornographic when it lacks "engagement of the soul." It is also true to say that the nonerotic life does not *play,* for "play is the erotic mode of activity," the essential way of being of a satisfied humanity, freely delighting or finding pleasure in life.[162] (Indeed, every animal is a "mode of play," says Hillman.) As the child analyst D. W. Winnicott has it: the "natural thing is playing."[163]

That one sense of nature is that of an erotic force means that when we repress our desires we negate our own essence, alienate ourselves from our natural powers, and deny our "deep hunger for communion" any satisfying food. Hence, Norman O. Brown's remark that "mankind, in all its restless striving and progress, has no idea of what it really wants. . . . mankind, unconscious of its real desires and therefore unable to obtain satisfaction, is hostile to life and ready to destroy itself."[164] As Freud demonstrated, however, desire is "immortal." When repressed it does not disappear but returns via neurotic symptoms. ("Drive out the natural and back it comes straightaway," observes Gaston Bachelard.[165]) Thus, while we may well use different terms to interpret the phenomenon of desire, as a transhistorical force it cannot be interpreted away.

Freedom and the Life Force. If the life force organizes or directs the shape of events, or courses through all beings in the way they body themselves forth and interact with one another, then what role does human agency or freedom play in relation to this mysterious force? The short answer is that our freedom lies in our being able to choose whether or not we "obey" the demands of the life force. We pay the price of suffering, however, if we decide against it; for there is no opting out of nature. As Percy Shelley said, freedom is "sweet bondage."[166] From the perspective of the previous chapter, we are most free when we work to realize those creative possibilities, in whatever situation we may find ourselves, that satisfyingly answers what our bodies are asking for; that is, when we are able to maintain an open, contactful, and responsive relation to the world. We are least free, on the other hand, when our lives are rigidly set in unconscious habit-patterns. On this view, the image of humans presented by deterministic philosophies (i.e., those which deny freedom) is in fact a pathological one. To be totally determined is to have no free room in which to act, is to have no "breathing space." Citing Kierkegaard's line that the "self of the determinist cannot breathe," Levin writes: "Breathing beings will suffocate unless they have *space* to breathe; a space, as it were, of possibility. Breathing beings will also suffocate unless they have *time* to breathe: a time that is not so pressing that it becomes impossible to breathe."[167] Anyone who knows what it is like to feel anxious or pressured—states in which it is hard to breathe—knows how claustrophobic our lived space can become and how tightly a dreaded future can squeeze in on us, such that we lose our ability to creatively and freely respond to the *present* moment.[168] Our deliberateness or agency, by contrast, depends on our maintaining a free and open realm in which to act or relate to others, on keeping a clear temporal and spatial distance between ourselves and the other-phenomena of our lifeworld. One of the tasks of experiential psychotherapy is to open up this existential clearing, to differentiate and back off the underdistanced otherness that presses in on us, or operates covertly in our background, so that we may then become more aware of it and enter into a freer or more caring relationship to it. For all of us, the more open this clearing becomes, the more are we able to use our freedom in making good contact with others, and so serving the life force of nature.

Although I have taken a relatively large block of text to stake out some terms for discussing nature, the goal of this interpretive exercise was not to promote Buddhism or humanistic psychology or Koyukon understanding or Heideggerian thought, but only to employ these to begin revealing a naturalistic landscape. I have been especially concerned to show that, as Snyder put it, "When humans know themselves, the rest of nature is right there."[169] I trust that I have established at least a minimum starting place, then, to pursue the outlines of a naturalistic psychology.

5
NATURALISTIC PSYCHOLOGY: A SKETCH

"If We Truly Experience Needs . . ."

If we truly experience needs that are in the long run incapable of satisfaction within the framework of a system dedicated to paving the world with asphalt, then it is no merely utopian exercise to loosen up the imagination so as to envisage an alternative world in which such needs might find satisfaction.

—John Rodman[1]

Throughout this book I am aiming to build up a sense for the centrality of the human-nature relationship in human existence, thereby disclosing this relationship as an ultimate concern. What I propose for this chapter is to pencil-in the main contours of a kind of psychology that would be of assistance to this concern. The discussion is divided into three sections: "Naturalism" introduces the general *spirit* of this psychology; "Life as a Hermeneutic, Sense-Making Journey" its general *principles;* and "Nature and the Human Life Cycle" its general *content.*

Naturalism

There is a nature of things, including human nature, whose right development can be violated.

—Paul Goodman[2]

[Human] nature leads into nature—the wilderness—and the reciprocities and balances by which man lives on earth.

—Gary Snyder[3]

Together, these two statements—one by a psychologist-sociologist (Goodman), the other a poet-ecologist (Snyder)—summarize much of what I mean by naturalism. Naturalistic psychology, as I am drawing it together, interprets the psychological in terms of the natural: approaches psyche in terms of both the natural ordering of our experience and the natural "others" who are prefigured in, or who call forth, our experiencing. It does not ignore the kind of problems with which other psychologists are occupied, but it reads these along naturalistic lines. The danger of the title "naturalism" is that it might be confused with a materialistic or natural scientific philosophy, which also goes by this name. And yet it has just too much resonance with what I am proposing—that psychologists be naturalists—for me to use any other. As Erazim Kohák has observed, moreover, the term does have a more generic meaning, suitable to my purposes:

> By speaking of "naturalism" in a generic sense . . . we shall mean any philosophy which recognizes the being of humans as integrally linked to the being of nature, however conceived, treating humans as distinctive only as much as any distinct species is that, but as fundamentally *at home* in the cosmos. . . . By "nature" in a similarly generic sense we shall mean the nature presented in lived experience, the primordially given cosmic context in which humans find themselves and to which they themselves belong in their bodies and minds, as humans are in fact aware of it, whether thematically or not, in their daily lived experience, not as it appears in the theoretical nature-constructs which seek to capture it.[4]

It is thus with an with an emphasis on the lived experience of human-nature continuity, and not on the models of natural science, that I am adopting the title of naturalism.

In forwarding a naturalistic psychology, I am essentially giving a psychological name to some perennial notions and articulating my own take on them. The idea that there is something right or meaningful or imperative or moral about lining ourselves up with a transcendent order of things is of course very old. For a recollective project, however, such a return to old ideas makes good sense. Again and again we must assert that to be claimed by the natural order means to belong to it, to be limited by it, and to feel its demands within our bodily experience. Only by allowing this—that we are of the natural order—will we ever come to respect the claims and limits of the larger natural world, for we will have then taken our place within it. Christopher Lasch writes, by contrast, that the "intellectual basis . . . of the modern cult of technology" is "the celebration of disembodied intelligence," an "incorrigibly escapist . . . fantasy of total control, absolute transcendence of the limits imposed on mankind."[5] Western history has in general been one of progressively rubbing out or concealing the claims and limits of nature.[6] According to Donald Worster, even the science of ecology has now become "permissive," with many scientists saying that there is little inherent organization in the natural world and so not much reason to limit the human modification of it.[7] We live in a world, notes Shepard, where "humility and [a] tender sense of human limitation is no longer rewarded. Yet we suffer for the want of that vanished world, a deep grief we learn to misconstrue."[8] In view of our society's consistent denial and narcissistic hatred of limits,[9] I am thus advancing a naturalistic approach that focuses *precisely* on such limits, and so aims to send up some sparks around what I believe is terribly at stake in our historical times.

Important to this undertaking is the convergence from manifold quarters on the notion of releasing ourselves to or *serving* something that is not strictly us. Fritz Perls, to begin, called the ego the *servant of the organism* (thus reversing the usual Freudian view).[10] Here, the lower-case "ego" refers only to that free agency which, as an aspect of the organism, deliberately sets the boundaries and performs the actions that will satisfy the needs of the organism (and which, whether as ego or Ego, is the *individual* sense of "human" in the human-nature relationship). "*Serving soul,*" writes Hillman, "implies letting it rule; it leads, we follow."[11] Ellen Chen likewise calls Taoism a religion that *serves life* by following "the way" of nature.[12] For Heidegger, we are *servants of being* or agents of possible world-disclosures. The Buddha, for his part, did not actually call his followers Buddhists, but *dharma servants* (or wayfarers). Knowing that, in his own words, one "lives unhappily who has nothing to venerate and obey," he committed *himself* to living "under the Dharma, honouring and respecting that."[13] Certainly the idea of *serving God* is familiar to all. From the German word *Gut,* the original meaning of "God" is "the Good One." Peter Mathiessen suggests that in this sense it is close to the Native American "Great Spirit" or "Great Mystery."[14] Says one primer on Native American spirituality, the "greatest of all lessons of the medicine wheel" is that the essence of our humanity is "to be found in *service to others.*"[15] Or as the Koyukon Indians believe: "the proper role of humankind is to *serve a dominant nature.*"[16] These are among the oldest, or at least the most basic, of intuitions about the essential business of humanity. Naturalistic psychology, accordingly, calls for a humbling of the self, an admitting that we emerge from and are beholden to serve a natural world much deeper and greater than our individual or personal selves.[17] A narcissistic culture, however, takes the *reverse* view, insisting that the world of nature serve *it.* When I look out on the dense buildings and roadways covering the earth and imagine instead living in a culture that genuinely serves nature, that would rather praise than pave, my grief rushes up inside me. The truth of the need to serve nature, I suggest, is in the tears.[18]

What, indeed, does a naturalistic approach have to say about *culture?* It certainly disagrees with the view that as cultural beings we have transcended nature or left the apes behind. But it does *not* go on from there to make "culture" some sort of enemy we need to get away from if we are ever to become more natural. Both of these positions only reinforce the human/nature dualism. An *interactive* view of nature and culture sees them, rather, as internally related moments within a unified and processual reality. From the Latin *cultura,* "culture" referred in its earliest uses to the tending of natural growth.[19] In this sense culture is essentially a verb, a *cultivating*, a kind of techne or artful attending to the life process.[20] When we conceive of culture as "an historically transmitted pattern of meanings embodied in symbols,"[21] such symbol systems may therefore be looked at in terms of how they serve the natural world and complete our own bodily nature. As Mary Midgley puts it: "What we build into our cultures has to satisfy our natural pattern of motives."[22] Note, moreover, that an interactive model reframes the old nature/nurture debate. The issue is not whether traits are innate or whether they are acquired (or some aggregate of the two), as if these were wholly distinct options, but how cultural patterns reorganize or affect our nature and how our nature always anticipates certain kinds of culturing. What matters, in other words (and to repeat a by now familiar line), is the reciprocity or dialogue *between* body and world, in which person and environment do not begin as independent entities making their separate contributions (as psychologists have historically conceived of them), but as poles within a single interactive process of being-in-the-world or meaning creation.[23]

Naturalism, then, does not mean turning away from culture but being *all the more demanding of it*. Erazim Kohák writes that "culture is not the contradiction of nature but rather the task of humans within it." It follows, furthermore, that the relationship between nature and culture is *asymmetric*. Our bodies are prior to any one culture, even as they anticipate a culture. As the grounding or governing moment of human existence, our own bodily nature thus "reserves the right to judge culture, and resist and revise it."[24] We often mistake the plasticity of human culture for the plasticity of human nature, entranced by the spectacle and variability of the former, while neglectful of the constraints and claims of the latter. Knowing this, we may examine our culture for just how willing it is to adjust *itself* to nature's demands. "A healthy culture," says Wendell Berry, "is a communal order of memory, insight, value, work, conviviality, reverence, aspiration. It reveals the human necessities and the human limits. It clarifies our inescapable bonds to the earth and to each other. It ensures that the necessary restraints are observed, that the necessary work is done, and that it is done well."[25] Snyder also remarks that it "has always been part of basic human experience to live in a culture of wilderness."[26] It is a simple fact that our culture is mostly geared to meet the needs of the political economic body, rather than the given needs of the body of nature. Naturalistic psychology, accordingly, cannot avoid criticizing this culture; and to this I turn more thematically in the final chapter.

Life as a Hermeneutic Sense-Making Journey

> *Remaining within the hermeneutic circle, can we found it on nature?*
> —Marjorie Grene[27]

As creatures of distance, we live in an interpreted, culturally mediated, historically changing world, and yet as creatures of nature we also live in a world that claims us from both below and outside of human history. I would like the idea that we are *hermeneutic creatures* to embrace both of these worlds—the historical and the natural—as one. So far, however, most hermeneutic thinkers have emphasized only that we belong to history. As Marjorie Grene remarks, "the stress on historicity seems to entail ignoring nature."[28] More strongly, Shepard writes that "the idea of history is itself a western invention whose central theme is the rejection of habitat. It formulates experience *outside* of nature and tends to reduce place to a stage upon which the human drama is enacted."[29] Not wind and crow, but history now teaches us our lessons. In arguing against biological reductionism, Heidegger spoke rather oddly of "our appalling and scarcely conceivable kinship with the beasts."[30] The mistake he made was to assume that affirming our kinship with other animals plunges us immediately into biologism. To the contrary, Grene argues, against Heidegger, that *not* to acknowledge our animality itself "constitutes an ontological omission," that is, it misses an essential aspect of our being.[31] My own project is exactly to articulate human existence *within* the process of life: to ground our historical meaning-making, or to formulate our experience, entirely *inside* the body of nature. This section aims to add some further weight to this undertaking.

In referring to life as a "hermeneutic sense-making journey," I am invoking the presence of the wing-footed Greek god Hermes, the go-between the divine and mortal spheres, deliverer and interpreter of messages from the gods to humans.[32] For all his mythological richness, however, my sense of the hermeneutic mode of existence comes less from the actual character of Hermes than from what hermeneutics has made in his name.[33] I start with the bias that all humans have an inherent desire to *understand deeply.* The same assumption is made by saying that a "thirst for experience is a part of all life," or that human existence "is innately disposed to an extremely broad experience."[34] Meaning may be invisible, yet it is what we live for. Humans are beings who are simply unable to live in a cosmos that does not—somehow—*make sense.* Clifford Geertz notes that chaos is a condition in which events are *uninterpretable;* where our intellect is baffled, our suffering unbearable, or our moral problems defiant of insight.[35] Chaos is intolerable; it nakedly reveals the void while offering no bearings. Thus, the more chaotic and insecure our world gets, the more must we devise symbolic means to keep our balance and ward off our nausea. The Cartesian search for absolute foundations, for instance, betrays an anxious existence whose sense-making is directed toward gaining control over or stabilizing a fluid and threatening reality, toward stilling the flux. Many delusions, if not all of them, are ironically based on this need to make sense, where our anxieties will not permit us a less distorted grasp of reality. The less existentially unified we are, the less tolerant we are of ambiguity or of contrary views, and the more insistent we are that our concepts be final, our world be unchanging. In short, then, it is by questioning into the process of sense-making that I wish to help find a way through to a more ontologically secure and so less violent mode of understanding—one that is experientially rich and in which nature, of course, figures prominently.

According to Paul Ricoeur every hermeneutics is, "explicitly or implicitly, self-understanding by means of understanding others"; while Hans-Georg Gadamer offers that it is only through others that "one learns one's own nature and limits."[36] What follows is a discussion of three principles, related to these basic interactive ideas, which I believe will be helpful in developing ecopsychology; three broad strokes I have placed on my own naturalistic canvas. The first holds that we are ordered by nature to participate ever-more widely in the world; the second that our language is always a "singing" of this world; and the third that all phenomena intertwine or mirror one another as a common "flesh." The virtue of these principles lies in their universality, in how we can apply them to what is familiar or agreed on in our current situation and then, with the understanding so gained, use them to open ourselves up and sense our way into those strange and possible places we are attempting to recollect (where I assume these principles still hold).

Ever-Widening Spheres of Meaning and Participation

> *Only the support of the familiar and common understanding makes possible the venture into the alien . . . and thus the broadening and enrichment of our own experience of the world.*
>
> —Hans-Georg Gadamer[37]

The title for this principle comes from Shepard, who writes that psychological maturity "celebrates a central analogy of self and world in ever-widening spheres of meaning and participation, not an ever-growing domination over nature, escape into abstraction, or existentialist funk."[38] The principle is that we are innately moved to differentiate and enter into progressively more encompassing realms of otherness, to dialectically widen out the ground of our being or the spheres of our understanding, thus developing an ever-growing horizon of awareness. It refers to the opening out of a life process, the moving into deeper and wider contact with the world, the building up of a sense of common ground or of belonging with others ("the widening and deepening of love"[39]), in the process of which we ourselves emerge, step by step, as the unique persons we are called to be. That human psychological development or individuation progresses as a relational project, as a process of bonding with and then separating from others, is well-recognized.[40] The ecopsychological maneuver is simply to assert that this process wishes to continue beyond the human realm, that our humanity is incomplete until we have established our kinship or social relations with the larger natural world and so satisfied our longing to feel at home in or at peace with the cosmos as a whole. As Abram writes, the human body is a "form destined to the world . . . a sort of open circuit that completes itself only in things, in others, in the encompassing earth."[41]

The successful graduation into ever-more subtle and complex realms of relationship occurs only under conditions in which we are able to maintain a *differentiated* rather than a *split* relation to others. As psychoanalyst Nancy Chodorow writes: "Differentiation . . . is not distinctness and separateness, but a particular way of being connected to others. This connection to others, based on early incorporations, in turn enables us to feel that empathy and confidence that are basic to recognition of the other as a self."[42] "Differentiation" refers to a process in which conditions are sufficiently good that we can open up some distance between ourselves and others, while not losing a sense of shared being or interconnection. Words like "separate" become ambiguous or problematic here, for although differentiation *does* involve a sort of separation, this separation is not a total break.[43] Indeed, it involves the incorporation of others, wherein having made good contact with them we come to experience their presence "internally" even in their physical absence. This is how a sense of kinship is born. Thus, when infants disrupt the field of infant care by separating from their caregivers, they are (under good conditions) engaging in a process of discovering-and-inventing an ever-widening reality to which they can belong.[44] Harold Searles, taking up this topic in an ecological context, wrote that psychological well-being is won not only by differentiating oneself from other humans but also by progressively differentiating oneself from one's *nonhuman* environment, "while developing in proportion as [one] succeeds in these differentiations, an increasingly meaningful relatedness" to it.[45] Splitting, on the other hand, is a defensive reaction emanating from a sense of basic insecurity and *inadequate* differentiation.[46] It occurs when our experience is still dominated by our own unmet needs, our "own exclusive subjectivity," which prevents us from reaching the stage of being able to recognize both the personhood of others and ourselves mirrored in them, and so achieving "a wider and more generous world view," an "enlargement of empathy and transcendence of the self."[47] Not surprisingly, splitting is the basic mode of Ego, the form of self that dominates nature, while differentiation belongs to the way of a spiritualized existence, which increasingly recognizes itself in the otherness of nature.[48]

As a hermeneutic unfolding, this journey of ontological expansion is one of making the unfamiliar or alien familiar, learning how it is similar to ourselves. We lean into novel or unfamiliar territory from that edge where the familiar leaves off, taking support from the relatively safe relations we have already secured. The "ventures of autonomy" undertaken by infants, in which they explore the space away from their caregivers and then return for what Margaret Mahler calls "emotional refueling," is perhaps the most visible example of this. In like fashion, we enter into or make sense of the world in increments, circularly enriching an experiential ground that makes still broader understanding, belonging, and communication possible. This process is well-described by anthropologist Colin Turnbull in his discussion of the first decades of life among the Mbuti hunter-gatherers of Zaïre. He characterizes these years as a series of rebirths, in which the person progresses "from one womb to yet another," each of these analogous to the former, yet experienced on a new or higher plane. The child thus moves through a series of developmental matrices that begin with the mother's actual womb and then extends outward to the mother herself; to the interior of the dwelling-hut; to the village camp; to the children's playground; and finally to the surrounding forest. Each transition to a new realm of otherness is the crossing of a critical juncture, a leap into the unknown. Thus when the mother for the first time brings her child out of the *hut* to greet the *camp* (both of which are spherical in shape), the "infant learns that there is a plurality of warm bodies, *similar* in warmth (which is comforting) but *dissimilar* in smells and rhythmic movements and sounds. If it is disconcerted enough to cry in protest, its mother immediately takes it back [to the hut] and puts it to her breast. Thus an initial model of predictability and security is reinforced."[49]

Note how the mother's caring actions help the child to navigate the latter's relation to the void. We are best supported to grow or phusically *emerge* as a differentiated being when we remain *grounded* in that sense of wholeness that comes from being lovingly connected to others.[50] To stand apart as an autonomous self is otherwise to risk a terrifying aloneness. A good developmental process, then, is one that "emphasizes relationships to others, so that intensified separateness does not maroon but establishes the self as ever more unique and yet more fully bonded to nonselves by chains of interaction, kinship, dependence, cooperation, and compliance."[51] Against our modern prejudice, Tim Ingold argues that hunter-gatherers generally do enjoy a kind of individualism, but unlike our own, theirs is "grounded in the social totality."[52] As he describes it, the un-folding of a life is at the same time an *en-*folding of others into one's own being—thus confirming Winnicott's observation that the assimilation of good others as a caring and affirming inner presence is essential to the capacity to enjoy or tolerate solitude.[53] In our own shaming society, we face the problem of the "mass" person or weak individual who lacks the inner security to break out of his or her conformity or confluence with the crowd. As individuals, we fear *living*—emerging as a differentiated self—because we lack the ontological security to do so, because it puts us too close to the void. We then also fear *dying*—the dedifferentiating of ourselves—because we have not yet lived. Existentialists typically look down on this fearful "herd" mentality, counseling us to courageously stand out from a meaningless nature, and so face the abyss. What they generally don't do, however, is trace the origins of our mass fear (as well as our grandiose, shame-based, limit-denying fantasies) to a loss of loving relations. They thus turn our sense of isolation into an essential fact of existence rather than a creation of our despiritualized and denatured historical condition.

Bearing these thoughts in mind, I also wish to conceive of this journey as a spiritual project. Under good conditions, it is the evolution of desire as the life force presses us on toward spirit, or the dissolution of Ego as we make good contact with others.[54] Using the notion of "the primitive" not pejoratively but as a way to evaluate civilized society, Stanley Diamond writes that "the primitive self cannot be reduced to an [E]go but is the result of a hierarchy of experiences, incorporated into an *increasingly spiritualized being* as maturation proceeds from birth through the multiple rebirths symbolized in the crisis rites, to ancestry of others."[55] Good conditions, as I define them, are those that do not lead to a reification or halting of experience, but rather allow for ongoing growth at the contact boundary, this being a zone of experience that is balanced *between* the twin terrors of isolation and fusion. Such conditions generally allow our desires to change their nature as the self is gradually transformed from an early state of near-total dependency on the service of others to one in which the wish to ourselves serve others is increasingly realized. In other words, the equilibrium won through the meeting of a need or completion of an experience is immediately disturbed by the further stirring of the life force, as it urges the self ever-more deeply into the world. "Here desire takes on the shape of Eros, or love, and unifies the self with object in ever-widening totalities."[56] Under bad conditions, on the other hand, our desires do not only remain a spur to further growth and challenge, but also become overfrustrated. The world then becomes a dangerous place from which we must protect ourselves and toward which we harbor some measure of hatred, our fears now fixing others into threatening aliens.[57] In this case, the experiential field cannot differentiate but, tragically, must split.

As a final point under this principle, I wish to stress that the spiritualization of the self is also its *sociation,* the widening of its social horizons, as the discussion above has already suggested. To be sociated is to derive our identity from our embeddedness within a society. "Living through participation in the life of others, the inner self becomes a congregation of the Other."[58] Parents are only one form of otherness in this journey, even if we get stuck on them in this society. To the growing child, parents play the role of nature, the source of being, but do so only as one phase or occasion in the larger human-nature dialectic that is human nature. As Kovel notes, viewing parents in this manner places our (albeit crucial) interactions with them within a spiritual framework and opens the possibility for a psychology that looks beyond (human) familial relations.[59] More specifically, the work of ecopsychology is to develop a psychology that embeds humans within a more-than-human society. The anthropocentrism that has so far prevented psychologists from doing so is an enormously blinding prejudice, which because it ignores our need to differentiate and relate to nonhuman others, contributes to that state in which the natural world remains a largely homogeneous and so threateningly alien presence.[60] In traditional societies where humans are but a minor presence in the landscape, not attending to social relations with the natural world is unthinkable. For the Mbuti, for instance, social life is permeated by one's relations to the forest. All Mbuti, young and old, "talk, shout, whisper, and sing to the forest . . . , addressing it as mother or father or both [depending on how they feel at the moment], referring to its goodness and ability to 'cure' or 'make good.'"[61] For the Koyukon, similarly, "the environment is like a second society in which people live, governed by elaborate rules of behavior and etiquette. . . . The surroundings are aware, sensate, personified. They feel. They can be offended."[62] Nelson tells a story of being with an elder who at one point begins speaking in earnest to a bird. "For how many thousand generations, I wondered, have people spoken and prayed to natural beings around them, as a customary part of daily life? At any other time in human history, this event would be as ordinary as talking to another person."[63] Going to the heart of the matter, he remarks that the failure of this kind of "understanding in our own culture is where the depth and poignancy of our own loss lies. Losing the recognition of spirituality in nature may be the most important transformation of the human mind in all of human history."[64]

That "nature is a social place"[65] is especially evident in the words spoken by a Navajo elder, Old Torlino, just before telling part of the creation story:

> I am ashamed before the earth;
> I am ashamed before the heavens;
> I am ashamed before the dawn;
> I am ashamed before the evening twilight;
> I am ashamed before the blue sky;
> I am ashamed before the sun.
> I am ashamed before that standing within me which speaks with me.
> Some of these things are always looking at me.
> I am never out of sight.
> Therefore I must tell the truth.
> I hold my word tight to my breast.[66]

Recall that the emotion of shame is associated with our very social sense. I do not read the shame expressed here as neurotic, but as the humbling of a self before the whole society of nature, an admitting of the fallibility of one's humanity, of one's capacity to do harm or show disrespect, at a spiritually significant moment. If, moreover, Old Torlino is able to feel some shame before the natural world, then we may speculate that in a violent society such as ours the discovery of a tremendous well of shame, including that related to our mistreatment of other-than-human beings, is an event waiting to happen for most of us. As Turnbull suggests, to be truly dedicated to Spirit is also to be dedicated to Society or to the greater social Self.[67] If nature is itself a social place, then the ecological crisis is both a spiritual crisis and a pathological disturbance in this largest of social fields.

Singing the World: Language . . . Meaning . . . Nature

> *The landscape and the language are the same/ For we ourselves are landscape and are land.*
>
> —Conrad Aiken[68]

Twentieth-century Western philosophy, in both continental and analytic traditions, has made language the key. As M. C. Dillon suggests, however, this has not overcome but merely extended the reign of dualism, for now it is language that is divorced from the rest of the world. Dillon focuses particularly on what he calls "semeiological reductionism," most exemplified by Derridean deconstruction, in which all sense-making is believed to be trapped and endlessly refracted within the play between linguistic signs, such that no reference is even possible to a reality outside of or transcendent to human language. I suggest that to adopt such a view would be the demise of ecopsychology; for it makes no room for the meaningfulness of the natural world outside of a purely linguistic constitution, nor, more fundamentally, does it admit to the origins of language from *within* this world, as an expression *of* it. What I wish to do here, then, is show what both ecological concern and phenomenological insight can bring to the debate on language, and the relevance of this topic for a naturalistic psychology. If, as Abram suggests, our current understanding of language and our forgetful manner of speaking are implicated in our alienation from nature, then as ecopsychologists we surely need a better grasp of the relationships among language, meaning, and nature. As with the nature/culture cleavage generally, the point is not to champion or pursue a reality free from language, or a language that is somehow purely "natural," but to recover a sense for the *power* of language as it serves and arises out of nature. To be sure, I feel that our symbolically starved bodies are hungering for more satisfying words, ones that will better disclose our inherence in the body of the earth, as well as make sense of our suffering. To address this situation is to enter into a massive topic in its own right, as people like Abram have skillfully begun to do.[69] In what follows, therefore, I return to the subject of language only for the purpose of bringing to light the one specific principle that concerns me here.

Merleau-Ponty, in naming this principle, held that "words, vowels and phonemes are so many ways of 'singing' the world." Different languages are thus different "ways for the human body to sing the world's praises."[70] What does he mean by this? Most simply, our linguistic intentions arise or issue from our bodily felt participation in the world, and so our verbal expressions are a "singing" of that world. Speech and thought, said Merleau-Ponty, are "the perceptible world's explosion within us."[71] In other words, the feelings that come *up* in us as we interact with the world need to symbolically burst *out* of us, like a big laugh that erupts from us when we see something funny, or, indeed, a song that demands to be sung, that spontaneously comes to us, overflows us, in a moment of pain or joy. To reject dualism is to realize that when we speak we are always giving voice to some worldly situation in which we are immersed, speaking from *inside* the world. This also means that as we come to live in a world more and more dominated by human artifacts, the world our language sings is increasingly a technological one. For the moment, however, I want to use the idea of "the world" in a broad sense, as "the natural world." "Indeed," remarks Abram, "if human language arises from the perceptual interplay between the body and the world, then this language 'belongs' to the animate landscape as much a it 'belongs' to ourselves."[72] Heidegger is remembered for saying that language is the "house of being." He did not, however, call this house a human prison. Language, he said, borrowing from the poetry of Hölderlin, is "the flower of the mouth. In language the earth blossoms toward the bloom of the sky."[73] Language is in this case a phenomenon of nature: it has sensuous, earthy roots, yet also the clarity and lightness of the sky. Hence, Merleau-Ponty's line that "in a sense . . . language is everything, since it is the voice of no one, since it is the very voice of the things, the waves, and the forests."[74]

What I have said so far is not the whole story, for words do not just come to us via some direct pipe from the natural world. Rather, there is a circular relation between the two. Merleau-Ponty held that "the body is, so to speak, predestined to model itself on the natural aspects of the world. But as an active body of gestures, of expression, and finally of language, it turns back on the world to signify it."[75] Language, in this view, originates as a kind of gesture that draws its meaning from our contact with the world, but our perception of this world is itself structured by the language already sedimented into it. That is to say, our linguistic symbols not only make the world intelligible but in doing so also *change* the world, bringing it forth in a way that favors a particular view or interpretation. The Merleau-Pontian interpretation I want to forward *here* is that language, on the one hand, and the phenomenal world, on the other, form two open systems which mirror and feed one another; that the world knows itself as it is reflected in language, and language knows itself only as it is reflected in the actual world.

Much current thought about language traces back to the structuralist Ferdinand de Saussure, who observed that language systems are not composed of independent linguistic elements but rather form organic totalities, with internal relations among their parts.

> In English, for instance, the sounded word "red" draws its precise meaning from its situation in a network of like-sounding terms, including, for instance, "read," "rod," "reed," and "raid," and in a whole complex of color terms, such as "orange," "yellow," "purple," "brown"; as well as from its participation in a still wider nexus of related terms like "blood," "rose," "sunset," "fire," "blush," "angry," "hot," each of which holds significance only in relation to a constellation of still other words, expanding thus outward to every term within the language. By describing any particular language as a *system of differences,* Saussure indicated that meaning is found not in the words themselves but in the intervals, the contrasts, the participations *between* the terms.[76]

Dillon calls this ecological characteristic of language its "infra-referentiality," indicating how all terms refer to one another *within* the given system. Following

Merleau-Ponty, however, he goes on to further identify the "extra-referential" character of language, noting that signs (or sign systems) also refer to the world *outside* of this language.[77] That is, the sense that words or phonemes reveal is not constituted by these alone, but in how they correspond to and make us aware of differentiations present within *the world itself,* how they bring to light some of the meaning that inheres in the way the *things themselves* internally relate. "Red" and "orange" have meaning not just because of linguistic play but because of apples and oranges (as it were). As Abram has noted, Merleau-Ponty "comes in his final writings to affirm that it is *first* the sensuous, perceptual world that is relational and weblike in character, and hence that the organic, interconnected matrix of any language is an extension or echo of the deeply interconnected matrix of sensorial reality itself."[78] It is thus only because we perceive the world itself as a kind of language—a field of expressive shapes, movements, sounds, tastes, smells, and so on—that human language, as an elaboration and ramification of this worldly logos, is even possible.[79] The great power of language inheres precisely in the correlation and interaction that obtains between these two systems, in the gestalt they form together. As a form of symbolization, language thus *does* have a privileged relation to truth, a unique power of disclosure, because every word, while always referring to the phenomenal world, also takes its place in a universe of historically sedimented speech, such that when we use any one word this whole linguistic universe is brought along with or implied in it.[80] (Music, painting, dance, and other nonverbal modes of poetizing do of course reveal meaning in important ways that verbal speech cannot. They nonetheless lack the systemic power of the latter.) This structure of double reference gives language its symbolic pliability and specificity, in that the vast infrareferential systems that make up our languages offer great flexibility and nuance in signifying or disclosing the world.[81]

Envisioning language thus, as a system that intertwines with and emerges from the world we experience, helps us to see how the alternative view could arise that language is a closed system unto itself. For the felt link between the two orders has become weakened to the point where language now appears to float somehow above the world we perceive—not of it, with it, or in it. As many continental thinkers have dealt with it, "language may now be said, in Roland Barthes' words, to 'celebrate itself' rather than to celebrate the world."[82] For Jacques Derrida and his followers, all signs endlessly refer to still other signs, such that the meaning of a text can never be decided or made present, being forever deferred.[83] Linguistic signs, that is, do not mediate our contact with the world but continually put it off.[84] This development is part of that modern syndrome in which the symbolic or formal loses its grounding in the experienced or felt. Gendlin therefore criticizes Derrida for assuming that word-use is governed by formal distinctions alone (schemes, kinds, logical constructs), rather than by an organic body sense that connects our speaking to our worldly situations.[85] What Derrida and other current thinkers do not recognize is the functioning of *experience* in our languaging, the shifting and unfolding of concretely felt meanings in steps of forward-moving living (it is this very lack of recognition, in fact, which makes the claim that meaning is forever deferred understandable). As Dillon further notes, the Derridian view is unable to account for the *origins* of language. Considered as the sole ground of meaning (even if this meaning be a mere mirage or effect), language must simply always have been.[86] In the view I am adopting here, this enacts the mistake of making what is derivative primary.[87] That is, seeing language as a closed system cuts it off from its worldly source, turns it into a system without origins. To the contrary, Merleau-Ponty unequivocally described the world as a cradle or a pregnancy of meaning, the "direction of all directions."[88] He therefore put language *after* the perceived world as his primary theme, claiming that language is in fact *founded* on this world. "In the end," he said, "language must signify something and not always be language about language."[89] In chapter two I discussed how all language is figurative, in that discourses appear only by taking on some of the world's figure, body, or physiognomy.[90] To give another example, the meaning of the words psyche, soul, anima, and spirit all come from "breath" or "wind," which evokes the way that life force, meaning, energy, and so forth, circulates through the world, belonging to nobody and everybody.[91] Critics like Dillon suggest that (post-)structuralist thought constitutes a denial of this original meaningfulness of the world and an intellectual retreat from it in general.[92]

It is worth noting that for primary oral peoples (peoples with no knowledge of writing) it would be virtually impossible to think of language as something that is closed off from the natural world. This is because the structure of their words and their stories explicitly derives from their concrete surroundings; the outer world tangibly lends form to and inspires their speaking. The languages of oral peoples are anchored in or held by their environments, not by systems of writing. As Walter Ong has observed, the advent of writing disrupts this relationship. For it acts to pull language away from the wider terrain in favor of a focus on the written word, thereby putting a new psychic distance between people and their environments and creating an interior mindscape entirely unknown to oral cultures.[93] Alphabetic literacy, in particular, has contributed to opening up the extreme distance that we now experience between ourselves and the natural world. As Abram notes, early writing systems consisted of glyphs or depictions of nonhuman entities (birds, sun, etc.), and so still acknowledged the more-than-human source of human language. The phonetic alphabet, however, is a stripped-down system of writing based on sound alone, on syllables and vowels; its characters (ABC . . .) make no reference to actual things in the world.[94] It thus definitively "short-circuits" the relationship between our speaking and the land. In other words, with the alphabet, our indebtedness to the natural world as the original site of all meaning is swept away. As Abram comments: "Only as the written text began to speak would the voices of the forest, and of the river, begin to fade."[95]

So this is our situation today: through a historical process of withdrawing our language from the land, we have reached the point where many thinkers now proclaim that our confinement within the written text is simply the way it is. This is not an acceptable situation for ecopsychology. If we are to reconnect our minds with the natural world, then we must reconnect our language with it as well. We must sing a more-than-human world. Ong and Abram are both careful to suggest that a return to primary orality is not necessary (even if it were somehow possible). Ong emphasizes that the shift from orality to literacy has not only entailed losses, but also what he sees as gains: an interior, introspective life, for example, and an awareness of the individual as distinct from the communal structures in which she or he is immersed. He would have us move forward with the gains, while also recovering an understanding for the primacy of the oral mode. Abram, for his part, writes that "there can be no question of simply abandoning literacy, of turning away from all writing. Our task, rather, is that of *taking up* the written word, with all its potency, and patiently, carefully, writing language back onto the land."[96] Abram has also spoken of the need to refrain from writing certain stories down, but to preserve them by simply speaking them aloud or enacting them, regularly, in the earthly places where these stories dwell (in the places where their more-than-human characters and events have a secret relevance related to the natural unfoldings in the land).[97] For if we and the earth are indeed to enjoy a reconciliation, he believes we will in fact have to periodically reenter a kind of oral mindscape. What can be safely said, in any case, is that the naturalistic task of returning language and meaning to the wider world is an experiential one; it will require that we expand our perception of, and dialogue with, other-than-human reality. As I discuss next, a good first step in undertaking this task is to recognize just how human-centered our current speaking is.

Given that all languages correspond to their speakers' perception of the world, the limits of our language are set by the limits of our perception.[98] If our engagement with others is narrowly or narcissistically focused, if the sphere of our care extends little beyond ourselves, then the world we sing will be correspondingly small and self-involved. To be sure, the language we speak today is increasingly entwined not with rivers, moss, and turtles, but with a web of cars, TVs, and telephones. The mechanical devices embedded in our social practices—clocks, steam engines, railways, hydraulic systems, telephone exchanges, computers, and the like—have, for example, been widely used by modern psychologists as a source of metaphors for describing the human mind.[99] "In the modern world," says Shepard, "where machines have largely replaced animals, it is perhaps inevitable that they should be treated as totems and seen as models of what we are."[100] David Leary calls this phenomenon—wherein we speak of ourselves and the rest of the world in terms of our own artifacts—the "boomerang effect."[101] Even as our words aim outward, little comes back to us but our own devices. This is a dangerous situation. Calvin Martin claims that words "are too perilous to be uttered out of a genuinely earthy context; they are too inherently powerful to be left unmoored, unaffiliated with place and the sentient beings there." Language, cut off from the wider natural world, goes its own delirious way. Or as Marcel Detienne writes: "As soon as mankind ceases to 'reverberate' to the world, the sickness penetrates language," which becomes "the victim of illusions produced by words."[102] Because our speaking is so disjunctive with the earth's own voices, Martin suggests that we have in a very real sense become less-than-human.[103]

The task, then, is to reopen the circuit between language and the larger world in order to permit into our language a vital return flow of meaning. In this, we again need acknowledge a crucial asymmetry: the living world outside of human language, the world of creeks and porcupines and leaves, even if revealed through language, is the given, primary reality, the ultimate social context to which our speaking must in good health remain faithful. As with much else of significance to ecopsychology, models of such faithfulness are best found among indigenous persons. Speaking of the Okanagan, for example, Jeannette Armstrong writes that "the land taught us our language. The way we survived is to speak the language that the land offered us as its teachings."[104] Sean Kane refers to the myth-telling of archaic peoples as a poetic "dialogue with nature," "an affectionate counterpoint to the earth's voices." A myth, he says, "is the power of a place speaking," conveying events as much from the perspective of the spirit world as the human. Such oral myths, moreover, are typically complex in the middle, but with "no pronounced beginning or end." This openness at the edges, then, deliberately allows for an influx of meaning from the surrounding wilderness.[105] We of the modern world are not myth-tellers, at least not of the oral sort described by Kane. We *are*, however, still people who, being of the natural order, are claimed by nature to use our language in its service. As Merleau-Ponty taught, the "call to language . . . originates from beyond language in an unspoken, or silence, that appropriates us or demands . . . a singing expression."[106] Language is not a closed system of verbal forms, but a mode of poetizing, of allowing for the disclosure of new meanings, new forms, in our dwelling on or listening to the earth.[107] Authentic speech, that is, is a response to our felt sense of what in the world needs to be said, to the "unspoken aspects of the world that seek expression." As before, I suggest that the demand for such speech gives us our embodied starting place.

Psychic Correspondence: One Flesh

> *The body . . . offers to him who inhabits it and senses it the wherewithal to sense everything that resembles himself on the outside. . . . If it touches [things] and sees them, this is only because, being of their family, itself visible and tangible, it uses its own being as a means to participate in theirs, because each exists as an archetype for the other, because the body belongs to the order of things as the world is universal flesh.*
>
> —Maurice Merleau-Ponty[108]

Shortly before his death, Merleau-Ponty noted to himself that: "A philosophy of the flesh is the condition without which psychoanalysis remains anthropology."[109] Such a philosophy, in other words, would provide the ontological basis for a psychology that reaches beyond the human sphere: for an ecopsychology (as we would say). But what is "flesh"? Merleau-Ponty had yet to finish working out this difficult metaphor at the time of his death, so there is no complete saying of what he meant by it. I do believe, however, that much of what this term implies *is* readily graspable once we enter into an interactive or ecological framework. For it points to how all phenomena interweave as a single cloth or "common tissue," how they are mutually informative in their commingling with one another—this being possible only because they are of the same elemental stuff.

> The flesh is not matter, is not mind, is not substance. To designate it, we should need the old term "element," in the sense it was used to speak of water, air, earth, and fire, that is, in the sense of a *general thing*.[110]

As the element of being itself, flesh is a medium more primary than mind and matter, which are differentiations *within* the flesh. In this case, language, too, is a kind of flesh; one that is "less heavy," or "more transparent," than other kinds.[111] As we saw above, language and the perceived world, although different, are not discontinuous. Rather, they resemble one another and are meaningful exactly in the way they reflect one another as different sorts of flesh.[112] Our bodies, moreover, are made of the same flesh as the world and the world shares in the flesh of our bodies.[113] Just as we speak of a shared or common humanity, so may we thus speak more broadly of a *common flesh*. I consider this Merleau-Ponty's way of saying that "we too are nature," of conceptualizing our embeddedness in, or continuity with, the wider natural world.[114] Something in us vibrates to the cry of wolves, to the play of bears; we are not some purely inward, acosmic stuff, but rather of the same flesh as bird song and snow. A deeply buried preunderstanding of our oneness in flesh is exactly what permits us to touch or understand one another. In other words, the nature or style of flesh is such that contact is *possible*. It "has a porous quality that allows, even requires, a coming and going through it; by definition, flesh 'breathes' or seeps, as well as containing or separating."[115] Given that the flesh is a single elemental fabric, each instance of contact is, furthermore, a case of flesh touching *itself*, of its folding back on or differentiating and mirroring itself. A calloused hand is thus flesh knowing itself as skin contacts (touches and is touched by) the rough surfaces of ropes and ladders, a delicate one as skin contacts the smoothness of pen and paper. To gather in this way the commonness or generalness of flesh has a decentering or transpersonalizing effect on the self, for all perceiving becomes not the activity of individuals, but of the world itself.

While Merleau-Ponty's formulation of the flesh may be an original contribution to Western philosophy, his ideas by no means stand alone. The poet

Rainer Maria Rilke, for instance, wrote that we "are set down in life as in the element to which we best correspond" and, moreover, that "when we hold still we are scarcely to be distinguished from all that surrounds us."[116] It is this theme of a *correspondence* between ourselves and others that I wish to pursue. At the heart of this philosophy is the idea that *like can only touch like;* that we can contact the world only when able to sense in *ourselves* something that resembles or resonates with it.[117] Bruno Snell held, for example, that "man could never have come to experience a rock anthropomorphically if he had not also experienced himself 'petromorphically.'"[118] "Things," in other words, "have an *internal equivalent in me*."[119] Bringing this principle into an ecological context, Shepard writes: "Wild species are true Others, the components of wilderness, and at the same time are the external correlates of our inmost selves."[120] The visible world, in other words, provides the tangible symbols to call forth or connect us with the intangible aspects of our own being. "We are selves composed of sleeping figures," says Shepard, "each a secret that can be awakened in acts of correspondence."[121] Other animals have always been used for human self-understanding, from totem animals to everyday metaphors (e.g., sloth, weasel), where some aspect of the animal's nature corresponds to or matches some quality in ourselves. The "otherness of stones and stars," meanwhile, "are models for thinking our humbleness in the universe, and they are the key to the strangeness of ourselves."[122]

Having introduced the principle of "one flesh," I wish to use it in what remains of this discussion to revisit a number of psychological notions, and so show further what a nondualistic and naturalistic psychology might look like. All of the interactive concepts I introduced in chapter three still apply. Here, I am only adding to that discussion.

Projection, first, is normally spoken of in negative tones. It is taken to mean the act of attributing some psychological content from inside ourselves to the outside world, such that we misperceive things. We anthropomorphize or person-ify our pets, think everyone is out to get us, or otherwise fill the world with fancy imaginings that exist only in our heads. No doubt our perception of others is often faulty. But the usual understanding of projection suffers both from a persistent dualism and from a limited and dismal view of imagination. Most important, our being is never located "inside" ourselves to begin with, but (as I have discussed at length) is always in-the-world, as a field phenomenon. Thus, how we imagine the world is not just a solipsistic act but is based on what sort of style of relating we have so far established with others, on how we are currently knotted into the world's flesh. We do not pollute things with our subjectivity; rather, they show up somehow in the light of our worldly existence. Medard Boss observed, in this regard, that "when the phenomena of my world confront me they reveal, of their great store of meanings, only those to which my perception—in the state of my existence at that time—is open."[123] We may note, then, that projection certainly does have something to do with how we are *attuned* to the world, but this attunement is a function of the ground of our existence, not some mechanism inside us. In this view, imagination is not simply a discrete mental faculty for making things up.[124] It refers instead to how *all* of our perception involves more than what is just immediately given to our senses, for we always participate in what we experience, imagining events in the context of the experiential background or felt biases we bring to them, the clearing our existence holds open. A snake may appear frightening to us, for example, because ours is the kind of existence wherein we imagine such animals biting us. We make sense of the world, that is, in a way that *corresponds* to the condition of our own existence, seeing in the world (projecting) that which resonates to the possibilities we can imagine from within the context of our own experiential history. Stated still otherwise: the visible surface of reality is the symbolic clue to its invisible depths, and it is only through imagining these depths that we reach into the hidden flesh of the world and so make contact with others *at all*.[125]

What, then, of projection in a negative sense? Consider the case I mentioned in chapter three, in which the person who slaughters wolves was said to repress all that is violent, irrational, insatiable, and disinhibited in himself and then to project these qualities onto wolves. I suggest that the real issue here is not projection per se, but the *quality* of this projection and the *poverty of contact* that obtains under a repressed condition. For even if his own "beastliness" is repressed—or, rather, precisely because of this—the wolf-hater's existence is *implicitly* attuned to the "beast"-like qualities in others. Wolves get singled out because their nature actually *does* correspond, if only trivially (i.e., because they are wild and predatory), to those qualities negated by the hunter. The wolves, that is, serve as the slimmest symbolic cue for calling forth the blocked and ugly meanings in the background of the hunter's life. The bias created by these off-base meanings then reveal the wolves in a relatively distorted or untruthful way. Where there is little contact with others, as here with the wolves, the imaginative component of our experience might therefore better be called *fantasy*. As Stephen Levine notes, imagination "is the means by which we reach out and connect with otherness," whereas fantasy "ignores actuality in creating images of pleasure or pain."[126] The way to dissolve fantasy projections is thus not to eliminate projection, but to make *better contact* with the world, thereby converting "fantasy" into "imagination" and owning our repressed feelings. The idea within a hermeneutic framework, to repeat, is that we can perceive others more faithfully only by more openly approaching them, letting them "talk back" to us, and so revising the imaginative biases by which we (necessarily) perceive them.[127] This amounts, in turn, to thickening up the sense of fleshy connection between us, recognizing ourselves in them, feeling our own flesh caught up with theirs. Indeed, Lopez remarks that we have broken our ancient contracts with other animals in two main ways: through a failure of everyday contact and through a related failure of imagination.[128] In a similar vein, the environmental researcher Tom Fleischner has called natural history an "antidote to projection" ("projection" in the negative sense), natural history being "the honest and honorable practice of learning as directly and expansively as possible from Nature."[129] The more experienced we are, the more complex or richly woven our existential ground, the more are we able to imagine the world truthfully (all else being equal). Philosopher George Santayana noted, in this regard, that our imagination, if it is not to be pure fantasy, "needs to be fed by contact with external things and by *widening vital rhythms.*"[130] We might ask ourselves, then, as I do in the next chapter, about what is feeding our imagination today.

The next notion I wish to consider is the *repressed unconscious.* I will not repeat my remarks from chapter three, except to remind the reader that what we repress are our world-bound intentions or meanings that are not completed, welcomed, acknowledged, or affirmed by others. In short, we become unconscious in those areas where our existence is not *mirrored,* and so where we cannot see or come to know ourselves. Repression, as Robert Romanyshyn says, thus "characterizes that condition of living in which experiences, which find no anchor in and/or reflection by the world, slip away from the world and are buried beneath it."[131] How might we apply this understanding to the idea of an *ecological* unconscious? I suggest, first of all, that within an interactive or interrelational scheme, distinguishing an "ecological" component of the psyche is a rather arbitrary or rhetorical business. I suggest, also, that calling the ecological unconscious (as Roszak does) a "repository" of "the living record of cosmic evolution," to which we need "open access,"[132] is in fact a dualistic way of conceptualizing it (for reasons I discussed in chapter three). The type of nondualistic view I would rather adopt here holds that we are born with certain kinds of world-relations or interactional patterns already bodily implied. To my mind, this view shifts the stress to our worldliness, to how we are attending to the process of moving into ever-widening spheres of meaning and participation. Gion Condrau and Medard Boss write: "Those world-relations which are prevented from being realized appropriately in an intentional, interpersonal manner must carry themselves out in the dark, mute spheres of existence where there are no thoughts or words, i.e., primarily in the somatic realm."[133] One way of understanding the ecological unconscious, then, is in terms of our frustrated or unconsummated inherent relations concerning the more-than-human world, relations which continue to be bodily implied under the encrustations of Western society and so which may still figure in our dreams and creative imagination. Rather than discuss further what these relations might look like, however, I leave this topic for my discussion in the final section on "nature and the human life cycle."

Our unconscious existence, in general, is sensed by us as the blocked or blind life that wants to come forth into some specific form. It is a feeling of being haunted by things not yet conscious, an aching for meanings not had, prefigured contacts not made—not only in relation to the human sphere, but also the more-than-human as well. The image that comes to my mind is that of a vast world, a million implied relations, collapsed or imploded in on a single isolated center: the repressed body. Today, with all these world-relations blocked or unreciprocated, with so much life unlived, distorted, and jammed in our bodies, it is no wonder that many people are suffering from chronic illnesses. This is also why one of the most important roles of a psychotherapist is to welcome and make a living connection with those parts of the client she or he has shamefully repressed or disowned. The therapist keeps the client's process company, mirrors her or his experience, right at the edge where something is becoming conscious, where some life wants to body forth into contact.

Moving on to the topic of *dreams*, we may again witness the general interactive manner of flesh. While dreams are often thought of as subjective events that belong entirely to the dreamer, as a projection *of* the dreamer, a philosophy of the flesh supports the idea that dreaming and waking worlds are better seen as intertwining or corresponding realms of being. Medard Boss was emphatic that we do not *have* dreams; rather, dreaming is a mode of existing in its own right.[134] Here, therefore, we do not collapse the dream world into the waking world but maintain that crucial dialectical or mirroring distance between them. This also fits with the notion that symbols in general express "a kind of correspondence between different worlds while maintaining a distinction."[135] Hillman thus asks: "Can we leave the [dream-] animal out there in its otherness and yet retain its psychological import and our kinship with it?"[136] His own answer is that:

> animals come into our dreams as guides, helpers, and saviors. . . . they teach us about something, but they are not part of us. The bear dream that one man had corresponds with his own earthy, shaggy nature, and therefore he can feel an affinity. But that bear is not his own shaggy nature. That reduces the bear to just a piece of himself and insults the bear—it interprets the bear away. The presence of the bear in the dream corresponds to qualities of the human soul, but is not reducible to it.[137]

My own training as a Gestalt therapist is to interpret dreams by identifying with the various dream elements in turn, acting the dream out as in a live drama, sensing how the various elements resonate metaphorically with one's own existence, and so gathering the dream's message in terms of what personal meanings it calls forth. While for some this method may well turn the dream into the sole possession of the dreamer, the Gestalt therapists Erving and Miriam Polster argue that such interpretation can also involve an *interplay* between, on the one hand, recognizing what aspects of oneself are "echoed" in the dream image and, on the other, a "healthy respect" for what qualities the dream image *itself* offers or brings to the dreamer, how the image *exceeds* the dreamer. They argue, that is, for a recognition of the "kinship" between the dreamer and dreamed.[138] Hence, when after paying much attention to crows in my neighborhood, dream-crows start entering into my night existence, I feel that I am being visited, not that I am merely projecting myself.[139] It is this fleshy reciprocation between ourselves and the otherness we experience, so well-exemplified in dreams, that is at the paradoxical or ambiguous heart of all experience: that our experience is ours, yet not ours; that in order to make contact with it we must identify with it, yet dis-identify from it; and that we are as one with the otherness we experience, yet different.

Finally, I return to the notion of *kinship*. I have left this notion for last because, as we have seen, a philosophy of the flesh suggests that kinship exists between all sorts of realms of reality, where there exists some common ground or likeness between them but where they necessarily maintain their distance and difference. In fact, in *every* moment of contact or act of correspondence we experience some commonality, sense the other as like unto ourselves. What is familiar is family. Following Merleau-Ponty, perception is "the mode of relatedness that separates us from ourselves and thereby brings us into contact with the things that teach us about themselves *and* ourselves."[140] For ecopsychologists, it is vital to note, in this respect, that prior to domestic times "animals served as delicate signs of the way the world goes, as elaborate metaphors and symbols, as spiritual beings, and as themselves."[141] As Gary Snyder asks:

> What do we learn from Wren, and Hummingbird, and Pine Pollen, and how? Learn what? Specifics: how to spend a life facing the current [salmon]; or what it is to perpetually die young; or how to be huge and calm and eat *anything* (Bear). But also that we are many selves looking at each other, through the same eye.[142]

Shepard gives particular emphasis to how, in the northern hemisphere, bears have since prehistoric times played a special role in the human imagination, with bear myths tackling "fundamental questions of human existence." He and Barry Sanders note that although every animal reflects some aspect of our humanity, the bear is a unique mentor in that her skills, personal qualities, and activities are so varied—and so resonant with our own.[143] As they also comment, "The most persistently and widely told tale ever devised to entertain and educate" is perhaps the story about a woman who married a bear.[144]

"To be kindred means to share consciously in the stream of life."[145] Entering this life-stream, as I discussed above, is a process of graduating into ever-widening spheres of social belonging. We most easily feel kinship with those who are closest to or most like ourselves, such as our parents and siblings. An expansion of self-understanding, however, requires that we develop our kinship with other-than-human beings, each species of which seems "to know a secret and to be wise in the metasocial fabric of the world."[146] Many animals, like the bear, are familiar enough that we can find metaphorical common ground with relative ease, whereas, as Shepard notes, plants generally have lessons for older, more subtle, minds.[147] What we are able to recognize as kin will always be a matter of how we are in our own particular ways attuned to the world. In general, however, the "highest order of maturity" is achieved, suggests Searles, when one is able to relate to, find likeness in, what on the surface seems *"most unlike* oneself."[148]

The general effect I have been after under this heading is the realization that all things correspond to (reflect, echo, mirror, metaphor, resemble) one another and only because of this have sense for us. This realization is common in the worlds of indigenous peoples, where the likenesses or analogies among things are a source of constant learning, where all things are potential symbolic mirrors—as is endlessly worked out in such instruments as the medicine wheels used by some Native North Americans.[149] The world experienced by primary peoples is often described as one with fluid boundaries, such that no absolute lines can be drawn among human, animal, and spirit realms; a world of metamorphoses, shape-shiftings, transformations. Joseph Epes Brown writes of the Lakota world that "the correspondence between levels of reality are as if one were the reflection of the other; they flow into each other in a manner that expresses a total, integrated environment."[150] A naturalistic psychology would explore these correspondences or resonances, would be a project of learning to recognize ourselves in what was formerly alien, of shifting ourselves along the kinship continuum or deepening our perception of the unity of the world's flesh. It would also emphasize that hyperdifferentiation or splitting is a possibility given in the very differential structure of the flesh, and that when we harden our boundaries, and so attenuate our sense of kinship with others, we suffer a spiritual loss.

Nature and the Human Life Cycle

Beneath the veneer of civilization, in the trite phrase of humanism, lies not the barbarian and the animal, but the human in us who knows what is right and necessary for becoming fully human: birth in gentle surroundings, a rich nonhuman environment, juvenile tasks with simple tools, the discipline of natural history, play at being animals, the expressive arts of receiving food as a spiritual gift rather than as a product, the cultivation of metaphorical significance of natural phenomena of all kinds, clan membership and small group life, and the profound claims and liberation of ritual initiation and subsequent stages of adult mentorship.

—Paul Shepard[151]

Paul Shepard maintained that an "ecologically harmonious sense of self and world . . . is the inherent possession of everyone, it is latent in the organism."[152] All humans, he said, are naturally ordered to undergo a psychogenesis in which "inherent predisposition" and "right experience" combine so as to key our speech and thought into the natural world.[153] The prospect he advanced is that today's high levels of stress and trauma, war and strife, social alienation, and ecological dysfunction are therefore the consequence of our having strayed from a general form of social life that is more in tune with the claims of wild nature and better suited to fulfilling our own generic expectations or needs.[154] Such ideas have greatly influenced my own, and it is to them that I wish to devote this section. Whether Shepard got all the details right seems to me beside the point. What is appealing is the vision of an unfolding of human life into ecologically mature adulthood, in which caregivers, mentors, and other-than-human beings provide good symbolic nutrition for completing the gestalts that the child's maturing body are organizing at any given time, thus revealing to him "the meaning of his own impulses, by providing them with an aim."[155] It is a vision in which our inherent world-relations find the specific kind of responses from others that will satisfy them, thereby lighting up the way to self-knowledge and to a sense of cosmic-at-homeness. I do not believe humans to be strangers on this earth. All along in this chapter I have in fact been working on the assumption that we all desire to be nurtured into loving relations with the cosmos, and that the achievement of same is a very real possibility. In what follows, therefore, my aim is to briefly consider some of the specifics.

Because this is an exercise in matters transhistorical, I must make some additional precautionary remarks. First, I think the idea of an inherent psychogenesis that includes other-than-human beings gains strength once we recognize a number of unfair prejudices working against it. Most obviously, developmental psychologists have effectively shut out the world of butterflies, ponds, and porcupines—a condition little changed since Searles first remarked on it forty years ago.[156] It has thus not occurred to researchers, furthermore, to ask about the possible ongoing *harm* of being restricted to domestic, human-dominated settings—as opposed to the more wild, multispecific sorts that have been the norm for all humans up until only recent times (considered on the scale of the deep past of our species). One important exception is the psychologist Gene Myers, who claims that the essence of our humanity lies not in our *discontinuity* from the rest of nature, as is normally assumed, but in our ability to sense our *commonality* with it all. Seen from this reverse perspective, maturity is the outcome not of transcending our animality or participation in nature, but of *realizing it* ever more fully.[157] Indeed, to see life as a quest for meaning and belonging on the largest of social scales is, as Edith Cobb said, to reorient psychology toward our "total relations with 'outerness,' with nature itself."[158] And then there is the prejudice that to posit a need for "nature" is romantic or nostalgic, the deluded product of an infantile longing for lost origins that never were. As I have discussed above, and will elaborate further below, my response to this charge is that our experience suggests otherwise. Finally, consider a comment made by the chief engineer for the Three Gorges hydroelectric scheme on the Yangtze River in China: "If we return to nature we cannot develop."[159] He meant *economic* development, of course. Yet "development" is a metaphor whose original meaning was biological, that is, natural. Insofar as it is prejudiced against nature, "economic development" is thus an oxymoron.[160] Indeed, I suggest that the engineer gets it exactly backward; for it is *only* by "returning to nature" that we can truly develop.[161]

That our bodily nature is self-organizing supports the kind of suggestion made by Shepard that we carry a preknowledge of what will be right for us as we extend ourselves out into the world, even if the particulars of this knowledge may be open to interpretive debate. My aim below, in this regard, is to put some relatively sure detail to the three principles I discussed above (ever-widening spheres; singing the world; one flesh). The more these principles are illustrated, and so reciprocally fleshed out, the more will they make sense, and the more will a certain scheme of human life become apparent. As with any other cyclic phenomenon, a human life is not without inherent organization. If nothing else, finally, I would stress that our psychological development is not only a process of going through our maturational sequences, but also of signifying the world—of coming to understand ourselves in relation to a more-than-human universe. This makes the topic of "nature and the human life cycle" of potential relevance to anyone who thinks about this relation. In what follows, I walk through the life cycle, focusing on the nature of infancy, childhood, and the adolescent transition into adulthood. This is another huge topic in its own right. I ask the reader, therefore, to bear in mind that my intention is not to offer an exhaustive treatise, but only an evocative sketch.[162]

Loving Mirrors for the Infant. That we are fleshy mirrors for one another is never more evident than in infancy. For it is through those intense and decisive interactions with her or his caregivers that the baby's self takes shape. Infant and caregiver are caught up in each other's being in such a way that simply undercuts any dualistic view of reality. The voices of caregivers awaken the infant's first smile; their faces reflect and give form to her or his first feelings.[163] Parent and infant famously exist in a state of mysterious synchrony, of mutual experiencing, where there is a "feeling mainline" between them.[164] Whereas early infants were once thought to be nonrelational or passive, a more recent view is that they are perceptually discriminating and interactive right from the start.[165] While newborns may not be reflectively aware of their difference from others, they nonetheless do live in their interactions, searching for nurturance from a source *outside* themselves.[166] The caregivers' mirroring responses, nurturing acts, and energetic adjustments, moreover, symbolize *for* infants the latter's preverbal experiencing, thereby carrying it forward. Infants make sense of their own experience, that is, primarily *through* their caregivers, as this is something that they are at birth not yet able to do for themselves via their own self-responses (at least that is what it seems). Indeed, these exchanges are part of the process whereby infants begin to satisfy their inborn desire to discover the world's meaning—what has been called their "cosmological urge." Even the child's play with her or his own body is what Erik Erikson called "autocosmic play."[167] This urge is evident also in those moments where infants interact with their *nonhuman* surroundings, as when, for instance, they interrupt their feeding in order to curiously gaze at something interesting, say a cat, that has caught their attention. Feeding, we may therefore note, is "capable of being usurped by a deeper hunger, namely the search for a comprehensible world."[168]

All these interactions are far from arbitrary, however. For as Gendlin writes: "Much more arrives at birth than a blank tablet. . . . The human infant implies the breast and the mother . . . . Infants come with good mothering already implicit, interpersonal communication already ongoing, the complexity of syntax already in place. They need not first be made from perceptions."[169] There is what Jean Liedloff calls a "continuum" between caregiver and child. Even if the baby refuses the breast, as sometimes happens, the baby-breast relation is still a general interaction-pattern of our species, and the fluid in the mother's breast still implies the infant in turn. When infants contribute their poetic babble to the dialogue at a social gathering, moreover, and cry in protest when taken away, it is hard not to recognize their "innate desire to be included in shared activity, to be acknowledged as a participant in the linguistic community."[170] Infant and caregiving environment are, then, a single field of mutually anticipated world-relations. As Goodman notes, the infant is a helpless being only when seen in isolation from the total social context that her or his existence implies. Regarded as part of the whole prefigured caregiving field, the child is not helpless at all.[171] Of significance to ecopsychology is the distinct possibility that the relational field implied by the infant's body *also* includes a richness of other-than-human beings. Although the most important relational matrix for the infant is no doubt human, Shepard suggests that the nonhuman *setting* for that nexus is thus also highly significant. He speaks of:

> a surround of living plants, rich in texture, smell, and motion. The unfiltered, unpolluted air, the flicker of wild birds, real sunshine and rain, mud to be tasted and tree bark to grasp, the sounds of wind and water, the voices of animals and insects and humans—all these are not vague and pleasant amenities for the infant, but the stuff out of which its . . . grounding [in the matrix of the earth], even while in its mother's arms, has begun. . . . it is a world bathed in nonhuman forms, a myriad of figures, evoking an intense sense of the differences and similarities, the beckoning challenge of a lifetime.[172]

In Winnicott's memorable words, "the whole procedure of infant-care has as its main characteristic a steady presentation of the world to the infant."[173] We may note, in this respect, that it is not at all unusual for parents to take their infants outdoors in order to introduce them to blue jays, squirrels, and such,[174] and to let them get into all those earthy things close at hand.

Reflecting on a lifetime of experience, Harold Searles wrote: "I am convinced . . . that lovingness is the basic stuff of human personality, and that it is with a wholehearted openness to loving relatedness that the newborn infant responds to the outside world."[175] Jean Liedloff likewise notes: "The feeling appropriate to an infant in arms is his feeling of rightness, or essential goodness. . . . All babies are good, but can know it themselves only by reflection, by the way they are treated. There is no other viable way for a human to feel about himself; all other kinds of feeling are unusable as a foundation for well-being."[176] I cannot imagine an infant who does not need to be loved simply because she or he is. For such is the foundation for loving relations toward both ourselves and others. The world-relations called for at this time are thus those reliable, responsive, and adaptive ones that will hold a safe space for infants and preserve their core feelings of continuity, trust, and innocence. No two babies are exactly alike; we enter the world with different genes, past karmas, destinies, personalities, or whatever. It is for this reason that I also emphasize the *general* need to have our *specific* needs lovingly recognized and adapted to by our caregivers. As Mary Ainsworth has documented, empathic and responsive caregiving[177] has a "buffering" effect even on infants born with constitutional difficulties.[178] Among most primal peoples, a continuous maintenance of closeness, and attendance to the infant's particular needs, reportedly results in children who are securely attached to their caregivers (i.e., who have a sure emotional tie with them) and so who cheerfully and freely explore the transitional space away from them.[179] Much study on attachment and separation by Western researchers also supports the idea that genuine independence is won *only* by having our early dependency needs well-met, despite the still frequently held belief that doing so only "spoils" children (especially males) or actually prevents them from becoming independent.[180] For the anxiously attached infant, who was perhaps *forced* to "grow up," life will predictably be marred by insecurities of all kinds, and much of life may be spent seeking little more than proof that one exists.[181] I stress this point because so many serious psychological disturbances surface in the wake of abuses occurring at this vulnerable stage in life. The so-called borderline personality disorder, for example, which involves chaotic or crisis-filled interpersonal relations and a severe fear of abandonment, is often traced by clinicians to poor attachment experiences in infancy, including situations in which the young child was punished for taking steps toward autonomy[182] (as well as to situations of early sexual and physical abuse[183]). Borderline personalities are also prevalent among men who batter their female partners—a significant finding given the current crisis of domestic violence.[184] In contrast to the traumatized infant, then, it is the well-loved baby who is generally able to spontaneously move on to the further stages of childhood with a relative absence of unfinished infantile business.

A Childhood Immersion in the "Natural World." Naturalists Gary Paul Nabhan and Stephen Trimble are not shy about claiming that "children need wild places" (nor is child psychiatrist Robert Coles, who comments in the introduction to their book that all "young people ache for nature").[185] The view worked out by these and other authors is that in childhood the innate urge toward meaning creation and social belonging takes the matrix of the earth as its locus. In a much-celebrated study on "the ecology of imagination in childhood," Edith Cobb wrote that "there is a special period, the little understood, prepubertal, halcyon, middle age of childhood, approximately from five or six to eleven or twelve—between the strivings of animal infancy and the storms of adolescence—when the natural world is experienced in some highly evocative way, producing in the child a sense of profound continuity with natural processes."[186] Cobb was convinced that what children want most is "to make a world in which to find a place to discover a self," and that their natural surroundings is the terrain in which to do it. Having graduated or separated from the earlier field of infant relations, children's emerging gestalt-making powers now direct them toward an aesthetic encounter with nature, for a joyful and wonder-filled revelation of creeks, groundhogs, and tadpoles. This period is a time that calls for imaginative play and wonder, for total absorption in and free exploration of the world. "The child learns that all life tells something and that all sound, from the frog calling to the sea surf, issues from a being kindred and significant to himself, telling some tale, giving some clue, mimicking some rhythm that he should know. There is no end to what is to be learned."[187] Just as we bond to caregivers in infancy, so do we—in this new phase of symbiotic immersion in the green world—need to become bonded to the earth. The "child must have a residential opportunity to *soak in a place,* and . . . the adolescent and adult must be able to return to that place to ponder the visible substrate of his own personality."[188]

Because the childhood need for nature is poorly recognized by most psychologists, I wish to make a couple of methodological remarks. First, I mentioned above that one of the main ways we discover needs is by tracing back along lines of suffering. The other is by paying attention to the fresh promptings of the life force: to where our bodily energy is genuinely pointing, to what is becoming newly figural in our awareness, to what tastes like nutritious or satisfying food. Within an experiential framework, especially, wherever there is spontaneous interest in the world, there we recognize an organismic need. For me, then, it is enough that (given supportive conditions) children are in general highly curious about and attracted to the world outdoors. They are themselves clearly saying what they need next in order to build up their existence, widen their self-boundaries, add further experiences to their life-gestalt, or discover-and-invent their "own increasing reality."[189] As Myers notes, in this regard, "the animal emerges for the infant and young child as a truly subjective other whose immediate presence is compelling. . . . cultural practices do not just create out of whole cloth (or fail to create) wonder at animals. Rather, such practices encourage or distort *a process already functioning* in its own way in the child."[190] Shepard also comments: "That children are interested in animals seems self-evident, . . . one of those 'givens' which in the past has not aroused the curiosity of psychologists."[191] Certainly, the continuing preponderance of animal characters in children's story books would support these views. This leads to my second methodological remark, which concerns, again, the human-centered prejudices of researchers.

In Myers book on children and animals, he discusses a number of these prejudices, saying that psychological theorists have to date "systematically obscured the importance of other species in our development," making them irrelevant or secondary to humans in the making of the child's world.[192] I will not try to reproduce all of Myers's helpful commentary, but only briefly highlight a few points. He discusses, for example, how the child's early and spontaneous sense of continuity with animals is erased by cultural lessons that lead to the creation of a "categorically human self." We are all familiar with the lowly status granted to animals (we insult people by calling them pigs, or rats, or just plain "animals!"). "The nursery school," says Myers, "is replete with boundary disputes, evaluation of the 'wild' or the 'animal' body, and with rigid distinctions, sometimes motivated out of a need to put at a distance that which is morally disturbing."[193] These biases against animals are then institutionalized in theories in which the chosen end points of developmental—rationality, self-consciousness, and so on—all involve an outgrowing of childhood animality. Because these theories measure maturity by the achievement of distance from an animal existence, they rule out from the start any consideration of the importance of animals to the child's growing self. The theories split the child into a simple animal body and a disembodied intellect, thereby making invisible the meanings that children might form in direct bodily felt contact with animals.[194] Against the assumption that the child's self is made only in the society of human language-users, Myers argues, by contrast, that a "sense of connection to the animal and by extension to a subjective [personified] ecology is a *telos,* or end, of development. It is a prepotent potential, and we might do well to consider its value."[195]

The broad task of childhood is *play.* From an experiential perspective, play is not just nonserious or trivial activity (as the cognitive development theorist Jean Piaget would have it[196]) but a means for extensive learning. Some degree of cultural transmission always takes place in the form of play, as in "playing house." For primal societies, especially, childhood play is allowed a central place. As Eaton et al. discuss it:

> In hunting and gathering societies play is the main activity of children throughout their waking hours, in contrast to other types of societies in which chores and schooling occupy large amounts of children's time after the age of six. Also, for hunting and gathering societies, the period of middle childhood—ages six to twelve

or so—is characterized by the encouragement of independence, . . . initiative, . . . flexibility, . . . and self-reliance, but not of obedience and responsibility [i.e., duties].[197]

In other words, there is a general lack of authoritarian parenting, especially of the sort that would humiliate the child, but a high degree of freedom given over to the child for play. In these societies, children learn through imitating the gathering and hunting activities of the adults, figuring out thereby which plants and animals make the best food, and coming to know the local natural history. There is thus little formal education. Rather, cognitive, physical, social, and emotional skills are acquired through all sorts of play, including the observation of adults and older children performing the everyday scenes of life, such as butchering, copulating, birthing, and dying.[198]

Of the many areas of play that characterize childhood, perhaps the most significant for our purposes is the imitation of animals. On the basis of much ethnographic study, Calvin Martin concludes that contact and reciprocity with nonhuman animals expresses a "universal human urge."[199] In childhood this urge is met in the form of play. Myers writes that translating "the shape of the animal's body into one's own—the key continuity—may be a *broadly shared characteristic of childhood*" across cultures.[200] "In the immensity of time," adds Shepard, "humans acquired, deep in their hearts, the expectation that animals signify. Insofar as they mediate between our conscious selves and the archetypal figures of our innermost being, childhood is a time of 'archetypal reminiscence' dependent on animals."[201] Anthropologist James Fernandez has likewise suggested that games of imitating animals are part of our "normal growth."[202] Through the playful recognition of themselves in the animal, children increasingly resolve their own inchoateness. For Myers and others, the reason why animals have a critical place in the life of children is because they:

> appear to be *optimally discrepant* social others . . . , offering *just the right amount of similarity and difference* from human pattern and other animal patterns to *optimally engage* the child. . . . animals are symbolic for the child . . . in the sense of confirming the child's own uniquely human self and representing and *furthering the living, feeling self* in a more vivid form than can other kinds of carriers of meaning.[203]

That is, children innately anticipate the kind of symbolic nutrition offered by animals. By this period the ground has been prepared for them to undertake the metaphorical leaps in self-understanding, and the widening of their social circles, that animals offer to them. In this way, their lives are *carried forward* into new realms of existing. "Each kind of animal gives concrete representation to an ephemeral and intangible element of the human self such as assertion, intimidation, affection, doubt, determination, kindness, anger, hope, irritation, yearning, wisdom, cunning, anticipation, fear, and initiative. Only when these feelings are discovered outside the self and then performed can such intense but elusive 'things' be made one's own."[204] In enacting other animals, moreover, children not only feel closer to them, but clarify for themselves just how they are *not* like animals. As Myers suggests, this has the effect of preserving the animal's otherness, of establishing a kinship based on shared qualities rather than pure identity. In such play the "vital natures of animals are encountered—and become our best defense against the conspiracy that animals are only machines or artifacts, and therefore against the lie that we ourselves are made of cogs, wheels, and wires."[205] In developing a connection with other animals, finally, children expand their own existential fields of care, not only to include these animals, but also the local terrains and larger ecologies to which they belong. (As Myers notes, the dilemma today is that to assist children in recognizing animals as genuine "social others," while also introducing them to a world that routinely violates animals, is to set them up for a good deal of grief. Hence: "If society were to really grasp what is at stake in child development, we might well reduce exploitation of animals to a minimum dictated by a stricter sense of necessity."[206])

What is perhaps most generally missing in our own Western childhoods is a culture of wilderness, wherein stories, rituals, everyday language, and day-to-day activities are all richly embedded in a more-than-human world. Trimble notes, for example, that:

> Pueblo Indian children learn about connections to the earth through virtually every experience in their culture. Beginning at about three years of age, Pueblo boys dance in their village plazas as animals, transforming themselves into the spirits of antelope and deer. They wear gray fox skins, deer-hoof and tortoise-shell rattles, parrot feathers, antler and horn headdresses, and skunk-fur gaiters. A little later, the girls may dance as parrots or buffalo mothers. The words of the songs, the symbols painted on costumes, and the choreographed gestures all connect the dancers with the earth: corn, clouds, the sun, rain, lightning, thunder, rainbows, evergreen trees. Life, growth, harvest.[207]

Despite my own joyful childhood experiences along the forest trail, I can little imagine what a difference in my perceptual universe it would have made to have been a member of such a culture as the Pueblo's—nor what it might have meant for the next phase of the life cycle.

Adolescent Initiation into a Sacred Adult Cosmos. One of the main tasks of a naturalistic approach is to identify those natural claims that are not being acknowledged or met by our society and to highlight the trouble this is creating. Our general misreading of the nature of adolescence provides a strong case in point. Having studied the human life cycle in a variety of cultural settings, Turnbull writes of adolescence that he "cannot think of a single culture . . . that handles this crucial stage of life more abysmally than we do."[208] While it is normal for us to view adolescence as a troublesome period that youth and their parents have to just survive somehow (or even as a kind of "mental illness"—sometimes officially[209]), other societies recognize it as a stage of great significance for both social and cosmic renewal, in which elders are called on to provide the cultural assistance necessary for youth to undergo a powerful symbolic rebirth into adulthood. As Turnbull thus notes: "Most of the adolescent behavior that is so puzzling to adults would be comprehensible if only they searched for the proper symbolic key."[210] In adolescence the carefree days of childhood wane as our maturing bodies ready us for the challenge of confronting our society and forming an adult identity, becoming part of our society in a new way. Our bodies naturally acquires sexual significance; we become highly sensitive to how others see us; and our minds search for a way to understand a cosmos that now bears down on us mightily. Struggling under the multiple burdens of physiological revolution, identity crisis, and spiritual awakening, it is not surprising that adolescents have developed a reputation for being difficult. I refuse to believe, however, that adolescents are "crazy" by nature; I argue instead (as do others) that the tragic mess our society makes of this stage of life demonstrates just how impoverished is its understanding of the cultural demands that our human nature makes on it.

A "humanistic" assumption of this book is that people are always making the best creative adjustments they can between their organismic needs and the situations in which they find themselves. We may well ask, then, about the general needs of adolescents; the kind of cultural conditions that are required to optimally meet them; and the creative adjustments that youth make when these conditions are lacking. This is essentially what Erikson did in his classic and still-valuable studies on youth. The following passage from *Identity: Youth and Crisis* sets the stage for much of what I want to discuss.

> In youth the tables of childhood dependence begin slowly to turn: no longer is it merely for the old to teach the young the meaning of life. It is the young who, by their responses and actions, tell the old whether life as represented to them has some *vital promise*, and it is the young who carry in them the power to confirm those who confirm them, to renew and regenerate, to disavow what is rotten, to reform and rebel.[211]

As this passage suggests, it is of the nature of adolescents to "talk back" to society (just as the saying goes). And this is because adolescence is the stage in life where our social status comes to a decision point, where we explicitly search for a form of social life or way of being that will satisfy our desire for a comprehensible and life-giving world. Youths offer their enthusiasm and faith to society, agree to regenerate or ensure the continuation of that form of society, only when it appears to offer them roles and ideals worthy of their *fidelity.* This fidelity, which Erikson describes as the naturally emerging power (or "vital virtue") of youth, can come to fruition or complete itself only if there is a "true community" available to house it—one to which the adolescent may genuinely be loyal or "true." Adolescents are "desperately seeking for a satisfactory sense of belonging," for a "defined personality within a social reality."[212] When, however, their elders fail to provide satisfying means to incorporate youth into the social whole, it is of the wisdom of their rebellious bodies to refuse that society, even if they themselves don't quite understand what they are doing.

Much of the adolescent activity that disturbs adults may thus be seen as forms of creative adjustment to an unsatisfactory situation. Gangs and cliques, for example, are "pseudo-societies" or "micro-societies"[213] that youths substitute for adult society, creating for themselves a community to which they can indeed be true. Gangs, said Erikson, are a "defense against a sense of identity confusion,"[214] as these offer a more satisfying identity for youth than is possible through membership in a corrupt or unwelcoming society-at-large. Even a "negative identity" is preferable to a bankrupt one, and even deviancy can be a form of loyalty to one's own nature.[215] Some adolescents adjust by withdrawing inwardly, while others become manifestly disturbed, disintegrating under their psychospiritual load. As Erikson argued, if we do not understand the need for (giving and receiving) fidelity, we will instead confirm the youth "by every act of the correctional or therapeutic authorities as a future criminal or a lifelong patient."[216] That is, rather than recognizing the intertwined needs of youth and society, our adult society effectively punishes and shames adolescents for how it has failed them. Instead of listening to the feedback offered by adolescents through their distress-filled activities, and taking responsibility for that distress, our elders call for more police and discipline. Punk rock and grunge music are adolescent ways of singing the world, are a kind of voice of nature. Adolescents, in other words, are natural mirrors for a society, even if our own society generally refuses to see itself in them, and even if our society is itself a broken mirror for reciprocally showing to adolescents their own "true" selves. Looking for a world to believe in, noble values to uphold, and cosmic meanings to embrace, the last thing adolescents "need" is wrong-headed social judgment.

In the general unfolding of adolescent life, two regions of existence that are highly figural, and so much in need of societal recognition, are the sexual and spiritual.[217] I thus want to consider these two in turn (even if they are tightly linked). First, the sexual. Sexual maturation spontaneously turns adolescents into a new kind of being, and so creates a discontinuity in their existence, makes them unfamiliar to themselves, at least to some degree. The bodily changes occurring at this time bring their ontological insecurity to a new apex and make them extremely self-conscious for that reason.[218] The pursuit of social acceptance by adolescents thus includes the desire for an identity in which their sexual being is actively affirmed, thereby bringing acknowledgment or celebration to the actual state of their youthful existence. For the most part, however, our society is not the kind that affirms sexuality as something good and sacred; and as a result many adolescents feel ashamed of their naturally emerging sexuality (for shame is the experience of feeling oneself rejected in the mirror of the other, or what amounts to much the same thing, not being mirrored at all). This is all pretty well-known. I raise the matter, though, in order to contrast our own society's handling of sexuality with that of some traditional societies (and also because leaving it out of the account would be another form of nonrecognition). Turnbull writes that: "In other cultures, where each stage of life is seen as having its own contribution to make to the well-being of society, adolescence is no exception. Instead of individual curiosity in sexuality being treated as shameful, it is encouraged to flower into exuberance, and that individual exuberance in sexual potency is then transformed into joy with the realization of the individual's wider social significance as a life-giver."[219] The anthropology literature is full of descriptions of sexual play among children. As Eaton et al. note, "a free and playful attitude toward sexuality during childhood is our ancestral heritage and may be most compatible with optimal psychological development."[220] The comparative religion scholar Mircea Eliade further notes that "for the entire premodern world, sexuality too participates in the sacred." In pubertal rites of initiation the sacredness of sexuality is revealed, thus lending the sexual play of childhood a spiritual meaning.[221]

Initiation rites, indeed, have been a traditional response to the spiritual needs of the pubertal human, in which females and males, in their own ways, undergo transformative experiences and are introduced to the sacred teachings of their communities.[222] This is not to say that initiation rites in all times and places have been or are universally virtuous. The ritual mutilation of female genitals, for example—performed today on millions of girls and women around the world, particularly in African nations—is a hideous act of violence aimed at controlling the emotions and sexual behavior of women.[223] Many anthropological accounts, moreover, describe male initiations that are terrifying and bloody ordeals.[224] What I wish to emphasize, then, is only the *need* for adolescent rites, and the importance of finding/inventing ritual forms that genuinely meet this need within the context of our own time and place. Good rites are "spiritual levers" that help propel the maturational process.[225] Adolescents, in short, need to be taken through a "powerful, tightly structured gestation," that will "tutor their suffering and dreaming," and "guide their feelings and fidelity."[226] As Eliade notes, "the experience of ritual death and the revelation of the sacred . . . exhibits a dimension that is metacultural and transhistorical."[227] In my own terms, I would assert that our bodies spontaneously organize themselves for or expect spiritual initiation. As above, we may support such an assertion by witnessing our basic interest in them, including the pervasive "initiation hunger" within our own society (about which, more below). Eliade comments that ethnologists frequently remark on the "intense interest" with which novices listen to mythological traditions and take part in ceremonial life, or the avidness they show in pursuit of the significance hidden within the myths they are being introduced to. What also led Eliade to call rites of passage "an existential experience that is basic in the human condition" was his recognition that even when initiatory patterns "lose their ritual reality," as they did in the West during the middle ages, they nonetheless persist in the mode of literary motifs in eagerly consumed stories.[228]

It is not my intention to offer much detail on the topic of adolescent initiation rites, as there is much existing literature that already does so.[229] I will only stress a number of points important for my purposes. The first is that such initiation is crucial for the sociation of the individual. Initiates in primal societies go through a process of separation from their families, of ritual death or descent, only through which process are they reborn as members of the wider community, their social place consolidated and recognized in a ceremony that usually follows on their return. The form of rites vary widely from culture to culture, of course. What is common, however, is that they reveal to initiates "the sacredness of life and of the world," as it is conveyed to them, for example, in origin myths. On a vision quest the initiate may be visited by a tutelary spirit or discover new planes of existence through ecstatic experiences. As Eliade notes, indigenous peoples generally believe that to live is to share in the sacrality of the cosmos. It is only through this ritual second birth into the spiritual realm, therefore, that the initiate attains full social standing as a human being.

One of the valuable contributions made by Shepard to this topic was his insight into the important role played by the earlier stages of the life cycle in readying the adolescent to comprehend this sacred dimension of ultimate meanings. Hence, the adolescent:

> will not put his delight in the sky and the earth behind him as a childish and irrelevant thing. He will graduate not out of that world but into its significance. So, with the end of childhood, he begins a life-long study, a reciprocity with the natural world in which its depths are as endless as his own creative thought. He will not study it in order to transform its liveliness into mere objects that represent his ego, but as a poem, numinous and analogical, of human society.[230]

Each stage of life lays down the preunderstanding for grasping the next. In this case, myths "and spiritual and cosmological concepts are communicated by allusion to a [now] familiar natural world."[231] The result is a form of spirituality that is tied to or grounded in a more-than-human place, one that initiates have already learned to love and feel themselves a part of.[232]

It is at this stage of life, moreover, that we are ordered to gather the metaphorical nature of reality *as such;* to achieve a symbolic level of perception. The adolescent passage is thus also "a transition in the imaginative faculty from a literal to a figurative place, from familiar temporal reality to the dreamtime."[233]

> Beginning in adolescence and continuing throughout life . . . metaphor and symbol
> in poetry and song as well as all other arts and myth . . . result . . . in the intellectual
> realization that things have more than a face value. Guiding the young in this work is
> the cultus, with all of its exercises in tutorial, myth, ceremony, and test, traditionally
> employed to open doors into maturity. A rich, literal knowledge of animal life is
> fundamental to this process, generating a respect for the natural community as a
> higher language, as clues toward wisdom in the immense panoply of nonhuman life,
> to which mature adults will look for the terms in which to describe a cosmology.[234]

For myself, I am most able to experience the world in an explicitly symbolic way
when I am lucid dreaming, in which I am aware that I am dreaming while still in a
dream state. In the days following such dreams the taste of lucidity permeates my
waking life, such that my existence becomes more spacious and filled with a kind
of luminous glow. Every being I encounter is potentially rich in meaning, has
some important message, some secret link to my own life. I thus imagine a mature,
earth-based spiritual life as one in which one feels enveloped in a mysterious-yet-
familiar world; where time and space easily slip out of their Cartesian dimensions;
where a million little resonances keep one paying attention; and in which new
revelations continually reform one's sense of the possible. As many seekers today
still understand, a symbolic perception of the world lifts one out of one's Ego into
a larger cosmic drama in which nothing, including oneself, has that substantial
reality of the literal viewpoint. To undergo a symbolic death and rebirth, for
example, takes the sting out of one's literal death. As Eliade notes, it even gives it a
positive value, for one realizes that death is merely the end of a mode of being, a
stage in the transformation of all things. And as Erikson observed, "healthy
children will not fear life if their elders have integrity enough not to fear death."[235]

    Not initiation into a sacred adult cosmos, but all sorts of perversions of it are
what we in the modern era generally live out. For us, it is senseless hazings and
literal descents rather than elaborately symbolic ordeals ritually completed. "In
many tribal cultures," writes the men's work leader Michael Meade, "it was said
that if boys were not initiated into manhood, if they were not shaped by the skills
and love of elders, then they would destroy the culture."[236] Good initiation rites
are designed to creatively resolve the tension between youth and society in a
way that is meaningful and of benefit to all. In their absence, social pathology
blooms—a notion well-captured in the suggestion that overcrowded prisons are
"houses of failed initiation."[237] Writes Meade:

> underlying the surface structure of schools, fraternities, sororities, maternity groups,
> military organizations, street gangs, rap bands, crack houses, meditation centers and
> prisons lie the bones and sinews of initiatory rites and symbols. Whenever life gets
> stuck or reaches a dead end, where people are caught in rites of addiction, possessed
> by destructive images, compelled to violent acts or pulled apart by grief and loss, the

process of initiation presses to break through. The most important reason to study rites of passage may be to see in the events erupting in the streets and at the borders and crossroads of our post-historic era the archaic energies of life renewing itself.[238]

At the heart of much of our modern trouble, that is, the life force is still pushing toward the completion of the initatory gestalt. "Instead of ritual descent and emotional resurrection," however, it is often the case that "complete death occurs; actual corpses pile up."[239] We may speculate with great seriousness, then, about the tremendous potential value of finding our way back to or reappropriating rites consciously enacted.

The human life cycle does not of course end at the beginning of adulthood. I have concentrated on the earlier stages of life both because of their formative significance and on account of the space restrictions of this chapter. In brief, however, we may note that adults themselves need to be needed, gaining their satisfaction through guiding the next generation and undertaking projects that are of service to others. Under good conditions adults ripen with age, continuing to learn lessons from a world still experienced as a constantly novel presence. They may then arrive at old age not as crippled and unwise adolescents, but as "memory banks, keepers of the lore and genealogy, healers, accumulators of useful social lessons (especially childrearing and the resolution of disagreement)" and tutors in ceremonial matters.[240] In their own way, by their proximity to death (and so to the spirit world), the old may also revitalize society, especially through their special connection to the young. A satisfying life, then, sees our basic desires met. "As the needs of adults in their prime to initiate and carry through their projects become fulfilled and age begins to reduce physical powers, desires are for seeing one's loved ones succeed, for peace, for less variety in experiences, to feel that things are moving through the cycle of life with less help from oneself, and ultimately, with no help, as the last of life's succession of desires is fulfilled and is replaced by none but the wish to rest, to know no more, to cease."[241] As Nietzsche said: "all that is ripe . . . wants to die."[242]

Despite the brevity of my presentation here, I hope to have demonstrated (or at least raised the possibility) that the human life process contains a great deal of underlying, naturally ordered demand; that there is much inherent structure to our human lives, and that this sets limits on us or gives us our place to be. My aim, in any event, has been to lay out a rough ground against which to contrast, and so better understand, the current situation within our own society. In the next chapter, it is to this needful situation that I more focally bring my naturalistic and experiential framework, in an effort to articulate the practical and critical tasks it implies.

6

MAKING SENSE OF SUFFERING IN A TECHNOLOGICAL WORLD

Technological Progress: The (Paved) Road to Happiness?

Man can survive *in appallingly anti-continuum conditions [those contrary to his transhistorical expectations] but his well-being, his joy, his fulfillment as a whole human being, can be lost. . . . the life force, in its ceaseless tending toward repair of damage and completion of the developmental phases, among its instruments employs anxiety, pain, and an array of other ways of signaling that things are wrong. Unhappiness in all its forms is the result.*

—Jean Liedloff[1]

In complicated times it is all the more helpful to have simple ideas. Like other ecological thinkers, my interest lies quite simply with the flourishing of all life—with a condition we might call *happiness*. The Buddhists say "may all beings be happy," which I hear as "may all beings thrive according to their own natures." In the previous three chapters I presented an interpretation of our own world-bound nature and of what the satisfactory unfolding of a human life generally entails. I also worked from the assumption, definitive of Buddhism, that if we are to find real happiness we have to know something about the basis of our suffering. Today, moreover (unlike in the Buddha's time), this means making sense of our suffering in a technological world. For this final chapter, then, I wish to more focally consider this general task to which my naturalistic and experiential approach points. I begin in the present section by examining the idea that currently rules over our society's thinking about what will make us happy, namely, technological progress. Norman O. Brown remarks that what humankind "is doing seems to be making itself more unhappy and calling that unhappiness progress."[2] Indeed, if the idea of technological progress is backward, as many argue, then I must make it the main butt of my own critical thought. The very process—technological progress—that is meant to enhance our lives will be seen in fact to betray "an impatience and even disdain for life, a contempt and defiance of our bodily, that is mortal, earthly existence."[3]

Not only the Buddha, but the likes of Aristotle, Francis Bacon, Marx, Freud, and the advertising industry all agree that the goal of life is happiness. This only makes sense, for we all want a good life, want to feel satisfied.[4] Indeed, one of Freud's central findings was that the "whole world may be against it, but still man holds fast to the deep-rooted, passionate striving for a positive fulfillment of happiness."[5] Where these various sources differ is over the route toward this happiness, and on the prospect of getting there. These days, it is primarily the advertisers who get listened to, for it is generally assumed that our happiness has something to do with technologically delivered commodity wealth, that "the good life is the goods life."[6] We need to note at this point, therefore, the close connection between economic and technological principles. A technologized reality, in other words, is an economized reality. To use Marxist terms, technological progress is of the essence of the capitalist mode of production,[7] is of a piece with its development. Associated with technology, then, is the steady concentration of wealth in the hands of the ruling class, the (in my terms) double violation of nature, the perpetual expansion and intensification of the capitalist marketplace, and in general, the relentless imposition of capitalist social relations. What I say about technology in this chapter thus carries on from my remarks at the end of chapter three on the economization of reality. Given that the promise of technological progress enjoys so much economic power and such a strong hold on the popular imagination, it will serve us, next, to consider the history of this promise.

In his book *Progress Without People,* David Noble[8] traces this history to an ideological transformation that occurred among monks in ninth-century Europe. It was at this time, observes Noble, that the "useful arts"—cloth-making, agriculture, weaponry and fortification, animal husbandry, mathematics, sculpture, and so on—were drawn into the Christian mythology of redemption. These arts, previously kept well out of the realm of religion and transcendence, suddenly took on a new significance, now being regarded as a vehicle for the salvation of "man" (women being excluded from the project of redemption), that is, for the restoration of his lost perfection and prelapsarian powers. What was to become modern technology thus had a religious and a masculine meaning right from the start, emerging as both a historical and salvationary force in the same stroke. It was not until the scientific revolution, however, that the "religion of technology" was brought "from the margins of Western history to centre stage, where it has remained."[9] Francis Bacon, in particular, gave bold definition to the masculine millennial project of modern technology. Human suffering, he said, was a needless scandal. Through the elevation and improvement of the "mechanical arts," directed toward the torture, inquisition, and subjugation of a female nature, it would be possible, he argued, to relieve "the inconveniences of man's estate"[10] and to finally erase man's sins by returning to him his divinelike powers. This religious theme was then carried into the industrial revolution of the nineteenth century, in which engineers were viewed as the "priests" of a new epoch, and in which the project begun in the ninth century was given its new name under industrial capital: "technology." At this time, worker opposition arose in Britain to the way that machines were being used by capitalists in creating a system of social domination that involved deskilling, wage slavery, and the destruction of communities. It was then, suggests Noble, that "middle-class apologists and optimistic economists" invented the idea of *inevitable* technological progress (as well as that of the virtue of competition) as a way to induce paralysis in this "Luddite" opposition to technology, and to prevent its recurrence. "Society" was similarly "discovered" as an entity that existed apart from the people who comprised it, having its own autonomous, "natural" laws, operating on the "hard logic of the market and the machine." In short, social progress and technological progress were equated and the system of capital promoted as an automatic process for delivering human happiness, "so long as people allowed it to follow its natural course."[11]

Of particular note is Noble's argument that the doctrine of technological progress derives its ideological strength from its abstract and future-oriented character, that is, from the manner in which it deflects attention away from the concrete and present moment. In other words, a high-altitude narrative about progress is used to explain away obvious human, social, and ecological losses as necessary costs along the way to a better future—those who suffer are enjoined simply to "look for future deliverance." Felt experience thus becomes largely irrelevant as the present tense is progressively replaced by fatalism and futurism, and as fantasies about technological development replace our contact with actual reality. This makes for a "proudly irrational framework," wherein we are told that we can't stand in the way of progress, even if it kills us, so sacrosanct and inevitable is it.

In today's secular society, technophiles now use an openly religious vocabulary. "We are as gods," some of them say, speaking (especially in magazines such as *Wired*) of the powers made available to them by the "new" technologies. "In space exploration, they are joining the angels; in artificial reproduction they are regaining Adam's male-only procreative powers; in artificial intelligence, they are overcoming the curse and the mortal bondage of the body; in genetic engineering, they are becoming once again God's partner in creation; in cyberspace they are recovering their rightful dominion over the universe, omniscient and omnipresent."[12] Technosalvationism, in sum, is the "shared delusion" of our age.

In contrast to the optimism of today's techno-boosters, it is helpful to consider the pessimism of Freud, who said that between happiness and unhappiness, the latter "is much less difficult to experience."[13] According to Freud, the three sources of human suffering are "the superior powers of nature" ("She destroys us—coldly, cruelly, relentlessly, as it seems to us"[14]), "the feebleness of our own bodies," and conflicts within human society.[15] Given this situation, he believed the best thing a person can do is become "a member of the human community, and, with the help of a technique guided by science, [go] over to the attack against nature, subjecting her to the human will"—even if humans shall "never completely master nature," including our bodies. Social problems, too (the third source of suffering), may be traced to "a piece of unconquerable nature," namely, our own hostile human nature which causes us to battle one another. We must therefore include *ourselves* in the attack on nature; that is, "every civilization must be built up on the coercion and renunciation of instinct."[16] Hence, the "principle task of civilization, its actual *raison d'être,* is to defend us against nature,"[17] both outside and in. With such views, Freud hopelessly dichotomized nature and culture, making our own organismic intentions the forces against which we must defend ourselves, and aligning himself with the idea of progress. Having made a necessity out of dissatisfaction, he concluded that the "programme of becoming happy . . . cannot be fulfilled." Rather, in exchange for the "security" offered by civilization, we pay the price of "a loss of happiness through the heightening of the sense of guilt."[18] What is admirable about Freud is his blunt acknowledgment that the technological domination of nature, even if necessary, brings no joy. In this respect, his vision is more honest than that of the optimists, for he did at least witness what was later to be called the "revolt of nature."

The revolt of nature is an aspect of what, in chapter three, I called the double violation of nature, and is a simple though compelling notion for refuting the promise of technological happiness. It was first named as such by Max Horkheimer, who saw civilization as a project of putting down or managing a nature increasingly in revolt, a revolt that is reaching "its peak in this era."[19] It is an easy enough notion to grasp. We experience the revolt of our own nature as our body's painful rebellion against repressing social and cultural conditions. I spoke in the previous chapter about the revolt of adolescent nature, and in the discussion above about the revolt of Luddites. Examples are endless. Much of the experience of depression that is widespread within Western culture can, for instance, also be read as a revolt of nature, our bodies saying "no" to the crushing demands and abuses of modern life. The revolt of nonhuman nature, on the other hand, manifests as mutating bacteria, mudslides, droughts, and the ecological crisis in general.[20] "As more of nature is domesticated and controlled, it becomes more compressed and dangerous. In the [atom] bomb, all the former wildness is concentrated . . . , pushed to an explosive end in the very heart of minerals themselves."[21] As William Leiss writes: "A vicious circle results, imprisoning science and technology in a fateful dialectic of increasing mastery and increasing conflict. The attractive promises of mastery over nature—social peace and material abundance for all—remain unfulfilled."[22] Any open recognition of the revolt of nature would spell disaster for the existing social order, as this would amount to an admission that technological progress is not the path to a heavenly future it is promised to be, but an ideology for safeguarding a vicious status-quo. The revolt of nature must therefore be mystified, as is done in at least two general ways.

The first is by manipulating or taking advantage of it. As Horkheimer argued, the "prevailing forces of civilization" use the revolt of nature "as a means to perpetuate the very conditions by which it is stirred up and against which it is directed."[23] The corporate world, in particular, has learned with a vengeance how to manipulate the revolt of nature. To take an obvious example, it profits from the alienation and interpersonal distance engendered by capitalist social relations by selling us the telephones we need in order to "reach out and touch somebody." Phones and other such commodities then "become necessary, a sign of progress, a proof of prestige for those who 'own' them."[24] Or the pharmaceutical companies sell us the antidepressants that gets us back to work. Peter Breggin says of psychiatry's appropriation of suffering: "The mental health professions, led by psychiatry, have rushed into the void left by the default of the family, the schools, the society, and the government. . . . By diagnosing, drugging, and hospitalizing children, psychiatry enforces the worst attitudes toward children in our culture today and exonerates those adult institutions that need reform."[25] As for the ecological crisis, the cooption of the environmental movement by the corporate sphere—recently dubbed "greenwashing"—immediately comes to mind. "Corporate environmentalism" is mostly a public relations exercise that portrays large corporations, such as car companies, as friends of "the environment" and that tends to redefine social-ecological problems in purely technical terms.[26] In an article that seeks to debunk the notion of "green capitalism," furthermore, Joel Kovel notes: "So seamless is capital's current moment of triumph, and so absent any appreciation that there might be alternatives to it, that the thought of whether its stewardship of the earth will *necessarily* bring about ecological catastrophe . . . scarcely enters anybody's consciousness."[27] Whenever "jobs" are pitted against "the environment," finally, the chance is missed to see the link between the revolt of human nature and that of nonhuman nature.

A second way the revolt of nature is controlled is by means of what has been called "mental health" oppression,[28] which is a blanket social force for the repression of it. An important ecopsychological point is that psychoanalysis was born only when the revolt of nature within the individual could no longer be ignored. Freud claimed that history itself has the character of an ever-increasing neurosis.[29] As civilization advances, our desires are frustrated more and more, not only by external pressures, but by our own internalized social authority, the superego. The result is massive psychic derangement. What Kovel calls "the mental health industry" is, then, the bureaucracy that has evolved for managing this crippled desire.[30] "Mental health" oppression refers to all the ways we are made afraid of seeming or actually becoming "crazy" and so entering this "mental health" system. To behave contrary to the rigidly prescribed patterns that keep the social machinery running is to risk being called "nuts" or being institutionalized for "losing control" of oneself. The effect is to keep our spontaneity in check and our problems all "inside." It is shameful[31] to be "weird" or different from the norm. There is an unwritten law, furthermore, which says that strong emotions, particularly distressful ones, should not be expressed; to be emotional is to be "weak," "hysterical," or "out of control."[32] The control of emotion, by contrast, is associated with people in positions of higher status and power, such as corporation heads (or psychiatrists). What is diagnosed as madness, moreover, is often more truthfully an attempt at healing, misperceived because of its high emotionality and seemingly bizarre nature.[33] Drawing on the work of Aihwa Ong, Ray Rogers has discussed the phenomenon of Malay factory women experiencing *hantu* spirit possessions, which results in epidemics of fits and "fugue states," as they move from a peasant culture to the culture of industrial factories. As Rogers observes, "those who operate the factories characterize these fits in terms of hysteria, thereby pathologizing and individualizing these conditions, and denying them their social significance."[34] Indeed, it is a tragedy that so many who refuse to "behave," and who protest their oppression in a passionate way, must live in fear of being called "nuts" or even being sent off to the hospital.[35] Eco-activists face a specific version of this fear. For as Noble notes, the ideology of technological progress is used to "define the bounds of sanity, of respectable discourse, of reasonable behaviour."[36] He comments, in this respect, that the relative merits of Luddism were not debated; rather, Luddites were "condemned as dangerous and demented." Those who care about spotted owls and grizzly bears, meanwhile, are all still liable to being called eco-nuts, eco-freaks, wackos, flakes, misanthropes, and other terms of mental dismissal.

To put it plainly, then, the progress of technology leads not to the fulfillment of our nature but to a natural rebellion that the ruling powers of our society must constantly turn to advantage, administer, or out-maneuver. With this argument I have aimed in this short opening section to introduce a naturalistic line of thought for unmasking the ideology of salvation through technology. Recalling the points I made in the previous chapter, I suggest that a naturalistic approach nakedly reveals the absurdity of believing that human happiness could ever be gained through the "progressive" immiseration of the rest of the natural world. (What, for example, becomes of our need to belong to and serve the natural world when our dominant ideology tells us that the natural world belongs to and is meant to serve *us?*) As Albert Borgmann has argued, the nature-dominating technological agenda nonetheless exploits our desire for happiness, promising us exactly what we most want even as it fails to deliver it. In the next section my task is to bring this criticism that much further home by bracketing this promise and taking a look at what kind of lives we actually live under technology, how we actually *experience* it. My goal is to thoroughly demonstrate the deep dissatisfaction and experiential impoverishment, essential to the functioning of capitalism, that betrays the promise of technology as a lie.[37] This sets the stage for the third section, in which I take up that ever-pressing question, What is to be done? Borrowing from Borgmann and others, I suggest that what a naturalistic and experiential approach leads to, broadly speaking, are practices that work with the life force in deliberately *countering* the pattern of technology. I want it to be very clear that such counterpractice does not involve getting rid of technology, but rather overcoming its current resourcist ontology and putting it back where it belongs: in the artful service of life. I also want to reemphasize my belief that it is the practical work of ecopsychology that will form the most fruitful basis for its theorizing. The most constructive theory will emerge, in other words, as we change ourselves in practice and as we develop concrete interventions capable of opening up new insights and avenues of understanding. To counter modern technology means refusing to live for an abstract future, and so recovering our lives in the concrete present. To make contact with present reality, however, is also to confront the painful feelings that are masked or numbed-out by our technological mode of living. In the final section, which concludes this book, I therefore address what I feel is an important aspect of this work: learning to collectively bear, find meaning in, and move through the suffering we inevitably uncover in the course of counterpractice.

Suffering Under Technology

We are as highly developed in psychopathology as in technology.
—Jules Henry[38]

Although we can no doubt develop a psychology that identifies our need for contact with wildlife, for rites of passage, and so on, the recognition of needs by psychologists has never been a guarantee that they will be met. For our society is not structured to care for life, to attend carefully to relationships and honor the growth or sacred unfolding of things. To be "successful" in today's society, one does not serve nature but rather the expansion of capital.[39] It is for this reason that ecopsychology will lack the necessary teeth to have much influence unless it is accompanied by critical thought or social analysis. Drawing on the concepts and traditions of my own naturalistic and experiential approach, I am here taking technology as the theme of my criticism. My basic critical strategy is a familiar one, namely, to frankly expose the suffering that is veiled by a reigning ideology and to generate in the reader some antipathy for this situation.[40] More exactly, I am aiming toward a sort of critical theory that takes a nonanthropocentric vision of happiness as its starting point (sketched out in the previous two chapters) and rejects the ideology of technological progress (something that Marx, for one, did not do). The initial challenge, however, is to find a pattern in our experience of technology that can then be countered in practice.

As a way to enter into this challenge, I begin with Fredric Jameson's remark that we are:

at the moment of a radical eclipse of Nature itself: Heidegger's 'field path' is after all irredeemably and irrevocably destroyed by late capital, by the green revolution, by neocolonialism and the megapopolis [*sic*], which runs its superhighways over the older fields and vacant lots, and turns Heidegger's 'house of being' into condominiums, if not the most miserable unheated, rat infested tenement buildings. The *other* of our society is in that sense no longer Nature at all.[41]

Jameson struggles to name what is now the "other" of our society, but claims that it may vaguely be conceived as the global network of power and control that comprises the world economic and social system of late capitalism—as it is embodied in technology. In his words, "technology may well serve as an adequate shorthand to designate that enormous properly human and anti-natural power of dead human labour stored up in our machinery, . . . which turns back on and against us in unrecognizable forms and seems to constitute the massive dystopian horizon of our collective as well as individual praxis." The problem presented here by Jameson is that we are *underdistanced* from the forces of technology and capital, and so that we lack free ground on which to get our critical footings.[42] Drawing on the work of Heidegger, Borgmann, and others, however, I suggest below that there is a specific pattern within the dynamics of technology, the discernment of which does help provide some of the necessary distance to win a degree of liberation from it. What I stress, then, is the vast difference between, on the one hand, a life patterned to the needs of human and nonhuman nature, to the rhythms of the life cycle, the land, the passage of the seasons, and, on the other hand, a life patterned to the needs of a technological society, to the rhythms of the market and machine. Because technology patterns or structures our lives it is no mere neutral set of instruments, as some like to claim. Rather, it determines—to the extent that we agree to live it—the sense, form, and telos of our existence. To recognize a pattern in technology is therefore to start making sense of it, seeing through it, and being more aware of the great disjunction between the promise of technological progress and the reality of our lived experience.

The Pattern of Technology. The former premier of Quebec, Robert Bourassa, said that "Quebec is a vast hydroelectric plant in the bud, and every day millions of potential kilowatt-hours flow downhill and out to sea. What a waste."[43] Heidegger claimed that the essence of our late modern epoch lies exactly in this technological mode of understanding. "Nature becomes a gigantic gasoline station, an energy source for modern technology and industry."[44] Or: "the earth now reveals itself as a coal mining district, the soil as a mineral deposit."[45] In other words, nature has for us become what Heidegger called a "standing reserve," in which all beings are leveled down to just so much extractable, transformable, exchangeable, transportable, raw material. Notice how in the following passage, in which Bill McKibben quotes a biotechnology spokesperson, animals are not so much objectified as "resource-ified."

Brian Stableford . . . promises that the "battery chickens" of the future, "whether they are being used to produce eggs or meat," will look very different from the birds of the moment. In fact the accompanying illustrations shows them looking like— well, hunks of flesh. This is because thanks to biotechnology, we might design chickens without the unnecessary heads, wings, and tails.[46]

"Before civilization," says Shepard, and certainly before biotechnology, "animals were seen as belonging to their own nation and to be the bearers of messages and gifts of meat from a sacred domain."[47] An initial point toward naming the pattern of technology, then, is that it involves more than just the addition of tools to our kit, but a profound alteration in how we perceive the natural world. Whereas a natural scientific mode of relating to nature reveals entities as brute objects, a technological mode degrades the being of things even further by revealing them as mere fodder for the megamachine. As Carol Bigwood notes, moreover, this shift in understanding constitutes a historical reversal, for (recalling the early Greek terms) techne "is no longer phusical but phusis in our modern age is technical."[48]

The reversal of which Bigwood speaks is that *from* "technology" understood as the human art of belonging to, participating in, or serving nature *to* nature understood as the servant of technology, as that which is dominated, controlled, formed, and put into order by humans. As Bacon put it, nature is "forced out of her natural state and squeezed and molded."[49] Biotechnologists, for example, aim to take over the original birthing powers of nature, to turn the genesis of life into a kind of purely human technology. The attempt, in general, to replace the creative powers of nature by those of a technology serving only human ends is increasingly converting the bio-sphere into a techno-sphere. As a mode of revealing, then, technology does not allow beings to spontaneously show themselves in accord with their own internal demands, their own rhythms of emerging and passing away, but rather forces or "challenges" them into being in a way utterly contrary to their essential natures. "The earth itself can show itself only as the object of assault. . . . Nature appears everywhere as the object of technology."[50] Technology, that is, is no longer a calling forth, a vocation, but a *provocation* of the earth.[51] As an exercise of ruthless power, however, this project is doomed. For as Heidegger remarked, in driving the earth "beyond the natural sphere of its possibility,"[52] by exceeding its limits, technology "devastates" or "exhausts" the earth. When it violently insists that the earth make itself wholly available and extractable, the technological mode does not let the earth rest or withdraw back into itself, but robs it of its nourishing mystery, burns it out. Precisely these words may also be used in reference to human beings, who within a technological frame are understood as "human resources," or as "mere disposable factors of production and accumulation,"[53] the result of which is the devastation and exhaustion of our humanity.

Having introduced the idea that technology currently signifies our whole manner of relating to and unconcealing reality, we may now consider what Albert

Borgmann means by "the pattern of technology." In formulating this pattern, Borgmann added to Heidegger's views the notion that resources are themselves refined into or disclosed as technological *devices*. A device, in turn, divides internally between a *machinery* aspect and a *commodity* aspect,[54] the latter of which is produced by the machinery. Borgmann uses the notion of a device very broadly. He claims, for example, that under this device paradigm an "animal is seen as a machine that produces so much meat. Whichever of its functions fails to serve that purpose is indifferent or bothersome."[55] (Notice how this sheds light on the passage above about headless chickens.) Similarly, at "pop concerts, reality is torn apart into a gigantic, intricate staging machinery and an alluring, hypercharged commodity."[56] What strikes me as most significant about this division of reality is that it acts to progressively eliminate or impoverish our world-relations. We may illustrate this point by observing the disappearance of world-relations which follows on the introduction of a new device—a central heating system, for example.[57]

Consider that prior to central heating many households relied on a woodburning stove, and that this stove was (and for some, still is) the focus for a world of bodily and social engagements. Trees in the forest had to be felled; and logs sawed, split, and stacked. This all had to be done, moreover, with an eye to the weather and the turning of the seasons. The lighting of the stove would mark the morning and fill the air with the smell of wood smoke. In the evenings, finally, people might gather around the stove to stay warm, tell stories, or play music. The point of this example (which I have obviously presented in a much-abbreviated fashion) is not to romanticize country living. It is simply to notice how our world-relations are altered by devices. The device in this case is a central heating system, which is a machinery for providing the single commodity of heat. In short, the furnace, gas lines, and fuel industry take over the web of living relations that formerly made up the wood-stove's world, leaving the householder only to adjust the thermostat and pay the bills.

Speaking more generally, what I want to suggest is that in the course of replacing our world-relations by machinery, whole regions of existence just drop out or find no symbolic satisfaction. As Borgmann notes, rather than "the fullbodied exercise of skill, gained through discipline and renewed through intimate commerce with the world . . . our contact with reality has been attenuated to the pushing of buttons and the turning of handles."[58] Part of the pattern of technology is for the machinery to become increasingly concealed, the perfect device being something like a panel of knobs and a screen, with an elaborate machinery hidden behind it. While, as I argued in the previous chapter, the natural unfolding of a human life involves making more and more of the world familiar and meaningful, the machinery of devices is designed precisely to be *unfamiliar*. To the extent that it is hidden, this machinery is simply *not experienced,* and to the extent that it takes over our living relationships, it therefore makes the satisfaction of our cosmological urge an impossibility. The pattern of replacing vital relations with machinery, that is, frustrates our world-making needs and so desiccates our reality. What remains of our lives, according to Borgmann, are the two principle activities that correspond to a reality now split between machinery and commodities: labor and leisure. Labor—a degraded form of "work"—consists of the construction, maintenance, and operation of the machinery, while leisure consists of the consumption or uptake of the commodities produced by it, wherein the real happiness is meant to be had. The pattern of technology, then, refers to the progressive replacement and/or substitution of our world-relations by, in labor, slim relations with an ever-more hidden and unfamiliar machinery and, in leisure, shallow relations with ever-more pervasive commodities—the overall effect of which is to dissolve the meaningful fabric of our lives. As notes Borgmann, "our once profound and manifold engagement with the world is reduced to narrow points of contact in labor and consumption."[59] I do not suggest that this pattern is the only way to understand our society, as there are many aspects of our social arrangements that it does not especially bring out.[60] What is fruitful about it, however, is that it helps tie together both technological and economic themes.[61] Our increasingly thin and meaningless laboring at the machinery and equally thin and meaningless consumption of commodities do not make us happy, for they do not offer us the kind of deep and wide contact with others that our bodies inherently demand. They are, however, the essential activities of a capitalist society, for they do create profits.

Necessary Suffering. Considered as a social system hostile to life capitalism is not simply disinterested in meeting our transhistorical needs. Rather, it has a real interest in actually fostering suffering, that is, an active opposition to genuine happiness is intrinsic to it. Kovel's words are to the point: "Were people either happy or clear about what they wanted, then capital's ceaseless expansion would be endangered."[62] Using the pattern of technology as my scheme, it is to this *necessitating* of dissatisfaction that I wish to turn next.

Part of the promise of technology is that it will alleviate our suffering by relieving us from toil. It would be ungrateful, to be sure, not to admit that certain instruments bring great benefits. Nonetheless, many of our burdens—the Baconian "inconveniences of man's estate"—are the inescapable demands placed on us by our own nature and by the natural others who address us. To be relieved of these burdens is, then, to be relieved of life itself. As Medard Boss writes, when we are disburdened "what is left is not just something negative, a nonburden, but the end of a life-giving engagement. . . . If a human being is deprived of such engagement, totally unburdened, he is robbed of the possibility of continuing to [exist] as a human being."[63] I believe this point goes very far, extending into many areas of social and cultural life that I will not pursue here (including the deskilling,[64] alienating, and unemploying of the labor-force, and the general *over*burdening of women with emotional duties that compensate for the dehumanizing effects of capitalist relations). What I want to suggest is that within an economized reality we are relieved of life exactly so that weakened or less satisfying versions of it can then be sold back to us for profit.[65] Take, for instance, the supermarket. It is a general human need to be skillfully engaged in the gathering/hunting, preparing, and presenting of food.[66] When this need is well-met, a meal is more likely to be a "ritual of gathering and remembrance, a communion in which the offering and the eating of food bonds us together into a community and installs us within the circle of life and its seasons."[67] A frozen dinner from the supermarket can be eaten after only six minutes in the microwave oven. Yet the consuming of such a disburdening and inconsequential commodity (perhaps in front of the TV set) hardly elicits our thanks; nor does it call forth a sense of our sacred membership within the community of all earthly beings, some of whose bodies we eat.

This returns us to that central feature of capitalist reality: commodity fetishism. The aspect of commodity fetishism that is important to consider here is that it involves an active mystification of our needing.[68] It is as if all our needs were such that they could be satisfied *only* by commodities; as if every felt intention pointed to a bottle of Pepsi or a jet ski. Unsure about our genuine needs, we interpret them according to what is both available and promoted to us for the meeting of them. In order to maintain this state of affairs, the economic order must then guard against our becoming aware of needs lying outside the field of commodity consumption: "Filtered through layers of commodities, the natural and human environment is progressively simplified, more smoothly ordered; the abrasive particles which might disrupt the flow of everyday normal experience— which might stir modes of feeling not dependent on the acquisition of [goods]— are trapped and removed."[69] Thus, for example, the tourist machinery serves up the natural world in commodity form, as scenery viewed through the windows of a tour bus, accompanied by postcards, travel guides, mass-made mementos, and so on. With such a thin experience, something like ecological consciousness is not likely to arise. Likewise, people must be convinced that the meeting of their nonmaterial needs—as for love, security, privacy, freedom, and so forth—are all bound to the purchase of commodities.[70] Our freedom, for instance, is supposedly realized when we are in a position to choose among a wide range of commodities. The Lotto 6/49 television ad asks us to "Imagine the Freedom" and then right away feeds us images of people recreating with the expensive toys they have bought with their lottery winnings. Finally, it is not only that our "needs" must be met by commodities, but also that they must *expand* so as to keep up with the expansion in the production of commodities themselves.[71] One way this is done is through the breaking down of existing needs into ever-more finely disconnected and numerous part-needs. Our lives then become an endless series of point to point correspondences between increasingly discrete needs and commodities. Thus do we purchase a plethora of bathroom products to meet a vast array of grooming needs—all of which have become components of our need for interpersonal respect, which has itself become a kind of "scarce resource that can only be appropriated through a fortunate selection and combination of the newest items in the marketplace."[72] Judged on the basis of our clothes, possessions, and the way we "sell" ourselves to one another, even we become just "another commodity offered up for consumption on the open market."[73]

Note that a dominant general mode of contact in our society is now *consumption*. The universal, unburdened consumption of commodities is in fact the fulfillment of the promise of technology.[74] Some portion of the goods and services we purchase do of course offer real satisfactions.[75] The smell of an old cotton sleeping bag reminds me of just how much joy and contentment I truly have experienced. I reserve the term *consumption,* therefore, for the process of using "up an isolated entity without preparation, resonance, and consequence."[76] It is a style of interaction which, to greater or lesser extents, has the character of an addiction, wherein any stirring of felt need or bodily tension leads straight away to the intake or enactment of the "drug" to which we are fixated. Consumption, accordingly, is a mode of experience that amounts mostly to tension relief, and not to any restructuring of the ground of our existence or carrying forward of our lives. It follows the same basic pattern of fleeting satisfaction over and over again. When we consume we do not unfold or expand our lives or deepen our understanding of the cosmos. To the extent that a commodity is disposable, moreover, we may well wonder about the depth of contact, or life-transforming meaning, it could ever offer to us. Knowing all this, it is all the more appalling to recall the words of the retailing analyst Victor Leblow, spoken following the Second World War:

> Our enormously productive economy . . . demands that we make consumption our way of life, that we convert the buying and using of goods into rituals, that we seek our spiritual satisfaction, our ego satisfaction, in consumption. . . . We need things consumed, burned up, worn out, replaced, and discarded at an ever increasing rate.[77]

Here is a naked admission that the ethical duty to consume was dictated not by any primary interest in happiness, in the demands of nature, but by the need to maintain the capitalist way of being at a certain phase in its historical development. Indeed, the truth of the matter is closer still to the lines suggested by Kovel.

> Monopoly capital, perpetually assaulted by the contradictions stemming from over-production, wants nothing more than a society of [people] not so dysfunctional that they cannot work or too sick to consume steadily, yet never satisfied either. The sugar with which capitalist industry loads its products is, to be sure, an obvious ruse to induce a chronic state of unsatisfaction. However, it would never matter in slightest unless it were offered to a sensibility that is bound to remain unsatisfied, one that will move on to new objects, to more commodities under the guise of food.[78]

In other words: "Capitalism works by not working."[79]

For more insight into this capitalist business of success by failure, we need only look to basic economic theory, where it is rationalized. More specifically, what we find in the first chapter of those introductory economics text books are *ideas about nature*. Human nature, first of all, is characterized by *unlimited want*. It is of our essence, that is, to be in a perpetual state of insatiable, limitlessly escalating, commodity-seeking desire. If this be our nature, goes the argument, then the social and economic system most "naturally" suited to it is capitalism. By a peculiar twist of logic, when we technologically ravage nature in an attempt to meet our limitless wants we are in fact being faithful to our own nature.[80] I have earlier stressed the importance of debating our symbolizations of nature, on the view that there are always better or worse interpretations. Here, we see that economists legitimate a violent economic order by relying on a bogus and unexamined theory of human nature. As Leiss notes, human nature is identified with "a state of radical, irreducible 'want,' 'lack,' or 'deficiency.'"[81] What is evident to me is that these are precisely the terms that describe the state of *shame*. Neoclassical economic theories build into their view of human nature a sense of ever-increasing need, and so of ever-increasing lack.[82] The reason they must do so is straightforward enough: capitalists profit by selling commodities; to sell commodities we must "need" them; hence, the system of capital is motivated to keep us "needy"—empty, hollow, and ashamed. In other words, by organizing society such that we can find little real nutrition for our deepest organismic hungers, our economic system *creates* the insatiability that economists then interpret as the essential human condition. Imagine, instead, if the first page of all economics text books were revised to say that human nature consists of praising and giving thanks for creation, of singing and dancing the cosmos, and of finding spiritual fulfillment through collectively caring for life and dwelling within our earthly limits. All the pages that followed would then have to drastically change. As is, by defining economics as "the study of the use of scarce resources to satisfy unlimited human wants," these texts set nature up as merely that from which scant resources must be wrested in order to supply the "upward spiral of production and consumption" on which rides an insatiable humanity.

Another way of criticizing our economic theories is to say that they enshrine and contribute to the inflation of Ego, the nature-dominating form of self, and so normalize a state of spiritual emptiness. This reveals capital as a sort of anti-spiritual force or as "a kind of flowering of Egoic being."[83] What results, however, is not the extinction of our spiritual needs, but the emergence of certain obsessions within our secular society that amount to painful attempts to satisfy the relentless spiritual impulse. Rather than witness this impulse, the corporate world invests in the delusions and cravings born of its frustration. In order to better get at this point, I wish to briefly look at four spiritually based delusional tendencies within our society, as identified by David Loy. The spiritual task, as considered here, is to find a way to resolve the anxiety of separation, wherein we feel the cosmic gap as a dread of annihilation and as a feeling that there is something wrong with us, that we are not real, that we are not enough, that we are *lacking*. One delusory route toward "being somebody," or overcoming our spiritual lack, is the quest for *fame*. When reality becomes equated with the glamorous world of celebrity, sold to us through every pore of the mass media, "to be unknown is literally to be nothing."[84] We fantasize, therefore, that fame will bring us the adoration and recognition we need to overcome our shame and unreality (remember the song: *Fame!*). A second delusory attempt at resolution is *romantic love*. In this case, we see our love partners only in the light of how they might fill in our own lack, might complete us, save us, make us whole, take us off to paradise.[85] Such fantasies make for hefty sales of pulp romance novels, soap operas, and pop music, but certainly not for the attainment of spirit. The third trend identified by Loy is what he calls the *money complex*. Here, we desire money as a means to happiness, and then make the acquisition of money a religious end in itself, even while doing so may make us miserable. Finally, the very idea of *technological progress* also bears a strong spiritual undercurrent, as I discussed in the opening section. The technological enterprise, says Loy, is "our effort to create the ultimate security, by transforming the entire world into our own ground."[86] In this event, the whole earth will testify to our reality. The idea of progress is the projection of a "lack-free time somewhere in the future" when the technological task has finally been completed, when we are saved. As Diamond has suggested, the idea of progress simply does not arise within "primitive" culture, for it was born precisely of the disequilibrium within the civilized world. For primal peoples progress "is a reality of personal growth, of progress *through* society, not *of* society."[87] Only a chronically nonsatisfied people are driven to fantasize about future fulfilment. And only a death-denying people are obsessed with using their technology for building immortality projects such as banking towers. The idea of progress is thus founded less on the aim of going *to* somewhere than on fleeing *from* "our own lack-shadow." As an effort to take over the world, in fact, technology "is a meaning-system without any ultimate meaning, because lacking any vision of cloture [*sic*] between humankind and cosmos."[88] It is poor food, in other words, for our cosmological hungers.

The Anticulture. Within a naturalistic framework, culture is viewed as a cultivating. From this perspective, our own technological culture is—in the main—an anticulture.[89] That is, it does not provide good symbolic forms (practices, beliefs, stories, etc.) for meeting the expectations of our own unfolding nature nor for keeping the balance with the more-that-human world. I hesitate to say much more on this point, feeling that I have already made it in a number of places. Given the centrality of the nature-culture interaction to my arguments, however, I wish to add a few more brief thoughts.

First of all, much of our shared symbolic life consists of the outpourings of what Horkheimer and Theodor Adorno called the "culture industry." Mass culture—what we would today call the whole sphere of entertainment, news, advertising, tourism, electronic reality, and "information" in general—was in their view a mechanically produced stream of commodious amusements, unabashedly calculated to be consumed rather than to offer any sort of "meaningful explanation of life."[90] Kovel has also taken up this criticism, drawing particular attention to the ideological function of mass culture: "It would be a grave mistake to think that the aim of the culture industry is to produce objects of real utility, enlightenment, or gratification. Rather, its concrete goals are to mystify, to titillate, and to frustrate; to take from people the organs of their own cultural resistance and to keep them hungry, restless, and confused, frantic in search of leisure, greedy for new commodities, and incapable of understanding much less changing their world."[91] I am not inclined to make my criticisms as strongly as does Kovel, having had some fine experiences in movie theaters and other such venues. I assume, furthermore, that the reader is well aware that a great deal of what is produced by the culture industry is rubbish. It is, though, the very obviousness of the superficiality of the bulk of mass culture that concerns me. As Horkheimer and Adorno note: "The triumph of advertising in the culture industry is that consumers feel compelled to buy and use its products even though they see through them."[92]

Daniel Boorstin calls advertising the characteristic rhetoric of technology.[93] Odd as it may seem, advertising is thus the definitive voice of our epoch, for in it "the promise of technology is presented both purely and concretely and hence most attractively."[94] Thus, advertisements that say "Drink Lots of Pepsi—Get Lots of Stuff" now tell us what we stand for. As with the consumption ethic, the advertising industry arose at a historical time when a surplus of commodities threatened to slow down the forward march of capital. Advertising, then, is a rhetoric of consumption which relies for its persuasive power on our dissatisfied and insecure condition, taking advantage of our unskillful desires. As Jean Liedloff observes: "Advertising has learned to capitalize on the longings of the [love] deprived public by holding out promises which seem to say, 'If you had this you would feel right again.'"[95] As a dominant form of symbolization, then, advertising is not much interested in our healing and growth—as is an authentic culture— but in selling us the goods any way it can. Again, many people seem to know all this. Yet we are not generally inclined to ask what an authentically life-serving culture might look like, nor to question the economizing of our reality. Consider, for instance, a television advertisement for a sport utility vehicle in which an earnest voice-over announces that it will "save your soul." Perhaps more than any other I have seen, this ad shows both how utterly vacuous is the promise of technology and how deep is our yearning.

My discussion on anticulture would be incomplete without considering the device of television. For as Borgmann suggests, "television remains the purest, i.e., the clearest and most attenuated, presentation of the promise of technology." It appears to maximally unburden us, freeing "us from the fetters of time, space, and ignorance," while also involving us in the nonstop celebration of commodity consumption that is television advertising.[96] The internet or virtual reality may soon replace television as the reigning symbol of technology's completion, yet it is my impression that TV still dominates the experience within most modern households.[97] What I wish to explore, in any event, is the huge role that television plays as a replacer of world-relations. Consider a claim from an ad for a TV station called The Life Network: "You don't have to live in the wilderness to experience the wonder of the great outdoors," because their "visually stunning programs" will bring "nature's most spectacular sites" to your living room. Thus can the very network of life now be consumed from the couch. Television's hidden machinery makes the whole world, including (it seems) the best bits of nature, fantastically available, so that we never need to get out of our pajamas. As the great disburdener, it makes virtually no demands on us, asking us to expend no more energy than is necessary to stay breathing and flip channels. The catch, though, is that in bringing us *the* world, television leaves us without *a* world of our own. As the principle of "ever-widening spheres" states, when an existence is realized in broader and broader circles of social belonging, the world's otherness can be articulated into a concrete network of meaningful interrelationships. TV, on the other hand, "articulates nothing but rather implodes, carrying its flattened image surface within itself."[98] For the experiences on the screen, even though we can see them, are not our own.

Normal Deprivation. The "most dangerous tendency in modern society," says Wendell Berry, "is the tendency toward the encapsulation of human order."[99] The danger Berry cautions against is the inclination to create a world consisting purely of humans and their artifacts. For when nonhuman life gets excluded, and so made alien, it inevitably gets destroyed—and yet it is just this excluded life that is essential to our own.[100] Ray Rogers describes the history of this encapsulating process in terms of a progressive "decoupling" of human society from the wider society of nature. As the west increasingly denied nonhuman beings any social standing, its connection to the natural world gradually shifted from one of "embedded" social relations to today's commodified and alienated relations. Rogers now sees this disembedding process coming to a kind of absurd completion in Martin Lewis's *promotion* of decoupling as "the most *ecological* course for human society." In his book *Green Delusions,* Lewis makes the case for a "Promethean" environmentalism that would "accentuate the gulf that sets us apart from the rest of the natural world," that is, that would conserve nature by placing it at an extreme distance from human society.[101] Decoupled humans would then conduct their lives in a "social, economic and technological milieu almost wholly removed from the intricate web of nature." What he does not adequately consider, though, is whether we would be happy.[102]

For all the hyperstimulation it provides, the quality of reality within a technological society suffers from a definite sameness. As the wild world is increasingly squeezed to the margins, it is replaced by a monotonous landscape of subdivisions, shopping malls, and electronic games. "The loss of wild others," writes Shepard, "leaves nothing but our own image to explain ourselves by— hence empty psychic space."[103] In a naturalistic sense, then, our experiential options are actually quite minimal.[104] We have in a sense been *deworlded,* not by being plucked by a scientist from out of our living context, but through the destruction of it. Thus we may ask: What is *left* of that nonhuman world or relational field our bodies imply or anticipate, and which we need in order to make earthly sense of ourselves?[105] What is now *available* to be symbolically called on in the making of ourselves? What sort of *self-understanding* do we form in interaction with the flesh of our own devices? (Recall the discussion in the previous chapter regarding the predominance of the machine metaphor.) In short, given that we exist not inside our skulls, but both in and as our world-relations, does not the denuding and violating of the natural world denude and violate *our own minds?* I submit that there is just nowhere in the great chain of decision making within a technological society where these kinds of questions get asked, where the deleterious experiential effects of replacing wild others with machines and commodities is properly considered—precisely because the pattern of technology itself sets the terms of the discourse. A large number of ecologically minded people have, however, thought long and worried hard about just these matters. Naturalist E. O. Wilson, for instance, writes that "on Earth no less than in space, lawn grass, potted plants, caged parakeets, puppies, and rubber snakes are not enough."[106] Insect ecologist Robert Michael Pyle likewise uses the phrase "the extinction of experience" to describe the loss of personal contact with wildlife that follows on the extirpation of local habitats.[107] Reminding us of the principle of "one flesh," Shepard writes, finally, that "our children, growing up with an inadequate otherness from which to rebound the elements of self, are in danger of becoming less than human."[108] Having largely destroyed a beautiful and mysterious world, we are less able to know our own corresponding beauty and mystery, all reality decaying to the mundane level of a video arcade. In the spirit of these witnesses, I suggest that most people in a technological society suffer from a form of "violent lack"[109] or experiential starvation; and that it is for ecopsychologists to highlight this condition.

My naturalistic argument, as always, is that our transhistorical environmental needs cannot be bypassed without generating trouble. Historian William Irwin Thompson argues, by contrast, that "those who were good at living with trees are on the way out, and those who are good at living with video display terminals and silicon tubes will be selected for. So cultures are actually selecting for a new postnatural environment."[110] In this view, there is no problem here, for nature is nothing but "the horizon of culture." Again, I believe this is a bad interpretation of nature. As our world is technologized and denuded of wild others, we do *not* "evolve"; rather, we suffer and then creatively adjust. As Shepard argues, our transhistorical urges are met in "perverted forms in modern society: our profound love of animals twisted into pets, zoos, decorations, and entertainment; our search for poetic wholeness subverted by the model of the machine instead of the body; the moment of pubertal idealism shunted into nationalism or otherworldly religion instead of ecosophical cosmology."[111] We settle for partial, secondary, or substitutive gratifications—we do the best we can, even when our best still has much pain and destructiveness in it. I believe that studying many of our contemporary behaviors as creative adjustments to an antinatural world would go a long way, therefore, toward discerning the transhistorical needs that are being thwarted by our society. John Livingston comments, for example, that the intensity of the house plant business expresses "a deep and primal need" for contact with other forms of life. "The geranium on the tenement windowsill is both an offering to the mysterious tidal pull of some distant biological memory, and a heartbreaking cry for help."[112] Indeed, the promise of studying such creative adjustments is that we might better hear this cry.

Some argue, nonetheless, that we are not experientially deprived at all. They say, for example, that the "computerized sensory immersion"[113] of virtual reality can in fact be richer, more thrilling, than the unsimulated reality of the natural world. Video games are widely available virtual realities of today, while something like Star Trek's holo-deck is the promise for tomorrow. Other kinds of artificial realities also offer experiences otherwise unavailable. At the West Edmonton Mall, for example, we can (on any day of the year) rent a rubber tube and take a ride on simulated rapids; towel off; and then go for a walk down an artificial version of Bourbon Street, New Orleans.[114] If our "wildest," most fantastic dreams can be virtually or artificially realized, if we can "improve" on reality, then why not do it? So go the arguments. Borgmann makes an important point when he observes that such arguments rely on dualistic biases. Hence, "'experience' no longer denotes a decisive encounter with reality but a certain subjective state engendered by whatever objective reality."[115] What we experience is an inner event, the result of so much sensory stimulation acting on our brains. The reality of the "outer" world, in other words, is a matter of some indifference.[116] Against this view, I posit the alternative one that "*the real is progressively given in contact.*"[117] Reality organismically unfolds and is built up through our interactions with *the world's otherness.* I said earlier that whatever we experience has some manner of reality. The term *reality* is used here, then, in a relative sense—as a designator of the strength or weakness of our contact with the world. To be more "in touch" with reality is to make better contact with, or to be dis-illusioned about, the situations in which we find ourselves. What is most "real," in this view, are the felt meanings we gather, or gestalts we form, in active, embodied, and concrete dialogue with the larger world of which we are a part.[118] The strongest, most satisfying reality, in short, is generally found-and-made in ever-widening spheres of meaning and participation,[119] and not simply in consumptive relations with a commodious, artificial, smoothed-over reality. To the virtual reality company whose motto reads "*Reality isn't enough anymore,*"[120] I therefore respond that there *isn't enough Reality anymore.*

Contesting the Pattern: Counterpractice

One can only insert oneself into [the social world] by taking one's place in the future-oriented productive juggernaut. But this now seems without any sense; the relation to the earth as raw material is therefore experienced as empty and alienating, but the recovery of a valid relation to the earth is the hardest thing once lost; and there is no relation to the absolute where we are caught in the web of meanings which have gone dead for us.

—Charles Taylor[121]

Given that modern technology pervasively, consistently, and perniciously patterns our lives, it must, says Borgmann, "be countered by an equally patterned and social commitment, i.e., by a practice."[122] Being in essential agreement with this view, I wish to use this section to present my own thoughts on what kinds of practice make sense from within an experiential and naturalistic framework, wherein the life process is regarded as an ultimate concern. The aim of counterpractice is to engage the word in a manner that lies outside the pattern of technology, thereby winning both a freer relation to technology and a more satisfying or contactful relation to reality. Counterpractice means clearing a non-technologized space for recovering and engaging in what are essentially human-natural activities; for meeting our transhistorical needs while at the same time dealing with our historical problem (or the problem of history). It means working with the life force, with the energy that is still in us, to take those small steps that feel right, given our specific interests and starting points. Master political programs, issued by central, theory-producing individuals, are against the spirit of an experiential approach. This is not to say that theories are unimportant, as they do play the crucial role of helping us to interpret modern life and consider our possibilities. An experiential approach, however, gives equal weight to taking guidance from our own particular experience of the concrete situations in which we are actually living our lives. What experiential practice highlights, in short, is the finding of just those specific actions that will both satisfy our living and contradict the repressive aspects of the existing social order. (To repeat, countering technology does not mean somehow eliminating it, but rather contesting its current pattern and reclaiming it as an artful serving of all life. While it is not my intention to lay out a specific program for building straw-bale houses and windmills, I do want this point to be clear.[123])

We need to remind ourselves that there is nothing inevitable about technological progress. Its "naturalness"—like that of the capitalist market place—is a kind of second nature, and, like any other pattern that we unconsciously and rigidly enact, its "laws" can always be disobeyed through aware and free action. As Noble comments, technological progress is not natural but *political*, it is "something people plan for and struggle over," something that reflects "social choices made by those who have the power to choose"[124] The exercise, then, is to ask what we might do with whatever is left of our own agency and power so as to deny to "technical devices . . . the right to dominate us, and so to warp, confuse, and lay waste our nature."[125] My own hope lies, in fact, with the possibility of large numbers of people developing a better gut-felt understanding of our technological existence and learning to deliberately refuse the ideology of progress—in ways ranging from the most intimate and personal to the most public and broad-based. There is no point in being naive about the forces geared against such a possibility, but no point in ignoring this possibility either.

Countering technology also means countering its future-orientation by attempting to embody what ultimately concerns us in this very present moment; it means refusing to turn our lives into a mere means to some end that never arrives. The charge is made, though, that any such antitechnological effort simply amounts to a foolish escape into the *past*. What this mistakenly assumes is that counterpractice entails winding the clock backward, tracing a direct line in reverse; when what it really involves is breaking or contradicting rigid patterns so as to liberate the life force and find creative ways to respond to *the present*. "We can't go back" is a resigned belief which leans on the ideology of linear progress in order to avoid looking at current possibilities.[126] The answer to "we can't go back" is that our bodies, being wild, have never stopped making their transhistorical demands, and that the natural world is still asking to be faithfully sung, still making its own demands. Going back really means *going in*—into the body, into the flesh of the world, and into a kind of mind-set where we are awake to the solicitations and commentaries being made by a more-than-human world. It will do us no good to say that this moment has passed us by.

Part of the problem for us ecological thinkers and activists, says John Rodman, is that "we lack a suitable myth that comprehends and integrates our feelings and perceptions, articulates our intuitions, allows our actions ritual status, and makes us intelligible to ourselves in terms of an alignment with a larger order of things."[127] What, then, might counterpractice contribute to this situation—where our ruling symbols lack meaning and our "ecological" feelings lack symbols? Joseph Campbell writes that the "most vital, most critical function of a mythology is to foster the centering and unfolding of the individual in integrity, in accord with himself (the microcosm), his culture (the mesocosm), the universe (the macrocosm), and that awesome ultimate mystery which is both beyond and within himself and all things."[128] In this chapter, I have identified one of our society's dominant mythologies with economic/technological progress. For "progress" is a narrative that tells us—even if few people probably "buy" it in these its baldest economic terms—who we are (commodious individuals); what our ethical duties are (production and consumption); what our relationship to the cosmos is (technological); and what life is all about (progress). The social good is served, says the myth, when the Gross Domestic Product goes up, and this is accomplished when individuals maximize the satisfaction of their limitless wants. Hence, self-interest constitutes our main social bond. As Loy remarks, however, all of this makes for a *defective* myth.[129] While it certainly does serve the mythological function of providing a story to direct our energies, and even while many do see it as a noble venture to serve future generations, "progress" ultimately provides no spiritual satisfaction, no cultural framework to integrate the individual into the cosmos, but only an increasing sense of lack and conflict. Pointing us in a better direction, the poet Robert Bringhurst writes that "Real myths are rich and nourishing. One of the things that makes them nourishing is that they are stories about others, about forces greater than ourselves."[130] Satisfying myths, that is, sing a more-than-human world. None of us knows exactly what kind of cultural story might ultimately replace the myth of progress. Inasmuch as counterpractices aim to expand the field of our existence or realm of our care, however, I suggest they are a way to actively foster the imaginative narrating or dreaming of a world that includes June bugs and ring-billed gulls, and so to welcome the eventual coming of a "real myth."[131] They are also a way to do the healing work—essential in my view—for recovering the *ability* to create and enact such myths, that is, to symbolize from, and live on the basis of, our own experience.

What makes this project so difficult is precisely that it is up against the technological war on (human) nature. Our civilized society has lost the bearings once provided by the larger natural world, our bodies, and earth-based mythologies. Creative adjustments to this situation come in the form of otherworldly, materialist, hedonistic, adventure-seeking, narcissistic, absurdist, literalist, scientistic, dystopian, apocalyptic, survivalist, technosalvationist, nihilistic, just-getting-by, economistic, reform environmentalist, and other life philosophies. Among all these, a genuine reconciliation with nature is strangely invisible. Recreation *in* nature is acceptable, but balanced and respectful coexistence *with* other-than-human beings—the general prescription of radical ecology and ecopsychology—is simply not admissible as a societal aim. Thompson writes, in a related way, that "nothing seems to be able to stop industrialization. . . . Like an enormous flood sweeping through a narrow valley, the torrent seems to pick up everything which stands in its way to include it in its own behavior. As you see romantic poet, anarchist, communist, and hippie swept up and floating in the rushing stream, you can see that the revolt cannot stop the flood but only lend a little color to the floating debris of history."[132] What I would emphasize about this historical flood is how it weakens us as individuals as we struggle just to stay afloat.

Being a psychological thinker, my concern is with what kind of shape we are in. On this, historian Russell Jacoby writes: "The modern individual is in the process of disintegration. To forget this is to abet the process not aid the resistance."[133] Witnessing this disintegration all too well, Horkheimer and Adorno lamented that our times simply lack "a revolutionary subject that might usher in the reconciliation of humanity with inner and outer nature,"[134] so far advanced is the process of psychic fragmentation. While my own outlook is less grim than theirs, I do regard the destruction of our experience as a core ecopsychological issue. As James Masterson observes, the so-called "'personality disorders' . . . are not only increasingly prevalent among people seeking professional help today, but also reflect major psychological themes in American culture at large: fear of abandonment, emphasis on the self to the exclusion of others, difficulties in intimacy and creativity and with the assertion of the real self."[135] One of the main elements of counterpractice I discuss below, then, concerns the historical need to strengthen our humanity—to get the water out of our lungs, as it were—so that we may indeed break the pattern of technology. As I discuss in the final section, such strengthening will be necessary if we are ever going to voluntarily face our suffering rather than continue to flee its message and increase our pain. As I discuss shortly, furthermore, I believe that simple, unambitious practices can also play an important role in this process.

In what follows, I first consider the basic function of counterpractice, that is, to provide a focus for our lives among the dispersing effects of our technological society. I then look more closely at the kind of political orientation that a naturalistic and experiential approach invites. Given the fundamental nature of ecopsychology's subject matter, its practices will inevitably overlap with those of other therapeutic and political ventures. Within my own approach, what distinguishes ecopsychological practice is explicit care for nature and experience, for the life process, for the natural moment of our existence—not just for getting us into the outdoors. I am therefore interested in promoting a wide range of practices, even if some will be less obviously "ecopsychological" than others. My discussion is more or less speculative, and necessarily broad, but not without a certain degree of experience on my part, and not without existing examples to point to. My aim is limited, then, to offering one *formulation* of the work that needs to be done, in the hopes of thereby contributing to it.

Focal Practice: Disciplined Engagement.[136] What first of all characterizes all counterpractice, as I am using the term, is that it both takes the form of a regular discipline and helps bring our lives into focus, providing them with a center. These are its baseline features. Through such practice, we rediscover a world outside of labor and consumption, where deeper satisfactions or more life-giving meanings may be experienced. There are no prerequisites for such practice other than that it be life-forwarding for the person involved. My daily meditation practice, for example, has opened up a universe of understanding and a sense of spiritual grounding that has nothing at all to do with the consumption ethic. As Gary Snyder has remarked, "The practice of meditation, for which one needs only 'the ground beneath one's feet,' wipes out mountains of junk being pumped into the mind by the mass media and supermarket universities."[137] Borgmann envisions a restructuring of our society not through any "external and violent blow," but by way of just such practice—by discovering for ourselves, and building an allegiance to, the good life that the forces of technology have progressively replaced with machinery and commodities.[138] If this sounds like an old pitch (meditation, voluntary simplicity, etc. have been around for a long time) I think that's because it is. What Borgmann adds to the cause is his elucidation of the pattern of technology, which he hopes will provide motivational fuel *for* focal-practices, including ones that are explicitly political. What I would add even further (as I discuss below), is that these practices become more possible when they include a commitment to the *healing* of practitioners, so that the latter are more capable of counterpractice in general.

In the sense used here, a discipline does not involve blind obedience to a coercive force. It is rather a freely chosen commitment to a form of regular practice that is of felt benefit, even if it may involve some difficulty. If technology is know by a pattern of disengagement, counterpractice is known by a pattern of deliberate contact-making. It is thus in the choices we make between either disengaging from or engaging with reality that we confirm or protest the rule of technology. One way of understanding a focal practice is to say that in it we become a participant rather than a spectator. So much of our experience today is of a vicarious sort—we watch movies in which other people exercise their dramatic skills, listen to music played by musicians who are not us, read books by authors who tell us of their spiritual quests, and so on. Focal practices, therefore, would include joining a theater group, meeting weekly with friends to play music, or taking up a concrete spiritual practice. These would counter the pattern of technology to the extent that they call for acquisition of skill, fidelity to a discipline, the broadening of sensibility, the making of good, bodily felt contact with others, and the preservation and development of life-giving tradition.[139] There are, however, any number of things that people might do as counterpractices. Shepard writes, for instance, that what "we can do is single out those many things, large and small, that characterized the social and cultural life of our ancestors . . . and incorporate them as best we can by creating a modern life around them. . . . given the pieces, the culture will reshape itself."[140] He lists a large number of such pieces, ranging from "participant politics" to "regular dialogue on dream experience," all of which are possible areas for the practical recollection of our nature. Inasmuch as any practice provides satisfaction for arrested world-relations, then, I think it fitting that ecopsychology get behind it. For as people start to enjoy real food, the TV sets and chocolate bars (in my experience) just spontaneously fall away.

An essential general practice for ecopsychology is to bring into focus the nonhuman life—of which there is often a surprising amount—that still remains within the interstices of our technological society. Richard Nelson, who has made this his own practice, remarks in an interview:

> Anyone can have [a] sense of moral and spiritual engagement with a place. One of the deep sources of that is to choose a place and focus on it in some way or another. It doesn't matter if it's your backyard in the city, or Central Park, or a farm field. It's to find a place in which you can feel deeply engaged, and then go back to it over a long period of time. . . . I think there's something very very important about that engagement.[141]

Ten minutes by bike from my house[142] there is a piece of land known as the Leslie Street Spit. Built of construction rubble, it was originally intended to form an outer harbor for the city of Toronto. While the planners were trying to decide what to do with the landform, plants started to take root in the soil dumped on it from the construction of a subway line. Now it is a park, rich with flowers, coyotes, muskrats, terns, cottonwoods, and other plants and animals, surrounded by a powerful body of water than meets a beautiful sky. It is also the destination for regular visits by my friends and me. I mention this place because, with rebar and slag jutting out all over the place, it is no pristine wilderness. Yet with every visit, it offers its gifts. On a recent trip, my wife and I looked up from studying a flower to find ourselves in the middle of a flock of ring-billed gulls feasting on June bugs that filled the air close to the ground. We felt right *inside* a feeding event, as if standing upside down on the surface of a lake watching a school of fish eat minnows. It was an exciting, funny, graceful, awful experience, whose meanings are still reverberating within me. And it is just the kind of nontechnologized encounter that is easily available to anyone who would make of such trips a counterpractice.

Counterpractice also entails a commitment to understanding others not as mere objects, resources, and consumers, but as ensouled persons with something to say. This, to be sure, is not the easiest of practices in a deanimated world. The great long-term significance of making such an ontological shift, however (one which I again feel will require much healing along the way), is that people "do not exploit a nature that speaks to them."[143] Abram suggests, in this respect, that we assume there is "some manner of spontaneity and sentience," some mode of aliveness, in all we encounter. He then recommends the practice of not speaking disrespectfully to or about *anything*.[144] Ursula LeGuin also writes: "Perhaps it is only when the otherness, the difference, the space between us (in which both cruelty and love occur) is perceived as holy ground, as the sacred place, that we can 'come into animal presence.'"[145] Practices that are dedicated to place are so important because they involve this kind of sacrilizing process, wherein through skillful dialogue with a specific locale it is allowed to disclose itself in its deeper meanings. Bioregionalism, ecological restoration, urban habitat renewal, and other such practices all involve this kind of intimacy, where the aim is to create social forms, develop technologies, and undertake projects that let the local ecologies be. Living in responsible and reciprocal relation to the land has always called for what the Anishinabe activist Winona LaDuke calls "intergenerational residency in place"—as there is just no substitute for local knowledge gained through firsthand experience and passed down through the generations. Indeed, the final overcoming of dualism will be a mending not only of the split between mind and body, but between mind and place. (Enforced dislocations of indigenous and other peoples are so cruel precisely because the enforcers assume the existence of a mind/place cleavage, whereas the people being dislocated often do not.[146])

Coming Back to Life.[147] The ecology movement works to defend and restore life on earth. The promise of ecopsychology is to assert that humans themselves participate in this life, and to encourage the work that brings us back to it. My own strategy is to criticize our society on the basis of its antagonism to the life process, and then to argue for a kind of politics that explicitly makes what Dorothy Dinnerstein has called "a deep turn toward life."[148] *Whatever* actions I am involved in, I want them to be healing and satisfying, for those are the kind that the life process calls for, that are meaningful; I want to act in ways that are at the same time a defense and restoration of human life. As I reviewed in chapter one, there is a growing recognition that when activists try to mobilize people on the basis of fear, guilt, and shame, they may well be adding to an immobilizing despair, apathy, and denial. What follows, then, are my own thoughts on what a difference it makes to our practice when our political acts are grounded in a dedication to, or appreciation for, our nature and our experience.

    I have already suggested that a pivotal issue for ecopsychology is the weakened state of our humanity. As the biosphere crumbles, so do we. The dreadful possibility is that we are sliding into a state in which most people are too distressed, are not in any kind of shape, to ever turn their attention to the betterment of society. Christopher Lasch refers to the emergence of a "minimal self," a self that "contracts to a defensive core," that retreats from any kind of emotional commitment to long-term causes, its main task being day-to-day survival. "The hope that political action will gradually humanize industrial society has given way to a determination to survive the general wreckage or, more modestly, to hold one's own life together in the face of mounting pressures."[149] I heard an author of a book about the unhealthy speediness of our society say that: "If we can't save society, at least we can save ourselves." For the beleaguered self, the need to work for social change simply does not become figural, for the conditions are not right for the organism to feel this as its most pressing need. The "permanent emergency of the individual"—"unable to think beyond itself"—"blocks the permanent and social solution."[150]

As a result of the disintegration of the self, politics in our times has largely been replaced by therapeutics—a development much bemoaned by many radicals. As Jacoby suggests, "the depletion of political concepts in favor of psychological and subjective ones is a by-product of the scramble for the remains of human experience."[151] Recall that the workings of capital require that the personal sphere become inflated, that we become ever-more needy. This is partly why the field of psychology looms so large in our age, and why social issues tend to get reduced to psychological ones. Within the circles of humanistic psychotherapy, for example, it is often assumed that personal transformation will somehow "magically extend" to the rest of society. As Isaac Prilleltensky notes, in their groups "humanists nurture each other and foster the belief that a better world is *inevitably* coming, without intervening in the real world."[152] Social activism becomes a kind of group therapy session. As much as anything else, what is perhaps revealed by the culture of personal growth is simply a "growing despair of changing society, even understanding it."[153]

A first step toward addressing this matter is to recognize that it is not only a moral issue, but a political issue in itself. What "needs to be criticized and condemned," writes Lasch, "is the devastation of personal life, not the retreat into privatism. . . . The trouble with the consciousness movement is not that it addresses trivial or unreal issues but that it provides self-defeating solutions" (because it does not address itself to the social structures that brutalize personal life in the first place).[154] If people are preoccupied with their own growth or survival, I think it is only fair to say that this reflects how very little our society is itself occupied with their growth and survival.[155] In my view, the best way to encourage individuals back toward society is therefore to be *all the more* attentive or sensitive to their personal experience. In this, I am agreeing with a large number of thinkers who argue that social movement toward greater freedom and happiness will occur only if the 'subjective conditions' are suitably prepared.[156] To concentrate on preparing these conditions is not the same as flattening out the psyche-society dialect in the psychologistic manner I just discussed. It is rather to give the personal sphere its due.[157] Roger Gottlieb writes that "the flaws of both communism and advanced capitalism can be overcome only if ordinary people achieve sufficient power and self-knowledge to shape social life in terms of the wisdom of their own experience and the demands of their own true needs."[158] This requires, in turn, that they develop (1) an *understanding* of how their lives have been deformed by their society, and (2) the *capacity* to act on that understanding, including the inner ability to make judgments independent of authorities and experts. (These two tasks clearly act in concert, for we take up a critical theory of society only to the extent that we are capable of bearing what it is trying to show us; and such a theory itself arises from or is complemented by our independent judgments or symbolizations of our own experience.) My discussion of the pattern of technology was addressed to the first of these tasks. A technological society, like any other, organizes our experience in a way that is consistent with or that corresponds to it. As many have noted, competitive, commodity-hungry, individualists are by their very essence not drawn to radical politics or cooperative action. To work from and toward a *different* understanding of ourselves, one that is both truer to our nature and incompatible with the order of technological society, is therefore a way to gradually turn ourselves out of this society and to energize ourselves toward the transformation of it. The challenge, as Paul Goodman expressed it, is "to live in present society as if it were a natural society."[159] Developing the ability and support to do so is the topic for the rest of this section.

Among the many efforts that people *are* making to better our society and its relationship with the natural world, the role I see for ecopsychology is to create the contexts that will help people recover their own nature and experience. This means, furthermore, being respectful of the position from which each person might begin such a recovery. If the life process be our concern, then I believe all people are entitled to keep themselves above what I call the *healing threshold.*[160] Below this critical threshold our lives spiral downward, we fall through the cracks and self-destruct, we lack the support (both inner and outer) to get on top of our pain and find our bearings. Above this threshold, our lives move forward, we gain strength, we enjoy the necessary support to learn, grow, and expand the spheres of our social concern—as we are naturally ordered to do. I am myself dedicated to creating a society in which all people are generally able to remain above this healing threshold (such a society being as far as I allow my utopian thinking go). The Buddhist Ken Jones takes a similar position: "The unequal burdens of [kar-maic] conditioning are compassionately recognized as well as the sacred individual freedom to relinquish them. Spiritual egalitarianism therefore honours individual differences and the importance of each person being able to develop their potential in their own unique way and at the pace proper to them."[161] My own vision is that of a society in which each person is supported in unfolding her or his life in the direction that her or his specific existence implies, whether it be to heal from childhood trauma, lead a movement to end poverty, or guide adolescents through their initiation rites. While I have no wish to add to the long list of elaborate political programs that never make it off the page of the text, I do want to mention two general areas of practice, already underway, that are indeed designed to help build a life-oriented society. The first includes the work of all those communities or forums that offer *support for the beleaguered self.* The second includes all those efforts that are contributing to the development of a culture that is *responsible to the human life cycle.*

Efforts to support the beleaguered self include the community workshops and other initiatives I discussed in chapter one which attempt to provide emotional and spiritual ground for activists and concerned citizens. Because my own experience in this area is primarily with a peer self-help psychotherapy group (Re-evaluation Counseling) and with the worldwide "focusing" community, I will base my discussion primarily on them. What is crucial about these two communities—

and others like them—is that they provide contexts within which we can re-emerge as human beings and turn our attention toward the larger world. I can think of three important ways that they do this.

The first is that they offer training in recovering our ability to work from our own bodily experience, to hear our own inner voice. If the violence of the modern world alienates us from this voice, then reconnecting with it is a counterpractice of historical significance. Overcoming dualism is no easy thing, no mere philosophical exercise, but a practical task that asks us to give ourselves over to the worldly demands of our bodies and to go through the often painful and scary process of thawing out our own flesh. We generally prefer to *stimulate* ourselves—to get excitement into our deadened bodies through bungy jumping and watching horror movies—rather than to *resensitize* ourselves. To the extent that we can do the latter, however, the benefits are tremendous, for (among other gains) we reclaim a centre for ourselves. Nothing compares to being able to speak our own truth, to having confidence in our saying because of the sureness of our feeling. There is an astonishing difference between going through life on the basis of stuck patterns, old ideas, introjected beliefs, habitual reactions, other people's opinions, superego warnings, expert advice, and archaic fantasies versus being aware of what we are bodily sensing in any given situation and listening for the needs, insights, fresh symbols, creative resolutions, and dialogical responses that flow from this source of organismic guidance. The goal of the focusing community is to make a space for all those bodies who are interested in working in this latter way, on the assumption that a society full of people capable of doing so will bear very little resemblance to the society of today. Meeting regularly with a "focusing partner" is one of the main forms of practice that comes out of this community. The person who introduced this popular self-help practice, Eugene Gendlin, writes: "The political context I am concerned about is the individual's own self-guidance by an inner source. Without this we cannot hope for any better political forms than we have now and have had throughout history."[162] In helping people to revitalize the concrete, experiential side of life, the focusing community is in its own way thus endeavoring to generate a populace of more capable social agents.[163]

The second way these efforts contribute to the making of a life-oriented society is that they locate social change work *within* the life process, making it part of the good life. The commitment is to develop, in Joanna Macy's words, "practical methods for embarking on social action, and sustaining and enjoying it, so that it is no longer seen as a daunting, demanding exercise in self-sacrifice. . . . so that our work for the world runs like an ever-refreshing stream through our lives."[164] In other words, the intention is to create conditions under which we can both discover what particular social action will be meaningful for us and acquire the emotional support to then do it. In this case, our organismic energy flows into the action because it meets a genuine need to engage the world on a matter that concerns us or in which we are interested. Re-evaluation Counseling (RC) is a worldwide network of communities dedicated to personal healing and social liberation, and to stressing the lively relationship that obtains between the two. To support healing, it teaches nonprofessional peers to counsel one another, primarily through weekly meetings with a partner in which each person takes a turn in the roles of "counselor" and "client." To support social change it holds workshops and develops theory about ending various forms of oppression. Personal counseling and social struggle are seen, moreover, as complementary and mutually enhancing activities. That is, the more we take action in the world, the more do we break or contradict our rigid, fear-based patterns. This leads to the emergence of the painful or distressful feelings that were hidden inside the pattern, which if addressed in counseling sessions may then find their healing resolution (rather than develop into conflict and burnout). Conversely, the more good counseling we receive, the more alive and clear-thinking we become in our activism. Outer and inner work thus unfold dialectically, to the benefit of both person and society.[165] I have myself witnessed many people within the RC community, through just these processes, develop rich world-relations, regain their personal powers, and take great love and skill out into the world.

Finally, the RC and focusing communities are dedicated to creating non-violent and caring environments—shelters from the storm—within which people may recover their inherent nature. Both communities foster relationships in which people listen to one another respectfully, empathetically, and nonjudgmentally, and in which one's basic goodness and creativity are routinely mirrored. In such a climate, people feel supported enough to take personal risks, let go of old patterns and self-interruptions, go into painful shame-linked feelings, and make more open contact with others. Because these communities bring many people of different backgrounds together, they also provide forums to learn about other people's life experiences and perspectives on the world. Within RC, in particular, great efforts are made to understand the common wounding that underlies all forms of oppression. As is widely recognized, the psychological dynamics between oppressor and oppressed groups form complex interlocking systems, wherein, for example, the oppressed introject and so "carry" the projected inferiority, weakness, rage, and so on of their oppressors. This is not the place to examine such dynamics. It is worth noting, however, that oppressors are generally reluctant to give up their "power" because "they are personally threatened, not simply with material loss but more significantly with patterns of managing their emotional lives. Given an equalitarian system, they would be called on to deal with their anxieties, angers, guilts, self-hatreds, and desires in new ways they cannot trust. They are thus committed to the styles of interaction that have lifted them to the position of superiority."[166] Because the RC community understands all this, it brings great compassion to both those in the role of the oppressor and of the oppressed (including an understanding of how we can occupy both roles because of the multiple and interwoven nature of oppressions). It thereby encourages the emotionally charged work of surrendering oppressive attitudes, forming alliances with other groups, and re-covering our humanity as we spit out the introjects that have distorted and harmfully limited our nature. I wish to emphasize, in sum, that it is only the strong affirmation of the inherent worth and loveability of all humans that makes this kind of work possible, as this provides the necessary context to sustain people, to ensure that they feel connected to others, as they come into contact with their feelings of shame and insecurity and as they attempt to forge links with previously hated and feared groups.

The second general area of counterpractice I want to highlight does not exclude the supportive ones I just discussed, but has a different focus, namely, attending to the human life-cycle. Here, the work is more recognizably "ecopsychological," in that the intention is to recollect our human nature in its fullness, a goal which emphatically includes cultivating mature relationships with a more-than-human, living reality. If not us, asks Audre Lorde, "who else will feed [children] the real food without which their dreams will be no different from ours?"[167] In my own terms, who but us will intervene to meet their transhistorical needs? Childhood today seems more and more about abuse and neglect rather than about loving delivery into the life stream—a situation that social workers, therapists, developmental psychologists, governmental agencies, child advocacy groups, and other bodies seem hard pressed to reverse. Every little bit helps, however. And I believe that ecopsychology's little bit is to hold out a vision that honors the unfolding of human life as a phenomenon of nature and then to take action in support of it. Most of the parents I know are isolated and stressed. Ecopsychologists might thus contribute as much to the making of an ecological society by allying themselves with today's overburdened parents and assisting with the care of their young as by trying to transpersonalize the self-sense of adults. The practice of the wild surely includes holding babies well. One way to counter the pattern of technology, in other words, is to nourish those who might do a better job of it than we do. While there is much that could potentially be done in this area, for the discussion here I will concentrate on two examples of practice that seem important to me: environmental education among children and wilderness rites among youth and adults.

Environmental education stands out for me because letting children play in wetlands and forests (as their bodies are naturally organized to do) could play such a key role in the developmental life of children. Unfortunately, environmental education largely conforms to the pattern of technology, at least as currently practiced where I live. In a recent review of Canadian environmental education, Constance Russell, et al. describe a basic tension within this field. Roughly speak-ing, a minority of educators favor approaches that recognize "the value-laden nature of education; the importance of cultural and ecological diversity; the com-bined movement toward social and environmental justice; and the challenge to anthropocentrism." The majority, on the other hand, are essentially committed to the status quo. As Anne Bell comments, "environmental education as it is widely practiced today, emphasizes above all the provision of information and the resolution of problems associated with pollution, waste reduction and disposal, and 'resource' management. Issues are understood primarily in terms of science, economics and pragmatic reforms geared in the first instance to human utility. Technocratic rationality predominates."[168] Environmental education is increasingly becoming science education, and its curriculum is largely driven by free, industry subsidized materials. It is thus less an opportunity for world engagement—for playful exploration and unstructured discovery of a living nature—than a "top-down . . . didactic teaching of pre-packaged knowledge,"[169] in which the pedagogical goal remains the technical mastery of reality. Its curricula also adopt big-picture approaches that use such abstract models as Spaceship Earth, nutrient cycles, and energy flows.[170] The middle-sized phenomena of traditional nature study, of mucking about with frogs and bugs, is replaced by CD Roms that deliver information to computer screens about managing planet earth.

In the main, then, environmental education is not a form of counterpractice. It *could* be, however. Russell, et al. speak appreciatively, for example, of "such school-based initiatives as habitat restoration, energy and waste audits, and bird and tree surveys," which indicate "a desire to situate [environmental education] in the immediate life contexts of students and in the intimacy of lived relationships with other life."[171] Given both the developmental need for immersion in wild nature and the fact that almost all children go to school, I think that much is at stake in the shape taken by environmental education. A naturalistic and experiential environmental education would design its curriculum not to satisfy industry but to reclaim a technologically obscured region of existence, one that is known by the excitement of incorporating wild others into a growing field of significant relations. As Gary Snyder comments, "It's not enough to be shown in school that we are kin with all the rest: we have to feel it all the way through."[172] Although environmental educators need not be ecopsychologists, ecopsychologists do need to be involved in environmental education. Indeed, my hope is that the work of ecopsychologists will become sufficiently influential that they can help to remove the handcuffs from those teachers who do wish to more concretely engage their students with the natural world, but whose lesson-plans, dictated from above, keep it otherwise.

In the previous chapter I made my views apparent about the need for adolescent initiation rites. One of the problems facing adults, however, is that we ourselves lack the knowledge and skill to mentor youth in the ways their nature demands. Stephen Foster and Meredith Little founded the School of Lost Borders precisely for this reason—to train elders in the work of leading wilderness rituals. As more people undertake such training, and as this work spreads, I am hoping it will do much to orient adolescents toward the natural world as the ground of their being and as the original domain for spiritual initiation. Amongst all the noise of technological adolescence, vision quests and other wilderness rites are counterpractices capable of bringing a transformative focus to the lives of many a confused youth. As Foster notes, such rites, which includes guidance from a council of caring elders, provide "an invaluable opportunity to make a difference in how at-risk youth see their future."[173] This kind of rite work, furthermore, is not just for adolescents. In his *The Four Shields: The Initiatory Seasons of Human Nature,* Foster (with Little) lays out an entire psychological model based on the seasons and other metaphors drawn largely from the natural world, and in which all the stages of life are incorporated. I myself undertook a wilderness quest at the time of my marriage, and the vision and understanding I gained on it remain a continual source of guidance and strength as I paddle my way forward in life. Rite work, in fact, explicitly involves all three of my naturalistic principles. It supports people in finding their place in both human and more-than-human society (i.e., in widening their spheres of belonging and responsibility); in perceiving a world beyond the boundaries of strictly human reality, and so in beginning to sing (or even "creatively mythologize"[174]) this wider world; and in learning to see their own lives symbolically mirrored and bound up in the flesh of all living things. All manner of rite work—an annual wilderness fast, for example, to refresh one's vision and maintain one's connection with the psyche of nature—can thus form a strong basis for counterpractice.

In sum, ecopsychology is a psychological intervention aimed at contributing to the transformation of society by encouraging or providing for the recovery of our nature and our experience, for the regaining of lost world-relations and life-meanings. It is an effort to remember that, and how, we are a part of the big life process; to get us back into the service of all life. What unites the diversity of counterpractical examples I offered in this section is their commitment to a more life-oriented cultural and social order. Examples, however, are only that. I am myself working toward becoming a wilderness rite of passage guide. Depending on one's cultural background and life-experience, however, a wilderness rite may be the last thing one is interested in undertaking, or that seems feasible. I also envision forming an organization for psychotherapists ("Ontario Psychotherapists for a New Society") that would advocate for social change based on the privileged knowledge therapists have about what our current society does to our humanity. I think we need keep an open mind, then, about just what forms our practice will take. If Freud got us onto the couch, where might ecopsychology get us to?

Whatever shape our practice does take, there can be little doubt that we need a lot more of it. That is why I have stressed the need to make the work *attractive,* which in turn means that it be *supportive* and that it have some *life* in it, some revitalizing juice. We can only hope that this kind of practice gains momentum. We might also take comfort in the fact that the process of change is quite mysterious. Despite my emphasis on the losses of the modern era, in order to be humble servants of nature we do not need to be all sorted out nor living in profound relation to Wolf and Eagle; we only need to be *present*. To come back to life is to realize that it is a process, one that involves taking countless steps that we can never quite predict, but which are most surely taken when grounded in contact with presently felt reality. Regardless of one's starting situation, to serve nature is to sense what the life force is asking for, what wants to unfold, move, happen, or come next. Today, moreover, perhaps more than at any other time, I believe that to be a servant of nature is to learn the essentially human art of bearing pain and suffering—as I discuss next.

On Bearing Pain and Suffering[175]

Life, as we find it, is too hard for us; it brings too many pains, disappointments and impossible tasks. In order to bear it we cannot dispense with palliative measures. . . . There are perhaps three such measures: powerful distractions, which cause us to make light of our misery; substitutive satisfactions, which diminish it; and intoxicating substances, which make us insensitive to it.

—Sigmund Freud[176]

Understanding comes through suffering.

—Aeschylus[177]

Rather than putting down the revolt of nature, I have said that we need to join it—need to join with the life force in rebelling against the repressive and exploitative aspects of modern society. Revolts are messy, though; and to join this one is to feel the pain and suffering that the pattern of technology both generates and acts to hide. Indeed, in the discussions above I have depicted the domination of nature as an entirely backward solution to the problem of pain and suffering. In the environmentalist's thinking about what it will take to reverse the ecological crisis, I suggest that this is a terribly overlooked factor. In this section I thus want to discuss the age-old truth that we can know ourselves, know our humanity, only if willing to consciously learn from our suffering. But how to bear it? The healing that goes on in a psychotherapist's office involves contacting those painful feelings we have previously been unable to bear, but which in a more supportive context can now be awarely experienced and completed. The same principle applies in all healing work: that the ground for the work—inner, interpersonal, physical, moral, conceptual, spiritual, ecological—must be strong enough so that we can maintain a sufficient distance from our unpleasant feelings to both *tolerate* and *move through* them. For the most part, our society lacks such contexts; it offers cotton candy and pills instead. It is thus no wonder that we have become so apathetic, for apathy (a-*pathos*) is precisely an insensibility to suffering. I suggest, in short, that we are just not going to be able to get it together, or do the radical work, unless we enjoy better self-knowledge—and that this implies creating the loving conditions under which we can feel, and so discover the meaning of, our pain and suffering. In the previous section I discussed some of the forums and communities that presently offer these kinds of conditions. What I concentrate on here is the specific need to make the bearing of pain and suffering a central principle of ecopsychological work. Gary Coates suggests that we view our historical suffering as an invitation to undertake a kind of rite of passage, through which we might renew our culture.[178] All such rites, however, involve preparation. As Venerable Myokyo-ni writes, the first step toward wholeness takes place "in the training yard, learning to bear with oneself, to bear emotional onslaughts, becoming gentle and stronger, acquiring not Bull-strength but bearing strength."[179]

Life strives toward happiness; suffering is a message that we're going the wrong way or that some painful state of affairs needs our attention. Our suffering, then, is a kind of life compass and teacher. Even the most vital people move their lives forward by responding to the tension of those bodily felt desires that urge them to take some action, make some sense. In a way, then, we are always making sense out of suffering. Inasmuch as we do not, our tensions inevitably grow. Hence, a society that knows little about suffering, that does much to avoid it, will know little about life (and so little about happiness). Consider, on this note, the biopsychiatrist Donald Goodwin's remark that "anxiety has no more survival value than a tension headache. Its elimination would be a blessing."[180] I understand anxiety as our feeling for the void. It thus both motivates the spiritual search and emerges strongly in people who have been traumatized and isolated. I understand tension headaches, furthermore, as symptomatic of repressed emotion, such as grief and anger. To argue for the "elimination" of these is therefore to grossly ignore their potential meaning. It is also to adopt that self-defeating approach for disburdening ourselves of suffering—itself rooted in anxiety—which I call "the strategy of violence."

The strategy of violence is to deal with the problem of pain and suffering by trying to annihilate what are perceived as the sources of distress. Richard Slotkin suggests that a dominant myth in the United States is that of "regeneration through violence." Originating with Puritan colonists, this myth holds that a new society is to be made through exorcising or attacking dark (corrupt, bad, threatening) forces, whether these be located in nature, Native Americans, Satan, or North Vietnamese. It, too, is a defective myth, however, in that it leads not to any kind of satisfaction, but only to a spiral of increasing violence and increasing guilt-anxiety.[181] All death, no rebirth. This myth, then, is part of the cultural background of a society that has become a kind of killing machine. My concern here is with how we turn this killing attitude toward ourselves, using drugs, for example, as "a weapon against the void."[182] Ours is a society that for the most part attempts to annihilate pain, to self-destructively go to war with it (whether the target be a recipient of our "projections" or our own bodies), rather than to recover the life that is locked up inside it. Why might this be so? Having started this chapter with a simple idea (happiness), I wish to also finish it with one: that we choose the strategy of violence only when we lack the contexts necessary to bear our pain and suffering, and so to stay above the healing threshold. When the pain of life is too great to bear, we use our aggression against it. All repression, for example, is a life-diminishing act of aggression against our natural selves. Drugs and alcohol desensitize or temporarily soothe us. And so on. The strategy of violence does not satisfy us precisely because it is not a positive search for fulfillment but a last-ditch quest for release from pain. The "fateful question" for our times is thus not, as Freud held, whether the instinct for life can win out over the instinct for death (the latter of which is an erroneous construction[183]), but whether or not we will choose to find collective ways to bear our pain and suffering, to strengthen ourselves, so that we can then stop negating life and instead get back to it. In the hope that we will, and in the face of all the evidence that we won't, I offer the following remarks.

To stay above the healing threshold we need a context for containing our pain that is larger or stronger than the pain itself (recall, for example, the contexts necessary to do the oppression-work within the RC community). Given the enormity of our pain, I suggest that our society needs very strong frameworks indeed. The strongest contexts, moreover, will in some sense always be spiritual. The recovery movement involves much spiritual practice (e.g., twelve-step programs) exactly because this puts people's pain into a more tolerable context. As the Gestaltist James Kepner also comments, the "reality of trauma and abuse, with its horror, hideousness, and inexplicable quality, simply cannot be held and made sense of within the individual person." Thus, "most survivors find some compelling need to develop a transcendent spiritual or philosophical framework."[184] This comes as no surprise, as religious symbols have traditionally helped people understand the cosmos in a way that makes their pain endurable. "As a religious problem," says Clifford Geertz, "the problem of suffering is, paradoxically, not how to avoid suffering but how to suffer, how to make of physical pain, personal loss, worldly defeat, or the helpless contemplation of others' agony something bearable, supportable—something, as we say, sufferable."[185] Our technologized and economized society does not encourage the creation of such cultural frameworks for bearing pain and suffering—only for avoiding and trying to kill it. This seems to me a fatal state of affairs. It is not my place to prescribe specific spiritual practices. I think it fair to say, though, that we are today called by nature, by the voice of our own pain, by the cry of the earth, to reoccupy the spiritual-ecological dimension of existence.

I have already mentioned efforts by people like Joanna Macy to promote spiritual practice and understanding within the ecology, peace, and social justice movements.[186] The Green Party activist Ken Jones does not mince words: "only some spiritual kind of conviction and training have the strength to bring about the necessary radical shift."[187] Or as Ram Dass has said, such training is necessary if we are to "keep our hearts open in hell."[188] Among the various dimension that make up my own practice, the most powerfully healing and strengthening have been those tied to a routine of Buddhist meditation and study. I have come to be less resentful of my pain, realizing that the work of life is exactly to learn from this suffering: to see how it attunes me to the pain of others; to develop the capacity to disidentify from it and so "breathe it through"; and to make out of it whatever small piece of work is mine to do in this lifetime.[189] I do not doubt, then, that the spread of such practice would be of great benefit to all—as would many other kinds of such practice. Whether our society undergoes a positive spiritual shift, whether it gets on top of its pain and violence, is obviously a matter that goes well beyond whatever interventions ecopsychologists might make. What I do want to stress, however, as a central theme of my own, is that the spiritual condition of our time is largely defined by the shame and isolation of the terrified Ego. The Catholic author Michael Higgens, in commenting on the hellishness of the twentieth century, characterizes hell precisely as a state of isolation (and so heaven as a state of communion).[190] I thus believe that the most basic requirement of a strengthening spiritual practice for our times is that it include a supportive response to this widespread condition of shame and isolation.

Shame is perhaps the hardest emotion to bear. When workaholics stop working, for example, they often feel engulfed by a sense of worthlessness, and so dive once again into further work. The more we matter-of-factly acknowledge the feeling of shame, however, and so give up the shameful feeling of having to run from it, the more compassionate will we become as a society. This is because shame is the emotion of rejection and isolation; to respectfully listen to shame is to hear a cry for love and community, for acknowledgment of both the goodness and fullness of our nature. Tuning into this cry—to those common feelings of inadequacy, inferiority, badness, unlovability, fear of abandonment, and so on—could thus be an ecopsychological undertaking of great historical significance, going right to the emotional core of our society. Our historical economic development, writes Kovel, "was won through the destruction of community. . . . From its basis and origin in the differentiated unity of primitive society, subjectivity has undergone a 'progressive' atomization and conflictual intensification with the intrusion, first of the state, then of the capitalist market, into the organic relationship between self, others, and nature. This results in the isolated, deeply problematic subject of today."[191] Hence: "A more or less universal separateness characterizes being under capital."[192] As so many people have realized, overcoming this loss of sociality is a matter of rebuilding community.[193] What is also called for, though, is acknowledgment of the terrible feelings of shame, hate, grief, and so on that the history of desociation has engendered. Whatever form our practice takes, I simply believe it needs to make room for the bearing of these feelings. The practice needed to transform this society, then, may look less like sitting on a meditation cushion and more like holding hands.

And what of the natural world? Bearing pain is always a matter of placing it in a larger context so that it both loses its overwhelming power and is given the space it needs to move. Several years ago I entered into some emotionally stormy waters. After one particularly sleepness night spent with my demons, and feeling all tight with my pain, I made my way to the kitchen for a mug of tea. I was sitting there alone when a cardinal began to whistle outside the window. "*The cardinal still sings*," I whispered . . . and then started to cry. The thick beauty of that song, the cool, pungent early morning air, and the crystallizing words that arrived on my lips, all combined to lift me out of my Ego—out into the enduring life stream beyond my own narrow existence—so that I was finally able to let the healing tears roll down my face. I am sharing this story for two points it illustrates. The first is that the more isolated we are the more pain we feel, that is, the more personal, cramped, and unbearable it becomes.[194] The second is that making healing connections with nonhuman others can involve the simplest of acts. Plainly put, any practice that helps reembed us within the society of nature, or expand the field of our care, cannot but help us bear our pain and suffering.

I vividly recall an Ojibway elder who, while talking before a group of people, said that he lacked the courage on his own to get up in front of a crowd. His strength came from his relationship with the spirit of Bear. If, indeed, it is our nature to seek empowerment from other animals, what more appropriate animal to lend us strength and help "bear" our pain than the bear? (Although there is apparently no etymological link between the verb "to bear" and the lumbering animal we call a "bear," the phonetic link is a fruitful one. Indeed, Hillman notes that such phonetic resemblances may "indicate profound connections."[195]) Shepard writes that our fascination and fear of bears suggests an "urge to be reunited with something lost and treasured, seen in the animal that most resembles us. It is almost as though in him we can see how great is our loss of contact with ourselves. Perhaps the bear can still serve as a pilot and messenger."[196] More generally speaking, I would note, if only suggestively, that if we are to consciously experience our historical suffering as a kind of rite of passage, we had best make it a prayer to the whole natural world.

Contrary to modern myth, the technological domination of nature does not relieve but ultimately exacerbates our suffering. Just what combination of contexts might provide the support for this wounded society to now bear its pain and suffering, for people to give up the fantasy of technological salvation and so come back to earth, is not something that can be predicted. Despite all my tentative commentary, my aim in this section was primarily to raise this topic, to stir up some areas of thought, and not to give any answers. I have attempted in this book to illustrate an approach that puts its faith in the process of feeling our way forward, not in coming up with the master solution. It is the natural governance of this process that is my greatest source of hope.

Last night I was in the pub talking with local environmentalists about their depression and despair. They also talked about their sense for the beauty and wonder of life, and their uncertainty about how to communicate that to the public, how to speak from their passion. As the discussion unfolded into the night it became clear to me that the work of ecopsychology is to help us "come out" as human beings. To come out is to say: "Yes, this is what I am; no apologies." A human being is a servant of nature, a plain member in the community of all life. For us today, however, to stand up and say this with an open heart is to make ourselves vulnerable; is to risk ridicule. We can nonetheless be confident in our vulnerability. As a psychotherapist I know that all people need to love and be loved, that they all suffer in some way or other, and that they are all basically good. As an ecopsychologist, I can now say with equal confidence that all people need to experience themselves as a part of the natural world, need to understand their own naturalness. The more we can, as ecopsychologists, build our alternative vision of humans and nature, the bolder we will become in encouraging others to speak out for a society that is consistent with this vision. Indeed, the promise of ecopsychology is to be a force for the therapeutic, recollective, and critical work that will help to make such a society a reality.

NOTES

Preface

1. Tom Athanasiou, *Divided Planet*, pp. 224–225.

Chapter 1

1. Editors comments, preceding Edith Cobb, "The Ecology of Imagination in Childhood."
2. Harold F. Searles, *The Nonhuman Environment*, p. xi.
3. In order to avoid awkwardness I will henceforth leave quoted male pronouns uneditorialized. In order to maintain gender neutrality in my own writing I will either use plural pronouns or use the phrases "she or he" and "her or him."
4. Searles, *The Nonhuman*, p. 23. Although Searles is a significant figure in the history of ecopsychology, he made only one other relevant contribution of which I am aware, the 1972 article "Unconscious Processes in relation to the Environmental Crisis." (His 1961 article, "The Role of the Nonhuman Environment" is adapted from his book.)
5. Although Searles was speaking as a psychiatrist, I use "psychology" as an umbrella term for all "psy" practice (psychiatry, psychotherapy, psychology, etc.).
6. Paul Shepard, *The Tender Carnivore and the Sacred Game*, p. xvi.
7. Theodore Roszak, *The Voice of the Earth*, p. 19.
8. Elan Shapiro, "Restoring Habitats, Communities, and Souls," p. 225.
9. Carl Jung, "Approaching the Unconscious," p. 85.
10. Roszak, *The Voice*, p. 302.
11. In addition to a personal unconscious composed of repressed mental contents, Jung proposed that we share a "collective unconscious" composed of archetypal contents, or patterns of experience, that have not derived from personal experience, but are rather universal to humanity. See Carl Jung, "The Concept of the Collective Unconscious" and "Instinct and the Unconscious" in *The Portable Jung*. On defining archetypes, see James Hillman, *Re-Visioning Psychology*, pp. xix–xxi.
12. Roszak, *The Voice*, p. 304.
13. Aldo Leopold, *A Sand County Almanac*, pp. viii and 204.
14. See Morris Berman, "The Cybernetic Dream of the Twenty-First Century."

15. Aldo Leopold, quoted in Mary-Ellen Hynes, "Walking in a World of Wounds: The Work of Donna Meadows," p. 10.

16. Leslie Gray, "Shamanic Counseling and Ecopsychology," p. 173. The only other contribution of which I am aware by a Native American is Jeanette Armstrong's moving "Keepers of the Earth."

17. James Hillman and Michael Ventura, *We've Had a Hundred Years of Psychotherapy—And the World's Getting Worse*, p. 51.

18. See Chellis Glendinning, "A Letter from Indian Country" and James Wright, "A Cauldron-Born Quest: Speculations on European Vision Quest Rituals."

19. Anthony Storr, "Man's Relationship with Nature," p. 21.

20. David Kidner, "Why Psychology Is Mute about the Environmental Crisis," pp. 365, 373.

21. Searles, *The Nonhuman*, p. 3.

22. Paul Shepard, *Nature and Madness*, pp. ix, 16, 108, 126, 124.

23. Tom Jay, quoted in Jim Cheney, "Postmodern Environmental Ethics: Ethics as Bioregional Narrative," p. 122. Emphasis removed.

24. Modern philosophy, it is widely acknowledged, has floundered among the various dichotomies issuing from the bifurcation of nature: spirit/matter, mind/body, human/nature, subject/object, knower/known, male/female, reason/feeling, inner/outer. As reality divided in two, so did philosophy, which split itself along the line of those siding with or giving primacy to "inner" reality (rationalists, idealists, intellectualists) and those taking the side of "outer" reality (empiricists, materialists, realists). Modern philosophy, then, is a story of the various attempts to give a complete account of reality from this divided—and so paradoxical—starting point, each effort failing to discover a convincing way to link the two disparate orders of being. (See Bernard Charles Flynn, "Descartes and the Ontology of Subjectivity.") While from our so-called postmodern vantage we can look back on modern philosophy and survey its many shortcomings, the problem of dualism has by no means been solved. Much current philosophy, for example, simply champions a "new spirit substance,. . . language detached from both breath and body" (M. C. Dillon, *Merleau-Ponty's Ontology*, p. x). And for the most part the natural sciences continue to take a materialistic view of reality; matter, after all, is what *matters* for such undertakings as biotechnology. In the realm of art, finally, Aniela Jaffé writes that modern visual art taken as a whole is itself symbolic of a "collective psychic rift." As civilization removed "man further and further from his instinctual foundation . . . a gulf opened between nature and mind, between the unconscious and consciousness. These opposites characterize the psychic situation that is seeking expression in modern art" ("Symbolism in the Visual Arts," p. 290). This rift has been played out, she says, through the two modern extremes of "great abstraction" (spirit) and "great realism" (matter).

25. See J. H. van den Berg, *The Changing Nature of Man*, Chapter Five.

26. James Hillman, "Anima Mundi: The Return of the Soul to the World," p. 74.

27. Carl Jung, "Approaching the Unconscious," in *Man and His Symbols*, p. 6.

28. Sendivogius, quoted in Hillman, "Anima," p. 71.

29. A polarity consists of a relationship between opposite poles wherein each is implicated in, or complementary to, the other—as in "yin and yang," or "up and down." The poles are inseparable from, and take their meaning from, each other, being differentiated from within a single field of reality. Dichotomies, on the other hand, consist of a splitting or dividing of the field into antagonistic or separate realities.

30. Hillman, "Anima," pp. 78–79. The painter Kadinsky similarly wrote that: "Not only the things of poetry, the stars, moon, wood, flowers, but even a white trouser button glittering out of the puddle in the street. . . . Everything has a secret soul" (quoted in Aniela Jaffé, "Symbolism in the Visual Arts," p. 292).

31. George Steiner, *Heidegger,* p. 69.

32. Hillman, *Re-Visioning,* p. 134. Emphasis mine.

33. Hillman, "Anima," pp. 88–89.

34. Hillman, *Re-Visioning,* p. 187.

35. My favourite introductions to phenomenology are in a series of articles by Eugene Gendlin, "Existentialism and Experiential Therapy," "Experiential Explication and Truth," and "Experiential Phenomenology;" and in a single article by David Levin, "Phenomenology in America." The second chapter of David Abram's *The Spell of the Sensuous* is another relatively straightforward introduction. More comprehensive, and challenging, studies include Herbert Spiegelberg, *The Phenomenological Movement;* D. Stewart and A. Mickunas, *Exploring Phenomenology;* and Pierre Thevenaz, *What Is Phenomenology? And Other Essays.*

36. Maurice Merleau-Ponty, *Phenomenology,* p. 92.

37. Merleau-Ponty, *Phenomenology,* p. xi. Or as he puts it otherwise: "Inside and outside are inseparable. The world is wholly inside and I am wholly outside myself" (p. 407). This, significantly, is to give psyche an ontological status, that is, is to conceive of psyche in terms of our primary understanding of being rather than a secondary domain of reality inside our heads—a move that also follows from an "existentializing" of psychology, where human existence is understood as being-in-the-world. How we grasp reality always depends on our mode or style of existing. It is not surprising, then, that in a note to himself (for a book on which he was working at the time of his death), Merleau-Ponty wrote: "I must show that what one might consider to be 'psychology'. . . is in fact ontology" (*The Visible and the Invisible,* p. 176). We might just as well say, conversely, that "ontology is psychology." In other words, once we externalize psyche or contest the mind/world split, then reality becomes psychological through and through. Thus does Hillman boldly conclude that "the psychological perspective is supreme and prior because the psyche is prior and must appear within every human undertaking. The psychological viewpoint does not encroach upon other fields, for it is there to begin with, even if most disciplines invent methods that pretend to keep it out. . . . psychology cannot be limited to being one field among others since psyche itself permeates all fields and things of the world" (*Revisioning,* p. 130).

38. Merleau-Ponty, *Phenomenology,* p. xi. See, also, p. 406.

39. David Abram, "Merleau-Ponty and the Voice of the Earth," p. 105. Hwa Yol

Jung had also made this connection in his 1972 article, "The Ecological Crisis: A Philosophical Perspective, East and West."

40. Merleau-Ponty writes, for example: "As I contemplate the blue of the sky I am not [dualistically] *set over against* it as an acosmic subject . . . ; I abandon myself to it and plunge into this mystery, it 'thinks itself within me' [i.e., as I lend my senses to it], I am the sky itself as it is drawn together and unified, and as it begins to exist for itself; my consciousness is saturated with this limitless blue" (*Phenomenology*, p. 214). He also calls perception "a coition, so to speak, of our body with things" (p. 320).

41. Abram, *The Spell*, p. 262.

42. James Hillman, "Aesthetics and Politics," p. 39.

43. See, respectively, Sarah Conn, "When the Earth Hurts, Who Responds?" and Elan Shapiro, "Restoring Habitats, Communities, and Souls." Another way of looking at this situation is to recognize that once the psyche is turned inside out, reality becomes psychological through and through (see note 37 above). If we are *in* the psyche, if all of our engagement with reality involves the soul in some way, then it is possible to consider any number of practices "psychological," let alone "ecopsychological."

44. The distinction I am making here—between ecopsychology in support of activism and ecopsychology as activism—can be a fine one. In her article "Personal Transformation and Social Change: Conversations with Ecopsychologists in Action," Mary Gomes talks with two people (Renee Soule and Amy Fox) who are "extensively engaged in both ecopsychology and environmental politics." In my reading, the emphasis in the article is on "bringing psychological sensitivity to the environmental movement" (p. 218), and not on reframing this movement as a form of ecopsychological practice in itself. Soule, for example, talks about how "ecopsychology can make an important *contribution* to activism" (p. 226, my emphasis). By bringing attention to its psychospiritual dimension, ecopsychologists may indeed play a role in changing the nature of activism. But the activism will still be activism. That said, I do want to leave space in this account for those who undertake ecological social action precisely as an effort at healing, or as an extension of their personal practice. As the green-Buddhist activist Ken Jones writes: "the distinction between personal Buddhist practice and social activism can be false; there is only one practice to be done" (*The Social Face of Buddhism*, p. 19). Indeed, the wise among us have always taught that everyday life is the primary theater of psychological and spiritual practice.

45. Joanna Macy, "Working Through Environmental Despair," p. 244. See, also, Anita Burrows, "Crying for the Manatees."

46. Joanna Macy, *Despair and Personal Power in the Nuclear Age*, pp. 2, 3.

47. Melissa Melamed, "Reclaiming the Power to Act," p. 9.

48. Roszak, "Where Psyche," p. 2.

49. This quotation is a composite from Theodore Roszak, "The Greening of Psychology" (*Gestalt Journal*), p. 16 and *The Voice of the Earth*, p. 38

50. Macy, *Despair*, p. xiii.

51. Theodore Roszak, "The Greening of Psychology" (*The Ecopsychology Newsletter*), p. 1.

52. Mitchell Thomashow, *Ecological Identity,* pp. 144, 151. Closely related to the psychology *of* activism is the psychology *within* activism. For his report, *The State of Environmentalists,* James Thornton interviewed approximately fifty U.S. environmentalists, many of them high profile mainstream activists and deep ecology supporters. His goal was to assess the emotional atmosphere in which they worked and to see how this atmosphere affected their sense of where the environmental movement was headed. In short, he found that the efforts of his subjects were dominated by hopelessness and anger. Many were strongly attached to their anger, and despite the dangers of burnout were "worried that if anger was not present, there could be no action" (p. 2). Thornton, a Buddhist, therefore finished his report by promoting training in "wisdom practices," such as meditation and group experiential work, so that environmentalists may become less angry and develop a more positive and clear-headed vision for their work.

53. Joanna Macy, *World as Lover, World as Self,* p. 185.

54. Sarah Conn, "Protest and Thrive," p. 11.

55. Macy, *Despair,* p. 69.

56. A more recent work by Joanna Macy and Molly Brown, *Coming Back to Life,* includes exercises from both "despair and empowerment" and "Council of All Being" workshops.

57. Council of All Being (CAB) workshops are based on the idea that deep ecology "remains a concept without power to transform our awareness and behavior unless we allow ourselves to feel—which means feeling the pain within us over what is happening to our world. . . . Often [this pain] arises as a deep sense of loss over what is slipping away— ancient forests and clean rivers, birdsongs and breathable air" (Joanna Macy and Pat Fleming, "Guidelines for a Council of All Beings Workshop," in John Seed, et al., *Thinking Like a Mountain,* p. 101).

58. Carl Anthony, "Ecopsychology and the Deconstruction of Whiteness," pp. 264, 273.

59. See Carolyn Merchant, *The Death of Nature.*

60. Cf. Martin Heidegger, "The Question Concerning Technology," in *The Question Concerning Technology, And Other Essays.*

61. See Carolyn Merchant, *Radical Ecology;* Carolyn Merchant, ed., *Ecology;* Michael Zimmerman, *Contesting Earth's Future;* and Michael Zimmerman, ed., *Environmental Philosophy: From Animal Rights to Radical Ecology.*

62. See Bill Devall and George Sessions, *Deep Ecology,* p. 70. For other overviews of deep ecology, see Arne Naess, "The Shallow and the Deep, Long-Range Ecology Movement. A Summary"; Bill Devall, *Simple in Means, Rich in Ends;* and Warwick Fox, *Toward a Transpersonal Ecology.* Practically speaking, deep ecology is a movement for cultivating "ecosophy" or "earth wisdom," which involves deepening one's sense of connection to earth and learning to "harmonize with the will-of-the-land" (Devall, *Simple,* pp. 10–11).

63. In a world viewed ecologically, things do not stand alone as self-contained, wholly independent, or static entities. Ecology is a perspective, rather, that regards all relations as *internal* relations: all phenomena are seen as interdependent processes, par-

ticipating in, structuring, or implying one another. My lungs, for instance, have no mean-ing without air to breathe; they imply air. Things link up, tie together, point to one another, form one whole.

64. Gary Snyder, Interviewed by Catherine Ingram, pp. 238–239.

65. *Self-realization* is the central norm in the particular ecophilosophy advanced by the person who in 1973 first gave deep ecology its name, Arne Naess. By Self-realization he means the broadening and deepening of the self to achieve as wide an identification with the world as possible. Fox decided (with some controversy) that Naess's philosophy is the most tenable and distinctive among the various approaches to deep ecology; he therefore used it as the basis for transpersonal ecology. See Arne Naess, "*Self*Realization: An Ecologi-cal Approach to Being in the World"; and Fox, *Toward.*

66. I consider George Bradford's "Toward a Deep Social Ecology" to be a relatively balanced critique of deep ecology. While Bradford is hard on the deep ecology movement for its failure to see the social and historical roots of its ecological and philosophical questions, he nonetheless does regard the basic insights and sensibilities of deep ecology (e.g., its poetic, animistic vision, and its respect for kinship with the land) as a "fundamental precondition for breaking out of the prison-house of urban-industrial civilization and creating a family of free cultures in harmony with one another and the Earth" (p. 418).

67. See chapter ten, "Character and Culture," in Devall and Sessions, *Deep;* and p. 2 of Devall, *Simple.*

68. I am taking cues here from Carolyn Merchant's brief summary of critiques of deep ecology in *Radical Ecology,* pp. 102–105.

69. Quoted in Bradford, "Toward," p. 419.

70. See Karren Warren, "The Power and Promise of Ecological Feminism."

71. Ariel Salleh, "The Ecofeminist/Deep Ecology Debate: A Reply to Patriarchal Reason," p. 214. Val Plumwood writes on this that the domination of women is an "illuminating model for many other kinds of domination, since the oppressed are often both feminized and naturalized" ("Ecosocial Feminism as a General Theory of Oppres-sion," p. 211).

72. Ariel Salleh, "Class, Race, and Gender Discourse in the Ecofeminist/Deep Ecology Debate," p. 229.

73. Ecofeminist Jim Cheney and others claim that the psychology of deep ecology is actually of an alienated masculine sort, in which relief is sought either through inflating one's ego to include the entire cosmos or through obliterating oneself through a holistic merger with the natural world. According to Zimmerman, on the other hand, he, Naess, and Snyder do not interpret Self-realization as a process of self-*expansion* but of self-*empty-ing,* of realizing the illusory nature or emptiness of the ego self (see *Contesting,* p. 314).

74. There are two ecofeminist-based articles in the main ecopsychology text (Roszak, et al., *Ecopsychology*), neither of which addresses the ecofeminism-deep ecology debate. Roszak, I should also note, does give some mention the ecofeminism-deep ecology debate in his *The Voice of the Earth.* I have, of course, not been able to outline all the features

of this debate, seeking primarily to indicate only that there *is* a debate. Deep ecology theorists have made numerous responses to their critics. See *The Trumpeter* 12:3 (1995); Warwick Fox, "The Deep Ecology-Ecofeminism Debate and Its Parallels"; and Zimmerman, *Contesting*.

75. Social ecology's main theorist is Murray Bookchin, although he is by no means its authoritative voice. His main work is *The Ecology of Freedom*, while *Remaking Society* is a more accessible introduction. While ecofeminism and social ecology share a focus on social and historical issues, they have differing philosophies and agendas. On this see Val Plumwood, "Ecosocial Feminism as a General Theory of Oppression." On Ecosocialism, finally, see James O'Connor's "Socialism and Ecology" and *Natural Causes*, as well as Kovel's forthcoming *The Enemy of Nature*.

76. I should note that there are a number of ecopsychologists besides Anthony (e.g., Allen Kanner, Mary Gomes, Jeanine Canty) who advocate for more of a multicultural perspective within ecopsychology. As far as I am aware, however, they have yet to publish any statements on the matter. I should also mention Renée Soule, who coauthored an article with Anthony ("A Multicultural Approach to Ecopsychology").

77. Anthony, "Ecopsychology," p. 264. "Environmental injustice. . . refers to the fact that poor communities are disproportionately harmed by industrial toxic pollution and that corporations and government—intentionally or unintentionally—build their worst toxic sites and store their most hazardous chemicals in and around these low-income neighborhoods. It also refers to the well-documented fact that local governments have excluded minority communities from environmental planning and that toxic sites have destroyed many traditional minority communities" (Ruth Rosen, "Who Gets Polluted?).

78. ". . . the kind of knowledge and insight that upsets institutions and threatens to overturn sovereign regimes of truth" (Joe Kincheloe and Peter McLaren, "Rethinking Critical Theory and Qualitative Research," p. 138).

79. Joel Kovel, "The American Mental Health Industry," p. 89.

80. Russell Jacoby, *Social Amnesia*, p. 125.

81. Norman O. Brown, *Life Against Death*, p. xvii.

82. Joel Kovel, "Therapy in Late Capitalism," in *The Radical Spirit*, p. 121.

83. Kovel, "Therapy," in *The Radical*, p. 119.

84. Dreyer Kruger, *The Changing Reality of Modern Man*, p. xiv. In addition to those cited here, my main sources for these views include David Ingleby (ed.), *Critical Psychiatry;* David Levin (ed.), *Pathologies of the Modern Self;* Joel Kovel, *The Age of Desire;* Issac Prilelltensky, *The Morals and Politics of Psychology;* Christopher Lasch, *The Culture of Narcissism;* and articles by Philip Cushman and Edward Sampson.

85. Tom Athanasiou, *Divided Planet*, p. 52. See also Brian Tokar, *Earth for Sale*.

86. As Kovel says, "*psyche* refers not to an isolatable thing but to a historically dynamic relation between a person and a social totality. . . . And if this is so, then the consequences for *psychology* are drastic, for it finds itself without the confident location of an object for its discourse" ("Mind and State in Ancient Greece," in *The Radical Spirit*, p. 224).

Kovel also has an interest in ecological politics, which makes his combination of social and psychological theory particularly helpful to ecopsychology. See, for example, "The Marriage of Radical Ecologies," p. 406.

87. See, for example, his "Things and Words."

88. I am referring here to Fox's *Toward a Transpersonal Ecology.* In his "The Deep Ecology-Ecofeminism Debate and Its Parallels," he defends deep ecology against criticisms made by ecofeminists and social ecologists, but his discussion there is not psychologically focused.

89. See, for example, the contributions in the journal *ReVision* (20.4, 1998), which are dedicated to the theme of "Ecopsychology and Social Transformation." In her "A Psychological Impact Report for the Environmental Movement," for instance, Melissa Nelson writes of how our "polluted thinking" creates a form of consciousness "that manifests in destructive beliefs and behaviours such as anthropocentrism, racism, sexism, nationalism, classism, greed, and aggressiveness" (p. 38).

90. Allen Kanner and Mary Gomes, "The All-Consuming Self," p. 83.

91. In his *Regarding Nature,* Andrew McLaughlin makes this same point in relation to the ecology movement in general.

92. Roszak, "Where Psyche," p. 15. Roszak is suggesting that if we could say with the "full weight of professional psychological authority" that humans are emotionally bonded to the earth, then this might "achieve the same legal and policy-making force that now attaches to physical hazards like toxic waste."

93. Sarah Conn, "When the Earth Hurts, Who Responds?," p. 162.

94. See, for example, Irene Harvey, "Schizophrenia and Metaphysics: Analyzing the DSM-III."

95. Joel Kovel, "A Critique of DSM-III," p. 135.

96. Conn does not view "the need to consume" as an individual issue, for example, but as "as a serious signal of our culture's disconnection from the Earth." She would therefore *revise* the DSM to include this larger context. My point, by contrast, is to suggest that ecopsychology keep its distance from establishment psychology altogether; that it stay radical, rather than reformist.

97. A point I first made in my, "Toward a More Radical Ecopsychology."

98. Roszak, *The Voice,* p. 55. Roszak refers, moreover, mostly to the "anti-psychiatry" movement of the sixties and seventies, in which psychiatrists such as R. D. Laing contended that the so-called mentally ill were expressing a sensible response to social conditions that were themselves mad. I have in mind, rather, the more sociologically and philosophically informed works of the critics listed above, that is, Kovel et al.

99. Charles Taylor, quoted in Raymond Rogers, *Nature and the Crisis of Modernity,* p. 166.

100. Stan Rowe, *Home Place,* p. 5.

101. Konrad Stettbacher, *Making Sense of Suffering,* p. 42.

102. The well-known ecologists Anne and Paul Ehrlich, for example, have written a book called *Healing the Planet,* in which there are headings about pollution, the ozone layer,

and so on—but none about healing humans. The danger that industrial society poses to human *physical* health have, of course, always been a focus of modern environmentalism. The environmental justice movement, which emerged in the mid-1980s, does include humans within its definition of "the environment," but focuses mostly on social rather than psychological issues (see Giovanna Di Chiro, "Nature as Community: The Convergence of Environment and Social Justice").

103. Joel Kovel, "Rejoinder to Kenneth J. Gergen," p. 407. Kovel asks, as I do: "if we are completely malleable [i.e., without a nature], then what can be postulated as the source of the drive toward freedom and the resistance to oppression?" ("On the Notion of Human Nature," p. 371).

104. John Rodman, "The Liberation of Nature?," pp. 89–90.

105. Gordon Wheeler, *Gestalt Reconsidered*, p. 34.

106. John Dewey, *Experience and Nature*, p. x.

107. John Welwood, "Meditation and the Unconscious: A New Perspective," p. 8.

108. See Eugene Gendlin, "A Philosophical Critique of the Concept of Narcissism." Gendlin uses the Women's Movement as an example of how everyday experience can imply social change, that is, how women's experience of social reality contests that reality because it oppresses them as women (pp. 296–297). Just so, in an ecodestructive society our everyday experience implies social change toward a more ecological one.

Chapter Two

1. John Livingston, *The Fallacy of Wildlife Conservation*, p. 15.

2. Albert Borgmann, *Technology and the Character of Contemporary Life*, p. 182.

3. Albert Borgmann, *Crossing the Postmodern Divide*, pp. 2–3.

4. Owen Barfield, *Poetic Diction*, p. 213.

5. Robert Socolow, quoted in Borgmann, *Technology*, pp. 185–186. Emphasis mine.

6. John Rodman, "The Liberation of Nature?," pp. 83–84.

7. Neil Evernden, *The Natural Alien*, p. 3. See, also, Neil Evernden, ed., *The Paradox of Environmentalism*.

8. Livingston, *The Fallacy*, p. 50.

9. I borrow this phrase from Raymond Rogers, *Nature and the Crisis of Modernity*, p. 150.

10. Ernest Laclau and Chantal Mouffe, commenting on Gramsci, in Marilyn Cooper, "Environmental Rhetoric in the Age of Hegemonic Politics," p. 241.

11. Borgmann also lists *the primacy of method* and *individualism* as defining features of the modern era, the main authors of these two features being Descartes and Locke, respectively. Ecopsychology, as should be evident by the end of this chapter, stands opposed to these two as well.

12. In his chapter on "Common Sense as a Cultural System," anthropologist Clifford Geertz writes: "As a frame for thought, and a species of it, common sense is as

totalizing as any other: no religion is more dogmatic, no science more ambitious, no philosophy more general." As a cultural system, however, rather than some immediately given native wisdom: "It can be questioned, disputed, affirmed, developed, formalized, contemplated, even taught, and it can vary dramatically from one people to the next" (*Local Knowledge*, pp. 76, 84).

13. Norman Denzin and Yvonna Lincoln, "Introduction: Entering the Field of Qualitative Research," p. 4.

14. A phrase I prefer over "abnormal," even if the latter makes for smoother English.

15. Tom Athanasiou, *Divided Planet*, pp. 44, 197.

16. Maurice Merleau-Ponty, *Phenomenology of Perception*, p. 24.

17. Martin Packer and Richard Addison, "Introduction," to *Entering the Circle*, p. 13. I am using the term "objectivism" here in a broad sense, as the position which insists that there must be some ahistorical, definitive framework that can serve as a foundation for all knowledge claims (see Richard Bernstein, *Beyond Objectivism and Relativism*).

18. See David Canter and Kenneth Craig, "Environmental Psychology"; Daniel Stokols and Irwin Altman, eds., *Handbook of Environmental Psychology;* and Russell Veitch and Daniel Arkkelin, *Environmental Psychology.*

19. Although David Seamon has made a call for a more phenomenological orientation to environmental psychology ("The Phenomenological Contribution to Environmental Psychology"), he did so precisely because the latter is so objectivistic in outlook.

20. Rachel and Stephen Kaplan, *The Experience of Nature*, pp. 1, 196.

21. David Kidner, "Why Psychology Is Mute About the Environmental Crisis," pp. 368, 370.

22. Kaplans, *The Experience*, pp. ix, 198.

23. I do not mean to demonize mainstream environmentalism. The radical critique does not make the concerns and efforts of the mainstream irrelevant, but rather points to the ways in which this mainstream, by itself, still supports the status quo.

24. Russell Veitch and Daniel Arkkelin, *Environmental Psychology,* p. 425.

25. Paul Stern, "Psychological Dimensions of Global Environmental Change," p. 295.

26. Ecopsychologists, of course, are not the only ones involved in such criticism, for the positivist conception of an "objective" nature (one unaffected by historical or social prejudice, human meaning or value, ideological distortion, and so on) is increasingly in disrepute. As historian Elizabeth Bird states: "Every aspect of scientific theory and practice expresses socio-political interests, cultural themes and metaphors, personal interactions, and professional negotiations for the power to name the world" ("The Social Construction of Nature," p. 256). For more specific treatments of this topic, see Donna Haraway's *Primate Visions,* in which, taking primatology as her vehicle, she examines how "themes of race, sexuality, gender, nation, family, and class have been written into the body of nature in western life sciences since the eighteenth century"; or Donald Worster's *The Economy of*

Nature, in which he traces the history of social metaphors embedded in the shifting theories of scientific ecology. In addition, a significant number of natural scientists (e.g., feminist scientists) have themselves put traditional natural science into question. See, for example, Evelyn Fox Keller, *Reflections on Gender and Science.*

27. Arthur Kleinman, *Rethinking Psychiatry,* p. 1.

28. As discussed at length in Maurice Merleau-Ponty, *Phenomenology.* A valuable, Heideggerian treatment of this topic is also given by Medard Boss in his *Existential Foundations of Medicine and Psychology.*

29. In a recent article ("The Myth of the Organicity of Mental Disorders"), Victor D. Sanua argues that after a hundred years of research into the brains, biochemistry, and genes of schizophrenics, no case can be made for an organic basis to schizophrenic suffering. Psychiatry leaves in its wake one discarded theory after another, each announced in its day with the claim that the "cause" of schizophrenia had finally been found. He asks: "Why do biopsychiatrists continue to attribute mental disorders to organic factors, while ignoring completely social factors which offer a more parsimonious explanation for the development of mental disorders?" (p. 61). As Judith Herman writes, "many or even most psychiatric patients are survivors of childhood abuse" (*Trauma and Recovery,* p. 122). Arthur Kleinman similarly comments that the genetic theory of schizophrenia "is now in complete disarray. Inheritance has not been proven. . . . There is still, after more than 30 years of intense biological investigation, no clear-cut understanding of the biology of schizophrenia. . . . This does not deter psychiatrists and those who write the advertisements for drug companies from asserting without any hesitation that schizophrenia is a biologically based disorder. This belief is the central tenet of professional orthodoxy" (*Rethinking Psychiatry,* p. 188, n. 1 for chapt. 3). While schizophrenia will always be a possibility within the vulnerable terms of the human condition, less "developed" countries reportedly have relatively low rates of it, with some small preliterate societies being almost entirely free of it. On the other hand, rates are globally highest in North America and some European societies (Kleinman, *Rethinking,* pp. 34–35). It has therefore been suggested that not only biology, but political economy plays an important role among the conditions that contribute to schizophrenia. The condition of the Western economy and "the development of capitalist modes of wage-labor in non-Western societies appear to lead to greater numbers of individuals manifesting schizophrenia and fewer of them improving" (Richard Warner quoted in Kleinman, *Rethinking,* p. 36).

30. The outspoken psychiatrist Peter Breggin calls schizophrenia not a disease but a psychospiritual crisis. Repeating a point made familiar by the antipsychiatry tradition, he argues that schizophrenic speech appears to have no meaning only when it is taken literally rather than metaphorically or poetically. He refers to one schizophrenic patient, Brugo, who was shown on the television program *60 Minutes* speaking about such things as being Adam and Eve's kin, being a Homo-erectus man, and about not yet being extinct. While the intention of the program was to demonstrate the nonsensibility of schizophrenic communication, Breggin heard Brugo *symbolically* discoursing about his "desperate need for

personal value and dignity, his identification with religion and humanity, and perhaps his awareness of primitive [*sic*] impulses stirring inside himself, as well as his fear of personal extinction" (Breggin, *Toxic,* p. 23).

There is a large body of literature arguing for the meaningfulness of schizophrenic experience, and protesting the medical model. James Glass, for example, writes that schizophrenics' delusional systems—obsessed as they are by themes of power, domination, enslavement, violence, and transformation—mirror the mentality of political programs and leaders that themselves paranoically divide the world into powerful and weak, seek to dominate others, and so on. "By being in the world," says Glass, "the schizophrenic conveys messages about social power; yet in its haste to banish the mad, society blunts their implicit criticisms and its symbolic meaning" ("Schizophrenia and Rationality," p. 431). David Levin, furthermore, says that in the speech of schizophrenia "there is always a painful truth about us, about family, society, world, which needs to be recognized." In particular, Levin suggests that the voice of schizophrenia is the most extreme manifestation of the pain inherent in modern dualism, wherein the inner self is isolated from the external world, cut off, lonely, empty, fearful of engulfment, and so on ("Clinical Stories: A Modern Self in the Fury of Being"). See also Peter Breggin and Mark Stern, eds., *Psychosocial Approaches to Deeply Disturbed Persons.*

31. Joel Kovel, "The American Mental Health Industry," p. 86. Eugene Gendlin's remarks are also relevant here: "I think that all our efforts to define schizophrenia—to classify it as a disease entity—will fail. Schizophrenia is something that *isn't.* Interaction *isn't.* Being alive toward other people *isn't.* Certainly there must be all sorts of chemical imbalances and organismic reactions as a result of this. If we can find chemical means to alleviate these, the individual may be more able to become reconnected. I doubt, however, that there can be a chemical or any other kind of cure without interaction. I think the *not* being, the cutoffness of interaction constitutes what we call schizophrenia" ("Schizophrenia: Problems and Methods of Psychotherapy," pp. 183–184).

32. See Sanua, "The Myth," p. 59.

33. The latest version of the American Psychiatric Association's *Diagnostic and Statistical Manual of Mental Disorders* (DSM-IV) includes "psychosocial and environmental problems" among its diagnostic axes. These problems nonetheless still have a minor presence in the manual, and their inclusion in no way makes the DSM a work of social commentary. Nor does the mention of these problems do much to change the predominantly medical ethos within the mental health setting.

34. Despite my concerns about biopsychiatry, I am not an outright opponent of psychobiological research, some of which has shed very helpful light on the physiological aspects of trauma (see, for example, Bessel van der Kolk, et al., *Traumatic Stress*). Nor do I think that it is always a bad idea to use psychiatric medication, especially for persons who have been traumatized and who are unable to "regulate" their overwhelming emotional reactions in other than self-destructive ways, or persons who have no other good options for reducing their suffering to the point where they can actually engage in a healing process or

manage their lives. What I do object to is the *reduction* of human suffering to a purely medical condition and human nature to biomechanics. It goes without saying that there would be less need for medication if the experience of trauma were not so common and if we had more humane and understanding environments in which to see our emotional and spiritual crises through. Kovel cites a case—Soteria House—where a "drug-free, nonmedical treatment environment worked better for acute psychosis and was far cheaper to boot." Yet, it "was perceived as a threat to the medical-pharmaceutical-insurance-government power structure, and was eliminated" ("Schizophrenic Being and Technocratic Society," pp. 345–347). See Loren Mosher, "Soteria: a Therapeutic Community for Psychotic Persons."

35. I am taking some of my cues here from Joel Kovel, "On the Notion of Human Nature: A Contribution Toward a Philosophical Anthropology" and "Things and Words."

36. As discussed in his writings on Freud in *The Conflict of Interpretations* and in *Freud and Philosophy.* The quote is from Kovel, "Things," p. 23.

37. Georgia O'Keeffe, quoted in Mical Goldfarb, "Making the Unknown Known," p. 180.

38. Hans-Georg Gadamer, "The Problem of Historical Consciousness," p. 86.

39. Richard Rorty, *Philosophy and the Mirror of Nature,* pp. 360, 373. John Dewey quoted on p. 379. On this point, see also John Caputo, *Radical Hermeneutics,* chapter eight.

40. Richard Palmer, *Hermeneutics,* p. 215.

41. J. H. van den Berg, *The Changing Nature of Man,* pp. 95, 96. Italics mine. "Natural understanding" is a phrase used to denote everyday, pretheoretical understanding.

42. Stanley Diamond, *In Search of the Primitive,* p. 122.

43. George Sessions, "Paul Shepard: Ecological Elder," p. 86.

44. Van den Berg, *The Changing,* p. 234.

45. Richard Nelson, "Searching for the Lost Arrow," p. 203.

46. Hans-Georg Gadamer, quoted in Bernstein, *Beyond,* p. 148.

47. It is this point, once again, that differentiates ecopsychology from environmental psychology.

48. By contrast Hans Peter Duerr suggests that normal scientists "mount the *defence* against what is strange" (*Dreamtime,* p. 126).

49. Hans-Georg Gadamer, "Practical Philosophy as a Model of the Human Sciences," p. 83.

50. Hans-Georg Gadamer, "The Universality of the Hermeneutical Problem," in *Philosophical Hermeneutics,* p. 5.

51. As related by Bernstein, *Beyond,* pp. 128–129.

52. Borgmann, *Crossing,* p. 51.

53. Rorty, *Philosophy,* p. 300. Rorty is here drawing on the views of Donald Davidson.

54. Kovel, "On the Notion," pp. 378–380. See also "Freud's Ontology—Agency and Desire."

55. Gadamer ultimately avoids this charge, for he claims that language always refers

back to lived experience, of which language is the articulation. The criticism here, however, is that his view of experience has little body. On this, see Jerald Wallulis, "Carrying Forward: Gadamer and Gendlin on History, Language, and the Body."

56. Eugene Gendlin, "Human Nature and Concepts," p. 5. I added the word "human" to indicate the possibility of nonhuman language and culture.

57. Eugene Gendlin, "A Philosophical Critique of Narcissism," p. 293.

58. David Abram, "Merleau-Ponty and the Voice of the Earth," p. 112.

59. Hermeneutics and phenomenology have a close relationship. While hermeneutics may not always be associated with phenomenology, Heidegger claimed in *Being and Time* that phenomenology is necessarily hermeneutical, working as it does to interpret or uncover phenomena. This "hermeneutic phenomenology" is distinguished from Edmund Husserl's "transcendental" phenomenology, the latter of which is conceived as an attempt to describe the pure structures of transcendental consciousness. While Merleau-Ponty held that his own work sprang most directly from the later Husserl, his writings are nonetheless best located in the tradition of hermeneutic phenomenology. Even Husserl's work can in retrospect be read as a hermeneutical undertaking.

60. My discussion here is drawing on Hubert Dreyfus, *Being-in-the-World*, pp. 16–23, and Martin Heidegger, *Being and Time*, p. 191. Dreyfus notes that there is no reason to believe that there are *any* theories, principles, or rules behind the "pervasive responses, discriminations, motor skills, and so forth" that make up our cultural practices. "Indeed, if one tried to state the rules for distance-standing, one would require further rules, such as standing closer if there is a noise in the background, or further away if the person has the flu, and the application of these rules would require further rules, and so on, always leading us back to further, everyday, taken-for-granted practices."

61. Such biases are in fact necessary for *any* inquiry to proceed, for they provide the initial organization or orientation for any kind of sense-making whatsoever. As Gadamer wrote: "Prejudices are biases of our openness to the world. They are simply conditions whereby we experience something—whereby what we encounter says something to us" ("The Universality," in *Philosophical*, p. 9). He was, accordingly, critical of the Enlightenment "prejudice against prejudices."

62. Palmer, *Hermeneutics*, p. 25.

63. Gadamer has been criticized for his notion of a "fusion of horizons" because it does not adequately account for the problematic aspects of dialogue or communication. Critics such as Jürgen Habermas rightly say that in describing fusion as a simple process in which preexisting traditions are mutually enriched, Gadamer does not sufficiently consider how communication is ideologically distorted and disrupted or how traditions can oppress people and limit their view of reality. For us, dialogue does not take place in some ideal community of equal participants but in a world riven with class interests and exploitative relations. While I believe there is merit in these criticisms, I also believe that the notion of a "fusion of horizons" does describe the everyday process by which meaning is transmitted and our biases are revealed. In other words, I think it is fair to use the term for the phenomenon it truly does describe, even if a critical hermeneutics must go beyond the

model of a simple fusing of horizons (i.e., dialogue under ideal circumstances) to also engage in the critique of ideology.

64. David Young and Jean-Guy Goulet, eds., *Being Changed.*

65. Richard Bernstein, *Beyond Objectivism and Relativism*, p. 141.

66. This point is made repeatedly in a recent issue of *Man and World*, 30 (1997), which is dedicated entirely to the topic of hermeneutics and natural science. Human/social scientists are increasingly adopting explicitly interpretive or qualitative approaches, although academic psychologists in particular have been slow to make the move. On the reluctance of the psychological mainstream to incorporate a hermeneutic perspective, see Kenneth Gergen, "Emerging Challenges for Theory and Psychology;" Stanley Messer et al., *Hermeneutics and Psychological Theory;* and Martin Packer and Richard Addison, eds., *Entering the Circle: Hermeneutic Investigation in Psychology.*

67. This is not to say, however, that there are not many scientists aware of hermeneutical issues.

68. Gadamer, "The Problem," p. 133.

69. Clifford Geertz, *The Interpretation of Cultures*, p. 96.

70. Baleen, quoted in Joel Kovel, *History and Spirit*, pp. 58–59.

71. Allen D. Kanner, "The Voice of the Earth: A Review," p. 170.

72. Robert Greenway, "The Wilderness Effect and Ecopsychology," p. 123. See also "Psychoecology as a Search for Language."

73. Christine Downing, "Poetically Dwells Man on this Earth," pp. 316–317. Emphases mine.

74. Peter Mathiessen, *The Nine-Headed Dragon River*, pp. ix–x. Charles Bergman, furthermore, echoes a common sentiment when he says: "increasingly we are coming to know nature through what is no longer available to us" ("The Curious Peach," p. 282).

75. Richard Nelson, *The Island Within*, p. 280.

76. Rogers, *Nature*, p. 152. Indeed, Rogers argues that a sense of loss is "the central battleground over which this divisiveness [between the radicals and the mainstream] struggles."

77. Erazim Kohák writes that "discourse seeks to communicate by evoking an experience shared" (*The Embers and the Stars*, 64). As I noted at the start of this chapter, however, the possibilities for communication become slim when one's experience is not shared by others (at least not on the surface). By focusing on what I presume is a common experience—loss—I am thus hoping indeed to evoke an "experience shared."

78. In his book *Radical Hermeneutics*, John Caputo does a good job of laying out what is at issue here. Caputo adopts Søren Kierkegaard's distinction between two basic orientations toward life: "recollection" and "repetition." Recollection is backward looking; it tries to regain something lost or forgotten, seeks to recover from a fall. Repetition, meanwhile, is forward looking; it is based on the idea that we come to know ourselves— repeatedly come back to ourselves—only by courageously pushing ahead through our difficulties, not by trying to recover some former innocence. The knock against recollection is that it "begins at the end instead of at the beginning, with the loss instead of the task" (p.

14). As Caputo describes it: "The love of repetition is happy, an earnest and exhilarating struggle, while the love of recollection is a nostalgic melancholy longing for a lost paradise, a dreamy wistfulness" (p. 15). I think, however, that this contrast is unfairly put. Repetition appears in such a positive light only because recollection is cast so negatively. This is the kind of binary strategy that Caputo is himself so adamant that we deconstruct (recollection is repetition's negated "other"). I would instead adopt an orientation that incorporates both motions, and that sees either motion on its own as problematic. A recollection that only looks backward, that spends all its time dwelling on losses and fantasizing about an idyllic past, is indeed an avoidance of present society, as well as a recipe for perpetual discontent. A repetition that lacks a recollective moment, however, is no less of a problem. For it misses utterly the genuine experience of loss; becomes insensitive to the deep "pain for home" (the etymological meaning of "nostalgia") that many people do in fact feel. At a time when our society is so obviously estranged from its "earth-home" (*oikos*), when such great numbers of people have been dislocated, when so much is disappearing, and when "soul loss" is such a common complaint, I just see no merit in dismissing all talk of loss as weak-willed or deluded chatter. I would ask the reader, then, not to confuse my use of the term *recollection* with Caputo's. For one thing, I am not trying to recall a golden era but rather our own human nature and our grounding in the more-than-human earth. I focus on *both* loss *and* task. I frame ecopsychology as a response to history, not a running away from it. Repetition, says Caputo, "is a living response which speaks against, protests, disavows the weight of tradition which has become leaden and lifeless" (p. 91). So would I describe the critical work of ecopsychology. It is in fact precisely through a process of recollection that I see ecopsychology helping us to find the strength and creativity to move forward. (Despite my disagreements with Caputo, there is much in his book that I would support, including his proposal for "an ethics of otherness, an ethics aimed at giving what is other as big a break as possible" (p. 260).)

As for the charge that to concentrate on our modern losses is to neglect or be ungrateful for what has in fact been gained, I will simply say that this is not necessarily the case. As should be apparent in this book, I am very much in support of the modern ideal of authenticity, as well as the modern goal of universal freedom and solidarity. In short, I seek to counter modernity only in its negative aspects; I want to get *beyond* modernity, not to duplicate precisely some premodern state of affairs. If I focus on the experience of loss it is only because I feel there is much important work to be done by doing so.

79. David Abram, *The Spell of the Sensuous*, p. 196.

80. On the relationship between theory and practice within an experiential framework, see Eugene Gendlin, "The Role of Knowledge in Practice."

81. The work of philosopher Eugene Gendlin has been crucial to me in validating such an approach.

82. Erazim Kohák, *The Embers and the Stars*, p. 55. Emphasis removed.

83. Paul Campbell, "Poetic-Rhetorical, Philosophical, and Scientific Discourse," p. 2.

84. Aristotle himself dedicated an entire book of his *Rhetoric* to the topic of individual and group psychology.

85. Hillman, *Revisioning*, pp. xvi, 213. The mind, says Hillman, has a poetic basis; it seeks meaning, not facts. Hence, to become less literal is to become more psychological— a point lost on those scientific psychologists who seek literal, objective accounts of psychological life.

86. It is worth noting, in this vein, that the traditional goal of rhetoric is to advance a persuasive case for how to deal with a collectively held problem that defies easy, single-discipline solution. "Rhetoric exists. . . because a world of certainty is not the world of human affairs. It exists because the world of human affairs is a world where there must be an alternative to certain [apodeictic] knowledge on the one hand and pure chance and whimsy on the other. The alternative is informed opinion." Rhetoric guides decision making, "where no method is inherent in the total subject-matter of decision" (Donald Bryant, "Rhetoric: Its Function and Its Scope," p. 39).

87. Borgmann, *Technology*, p. 240.

88. I am borrowing here from Charles Taylor, who, in the same spirit as Borgmann, has written that: "As our public traditions of family, ecology, even polis are undermined or swept away, we need new languages of personal resonance to make crucial human goods alive for us again" (*Sources of the Self*, p. 513).

89. Owen Barfield, "The Meaning of the Word 'Literal,'" p. 57. Emphasis mine.

90. Barfield, *Poetic*, p. 63. Emphasis removed.

91. Ralph Waldo Emerson, quoted in Barfield, *Poetic*, p. 179. Heidegger likewise wrote: "Poetry proper is never merely a higher mode of everyday language. It is rather the reverse: everyday language is a forgotten and therefore used-up poem, from which there hardly resounds a call any longer" (quoted in Charles Taylor, "Heidegger, Language, Ecology," p. 269, n. 32). Or as Paul Ricoeur says: "Every metaphor is a poem in miniature" (quoted in Véronique Fóti, "Alterity and the Dynamics of Metaphor," p. 307).

92. There is therefore no sharp line between literal and figurative speech, but only different degrees of metaphorical "twist" that may still be felt in a word or phrase. The point of this paragraph—that the metaphoric-poetic mode is primary—has been well established by many others. In addition to the works by Burke, Barfield, Romanyshyn, and Campbell cited in this section, see Eugene Gendlin's numerous writings on metaphor and experience; Merleau-Ponty's writings on speech/language in *Phenomenology of Perception* (as well as Jerry Gill's study, *Merleau-Ponty and Metaphor*); Heidegger's *Poetry, Language, Thought;* and, for psychological perspectives, James Hillman's *Re-Visioning Psychology;* Ronald Valle and Rolf von Eckartsberg, ed.'s *The Metaphors of Consciousness;* and David Leary, ed.'s *Metaphors in the History of Psychology.*

93. Edmund Burke, quoted in Campbell, "Poetic-Rhetorical," p. 3.

94. Paul Campbell, *Rhetoric-Ritual*, p. 21. The word *rhetoric* traces back to a prehistoric Indo-European base, *wer-*, which means "speak, say," and which also gives us *word* and *verb*.

95. Mikhail Bakhtin, *Speech Genres and Other Late Essays*, p. 92, emphasis removed. The modern scientific and philosophical dream, by contrast, was to discover the literal foundations of reality without having to resort to using figurative, rhetorical language in order to persuade one's audience toward the truth. Thus, in 1667 Thomas Sprat wrote of the Royal Society of London that it had "endeavored to separate the knowledge of Nature from the colours of *Rhetorick,* the devices of *Fancy,* [and] the delightful deceit of *Fables*" (David Leary, "Psyche's Muse," p. 8).

96. Campbell, "Poetic-Rhetorical," p. 5.

97. Hans-Georg Gadamer, "On the Scope and Function of Hermeneutical Reflection," in *Philosophical Hermeneutics,* p. 24. See also "The Hermeneutics of Suspicion," in which Gadamer notes that there is a "deep inner convergence with rhetoric and hermeneutics."

98. Borgmann, *Technology,* p. 178.

99. "World" refers here to the everyday context or interrelational whole in which we gather the meaning of things according to our practical, concernful involvement with them. To the extent that natural scientists attempt to rub out any such involvement, their methods "deworld" nature—disclose it in only its thinnest, decontextualized, meaning-shrunken dimensions. On this, see Dreyfus, *Being,* chapter eleven.

100. Aristotle made a distinction between *epi-deictic* and *apo-deictic* discourses, both of which seek to *demonstrate* something, the latter by means of scientific proof, the former by means of displaying or showing forth some phenomenon. I believe that Borgmann uses the simple term *deictic* in place of Aristotle's *epideictic.* Relating these two forms of discourse in his own way, Gadamer wrote that the "hermeneutical experience . . . is the matrix out of which arises the questions that it then directs to science" ("On the Scope," in *Philosophical,* p. 40).

101. As Medard Boss argues in *Existential Foundations of Medicine and Psychology,* for example, all medical interventions should in principle take their bearings from the existence of the person, from the meaning of a medical condition within the world of the patient. Even to fix a broken leg, for example, is more than just treating bone matter. For the meaning of the break is that one can no longer play with one's friends, go to work, walk to the store, go on a canoe trip. The break is essentially an injury to one's existence, which shrinks as a consequence. Hence, the real significance of medical treatment is that it restores one's freedom to engage the world, returns one to one's former life. Why else fix the bone? A broken bone may, however, further symbolize to a person that she or he is "breakable," a loser, a victim, or some other disturbing existential meaning, in which case applying plaster to the bone will of itself not be an adequately human response. All the more so is the sufficiency of purely medical treatment a question in the case of psychic suffering, as I discussed above.

102. Kohák, *The Embers,* p. xii.

103. Joanna Macy, *Despair and Personal Power in the Nuclear Age,* p. 146.

104. Wendell Berry, *The Unsettling of America,* p. 107. I do not wish to give the impression that statistics have no place in ecopsychological (or any other) inquiry, but do

offer Gadamer's caution that "what is established by statistics seems to be a language of facts, but which questions these facts answer and which facts would begin to speak if other questions were asked are hermeneutical questions. Only a hermeneutical inquiry would legitimate the meaning of these facts" ("The Universality," in *Philosophical,* p. 11).

105. Borgmann, *Crossing,* p. 5.

106. Borgmann, *Technology,* p. 179. Borgmann mentions, in particular, the poetic prose of Henry Thoreau and Herman Melville.

107. Norman O. Brown, quoted in Hillman, *Revisioning,* p. 149.

108. On this, see Barfield, *Poetic.*

109. Calvin Martin, *In the Spirit of the Earth,* p. ix.

110. Gary Snyder, *The Old Ways,* p. 13. Also on p. 51 of *A Place in Space.* See also Borgmann, *Technology,* p. 26.

111. Borgmann, *Technology,* p. 26.

112. In Borgmann's words: "Something is going on that needs to be illuminated and understood. Yet. . . it will not be captured in the modes of explanation that are proper to the sciences and to the great focal powers of the past, i.e., through apodeictic or [epi-]deictic explanations. But there is a third possibility of explaining, one where we try to comprehend the character of reality by discovering its predominant pattern. A pattern is more concrete and specific than a [scientific] law and yet more general and abstract than a unique focal thing. To illuminate reality by disclosing its pattern is a quasi-deictic explanation. Let us call it paradeictic or paradigmatic explanation" (*Technology,* p. 73).

113. A point also made by Dreyfus about phenomenological inquiry in his *Being-in-the-World.*

114. Borgmann, *Technology,* p. 179.

Chapter Three

1. With a nod to Neil Evernden, who used this phrase as the title for the third chapter of his *The Natural Alien.*

2. Stanley Diamond, *In Search of the Primitive,* p. 119

3. John Livingston, *The Fallacy of Wildlife Conservation,* p. 100. A conclusion shared, incidentally, by David Abram in *The Spell of the Sensuous,* p. 268.

4. Evernden, *The Natural,* p. 33.

5. Livingston, *The Fallacy,* p. 115.

6. R. D. Laing, *The Politics of Experience,* p. 12.

7. Hans-Georg Gadamer, *Truth and Method,* p. 346.

8. David Levin, "Psychopathology in the Epoch of Nihilism," p. 33.

9. As a popular movement in mid-twentieth-century Europe, existentialism became associated (especially under the influence of Jean-Paul Sartre) with the idea that existence precedes essence, that is, that our nature is purely what we choose it to be through our free actions. I oppose that idea, so do not want my use of the term *existentialism* to be

limited to it. I am using the term more broadly, to indicate an emphasis both on the primacy of experience and on a confrontation with the ultimate concerns in life (death, freedom, meaning, suffering, the human place in nature, etc.). In this sense, Buddhism, for example, is a kind of existentialism. My specific goal is to develop a kind of "ecological existentialism," wherein the ultimate concerns of life are worked out in the context of our membership within the community of all life. As a Buddhist-ecologist, Gary Snyder seems to me an example of someone practicing this kind of existentialism.

10. Eugene Gendlin, *Experiencing and the Creation of Meaning*, p. 15.

11. Maurice Merleau-Ponty, *Phenomenology of Perception*, p. 166.

12. Mikhail Bakhtin made a similar existentialist point: "Contemporary man feels sure of himself, feels well off and clear-headed, [only] where he is essentially and fundamentally not present. . . . The course from a premise to a conclusion is traversed flawlessly and irreproachably, for [he himself does] not exist on that course. . . . But he feels unsure of himself, feels destitute and deficient in understanding, where he has to do with himself" (*Toward a Philosophy of the Act*, pp. 20–21). Middle sentence is out of original order.

13. Gendlin, *Experiencing*, pp. 15–16.

14. See David Levin, "Psychopathology in the Epoch of Nihilism," p. 29.

15. Theodore Roszak, "Where Psyche Meets Gaia," p. 15.

16. Theodore Roszak, *The Voice of the Earth*, pp. 94–95. Emphasis mine. Roszak also comments: "If any part of an animist sensibility is to be reclaimed, the project will have to integrate with modern science. Nothing else will qualify as an honest intellectual effort." My discussions in part one, especially concerning Hillman's and Abram's work, should suffice to indicate my utter disagreement with Roszak on this point.

17. Max Horkheimer, *The Eclipse of Reason*, p. 3. "Reason" here refers to *instrumental* reason—not to be confused with critical, practical, spiritual, or other kinds of reason. Even Issac Newton cautioned that "Reasoning without experience is very slippery" (quoted in Carolyn Merchant, *The Death of Nature*, p. 284).

18. Paul Shepard, *The Tender Carnivore and the Sacred Game*, p. xii.

19. Hence, even Shepard's statement is misleading, for scientific data may of itself only assist, and not guide, a redirection of society. On the folly in presuming that it may, see Neil Evernden, *The Social Creation of Nature*. On the dangers of defending nature by speaking in ecological abstractions (e.g., complexity, diversity, integrity, etc.), rather than by offering testimonials and appeals based on lived experience, see Albert Borgmann, *Technology and the Character of Contemporary Life*, pp. 186–187.

20. Laing, *The Politics*, p. 51.

21. Hans Peter Duerr, *Dreamtime*, p. 115.

22. The discussion under this heading and the next draws particularly heavily on the work of Eugene Gendlin. Indeed, I use many of his phrases throughout. I wish, then, to indicate here my colossal indebtedness to Gendlin.

23. Eugene Gendlin, "A Theory of Personality Change," p. 129.

24. Martin Heidegger, quoted in David Levin, *The Listening Self*, p. 219.

25. Gendlin, *Experiencing*, p. 162.

26. In the early 1930s, Heidegger believed that Nazism was a necessary violence for halting the decline into nihilism and for reversing the devastation of the Earth wrought by modernity. The danger of using Heidegger's thought is that it includes hierarchical and authoritarian views that can still conceivably be used to justify fascist causes. My position on the Heidegger question is essentially that of Thomas Sheehan's: "If Heidegger himself felt free, even for awhile, to put not just his person but also the major categories of his philosophical thought at the service of Nazi foreign and domestic policy, then one would do well to ask whether those categories are really as free of economic, social, and political interests as most Heideggerians contend. The point is not to condemn a man for his past but to learn something about oneself in the present, not to dismiss Heidegger's philosophical work out of hand but likewise not to join the Perpetual Adoration Societies that currently thrive among the Heideggerian faithful in Europe and America. The task, for those who care to take something from Heidegger, is to learn how to read him critically, both his life and his works, not to swallow his philosophy whole but to sift it for what is still of value and what is not." ("Reading a Life: Heidegger and Hard Times," p. 92). Although I am still in the process of learning to read Heidegger critically, I believe that the elements of his thought I have drawn on bear no necessary connection to fascism. The task of saving what is profound and essentially human in Heidegger's thought, while rejecting what is dangerous and inhuman, is one that I plan to take up more fully in future works.

27. See Gendlin, *Experiencing*, p. 125, n. 17 and p. 134.

28. Merleau-Ponty, *Phenomenology*, p. 403.

29. As recounted in Merleau-Ponty, *Phenomenology*, pp. 197–198. See also Jerry Gill, *Merleau-Ponty and Metaphor*, pp. 29, 121.

30. Maurice Merleau-Ponty, *The Visible and the Invisible*, p. 215.

31. Neil Bolton, "The Lived World: Imagination and the Development of Experience," p. 9.

32. John (Fire) Lame Deer and Richard Erdoes, *Lame Deer*, p. 162.

33. Maurice Merleau-Ponty, "The Concept of Nature I," p. 70.

34. Friedrich Nietzsche, *The Will to Power*, p. 131.

35. Duerr, *Dreamtime*, p. 57.

36. See David Noble, *The Religion of Technology*.

37. The "corpse is the body abandoned and invented for the space of explanation" (Robert Romanyshyn, "The Human Body as Historical Matter and Cultural Symptom," p. 165).

38. Romanyshyn, "The Human," p. 173.

39. Sigmund Freud, *New Introductory Lectures on Psychoanalysis*, p. 106. Emphasis mine.

40. Alan Watts, *Psychotherapy East and West*, p. 168.

41. Sigmund Freud, "The Future of an Illusion," p. 194.

42. On violent practices designed to break children of unwanted natural tendencies see Alice Miller, *For Your Own Good*.

43. Michel Foucault, *Madness and Civilization*, pp. 73–74.

44. "The core of our being. . . is formed by the obscure *id*, which has no direct relations with the external world" (Sigmund Freud, *An Outline of Psychoanalysis*, p. 108).

45. See Eugene Gendlin, "A Philosophical Critique of the Concept of Narcissism: The Significance of the Awareness Movement."

46. Eugene Gendlin, *Focusing-Oriented Psychotherapy*, p. 304. Emphasis mine.

47. This exercise is the briefest of introductions to focusing. Gendlin has presented focusing in a variety of forms: popularly in *Focusing*; psychotherapeutically in "A Theory of Personality Change" and *Focusing-Oriented Psychotherapy*; and philosophically in *Experiencing and the Creation of Meaning*.

48. Eugene Gendlin, *Focusing*, p. 76. Emphasis removed.

49. Gendlin, *Focusing*, p. 76. Emphasis mine.

50. Susan Griffin, *A Chorus of Stones*, p. 330.

51. See Gendlin, "A Philosophical Critique."

52. Eugene Gendlin, "The Wider Role of Bodily Sense in Thought and Language," p. 194.

53. I am using this term in the strong sense (as discussed by Richard Bernstein in *Beyond Objectivism and Relativism*), that is, in reference to the position that because all truths are relative to a particular (social, cultural, theoretical, geographical, personal, . . .) context, there are no grounds for judging one view better than another. I agree that truths are relative, but argue in this paragraph that the life process gives us our ground.

54. See Carol Bigwood, *Earth Muse*, p. 46.

55. Martin Dillon, *Merleau-Ponty's Ontology*, p. 101.

56. "The dead end of postmodernism," says Gendlin, "arises when one discounts the role of experience because it is never pure, never without conceptual forms and distinctions already implicit in it, and then discount those because they are never purely logical, but always involve experience" ("How Philosophy Cannot Appeal to Experience, and How It Can," p. 6).

57. Eugene Gendlin, "Neurosis and Human Nature in the Experiential Method of Thought and Therapy," p. 140.

58. Eugene Gendlin, "Experiential Phenomenology," p. 292.

59. This is perhaps the central point of Gendlin's whole philosophy of language.

60. Livingston, *The Fallacy*, p. 59.

61. Merleau-Ponty, *Phenomenology*, p. 184.

62. Eugene Gendlin, "Reply to Wallulis," in David Levin, ed., *Language Beyond Postmodernism*, p. 287. I have modified this sentence to clarify its meaning.

63. Hans Jonas, *The Phenomenon of Life*, p. 25.

64. This is an argument made by Martin Heidegger in *Being and Time*, where he suggests, for example, that any effort to "prove" the existence of the "external world" "presupposes a subject which is proximally *worldless* or unsure of its world, and which must, at bottom, first assure itself of a world" (p. 250). See also Eugene Gendlin, "*Befindlichkeit:* Heidegger and the Philosophy of Psychology."

65. Frederick Perls et al., *Gestalt Therapy*, p. 332.

66. The words *mind* and *mean* both mean *intend*, sharing as they do the common Indo-European base, "men." Given that meaning and intentionality are both bodily based, then so is the mind. Simply put: "psychological events are body events" (Eugene Gendlin, "A Small, Still Voice," p. 59).

67. Merleau-Ponty, *The Visible*, p. 271.

68. Medard Boss, *Psychoanalysis and Daseinsanalysis*, p. 33.

69. Boss, *Psychoanalysis*, p. 33, emphasis mine.

70. Perls, et al., *Gestalt*, p. 229.

71. The prehistoric base "per-" denotes trial, test, peril.

72. Frederick Perls, *Gestalt Therapy Verbatim*, p. 42.

73. Paul Shepard, *The Others*, p. 13.

74. Gordon Wheeler and Daniel Jones, "Finding Our Sons: A Male-Male Gestalt," p. 75.

75. Fritz Perls, *The Gestalt Approach and Eye Witness to Therapy*, pp. 33–34.

76. Gary Snyder, "Fear of Bears" (Afterword to Paul Shepard and Barry Sanders, *The Sacred Paw: The Bear in Nature, Myth, and Literature*), p. 209.

77. Shepard notes that *meat* means *mate* (from the Old German *gemate*)—"one with whom food is shared." Similarly, in the Sanskrit *madati* means "rejoice." Shepard suggests therefore that "meat" most originally signifies "celebrated sharing."

78. Despite that I am here using the concept of "need," my intention is not to introduce a biologically reductive position. My intention, rather, is to maintain an existentialist or experiential perspective while yet locating existence within the life process (as Gendlin does in his *A Process Model*). I believe that any misunderstanding this strategy produces will be worked out in chapters four and five.

79. See James Kepner, *Body Process*.

80. Wheeler and Jones, "Finding," p. 78.

81. Perls et al., *Gestalt*, pp. 340, 342.

82. See Frederick Perls, *Ego, Hunger and Aggression* and Laura Perls, *Living at the Boundary*.

83. Contacting thus has two poles, involving both *confluence*, in which we flow together with the other, and *resistance*, in which we maintain our difference from the other (Gordon Wheeler, *Gestalt Reconsidered*, p. 110). Or in James Kepner's words, it is 'dissolving to some extent our sense of boundedness, and then return[ing] to a more bounded sense of self' (*Body*, p. 195).

84. "What makes life 'meaningful' to the acting organism is . . . [s]imply that which secures and guarantees the forward momentum of its action" (Ernest Becker, *Angel in Armor*, p. 7). See also Merleau-Ponty, *Phenomenology*, p. 428.

85. Perls, *Gestalt*, p. 3.

86. This follows from his view that for the "well-adjusted" person "the self is primarily a reflexive awareness of the process of experiencing. It is not a perceived object, but something confidently felt in process. It is not a structure to be defended, but a rich and changing awareness of internal experiencing" (quoted in Gendlin, "A Theory," p. 110).

87. Eugene Gendlin, "The Role of Knowledge in Practice," p. 276.

88. Gadamer, *Truth,* p. 356. Emphasis mine.

89. That is, despite that Gadamer recognizes experience as a dialectical process, he only conceives of it as one of formal negation, without a natural, organizing moment: our expectations can only come from the forms we have already acquired. For anything new to happen, it must therefore be a painful contradiction of some earlier form, rather than a satisfying lending of good form to a genuine bodily need. Gadamer's philosophy of experience thus does contain a pessimistic element, even as he openly denies it.

90. As Joel Kovel notes: "Neurosis is living proof of the tension between the human subject and the objective social order; it only comes into existence so far as these are incongruent" ("Therapy in Late Capitalism," in *The Radical Spirit,* p. 123).

91. Morris Berman, *The Reenchantment of the World,* p. 164.

92. In *Civilization and Its Discontents* Freud speculated that all of civilized society might be neurotic. In 1955 Erich Fromm coined the phrase "the pathology of normalcy," arguing, indeed, that "the fact that millions of people share the same forms of mental pathology does not make these people sane" (*The Sane Society,* p. 23). Abraham Maslow later spoke of "the psychopathology of the average."

93. To be clear, I use the term *problem* broadly: to include any tension between body and world that calls for some action and resolution, not just those technically or formally defined ones.

94. The theory of creative adjustment, as developed by Paul Goodman, is presented in part two of Perls, et al., *Gestalt Therapy.*

95. Konrad Stettbacher, *Making Sense of Suffering,* p. 33.

96. On understanding social oppression as nature domination, Kovel writes that "the major forms of social domination, of class, of race and of gender, are each mediated through the domination of nature-as-body. In class domination, the oppressed body of the slave/serf/worker is repressed and converted into a machine for the aggrandizement of the master; in racial domination, sensuousness is lost by the master, who splits off bad [shame-bound] parts of the self and invests them in the body of the oppressed; while in patriarchy, female parts of the self are degraded, repressed and conquered in the body of the woman" ("The Marriage," pp. 412–413).

97. Perls, et al., *Gestalt Therapy,* p. 260.

98. As discussed in the context of Gestalt therapy by Kepner, *Body,* p. 98.

99. Laing, *The Politics,* p. 64.

100. Perls et al., *Gestalt Therapy,* pp. 264–265.

101. Stettbacher, *Making Sense,* p. 15.

102. Stettbacher, *Making Sense,* p. 26.

103. Perls et al., *Gestalt Therapy,* p. 375.

104. On this see Gendlin, "A Theory," p. 142.

105. Carl Rogers, "Ellen West—And Loneliness," p. 165.

106. Miller, *For Your Own,* p. 85.

107. Carl Rogers, "A Therapist's View of the Good Life," p. 195.

108. This is not to say that introjection is not an *aspect* of contact making. In learning a new field of study, for example, we must take in much material and only gradually come to develop our own views in relation to it. What is contrary to the organism is to *never* bodily evaluate that which has been swallowed. See Gordon Wheeler, *Gestalt Reconsidered.*

109. Perls et al. *Gestalt Therapy,* p. 190.

110. Quoted in Rogers, "Ellen West," p. 173.

111. See Perls et al. *Gestalt Therapy,* p. 265.

112. Bakhtin, *Toward,* p. 51. In Perls words: "fantasy is diminished reality and thinking diminished acting" (*The Gestalt,* p. 53). John Dewey's comments are also significant: "Philosophical dualism is but a formulated recognition of an impassé in life; an impotence in interaction." Hence the various "forms of subjectivism register an acceptance of whatever obstacles at the time prevent the active participation of the self in the ongoing course of events" (*Experience and Nature,* pp. 241–242). In other words, the social context that gives rise to dualistic thought is one that frustrates worldly engagement or organismically satisfying interaction.

113. Jeannette Armstrong, "Keepers of the Earth," p. 319.

114. Gendlin, *Focusing-Oriented,* p. 246.

115. Hence, "all psychiatric diagnoses are basically only sociological statements" (Boss, *Psychoanalysis,* p. 56).

116. J. H. van den Berg, *A Different Existence,* chapter three.

117. See chapter three, "Disconnection," in Judith Herman, *Trauma and Recovery.*

118. In the discussion that follows I am drawing heavily on Robert Lee's, "Shame and the Gestalt Model," and Gordon Wheeler's, "Self and Shame: A New Paradigm."

119. See Lee, "Shame."

120. Shame and guilt are both emotions arising from negative (self-)evaluation, but have different contexts or felt meanings. In guilt we feel that we have *done* something bad, have broken a moral code, whereas in shame we feel that we *are* bad, not enough, and so forth. Intense guilt can, however, lead to shame, for the doing of wrong deeds does imply that it is of our nature to be bad. To not act on or make reparations for our guilty acts, moreover, does generate feelings of inadequacy, which will then lead us into a "shame-guilt bind." (See chapter fifteen, "Shame," in Gary Yontef, *Awareness Dialogue and Process: Essays on Gestalt Therapy.*) Note, also, that the polar opposite of shame is pride, whereas the opposite of guilt is innocence.

121. Freud, for instance, denied to our nature any positive social impulses. In his dualistic model of human nature, relationships are purely instrumental: I depend on others only to the extent that they serve as objects for the discharging of my sexual and aggressive drives.

122. Wheeler, "Self and Shame," p. 48.

123. Wheeler, "Self," p. 49.

124. Gordon Wheeler and Daniel Jones, "Finding Our Sons," p. 84. I am drawing on this article throughout this paragraph.

125. Iris Fodor, "A Woman and Her Body: The Cycles of Pride and Shame," pp. 235, 265.

126. Becker, *Angel*, pp. 150–151.

127. Boss, *Psychoanalysis*, p. 144. Emphasis mine.

128. See Perls, et al. *Gestalt Therapy*, pp. 430–432. Gendlin thus says that "neurosis involves sensing more meanings than are livable" ("Neurosis and Human Nature," p. 148).

129. Gendlin, "A Theory," p. 137.

130. Wheeler and Jones, "Finding," pp 75, 80. Emphasis mine.

131. Robert Romanyshyn, "Unconsciousness: Reflection and the Primacy of Perception," p. 159. See also J. H. van den Berg, "What Is Psychotherapy," pp. 347–348.

132. My friends were following the theory of Re-evaluation Counseling, which holds that healing occurs through giving respectful attention to people as they complete old emotional experiences. See Phyllis Bronstein, "Re-Evaluation Counselling: A Self-Help Model for Recovery from Emotional Distress."

133. See Phyllis Bronstein, "Promoting Healthy Emotional Development in Children."

134. See Eugene Gendlin, "A Phenomenology of Emotions: Anger."

135. John Welwood, "Meditation and the Unconscious: A New Perspective," p. 4.

136. Paul Goodman suggests that Freud was unable to connect his patients' spontaneous mental contents with either their bodies or their environments because he passed over the body in favor of a purely verbal therapy. Needing to account for the apparent autonomy of these contents, however, he was then forced to confusedly posit the unconscious as an independent realm of its own (Perls et al., *Gestalt Therapy*, p. 440).

137. See, especially, Gendlin, "A Theory."

138. Merleau-Ponty, *Phenomenology*, p. 381. As he remarked, what he became aware of in a moment of insight "was not, from the start, a *thing* hidden in my unconscious. . . but the *impulse* carrying me *towards* someone" (emphasis mine).

139. Deborah Rinzler, "Human Disconnection and the Murder of the Earth," p. 102.

140. The word *attenuation* is used by Daniel Boorstin to describe the "thinning out or flattening of experience" that has come with the modern homogenizing of everyday life (see chapter ten of *Democracy and Its Discontents*). The phrase "the extinction of experience" is used by insect ecologist Robert Michael Pyle to describe the loss of personal contact with wildlife which follows on the extirpation of local habitats (as discussed in Gary Paul Nabhan and Sara St. Antoine, "The Loss of Floral and Faunal Story: The Extinction of Experience"). The "waning of affect" is a phrase used by Fredric Jameson in his discussion of the depthlessness of postmodern culture ("Postmodernism, or the Cultural Logic of Late Capitalism," pp. 61–62).

141. The symptoms of this personality include "contactlessness, isolation, fear of falling, impotence, inferiority, verbalizing, and affectlessness" (Perls et al., *Gestalt*, p. 317).

142. Joel Kovel, *History and Spirit*, pp. 12–13.

143. Gendlin, *Focusing*, p. 114.

144. Jean Liedloff, *The Continuum Concept*, p. 24. Even the least pessimistic of witnesses, such as the Buddhist Jack Kornfield, speak of how "a deep loneliness and inner poverty" contribute to our society's "pervasive sorrow" (*A Path With Heart*, p. 24).

145. Says Glendinning: "Just about everybody I know who is serious about personal healing, social change, and ecological rebalancing is in recovery: recovery from personal addiction, childhood abuse, childhood deprivation, the nuclear family, sexism, racism, urban alienation, trickle-down economics, combat service in the trenches of the gender wars, the threat of extinction, linear thinking, the mind/body split, technological progress, and the mechanical worldview" (*My Name Is Chellis and I'm in Recovery from Western Civilization*, p. ix).

146. Perls et al. *Gestalt*, p. 333.

147. Joel Kovel, "Things and Words," p. 49. Hence, "the unconscious must be primarily grasped as the indwelling, subjective record" of the "uneasy" relationship between human society and nature. Next quotation, p. 48.

148. See Joel Kovel, "Mind and State in Ancient Greece," in *The Radical Spirit*, p. 220.

149. See Kovel, *History*. This is not to ignore the existence of a considerable body of psychoanalytic social criticism. For an anthology dedicated to juxtaposing socialist with psychoanalytic theories and practices, for example, see Barry Richards, ed., *Capitalism and Infancy*.

150. *Toronto Star*, June 21, 1995, p. C2.

151. Kovel, "The Marriage," p. 411. As Kovel notes elsewhere, "capitalism is not so much a species of economy as it is a kind of society which deifies the economic in order to produce capital" ("On the Ontology of Capital," p. 2).

152. Wendell Berry, *The Unsettling of America*, p. 138. ". . . , to put these [material, social, spiritual] sources under the control of corporations and specialized professionals, and to sell them to us at the highest profit."

153. How much this is the case is suggested in Roger Gottlieb's discussion of the nuclear family: "The male-dominated nuclear family is a highly mobile unit for an economy which needs to shift its labor force to changing areas of investment. The nuclear family also tends to create people who think of themselves primarily as individuals rather than as members of communities or classes. This self-understanding makes political organizing and mass radical movements extremely difficult. Having women do the household and emotional labor necessary to 'reproduce' male laborers and raise new ones cheapens the reproduction of workers—and thus the cost of labor for capitalists. Women's inferior social status also allows capitalists to pay them less and treat them worse than men. Additionally, the atomized nuclear family is necessarily a high-consumption family, providing an ever-growing market for consumer goods. Finally, the power that men enjoy over women makes up in a psychic sense for the powerlessness they experience on the job. After a day of demanding and at times degrading paid labor, a man may exercise power at home while he

is catered to by his wife. At the same time, the authoritarian, nonegalitarian relationships within the home perfectly prepare children for a public world defined by hierarchy, competition, and unequal power" (*Marxism,* pp. 137–138).

154. Joel Kovel, *The Age of Desire,* p. 113.

155. Some factories are now openly "managed by stress." That is, the pace of production is continually speeded up "to find out where the weaknesses and soft spots are, so that new designs and procedures can be implemented to increase the pace and performance." The consequence is reportedly a historically high level of mental and physical pathology among workers (including chronic fatigue) as they are progressively transformed into high velocity machinery (chapter twelve of Jeremy Rifkin, *The End of Work*). As David Noble also writes: "In the wake of five decades of information revolution, people are now working longer hours, under worsening conditions, with greater anxiety and stress, less skills, less security, less power, less benefits, and less pay. Information technology has clearly been developed and used during these years to deskill, discipline, and displace human labour in a global speed-up of unprecedented proportions" (*Progress Without People,* p. xi).

156. Raymond Rogers, *The Oceans are Emptying,* p. 9.

157. Raymond Rogers, *Nature and the Crisis of Modernity,* p. 1.

158. Rogers, *Nature,* p. 160. Because the ecological crisis predates capitalism the latter cannot entirely be blamed for the former. To the extent that the system of capital defines our society, however, it is the current antagonist. On this, see Joel Kovel's forthcoming *The Enemy of Nature.*

159. Rogers, *Nature,* p. 12. Winona LaDuke offers an indigenous person's perspective on this topic in her "From Resistance to Regeneration."

160. Vandana Shiva, "The Impoverishment of the Environment: Women and Children Last," in Maria Mies and Vandana Shiva, *Ecofeminism,* p. 75.

161. Horkheimer, *The Eclipse,* p. 94. Emphasis mine.

162. For discussions of the work of other critical theorists on this topic see Henry Blanke, "Domination and Utopia: Marcuse's Discourse on Nature, Psyche, and Culture" and Robyn Eckersley, "The Failed Promise of Critical Theory."

163. As William Leiss clarifies, the "notion of a common domination of the human race over external nature is nonsensical" (*The Domination of Nature,* p. 122). Rather, the artificial separation of human society and the natural world masks the way in which ruling groups dominate other social groups, who are put to work in exploiting nonhuman nature. The domination of nature, as a "species project," has thus historically arisen as an ideology for concealing social contradiction.

164. Kovel, *History,* p. 205.

165. Kovel, *The Age,* p. 125. Middle sentence is from p. 172. Kovel is currently preparing a manuscript entitled *The Enemy of Nature.*

166. Tom Athanasiou, *The Ecology of Rich and Poor,* p. 171. See, also, James O'Connor, "Socialism and Ecology." These points are basic aspects of Marx's theories of exploitation and capitalist development.

167. See Christopher Lasch, *The Culture of Narcissism* and Joel Kovel, "Narcissism and the Family," in *The Radical Spirit*.

168. "For all his inner suffering, the narcissist has many traits that make for success in bureaucratic institutions, which put a premium on the manipulation of interpersonal relations, discourage the formation of deep personal attachments, and at the same time provide the narcissist with the approval he needs in order to validate his self-esteem" (Lasch, *The Culture*, p. 91).

169. John Rodman, "The Liberation of Nature?," pp. 114–115. Emphasis mine.

170. Livingston, *The Fallacy*, p. 116.

171. William Leiss, *The Limits of Satisfaction*, p. 3.

172. See Athanasiou, *Divided*, p. 14.

173. Leiss, *The Domination*, p. 151.

174. David Levin, "Psychopathology in the Epoch of Nihilism," p. 26. In his *Nihilism Incorporated*, Arran Gare similarly identifies the dominant theme of the modern age with an inherently nihilistic mechanistic materialism. He traces the ecological crisis and other modern problems to this meaning-denying world-orientation, albeit in different terms than my own.

175. Jules Henry, quoted in David Levin, "Clinical Stories: A Modern Self in the Fury of Being," p. 512.

176. Evernden, *The Natural*, p. 124, emphasis mine.

177. Evernden, *The Natural*, p. 126.

178. Romand Coles, "Ecotones and Environmental Ethics: Adorno and Lopez," p. 244.

179. Laing, *The Politics*, p. 24.

180. Horkheimer, *The Eclipse*, p. 100.

181. Barry Lopez, *Of Wolves and Men*, p. 140. See also Keith Thomas's *Man and the Natural World*, in which he chronicles early modern English attitudes toward animals. "Men attributed to animals the natural impulses they most feared in themselves—ferocity, gluttony, sexuality—even though it was men, not beasts, who made war on their own species, ate more than was good for them and were sexually active all the year round" (pp. 40–41).

182. Rinzler, "Human," p. 106.

183. Audre Lorde, "Poetry Is Not a Luxury," p. 127.

184. Even if it is one of "immeasurable need," "nameless sorrow," "growing and spreading peacelessness," and "mounting confusion" ("What Are Poets For?," In *Poetry, Language, Thought*, p. 93).

185. Alice Miller, *Breaking Down the Wall of Silence*, p. 144.

186. This is a recurrent theme in Alice Miller's work.

187. See Ynestra King, "The Ecology of Feminism and the Feminism of Ecology."

188. Ynestra King, "Healing the Wounds: Feminism, Ecology, and the Nature/Culture Dualism," p. 117. Emphasis mine.

Chapter Four

1. Wendell Berry, *The Unsettling of America,* p. 130.

2. Anthony Barton, "Humanistic Contributions to the Field of Psychotherapy: Appreciating the Human and Liberating the Therapist," p. 215. Emphasis removed.

3. While human specialness is a defining concern of humanism generally, the extent to which specific humanistic psychologists posit a human/nature divide varies. Existential psychologists (who are most often placed in the humanistic camp) such as Rollo May are probably the most committed to such a division, saying that humans, "cast on this barren crust of earth aeons ago," have to willfully make their own meaning in an intrinsically meaningless and indifferent world. However, one of my favorite humanistic authors, Eugene Gendlin, has a strong interest in what ethology can teach us about the continuity between human and nonhuman nature, and emphasizes our kinship with plants. There is much in Gestalt therapy, furthermore, that opens toward the natural world, and Fritz Perls speculated that awareness is a property of the entire universe (making him a quasi-animist). My comments, then, are aimed at humanism as its main authors have presented it over the years and also at the fact that, quite simply, humanistic psychology could by no means as yet be called an ecopsychology. For overviews of humanistic psychology, see Frederick Wertz, ed., *The Humanistic Movement: Recovering the Person in Psychology;* and Joseph Royce and Leendert Mos, *Humanistic Psychology: Concepts and Criticisms.* I should also say that although I am throughout this book blending hermeneutic and humanistic psychological sources, there are notable differences in their general outlooks, as Louis Sass has discussed in his "Humanism, Hermeneutics, and the Concept of the Human Subject." Granted Sass's distinction, humanistic psychology and hermeneutics are both "humanistic" in the sense of being human-centred, which is the general point I am after. I might thus have more broadly called this chapter "From Humanism to Naturalism."

4. Amedeo Giorgi, "Whither Humanistic Psychology?," pp. 312, 318.

5. Erich Fromm, quoted in David Kidner, "Why Psychology Is Mute About the Ecological Crisis," p. 366.

6. Noteworthy here is William Cahalan's effort to ecologize his Gestalt therapy practice (see "Ecological Groundedness in Gestalt Therapy"); as well as the efforts of those with articles in a special issue of the *The Gestalt Journal* on ecopsychology (18.1, 1995). See also *The Humanistic Psychologist's* special issue on ecopsychology (26.1–3, 1998).

7. See, most notably, David Ehrenfeld, *The Arrogance of Humanism.*

8. Roy DeCarvalho, *Founders of Humanistic Psychology,* p. 82.

9. David Levin, commenting on the failures of humanism, in "Clinical Stories: A Modern Self in the Fury of Being," p. 487.

10. Hans Peter Duerr, *Dreamtime,* p. 110.

11. Graham Parkes, "Human/Nature in Nietzsche and Taoism," p. 356.

12. On these general themes, see Joel Kovel, "On the Notion of Human Nature: A Contribution Toward a Philosophical Anthropology."

13. Plural realism is Hubert Dreyfus's term for the stance of Heidegger's later thinking. I am, however, additionally qualifying the term along my own lines. Says Dreyfus: "For a plural realist there is no point of view from which one can ask and answer the metaphysical question concerning the one true nature of ultimate reality. . . . for Heidegger different understandings of being reveal different sorts of entities, and since no one way of revealing is exclusively true, accepting one does not commit us to rejecting the others" (*Being-in-the-World*, pp. 262–263). In *Being and Time*, the early Heidegger had already said that "an entity can show itself from itself in many ways, depending in each case on the kind of access we have to it" (p. 51). He also did not dispute that what is represented by modern natural science "is indeed nature itself," but was adamant that this "objective" nature is "only *one* way in which nature exhibits itself" ("Science and Reflection," in *The Question Concerning Technology and Other Essays*, p. 174).

14. Simone Weil, quoted in Ken Jones, *The Social Face of Buddhism*, p. 315.

15. This is not the place to discuss the relative ecological merits of Buddhism. On these topics, see Ian Harris, "How Environmentalist is Buddhism?" and "Buddhist Environmental Ethics and Detraditionalization: The Case of EcoBuddhism;" Alan Badiner, *Dharma Gaia: A Harvest of Essays in Buddhism and Ecology;* Martine Batchelor and Kerry Brown, *Buddhism and Ecology;* and D. T. Suzuki, "Nature in Zen Buddhism."

16. Gary Snyder, *A Place in Space*, p. 187.

17. These three categories correspond to those discussed by Raymond Williams in his *Keywords*.

18. See Sean Kane, *Wisdom of the Mythtellers*.

19. This is my own version of James Wright's suggestion that while it is important for Euroamericans to draw on Euroamerican traditions, the work of eco-spiritual renewal must still rely to some extent on indigenous knowledges. In his own wilderness quest work, Wright has chosen to perform a "literary archeology" of European mythology in order to retrieve the skeletons of rites that he feels are hidden in the old myths. He admits, nonetheless, that without "direct experience of some of [the] North American ways, . . . the work of reanimating the old European forms would be virtually impossible" (*The Bones of Metamorphosis*, p. 19). Caught between using ritual forms native to North America or reimagined forms indigenous to old Europe, Wright counsels that "we must do some of each"—while insisting that as an archetypal pattern, found across cultures, "the core vision quest experience does not belong to any one people."

I assume that it is clear to the reader that I claim no authoritative knowledge of indigenous ways—that I am using such general notions as can roughly be grasped not as a guide to those ways, but primarily as a means to come back to and show up my own theme of loss and longing. I am aware, moreover, that disharmonious relations with the natural world, warfare, starvation, and questionable gender arrangements are not unheard of amongst primal peoples. These things do not of themselves, however, erase the general relevance of indigenous teachings for undertaking the recollective task at hand.

20. John Livingston, *The Fallacy of Wildlife Conservation*, p. 101.

21. Richard Nelson, *The Island Within*, pp. 245, 249.

22. Robert Avens, "Heidegger and Archetypal Psychology," p. 185.

23. Martin Dillon, "Merleau-Ponty and the Reversibility Thesis," p. 368.

24. I developed the idea of a kinship continuum from Dillon, "Merleau-Ponty," p. 378; as well as from Joel Kovel, "Human Nature, Freedom, and Spirit," in *The Radical Spirit*, pp. 300–301; and the writings of Paul Shepard.

25. Douglas Kirsner, *The Schizoid World of Jean-Paul Sartre and R.D. Laing*, p. 68. In Sartre's novel, *Nausea*, even the protagonist's own hand is a source of disgust.

26. In truth, Sartre's world is *conceivable*, but never quite *achievable*, as a person with no common ground with others could never make contact with them. Similarly, nirvana is a temporary state only, so could never be regarded as a day-to-day form of life.

27. Gary Snyder, *The Practice of the Wild*, p. 8.

28. A point I take from M. C. Dillon, "Erotic Desire," p. 158.

29. Joel Kovel, *History and Spirit*, p. 152.

30. Joel Kovel, "On the Notion of Human Nature," p. 375.

31. Contacting, recall, occurs across a boundary zone of "me and not-me." We are never identical with that which we contact, no matter how much we may be identified with it. Even when in such "nondual" states of awareness as meditation or absorption in a task, we are still in contact with the world. As the Zen author D. T. Suzuki writes: "The mountains do not vanish; they stand before me" ("Nature and Zen Buddhism," p. 241).

32. The idea of some "optimal distance" is present, in one form or another, in all experiential practices of which I am familiar. T. J. Scheff discusses the relation between "aesthetic distance" and "optimal distance" in his *Catharsis in Healing, Ritual, and Drama*. The notion of finding the "right distance" from a felt sense is a central feature of the practice of focusing. The Buddhist idea of a "middle path" also suggests an optimal balance between the extremes of sensual indulgence and asceticism, or a zone of experiencing in which one can face one's suffering while not being overwhelmed by it. Merleau-Ponty, finally, writes that: "For each object, as for each picture in an art gallery, there is an optimum distance from which it requires to be seen, a direction viewed from which it vouchsafes most of itself: at a shorter or greater distance we have merely a perception blurred through excess or deficiency" (*Phenomenology of Perception*, p. 302).

33. Joel Kovel, "The Marriage of Radical Ecologies, p. 411.

34. Paul Shepard, *The Others*, p. 5. Emphasis mine.

35. Richard Nelson, *Make Prayers to the Raven*, pp. 20, 33, 76.

36. Kane, *The Wisdom*, p. 105.

37. Barry Lopez, "Renegotiating the Contracts," p. 14.

38. Calvin Martin, *In the Spirit of the Earth*, p. 19.

39. For a poetic and touching consideration of this, see chapter eleven of Ursula LeGuin, *Buffalo Gals; And Other Animal Presences*. See also Colin Turnbull, *The Human Cycle*, pp. 51–52, 183–184.

40. Gordon Wheeler, "Self and Shame: A New Paradigm for Psychotherapy," p. 49.

41. "For us, being is discontinuous—and yet this discontinuity is experienced as loss, and life is spent trying to overcome it. It comes naturally to us, then, to sense nonbeing

along with being, and to try to rejoin the two, that is, to be spiritually. For nonbeing [the gap] is the space between the discontinuities." (Joel Kovel, *History and Spirit,* p. 81).

42. Kovel, *History,* p. 83.

43. Egoic "being is self-experience in which the rationalistic, all knowing 'I' crowds out every other self-phenomenon. In the egoic topology of the self, ontological space is occluded by the I-centre" (Kovel, "Human," p. 299). My presentation here on the Ego and the void is of necessity a great simplification of a complex topic. The three articles by David Loy in the bibliography offers some further discussion.

44. David Loy, "Avoiding the Void: The *Lack* of Self in Psychotherapy and Buddhism," p. 172.

45. Bertram Karon and Leighton Whitaker, "Psychotherapy and the Fear of Understanding Schizophrenia," pp. 39–40.

46. This is a variation on Gary Yontef's "twin dangers" (*Awareness, Dialogue, and Process,* p. 463). See, also, Irvin Yalom, *Existential Psychotherapy,* pp. 143–147.

47. Judith Herman, *Trauma and Recovery,* p. 93. For a discussion of this dynamic in the lives of physically and emotionally abusive men, see Donald Dutton, *The Abusive Personality: Violence and Control in Intimate Relationships.*

48. See William Bridges, *Transitions.*

49. Max Horkheimer, *The Eclipse of Reason,* pp. 105, 106.

50. Kovel, "Human Nature," in *The Radical,* p. 300.

51. Passages taken from Snyder, *The Practice,* p. 19, and from Gary Snyder quoted in Paul Shepard, "A Post-Historic Primitivism," p. 82.

52. Erich Fromm, *The Art of Loving,* p. 8. Emphasis removed.

53. See M. C. Dillon, "Toward a Phenomenology of Love and Sexuality: An Inquiry into the Limits of the Humans Situation as They Condition Loving."

54. Martin Heidegger, *Introduction to Metaphysics,* p. 14.

55. Paul Shepard and Barry Sanders, *Sacred Paw,* pp. xix, 57.

56. John Livingston, *Rogue Primate,* p. 104.

57. "The gap between nature and ourselves is healed by attempting to sway as humans within the rhythms of nature, swinging to and fro with the coming-to-be and passing-away inherent in all life" (Carol Bigwood, *Earth Muse,* p. 197).

58. David Abram, *The Spell of the Sensuous,* p. 169.

59. Kane, *The Wisdom,* p. 40.

60. Jacob Boehme, quoted in Norman O. Brown, *Life Against Death,* p. 130.

61. On this see Martin Heidegger, "The Age of the World Picture," in *The Question Concerning Technology and other Essays;* and Robert Romanyshysn, "The Despotic Eye: An Illustration of Metabletic Phenomenology and Its Implications."

62. Owen Barfield, *Saving The Appearances,* p. 95.

63. Cf. Heidegger's comments: "Color shines and wants only to shine. When we analyze it in rational terms by measuring its wavelengths, it is gone. It shows itself only when it remains undisclosed and unexplained. Earth thus shatters every attempt to penetrate into it. It causes every merely calculating importunity upon it to turn into a destruc-

tion. . . . The earth appears openly cleared as itself only when it is perceived and preserved as that which is by nature undisclosable, that which shrinks from every disclosure and constantly keeps itself closed up" ("The Origin of the Work of Art," in *Poetry, Language, Thought,* p. 47).

64. Barry Lopez, *Of Wolves and Men,* p. 4.

65. S. N. Tandon, "Dharma—Its Definition and Universal Application," p. 11.

66. Lawrence Hatab, *Myth and Philosophy,* p. 35. This is not to equate the outlooks of Buddhists, western phenomenologists, and various mythological peoples, all of whom will of course have their own specific understandings of things, even as they share an experiential approach.

67. Shepard, *The Others,* p. 326. James Hillman similarly remarks that: "Multiple personality is humanity in its natural condition. In other cultures these multiple personalities have names, locations, energies, functions, voices, angel and animal forms" (*Archetypal Psychology: A Brief Account,* p. 51. See also *Revisioning Psychology,* p. 203). Indeed, in indigenous societies, and up until about the seventeenth century in our own culture, "the otherness of the self has been axiomatic" (Michael Holquist in the Introduction to M. M. Bakhtin, *Art and Answerability,* p. xxvi).

68. On some such varieties of private otherness, see Roger Levin, "Multiple Personality, Transpersonal Guides, and Malevolent Possessions: Discriminating Kinds of Alterity in a Psychotherapy Case by Means of Bodily Felt Sensing."

69. Eugene Gendlin, "The Client's Client: The Edge of Awareness," p. 81. The felt sense is thus the source of all our inwardly arising symbols, the place where we discover the aims or intentions, the needs or claims, of the soul itself (the soul being the personification of the unconscious). In what could serve as a description of the felt sense, Hillman alludes to soul as "an inner place or deeper person or ongoing presence" below our normal consciousness (*Revisioning,* p. xvi).

70. James Hillman calls this the "personal/impersonal paradox of the soul" (*Revisioning,* p. 105; see also pp. 31, 46–51). I would also call it the identity/dis-identity paradox.

71. Hillman, "The Animal," p. 320.

72. The best descriptions of this process are contained in the work of Ann Weiser Cornell, including *The Focusing Student's Manual* and *The Power of Focusing.* Gendlin, furthermore, emphasizes the importance of *thanking* whatever comes to us in focusing, *loving* and appreciating our dreams; in short, of developing a respectful personal relationship with all "inner" contents. See also Hillman, *Re-Visioning,* pp. 31, 139.

73. James Hillman devotes the first chapter of *Re-Visioning* to this point.

74. See Hillman, *Revisioning* and Robert Sardello, *Love and the Soul.*

75. Shagbark Hickory, "Environmental Etiquette/Environmental Practice: American Indian Challenges to Mainstream Environmental Ethics," p. 121. As Nelson also notes: "weather is the most fully personified element in the Koyukon physical world. The interchange between people and these conscious entities is fairly elaborate and intense" (*Make Prayers,* p. 40).

76. Martin Heidegger, "The Fieldpath," p. 456.

77. There is, in fact, a great deal of literature on such communication. See, for example, Stephen Foster and Meredith Little, *The Roaring of the Sacred River;* Stephanie Kaza, *The Attentive Heart: Conversations with Trees;* and the last two chapters of John Livingston, *The Fallacy of Wildlife Conservation.*

78. I can, for example, *generally* distinguish among the kind of experiences I have in downtown Toronto; on a canoe trip in Algonquin Park; and in those even-less-humanized places where there are no trails, designated campsites, or line-ups at portages. This does not mean, however, than I do not have wild encounters in downtown Toronto, nor that I am always optimally attuned or open to the big outdoors when I am in them.

79. John Livingston, *Rogue Primate,* p. 104.

80. Even the most cursory glance at the Buddhist doctrine of karma is enough to realize that to comprehend it in any depth requires much practice and insight.

81. Richard Nelson, Interview. "Life-Ways of the Hunter," p. 84. Sean Kane similarly writes: "In dealing with nature or any of her people, the one thing you can be really sure of is that beings are intelligent and therefore easily insulted, and that acts have consequences. For life in a playground of intelligent roving energies, that is perhaps the best advice. What goes around comes around" (*The Wisdom,* p. 240).

82. Tandon, "Dharma," p. 12. These ideas are discussed well in a Taoist context by Roger Ames, "Taoism and the Nature of Nature."

83. Bruce Foltz, *Inhabiting the Earth,* p. 125. Emphasis mine.

84. James Hillman, "The Animal Kingdom in the Human Dream," pp. 314, 325–326.

85. Martin Heidegger, "What Are Poets For?," in *Poetry, Language, Thought,* p. 101. Heidegger quotes Nietzsche: "How can anything dead 'be'"? See also Foltz, *Inhabiting,* pp. 132–134, from which I am taking most of this discussion. As Foltz observes, *Zoe* is itself from the Greek root '*Za-,*' which means a strengthening or intensification.

86. Tandon, "Dharma," p. 10.

87. As John Caputo notes, everything in a "hermeneutic interpretation. . . comes down to its ability to provoke in us the ultimate hermeneutic response: '*That* is what we are looking for. That puts into words what we have all along understood about ourselves'" (*Radical Hermeneutics,* p. 81).

88. Martin Heidegger, "The Question Concerning Technology," in *The Question Concerning Technology, And Other Essays,* p. 10.

89. Kane, *The Wisdom,* p. 234.

90. Hillman, "The Animal," p. 324. Hillman's comments are inspired by the biologist Adolf Portmann.

91. Owen Barfield, *Poetic Diction,* p. 180. Bernard Berenson similarly wrote that what he perceived in art was the appearance of *living motion,* even in works of stone (as discussed in Edith Cobb, "The Ecology of Imagination in Childhood," p. 131).

92. Martin Heidegger, quoted in Eugene Gendlin, "Dwelling," p. 139. As this line suggests, Heidegger regarded written poetry or "poesy" as only one of many possible modes of poetizing or bringing forth.

93. James Hillman, "Aesthetics and Politics," p. 76.

94. Richard Avens, "Heidegger and Archetypal Psychology," p. 199. Emphasis mine.

95. See Eugene Gendlin, "Nonlogical Moves and Nature Metaphors" and "Dwelling."

96. Whatever sense we make, it is always from a bodily feeling, is always *phys*-ical. Thus, says Avens, *physis* "as *logos* (physio-logy) is also the soul (psycho-logy)" ("Heidegger," p. 198). Vincent Vycinas observes, in this respect, that: *"Logos,* as cut off from *physis* and standing by itself or for itself, becomes the perverted *logos,* logic. *Physis,* on the other hand, when thought of separately from *logos,* becomes perverted *physis,* matter" (*Earth and Gods,* p. 196). David Abram makes a similar point when he notes that when reflective reason fails to acknowledge or loses conscious awareness of its "rootedness in . . . bodily, participatory modes of experience" it becomes "dysfunctional" (*The Spell of the Sensuous,* p. 303). On the original unity of *physis* and *logos,* see Martin Heidegger, *An Introduction to Metaphysics,* pp. 115–196.

97. Paul Klee, quoted in Mica Goldfarb, "Making the Unknown Known: Art as the Speech of the Body," p. 188. J. Macmurray likewise wrote: "The artist is not abnormal, but simply the normal human individual. Not of course the average human being, after education and the constraints of social and physical necessity have succeeded in suppressing and stunting his natural capacity" (Quoted in Neil Bolton, "The Live World: Imagination and the Development of Experience," p. 14).

98. Sigmund Freud, quoted in Norman Brown, *Life Against Death,* p. 67.

99. Frederick Perls et al., *Gestalt Therapy,* pp. 235, 321, 323. The psychoanalyst D. W. Winnicott claimed that creativity "belongs to being alive." Hence, the person who lives creatively feels that "life is worth living." An uncreative and conformist mode of existence, by contrast, "is a sick basis for life" (*Playing and Reality,* pp. 65, 67).

100. See Carl Bigwood, *Earth Muse* for lengthy discussions of this theme.

101. George Steiner, *Heidegger,* p. 132.

102. Martin Heidegger, ". . . Poetically Man Dwells . . . . ," in *Poetry, Language, Thought,* p. 216.

103. Martin Heidegger, "Building Dwelling Thinking," in *Poetry, Language, Thought,* p. 149. We can tell when our dwelling has become unpoetic exactly "because it is in essence poetic" (Heidegger, ". . . Poetically," in *Poetry,* p. 228).

104. Martin, *In the Spirit,* pp. 10, 15. Otherwise put, indigenous societies judge "ecstatic communication with the earth to be humanity's greatest prerogative and calling" (p. 133).

105. See Shagbark Hickory, "Environmental," pp. 114–115; and Jeanette Armstrong, "Keepers of the Earth."

106. Bigwood, *Earth,* p. 206. John Livingston has suggested that the best word he can find to describe bird song is "celebratory" ("The Dilemma of the Deep Ecologist," p. 68). I do not doubt, then, that others creatures also revel in creation. I would suggest, though, that it is the special business of humans to create cosmologies.

107. The story is told by the Haudenosaunee statesman Leon Shenandoah, quoted in Chellis Glendinning, *My Name Is Chellis and I'm in Recovery from Western Civilization,* pp. 211–212. As Joseph Bruchac observes, in Native American traditions "Animals are recognized not only as spiritual beings but, in some ways, as being wiser than humans. A bear never forgets that it is a bear, yet human beings often forget what a human must do. . . . This potential for confusion was true for Native people long before the coming of Europeans (though Europeans have raised the art of spiritual confusion to a new level!) That is why the traditional teachings remain so important. They remind human beings how to take care" ("Understanding the Great Mystery," p. 101).

108. See Kovel, "On the Notion." For an example of weak denial, see chapter two of Clifford Geertz, *The Interpretation of Cultures.*

109. See Eugene Gendlin, "Neurosis and Human Nature in the Experiential Method of Thought and Therapy."

110. Eugene Gendlin, "Human Nature and Concepts," p. 4.

111. For arguments by a phenomenologist who claims that it "cannot seriously be doubted today that there *is* a *given* biological nature," a "transhistorical order not reducible to social conditioning," see David Levin, *The Listening Self* and "Visions of Narcissism." Eugene Gendlin also argues that the "dreadful error" of many modern thinkers has been "to think of humans as mere creations of culture, created out of nothingness, disclosed in the midst of an abyss" ("Reply to Hatab," in David Levin, ed., *Language Beyond Postmodernism,* p. 247). "From Descartes to Heidegger. . . there are only cultural humans: there is no human" ("The Small Steps of the Therapy Process," p. 209). More, he says that because the "conviction that there is no human nature" leads to a nonrecognition of our shared humanity it also leads to bloodshed based on the notion that one group of people's culture is superior to another's (see "Reply to Hatab").

112. Merleau-Ponty, *Phenomenology,* p. 254. Emphasis mine. I do not want to make Merleau-Ponty say what he did not intend. While he clearly felt that we are born already organizing our experience according to an ancient dialogue between body and world, he did not go as far as I do in positing a transhistorical human nature.

113. Frederick Perls, et al., *Gestalt Therapy,* p. 440.

114. Eugene Gendlin, *Focusing-Oriented Psychotherapy,* p. 281.

115. Eugene Gendlin, "A Phenomenology of Emotions: Anger," p. 373. Emphasis mine.

116. Eugene Gendlin, "A Philosophical Critique of the Concept of Narcissism: The Significance of the Awareness Movement," p. 264.

117. See Gion Condrau and Medard Boss, "Existential Analysis"; Medard Boss, *Existential Foundations of Medicine and Psychology;* and Christine Downing, "Poetically Dwells Man on This Earth," p. 315.

118. Joel Kovel, "Things and Words," p. 53.

119. See Kovel, "Things." As Kovel offers: "Secure and coherent intimate human relations . . . have been established as a transhistorical human need—that is, a necessary

condition for the development of real human power, as against infantile impotence" ("Narcissism and the Family"). See, also, Alice Miller, *The Drama of the Gifted Child.*

120. The quote continues: "An analogous argument would be that because some societies do not define fruit and leafy vegetables as edible they are not required in the diet. Unless one could show that scurvy, rickets, and other diseases of poor nutrition were absent, the argument about cultural variation in diet would not be credible. Because of this lapse, the cultural-specific position of the arbitrariness of emotional expression should probably not be given much weight" (Thomas Scheff, "Toward Integration in the Social Psychology of Emotions," p. 339). Noteworthy, also, is the claim of Harvey Jackins that in counseling people from every corner of the world, he has discovered that they all appear to have been wounded in the same general ways and to have the same need to express the same repressed emotions (which seem to be of a cross-cultural nature). Jackins is the International Reference Person for a form of peer-counseling practiced in over eighty countries. (See Harvey Jackins, *How "Re-evaluation Counseling" Began,* p. 14; and *The List.*) Mary Hendricks similarly writes that the process of focusing "seems to get at a variable more fundamental than cultural differences" ("Focusing Oriented/Experiential Psychotherapy"). Finally, Shepard offers that most anthropologists have been "hell-bent on the study of cultural differences," while evincing little interest at all in "species characteristics" (*The Only World We've Got,* p. xii).

121. Victor Frankl, *Man's Search for Meaning.* Of course, the need for meaning cuts across all the rest, which only goes to show that there are our needs can be articulated in various ways.

122. I emphasize some developmental needs in the following passage from Judith Herman: "In [a] climate of profoundly disrupted relationships the child faces a formidable developmental task. She must find a way to form *primary attachments* to caregivers who are either dangerous or, from her perspective, negligent. She must develop a way to develop a *sense of basic trust and safety* with caretakers who are untrustworthy and unsafe. She must develop a *sense of self* in relation to others who are helpless, uncaring, or cruel. She must develop a *capacity for bodily self-regulation* in an environment in which her body is at the disposal of others' needs, as well as a *capacity for self-soothing* in an environment without solace. She must develop the *capacity for initiative* in an environment which demands that she bring her will into complete conformity with that of her abuser. And ultimately she must develop a *capacity for intimacy* out of an environment where all intimate relationships are corrupt, and an *identity* out of an environment which defines her as a whore and a slave. . . . Though she perceives herself as abandoned to a power without mercy, she must find a way to preserve *hope and meaning.* The alternative is utter despair, something no child can bear" (*Trauma,* p. 101).

123. The same can be said, inversely, for the process of affirming the common *joys* we experience, such as the universal delight at a baby's smile.

124. See Judy Steed, *Our Little Secret.*

125. Paul Shepard, *Coming Home to the Pleistocene,* p. 134.

126. See Jean Liedloff, *The Continuum Concept.*

127. Chogyam Trungpa, *Shambhala*, pp. 9 and 10. I have taken liberties with the ordering of the quotations.

128. Jack Kornfield, *A Path with Heart*, p. 50.

129. It may be objected that humanistic psychology and Buddhism have differing views of our basic goodness. Whereas numerous humanists suggest that we are simply born good, Buddhists suggest that we are *re*born carrying patterns of bad karma from previous lifetimes. Despite this difference, what is common to humanism and Buddhists is the belief that we free ourselves from suffering and make better contact with our basic nature primarily through our own efforts. Although humanists generally trace our suffering to hurtful experiences, they do not advocate victimhood, but rather the taking of responsibility for our wounds, for becoming more accountable for our behaviors, and for developing the awareness to personally grow. Buddhists similarly advocate that we take responsibility for all our past karmas, for our reactions in the present, and for the work of becoming more enlightened or attained. In other words, for both Buddhism and humanism our basic goodness is something that can be relied on, that is assumed as an ultimate truth, and yet which is not realized without our taking responsibility for this realization.

130. The idea of innate human goodness has not gone uncriticized (see, for example, F. C. Thorne, "Critique of Recent Developments in Personality Counselling Therapy"). Critics say, for example, that the presence of so much antisocial or oppressive behavior in the world makes the idea of innate goodness untenable; or they say that humanists set up a false duality between a good human nature and a bad human society, the latter of which is regarded as the sole source of our trouble. Because it is not the purpose of this book to defend humanistic psychology or Buddhism against its critics, I do not intend to pursue these debates at any length. I would like to assert, however, that pointing to our bad karma does not by itself refute the idea of basic goodness. Indeed, Buddhists emphasize precisely that the world is full of greed, hatred, and delusion, while *still* maintaining that we and the world are basically good—a goodness that can be gradually realized or understood with practice. While wholeness and goodness define our original condition, we live in forgetfulness or ignorance of this fact. How this might have become so is the topic for numerous cultural narratives, as I discussed above. Regardless of how we might understand this "fall" into ignorance and violence, what seems most significant to me is that the process of awakening to our essential nature or unity, of spontaneously reclaiming it in the course of healing and growing, is well-documented and widely experienced by all sorts of practitioners, including humanists and Buddhists. Goodness and badness in this case are not dualistically opposed but are related via our condition of ignorance, forgetfulness, woundedness, and so on.

131. Gary Snyder writes: "There is nothing in human nature. . . which intrinsically requires that a culture be contradictory, repressive and productive of violent and frustrated personalities. . . . One can prove it for himself by taking a good look at his own nature through meditation. . . . To make 'human nature' suspect is also to make Nature—the wilderness—the enemy" (*Earth Household*, pp. 91, 115).

132. Richard Nelson. "Life-Ways of the Hunter," p. 96.

133. Russell Jacoby, *Social Amnesia,* p. 31; Kovel, "Human Nature," in *The Radical,* p. 303.

134. Jeanette Armstrong, interviewed on the Canadian Broadcasting Corporation radio program, "From Naked Ape to Superspecies."

135. See Peter Mathiessen, "Native Earth" and Joseph Bruchac, "Understanding the Great Mystery."

136. Heidegger, *An Introduction,* pp. 125, 134.

137. John (Fire) Lame Deer and Richard Erdoes, *Lame Deer,* p. 120.

138. Joel Kovel, "The Marxist View of Man and Psychoanalysis," in *The Radical Spirit,* p. 169.

139. Nelson, "Life-Ways," p. 92.

140. Nelson, *Make Prayers,* pp. 138, 225.

141. Martin, *In the Spirit,* p. 8.

142. Matthiessen, "Native," p. 22. Mathiessen continues: "Nature itself is 'the Great Mystery,' the 'religion before religion'. . . Respect for nature is respect for oneself, . . . since man and nature, though not the same thing, are not different." Joseph Epes Brown writes: "Throughout virtually all indigenous American Indian traditions, a pervasive theme has been that all forms and forces of all orders of the immediately experienced natural environment may communicate to human beings the totality of that which is to be known of the sacred mysteries of creation, and thus of the sacred essence of beings and being" (*The Spiritual Legacy of the American Indian,* p. 26). See also Barre Toelken, "Seeing with a Native's Eye: How Many Sheep Will It Hold?," p. 14.

143. Stan Rowe, *Home Place,* p. 75.

144. Mathiessen, "Native," p. 7.

145. "For the Navajo . . . almost *everything* is related to health . . . one needs not only medicine, the Navajo would say, but one needs to reestablish his relationship with the rhythm of nature. It is the ritual as well as the medicine which gets one back 'in shape'" (Toelken, "Seeing," pp. 14–15).

146. Abram, *The Spell,* p. 22.

147. These four are Re-evaluation Counseling, Vipassana meditation, Gestalt therapy, and focusing.

148. Vipassana simply means "insight" or "wisdom." Vipassana meditation is based on the original discourses of the Buddha, being associated with the earliest, or Theravaden, stream of Buddhism. For a discussion of how crucial the condition of one's posture is for the experience of sitting meditation, see Will Johnson, *The Posture of Mediation.*

149. Martin Heidegger, "What Is Metaphysics?," in *Basic Writings,* p. 108. My emphasis.

150. In *The Attentive Heart: Conversations with Trees,* for example, Stephanie Kaza describes how she draws on her Zen Buddhist training to listen to trees. It was encouraged, furthermore, in my own training for an extended wilderness quest (on which topic, see Stephen Foster and Meredith Little, *The Roaring of the Sacred River*).

151. A topic extensively treated by Kovel in *History.*

152. Kovel, "On the Notion," p. 389. "Desire wants fusion with the ground of its being and the undoing of the distinction between humanity and nature" (Kovel, *History,* p. 144).

153. Charles Bergman, "'The Curious Peach:' Nature and the Language of Desire," p. 282.

154. Kovel, *History,* pp. 124, 159.

155. Kovel, *The Age,* pp. 72, 83. "There is no intrinsic need . . . for desire to be problematic unless the society in which it emerges is self-estranged and estranged from nature" (p. 72).

156. Kornfield, *A Path,* p. 88.

157. Perls et al., *Gestalt,* p. 408.

158. David Levin, *The Body's Recollection of Being,* p. 2. See also his "Eros and Psyche: A Reading of Merleau-Ponty."

159. Sigmund Freud, *An Outline of Psychoanalysis,* p. 20.

160. As the Jungian Erich Neumann observed, Eros is the "archetype of relatedness."

161. Terry Tempest Williams, Interview. "Terry Tempest Williams," pp. 310, 312; Audre Lorde, "Uses of the Erotic: The Erotic as Power," p. 209. Emphasis mine. "When I speak of the erotic, then, I speak of it as an assertion of the lifeforce of women; of that creative energy empowered, the knowledge and use of which we are now reclaiming in our language, our history, our dancing, our loving, our work, our lives" (p. 210).

162. Brown, *Life,* pp. 33–34.

163. D. W. Winnicott, *Playing and Reality,* p. 41.

164. Norman O. Brown, *Life Against Death,* p. xvii.

165. Gaston Bachelard, quoted in Shepard, *The Others,* p. 291.

166. Percy Shelley, quoted in Livingston, *Rogue,* p. 196. Understood in this way, human nature takes on a dual aspect. In his study of Freud, for example, Paul Ricoeur concluded that human existence is a combination of *desire* and *effort* ("Existence and Hermeneutics," in *The Conflict of Interpretations,* p. 21). I take "effort" to be the realm of our free will, agency, or volition, which we are charged by nature to use in its service, whether we take up this responsibility or not. Kovel likewise suggests that the two main categories of human nature are *desire,* the transhistorical aspect of our nature, and *praxis,* which is the freely chosen, organized, purposeful activity by which a society transforms the conditions of its existence and so makes history (Kovel, *The Age,* pp. 52, 236).

167. David Levin, "Logos and Psyche: A Hermeneutics of Breathing," p. 132.

168. This is borne out as well in the etymology of *anxiety* and *angst,* which come from the Indo-Germanic root "angh," meaning "to constrict."

169. Gary Snyder, *The Practice of the Wild,* p. 68.

Chapter Five

1. John Rodman, "The Liberation of Nature?," p. 113. Emphasis mine.

2. Paul Goodman, *New Reformation,* p. 207.

3. Gary Snyder, *Earth Household,* p. 127.

4. Erazim Kohák, *The Embers and the Stars,* p. 8. Perhaps clarifying this matter a little further, the social theorist Ted Benton refers to any approach that reduces social reality solely to natural scientific explanation (e.g., sociobiology, neo-Malthusianism) as "over-naturalistic." (Ted Benton, "Biology and Social Theory in the Environmental Debate," pp. 39–40).

5. Christopher Lasch, quoted in David Noble, *Progress Without People,* p. 128.

6. See William Leiss, *The Domination of Nature,* pp. 178–187; Carolyn Merchant, *The Death of Nature;* and Max Oelschlaeger, *The Idea of Wilderness.*

7. Donald Worster, "The Shaky Ground of Sustainability," pp. 140–142. This makes the point further that the concerns of ecopsychology cannot be articulated by natural scientific discourse alone.

8. Paul Shepard, *Nature and Madness,* pp. 14–15.

9. Hatred of limits is a symptom of grandiosity or narcissism. Because narcissists have such little self-esteem, they feel driven to win the esteem of others by becoming larger-than-life, denying their bodily limits, becoming kings of the world. That our society's ecocidal relationship to nature betrays a narcissistic pattern is obviously a topic for further ecopsychological inquiry. As Allen Kanner notes, there is a "narcissistic thread" that runs through "the many historical, political, and economic trends" that contribute to the global environmental crisis ("Mount Rushmore Syndrome: When Narcissism Rules the Earth," p. 102).

10. Frederick Perls, *Ego, Hunger and Aggression.* The ego in this view is not a substance but a process, coming into existence as required by our life situations. Note that for Freud the Id (nature) is mastered by and put in service of the *Ego,* that is, Freud's view is the reverse of Perls's.

11. James Hillman, *Re-Visioning Psychology,* p. 74. Emphasis mine.

12. Ellen Chen, *The Tao Te Ching,* p. 3.

13. Bhikku Nanamaoli, *The Life of the Buddha,* p. 37. I have changed *dhamma* to *dharma.*

14. Peter Mathiessen, "Native Earth," p. 12.

15. Four Worlds International Institute for Human And Community Development, *The Sacred Tree,* p. 47. Emphasis mine.

16. Richard Nelson, *Make Prayers to the Raven,* p. 240. Emphasis mine.

17. On this humility, Perls writes: "The organism knows all. We know very little" (*Gestalt Therapy Verbatim,* p. 23); while, echoing a common Native American belief, a Koyukon Indian comments that "Each animal knows way more than you do" (*Make Prayers,* p. 225).

18. I disagree with the view that whatever grief I experience in relation to the paving of the earth merely reflects my own personal neurosis. In her lovely article "Crying for the Manatees: Youth and Our Endangered World," Anita Barrows discusses how children can be hurt in ways that result in their being particularly *attuned* to the violence done to

wildlife. While it would be possible to fix a psychodiagnostic label on many of these children, this is not good grounds for dismissing their perceptions.

19. Raymond Williams, *Keywords*, p. 87. *Cultura* itself traces to *colere*, whose meanings included "inhabit, cultivate, protect, honor with worship."

20. See Carol Bigwood, *Earth Muse*, pp. 207–223.

21. Clifford Geertz, *The Interpretation of Cultures*, p. 89. The quotation continues: "a system of inherited conceptions expressed in symbolic forms by means of which men communicate, perpetuate, and develop their knowledge about and attitudes toward life."

22. Mary Midgley, *Beast and Man*, p. 29. See also p. 286.

23. See Deborah Kleese, "Toward an Ecological Epistemology for Psychology"; Paul Shepard, "Wilderness Is Where My Genome Lives," in *Traces of an Omnivore;* and Marjorie Grene, "The Paradoxes of Historicity."

24. Lionel Trilling, quoted in Paul Shepard, *Coming Home to the Pleistocene*, p. 38. Noting that an authentic culture takes nature as its "guide in the task of cultivation," Kohák remarks: "If, in the course of the last three centuries, we have become increasingly marauders on the face of the earth rather than dwellers therein, it is not because we have become more distinctively human, more distinctively cultured, but rather because we have become less so" (*The Embers*, p. 91).

25. Wendell Berry, *The Unsettling of America*, p. 43.

26. Gary Snyder, *The Practice of the Wild*, p. 7.

27. Grene, "The Paradoxes," p. 28.

28. Grene, "The Paradoxes," p. 29. Note that I am here addressing the problem of finding a discourse that lies "between the human and the natural," for (as Grene observes) human science is said to correspond to the historical, natural science to the nonhistorical. History (humans) and nonhistory (nature) thus share no common ground.

29. Paul Shepard, quoted in David Abram, *The Spell of the Sensuous*, p. 181. Emphasis mine. See, also, "A Post-Historic Primitivism," pp. 40–47; and *Nature*, pp. 54–58, 144.

30. Martin Heidegger, "Letter on Humanism," in *Basic Writings*, p. 206.

31. For all his talk of earth and sky, Heidegger was thus ultimately unable "to place man within an organized nature." "Only if we can place ourselves . . . *within* nature," says Grene, "only then can we save the concept of historicity from the self-destruction to which it seems so readily susceptible" ("The Paradoxes," p. 29).

32. Hermes is a complex character—guide of souls, inventor, trickster, bringer of both luck and misfortune, thief, source of wild versus domestic order, god of fertility. Walter Otto called the world of Hermes a "basic image of living reality," a complete form of existence, where one journeys after the full sweep of human experience while keeping a good-humored spiritual detachment about it all. See Karl Kerényi, *Hermes: Guide of Souls* and Kane, *The Wisdom.*

33. Kerényi notes the connection between hermeneutics and Hermes: "Hermes is *hermeneus* ('interpreter'), a linguistic mediator, and this not merely on verbal grounds. By nature he is the begetter and bringer of something light-like, a clarifier, God of ex-position

and inter-pretation . . . which seeks and in his spirit . . . is led forward to the deepest mystery" (*Hermes,* p. 88). Despite that Hermes figures in my thinking, I am reluctant to wholly embrace him as a symbol for my psychology, for two reasons. The first is that I wish to work in broad principles, rather than in the details of Hermes' world. The second is that I am mindful of the fact that within indigenous traditions the messengers of the divine are not in human but *animal* form. The bear, for example, "has for thousands of years been the master of souls, bodies, and minds in transition," guarding the underworld and bringing "to the people a message of good ecology and good relations between them and the sacred powers that govern the world" (Paul Shepard and Barry Sanders, *The Sacred Paw,* pp. xv, xviii, 72). Likewise, in "the Haida mythworld, the messengers are the loon and pie-billed grebe, birds of good omen" (Kane, *The Wisdom,* p. 110). What I am going for in this section, then, is simply a view of human existence that is inspired by hermeneutic thought, and in which messages or gifts are welcomed from all sorts of others.

34. Claudio Naranjo, *The Techniques of Gestalt Therapy,* p. 5; Medard Boss, *Existential Foundations of Medicine and Psychology,* p. 282.

35. Clifford Geertz, *The Interpretation of Cultures,* p. 100. Geertz is also drawing on Susan Langer.

36. Paul Ricoeur, "Existence and Hermeneutics," in *The Conflict of Interpretations,* p. 17; Hans-Georg Gadamer, "The Problem of Historical Consciousness," p. 87.

37. Hans-Georg Gadamer, "The Universality of the Hermeneutical Problem," in *Philosophical Hermeneutics,* p. 15.

38. Shepard, *Nature,* p. 14.

39. Medard Boss, *Meaning and Content of Sexual Perversions,* p. 37.

40. This is the particular terrain of an area of psychoanalysis known as "object relations." See, for example, Margaret Mahler, et al., *The Psychological Birth of the Human Infant;* D. W. Winnicott, *The Maturational Processes and the Facilitating Environment* and *Playing and Reality;* and Jay Greenberg and Stephen Mitchell, *Object Relations in Psychoanalytic Theory.* This principle comes out clearly, as well, in Erik Erikson's work on psychosocial development, in which he assumes that "the human personality in principle develops according to steps predetermined in the growing person's readiness to be driven toward, to be aware of, and to interact with, a widening social radius" (*Childhood and Society,* p. 270). Finally, the principle of ever-widening spheres also comes out of the field of "attachment theory," first formulated by the psychiatrist John Bowlby. See, for example, Bowlby's *A Secure Base;* Mary Ainsworth, *Patterns of Attachment;* and Michel B. Sperling and William H. Berman, *Attachment in Adults.*

41. David Abram, *The Spell of the Sensuous,* p. 62.

42. Nancy Chodorow, "Gender, Relation, and Difference in Psychoanalytic Perspective," p. 11. Emphasis removed. I am partly drawing on Chodorow in the rest of this paragraph as well.

43. Winnicott thus speaks of the seeming paradox that there can be a "separation that is not a separation but a form of union" (*Playing,* p. 98)—in other words: kinship.

44. Frederick Perls et al., *Gestalt Therapy,* p. 270.

45. Harold Searles, *The Nonhuman Environment*, p. 30.

46. For Chodorow, it is especially important to see this in boys, who in the absence of parenting by men must establish their male identity by splitting away and overasserting their difference from women (mother).

47. Edith Cobb, *The Ecology of Imagination in Childhood*, p. 70.

48. Joel Kovel, *History and Spirit*, p. 85. "Splitting . . . is the basic property of domination, whether of class, sex, race or, more generally, of nature itself. . . . Differentiation . . . represents what we [ideally] strive for: it is the outcome of human nature in the direction of ecological interrelatedness and the essential unity of all beings" (Joel Kovel, "Human Nature, Freedom and Spirit," in *The Radical Spirit*, p. 292).

49. Colin Turnbull, *The Human Cycle*, p. 36. Emphasis mine. The detailed discussions in Turnbull's entire book admirably bring out much of what I am attempting to say in this section.

50. I should note that humans are not the only species to experience anxiety before the void or to go through a developmental process of attachment and separation, both of which are highly noticeable among primates generally. As Hans Jonas suggests, the various forms of life are more or less precarious depending on how mediated their relationship is to the world, how much of a gap they sense. "Imaging and speaking man," however, has achieved the most extreme degree of such mediacy (*The Phenomenon of Life*, pp. 183–187).

51. Shepard, *Coming*, p. 45.

52. Tim Ingold, *The Appropriation of Nature*, p. 223. For the hunter-gatherer, "there is no contradiction, no conflict of purpose, between the expression of individuality and his generalized commitment to others. Since the world of others is enfolded within his own person, these are one and the same" (p. 240).

53. D. W. Winnicott, "The Capacity to Be Alone," in *The Maturational Processes and the Facilitating Environment*.

54. I am adapting here from Kovel, *History*, p. 181.

55. Stanley Diamond, *In Search of the Primitive*, p. 170. Emphasis mine.

56. Joel Kovel, *The Age of Desire*, p. 74. My discussion here on desire is in general inspired by Kovel.

57. In actuality, we typically experience life as a relative mix of goodness and badness, which leads to a complexly compartmentalized inner life.

58. Kovel, *The Age*, p. 255. The notion of "sociation" comes from Kovel.

59. See Kovel's excellent discussion in *History*, pp. 81–82.

60. As Kovel writes: "The more alienated a society or person, the more horrific the Otherness" (*History*).

61. Turnbull, *The Human*, p. 30. Hence: "With the Mbuti we see the concept of the family as a constantly expanding universe, beginning with the nuclear family and ultimately embracing the whole forest, the entire extent of their experience at any moment" (p. 59).

62. Nelson, *Make Prayers*, pp. 14, 226, 238. Reports such as Nelson's and Turnbull's are ubiquitous. Musicologist Marina Roseman, for example, observes that the Temiar, a rain-forest people of the Malay peninsula, do not alienate "flowers, trees, or cicadas as

inherently different and distant," but "stress an essential similarity." They "receive inspiration and constant regeneration from interaction with the essences of mountains, rivers, fruits, and creatures of the tropical rain forest. . . . The jungle is a social place" (quoted in Shepard, *Coming*, p. 42).

63. Richard Nelson, *The Island Within*, p. 276.

64. Richard Nelson, "Life-Ways of the Hunter," p. 88.

65. This idea forms part of the nucleus of Ray Rogers's thesis in *Nature and the Crisis of Modernity*.

66. Old Torlino, quoted in Abram, *The Spell*, p. 70.

67. Turnbull, *The Human*, p. 149.

68. Conrad Aiken, quoted in Edith Cobb, "The Ecology of Imagination in Childhood," p. 129.

69. The middle chapters of Abram's *The Spell of the Sensuous*—namely, "The Flesh of Language," "Animism and the Alphabet," and "In the Landscape of Language"—are all dedicated to this topic. I will be making reference to others besides Abram in due course, especially Merleau-Ponty, but see also Kohák, "The Gift of the Word" in *The Embers*, pp. 47–66.

70. Maurice Merleau-Ponty, *Phenomenology of Perception*, p 187.

71. Merleau-Ponty, quoted in Dillon, *Merleau-Ponty's*, p. 215.

72. Abram, *The Spell*, p. 82. Hence Merleau-Ponty's remark that "language has us. . . it is not we who have language. . . . it is being that speaks within us and not we who speak of being" (*The Visible and the Invisible*, p. 194). By "being," Merleau-Ponty here means the world in its nonthematic, inexplicit, or horizonal character.

73. Martin Heidegger, *On the Way to Language*, pp. 98–99.

74. Merleau-Ponty, *The Visible*, p. 155. In making this point, Merleau-Ponty is borrowing from Valéry.

75. Maurice Merleau-Ponty, "An Unpublished Text by Maurice Merleau-Ponty: *A Prospectus of His Work*," in *The Primacy of Perception*, p. 7.

76. Abram, *The Spell*, p. 83.

77. In addition to Abram's work, my other main source, Dillon's *Merleau-Ponty's Ontology*, offers much discussion that helps elaborate this principle beyond what I am able to do here.

78. Abram, *The Spell*, p. 84. Emphasis mine. See also Dillon, *Merleau-Ponty's*, p. 218.

79. Abram, *The Spell*, pp. 80, 84.

80. "Alone of all expressive processes, speech is able to settle into a sediment and constitute an acquisition for use in human relations" (Merleau-Ponty, *Phenomenology*, p. 190). Words thus also have a transparent quality, going right to the things they disclose while keeping themselves nonfigural, just as we see *with* our eyes while having no thematic awareness *of* them (unless something gets in them, we develop cataracts, or whatever).

81. This unique disclosive ability of words is suggested, says Abram, in the Old

English word "spell," which came to mean not only correctly arranging the letters of the name for some entity but in so doing to also "effect a magic" or cast a "spell" over that entity, that is, to summon it forth in some way (*The Spell,* pp. 89, 133).

82. Paul Ricoeur, "The Metaphorical Process as Cognition, Imagination, and Feeling," pp. 150–151.

83. See Christopher Norris, *Deconstruction,* and Robert Mugerauer, *Interpreting Environments.*

84. Dillon, "Merleau-Ponty and Postmodernity," p. xxiii. As Dillon suggests, by contrast: "sedimented language, the store of knowledge wrested from the perceived world, does not screen us from the world; rather it provides the means of articulating the world and adding to that store" (*Merleau-Ponty's,* p. 201).

85. Eugene Gendlin, "Nonlogical Moves and Nature Metaphors." Derrida's strategy is to show that language is metaphorical and so that it can never re-present some original or objective reality, as the modern tradition has sought to do; he wants to show that there is no such reality, but rather constant slippage. Gendlin argues, however, that in knocking the representational model, Derrida is at the same time holding onto it, that is, he retains a dated theory of metaphor. He thus does not go *far enough* in his criticism, or pose any alternatives. That is, Derrida misses the creative, originating power of language-use, wherein we sense *more than* our existing concepts and distinctions; "misses the texture of life and usage" that word-use *opens up;* misses, finally, the way that metaphors call forth bodily felt meanings, bring experiential effects, as part of an ongoing life process, rather than simply mis-represent some original reality that is nowhere to be found.

86. Dillon, *Merleau-Ponty's,* p. 187.

87. Walter Ong has criticized Derrida and other "textualists" precisely on this point. Ong says that textualist regard the text as a closed system because they view it in historical isolation, instead of tracing it to its verbal source in primary orality. See *Orality and Literacy,* pp. 168–169. In other words, they take the text as primary when it is in fact secondary.

88. Merleau-Ponty, *Phenomenology,* pp. 429–430. "The only pre-existent Logos is the world itself" (p. xx). I think it is odd that Barfield should have to argue that "if language is 'meaningful,' then nature herself must also be meaningful." How could it be otherwise? As Barfield notes: "The denial of any . . . inner being to the processes of nature leads inevitably to the denial of it to man himself" ("The Rediscovery of Meaning," pp. 12, 15).

89. Merleau-Ponty, quoted in Dillon, *Merleau-Ponty's,* p. 201. Note that although this statement may serve as a response to Derrida, it was written a number of years before Derrida's major works appeared, by which time Merleau-Ponty had already died. See also M. C. Dillon, "Merleau-Ponty and Postmodernity."

90. See Ricoeur, "The Metaphorical," p. 142.

91. Hence Merleau-Ponty's comment: "There really is inspiration and expiration of Being" ("Eye and Mind," in *The Primacy of Perception,* p. 167). See, also, Abram's chapter on "The Forgetting and Remembering of Air," in *The Spell.*

92. I do not doubt the critical value of Derrida's efforts to disrupt received habits of

thought. As Joel Kovel comments, however, whatever liberation Derrida promises is largely undone by his flight into the cage of text. "There is nothing to be said within language—yet nothing but language: surely one of the bleakest perspectives ever advanced on the human condition." (*History,* p. 281, n. 48). On intellectual retreatism, see also Dillon, "Merleau-Ponty and Postmodernity," pp. xxii–xxiii.

93. "More than any other single invention," writes Ong, "writing has transformed human consciousness" (*Orality and Literacy,* p. 78). Ong is careful to note, however, that the shift from orality to literacy is not the only historical force that has brought about changes in "psyche and culture." "Developments in food production, in trade, in political organization, in religious institutions, in technological skills, in educational practices, in means of transportation, in family organization, and in other areas of human life all play their own distinctive roles. But most of these developments, and indeed very likely every one of them, have themselves been affected, often at great depth, by the shift from orality to literacy and beyond, as many of them have in turn affected this shift" (p. 175).

94. As Abram observes, the letters of our alphabet *can* in fact still be traced to earlier pictorial signs. In the early Semitic *aleph-beth,* for example, the first letter, *Aleph,* is also the ancient Hebrew word for *ox.* This letter is (from our perspective) an upside-down version of our own letter *A,* with two ox horns pointing upward (*The Spell,* p. 101).

95. Abram, *The Spell,* p. 254. Emphasis removed.

96. Abram, *The Spell,* p. 273.

97. Personal communication, November 2000.

98. See M. C, Dillon, *Merleau-Ponty's,* p. 256, n. 61.

99. See Kurt Danzinger, "Generative Metaphor and the History of Psychological Discourse," pp. 348–352. On psychology's general adoption of the modern world's economic-technological character, David Leary comments that throughout the field one finds a "cult of efficiency," a preoccupation with productivity, a language dense with technological analogues (calling our senses, for example, "signal detection devices"), and many other features of an engineering vision ("Psyche's Muse," pp. 51–52, n. 53). Currently, the clearest example in psychology of using machine metaphors is cognitive psychology's adoption of the computer as an image to describe the human mind.

100. Paul Shepard, *The Tender Carnivore and the Sacred Game,* p. 231. Roughly speaking, totemism is the practice in which a society perceives itself homologously to certain totemic beings who act as symbols for organizing the whole community.

101. Leary, "Psyche's Muse."

102. Marcel Detienne, quoted in Calvin Martin, *In the Spirit of the Earth,* p. 2.

103. Martin, *In the Spirit,* pp. 94, 107. Martin did not actually use the phrase "less-than-human," but rather "we are not now true humans." I used "less-than-human," however, because it indicates what becomes of us when we cleave ourselves off from what is "more-than-human."

104. Jeannette Armstrong, "Keepers of the Land," p. 323. As Armstrong also notes: "The Okanagan word for 'our place on the land' and 'our language' is the same."

105. Kane, *The Wisdom,* pp. 14, 79, 166. Like Abram, Kane offers that our own

language has become domesticated, "no longer wild in the sense of resonating with the cries of forest animals" (p. 235).

106. Dillon, *Merleau-Ponty's*, p. 235. See also p. 195.

107. See Eugene Gendlin, "Dwelling." Gendlin also notes: "If words were only discursive forms [i.e., lacking in an experiential dimension], then they could not say something new, nor something that does not follow from their established patterns. Then what words *newly say* has to be considered only a contradiction or a rupture" ("How Philosophy Cannot Appeal to Experience, and How It Can," p. 36).

108. Merleau-Ponty, *The Visible*, pp. 135, 137.

109. Merleau-Ponty, *The Visible*, p. 267. Merleau-Ponty noted to himself that his philosophy "must be presented without any compromise with *humanism*, nor *naturalism* [natural science], nor finally with *theology*" (p. 274). In other words, he was convinced that philosophy could not proceed so long as it retained the traditional cleavages among humans, nature, and God. Jerry Gill, in fact, calls Merleau-Ponty's outlook a "naturalistic theism," indicating the latter's belief that God is not above the world but *is* the world, in the sense of a nonthematic logos (*Merleau-Ponty and Metaphor*). Merleau-Ponty's philosophy of the flesh was presented in a limited number of places, primarily *The Visible and the Invisible* (specifically, chapter four, "The Intertwining—The Chiasm," and among his "Working Notes"); and the article "Eye and Mind." For a brief explication see M. C. Dillon, "Merleau-Ponty and the Reversibility Thesis."

110. Merleau-Ponty, *The Visible*, p. 139. Thus flesh denotes the commingling or intertwining of subjective and objective reality, for example, I experience my body's intentionality, I aim at the world with my hands and feet, yet only because I can see these parts of my body as objects am I able coordinate my subjective actions.

111. Merleau-Ponty, *The Visible*, p. 153.

112. Merleau-Ponty himself said that language "is founded on the phenomenon of the mirror . . . or the echo, . . . on the magical action of like upon like" (quoted in Dillon, *Merleau-Ponty's*, p. 206).

113. "Where are we to put the limit between the body and the world, since the world is flesh?" (Merleau-Ponty, *The Visible*, p. 138; see also p. 248). Ecological thinking places phenomena in con-text, within the larger text-ure, fabric, or weave, of life. The ultimate "text," then, is the flesh of the world.

114. Indeed, Merleau-Ponty also noted to himself to: "Do a psychoanalysis of nature: it is the flesh, the mother" (*The Visible*, p. 267).

115. Gill, *Merleau-Ponty*, p. 60. Recall my discussion of the contact boundary in chapter three. In the terms used here, we would say that our flesh faces both inward and outward at this boundary.

116. Quoted in David Strong, *Crazy Mountains*, p. 155.

117. Thus did Heidegger say that "perceiving is responding (resonating)" (quoted in Avens, "Heidegger," p. 197). Experiential psychotherapists understand this well, for they are always sensing into their *own* bodies in order to sense what might correspondingly be going on for their clients.

118. Owen Barfield, "The Meaning of the Word 'Literal,'" p. 56. As the Roman philosopher Plotinus put it: "All knowing comes by likeness" (quoted in Hillman, *Revisioning*, p. 99).

119. Merleau-Ponty, "Eye and Mind," in *The Primacy of Perception*, p. 164. Emphasis mine. "We understand the thing as we understand a new kind of behaviour, not, that is, through any kind of intellectual operation of subsumption, but by taking up on our own account the *mode of existence* which the observable signs adumbrate before us" (*Phenomenology*, p. 319; emphasis mine).

120. Shepard, "Wilderness," in *Traces*, p. 221.

121. Paul Shepard, "The Ark of the Mind," p. 59.

122. Paul Shepard, *Thinking Animals*, p. 191. As many have commented, we experience the world as a unified whole only because of the way that things resemble or imply one another, and so hang together in our perception of them (see, for example, Isaiah Berlen's comments in David Leary, "Psyche's Muse," p. 29, n. 12). Trees are like flowers, flowers are like us, and we are like stones and stars (and this sentence is like a Gary Snyder poem, in *No Nature*, p. 287). Everything overlaps, mirrors, bleeds into, stretches away from, or "metaphors," everything else.

123. Boss, *Existential*, p. 76. Recall that self and world form a single unit, both being disclosed within the same clearing of being or horizon of understanding. Thus for scientists to experience the world as a dead place, they must actually deaden *themselves*— must adopt a mood or mode of attunement that is "calm, cool, and collected." In studying vision, Descartes, for example, chose to take "the eye of a newly dead man" (quoted in Robert Romanyshyn, "The Despotic Eye: An Illustration of Metabletic Phenomenology and Its Implications," p. 93; see also van den Berg, *Things*, pp. 20–21).

124. Indeed, according to a philosophy of flesh no such independence of mental functions is even possible, for all aspects or regions of existence continuously play into or mirror one another. What we perceive, for example, cannot be cleanly separated from how we are moving our bodies, what emotions or desires we are feeling, what we are thinking, or what kind of language we have acquired. All of these are intertwined aspects of a single bodily existing.

125. Please note how this discussion ties into much of what I talked about in chapter two concerning the impossibility of achieving an unbiased knowledge of reality. On the necessary of projection for the making of contact see also Abram, *The Spell*, pp. 58, 275–276, n. 3; and Gordon Wheeler, *Gestalt Reconsidered*. Quite simply, if others are so different from ourselves that we can't imagine what it is like to be them or what they are experiencing, then we can't make any contact. This is also why psychotherapists are often people who have been much wounded themselves, for this helps them to see, understand, and make contact with other people's wounds. On the imaginative component within all experience, see Neil Bolton, "The Lived World: Imagination and the Development of Experience."

126. Stephen Levine, *Poiesis*, pp. 33, 41.

127. In the usual understanding of projection, by contrast, the idea that we misper-

ceive the wolves can only mean that there exists some correct or objective, perhaps scientifically determined, perception of wolves.

128. Barry Lopez, "Renegotiating the Contracts." *Parabola* 8.2 (1983), p. 16.

129. Personal communication, August, 2000; and "Revitalizing Natural History," p. 87.

130. George Santayana, quoted in Kenneth Burke, *A Rhetoric of Motives*, p. 82. Emphasis mine. In concluding the controversial anthology, *Uncommon Ground*, William Cronon writes: "Nature is a mirror onto which we project our own ideas and values; but is also a material reality that sets limits . . . on the possibilities of human ingenuity and storytelling. . . . The nonhuman world is real and autonomous, a place worthy of our respect and care, but the paradox of our human lives is that we can never know that world at first hand. Instead, we see it through the lens of our own conceptions and simulations, which never map onto the real world in a perfect one-to-one correspondence" (p. 458). While I am in support of recognizing both the otherness of the natural world and the role of projection in our understanding of it, I believe that Cronon's conception of projection is dualistic, for it makes "the real world" inaccessible. As a plural realist I suggest, rather, that we *do* contact reality, even if we can do this in better or worse ways. Reality, in short, is not some objective, material realm we distortedly perceive through our various lenses, but the meanings we gather in our fleshy commerce with others.

131. Robert Romanyshyn, "Unconsciousness : Reflection and the Primacy of Perception," p. 158.

132. Theodore Roszak, *The Voice of the Earth*, pp. 303, 320.

133. Gion Condrau and Medard Boss, "Existential Analysis," p. 503.

134. Medard Boss, *Existential*, p. 261. See also Medard Boss, *The Analysis of Dreams*.

135. André de Koning, "Reflections on the Heart," p. 142.

136. James Hillman, "The Animal Kingdom in the Human Dream," p. 321.

137. James Hillman, "Animal Presence," pp. 126–127. Elsewhere, Hillman has pleaded that we not view dream animals as mere symbols of our instincts or dangerous subjective forces inside us, but in "motifs of learning from the animal, amazed by its beauty, touched by its pain, reconciliation with it, being borne, helped, saved by the animal" ("The Animal Kingdom in the Human Dream," p. 329). In *The Dream and the Underworld*, he also notes that dream animals do not merely represent instincts because "they are not images *of* animals, but images *as* animals" (p. 150). Medard Boss makes similar remarks in *The Analysis of Dreams* (e.g., pp. 105–107), even if his theoretical framework differs in other respects from Hillman's.

138. Erving and Miriam Polster, *Gestalt Therapy Integrated*, pp. 266–268. As Gendlin, Jungians, and other also emphasize, it is important to establish a reciprocal relation with dreams, to treat them lovingly and respectfully, to welcome them, pay attention to them, thank them. In this way, the dreams themselves come to offer more to the dreamer.

139. I thus agree with the distinction made by Gary Snyder: "Animals come into myth or dream not as projections, but as a way to speak to the human mind. In one sense, you can say that's a projection, but the fact is we couldn't have animals in our dreams if there

weren't real animals. There is some kind of information that is exchanged there" ("Hanging Out with Raven," p. 140).

140. Dillon, "Merleau-Ponty and Postmodernity," p. xxiii. Emphasis mine. We are "separated from ourselves" in that we exist only in our interactions with others; and that in order to contact the other we must reach across a distance, finding ourselves both here in our bodies and over there, absorbed in another who correspondingly mirrors or informs us of who we are or what we can be. Thus it is only in being separated from myself that I may come back to myself changed—the other creates the distance I need in order to see myself.

141. Shepard, *The Others,* p. 281.

142. Gary Snyder, *A Place in Space,* p. 187.

143. "Many features of the bear—especially the many races of the brown bear—place it in correspondence to humanity. Its size, appearance, mobility, dexterity, omnivorousness, reproduction, annual cycle, length of life, social behavior, and intelligence have an eerie relation to our own. These characteristics are the source of enduring speculative analogy and psychological tension. . . . The bear is the only familiar omnivore whose size approximates our own. . . . It has an expressive face, binocular vision, vocal and gestural responses, sitting and bipedal stances, almost no tail, and fine dexterity. . . . And yet the bear is vividly other—huge, furry, long-muzzled, long clawed, quadrupedal—in these things nothing like a man" (Shepard, "The Ark," p. 58).

144. Shepard and Sanders, *The Sacred,* p. 59. Gary Snyder also includes a version of this story in *The Practice of the Wild.*

145. Paul Shepard, "The Unreturning Arrow," p. 211. Emphasis removed. Although I have not pursued it here, this idea suggests an affinity between the notions of flesh and that of the life force. Anita Barrows has, in this vein, called for a type of developmental psychology that would emphasize "the wordless stratum of the child's being, which is . . . a life-force made manifest, a porous, permeable, sensitive essence intertwined with all other such essences, affecting and affected by them with its every breath" ("The Ecopsychology of Child Development," p. 110).

146. Shepard, *The Sacred,* p. 72. By "species" I mean to suggest more than just the plant and animal world.

147. Shepard, *Thinking,* p. 72. See, also, "Phyto-resonance of the True Self," in *Traces of an Omnivore.*

148. Harold Searles, quoted in Shepard, *Nature,* p. 14.

149. For a "wheel" teaching which combines Native American and old European sources, and which is intended as a contribution to the ecopsychology literature, see Steven Foster, with Meredith Little, *The Four Shields.*

150. Joseph Epes Brown, "The Bison and the Moth: Lakota Correspondences," p. 13.

151. Paul Shepard, "Nature and Madness," p. 39.

152. Shepard, *Nature,* p. 128.

153. Paul Shepard, "On Animal Friends," p. 279.

154. Shepard, *Coming Home,* p. 5.

155. Merleau-Ponty, *Phenomenology,* pp. 184–185. The following sentence also borrows from Merleau-Ponty.

156. See Searles's remarks from chapter one. Anita Barrows recently noted that "from the earliest moments of life the infant has an awareness not only of human touch, but of the touch of the breeze on her skin, variations in light and color, temperature, texture, sound. No one who has spent time watching an infant could fail to notice this; yet the theorists on whose work our current understanding (and therapies) have been based fail to account for its importance—indeed, even for its presence" ("The Ecopsychology," p. 103).

157. Gene Myers, *Children and Animals,* p. 143. This is the same point made above by Searles. Shepard also writes: "We do not graduate from animality but . . . into and through it" (*Thinking,* p. 3).

158. Cobb, "The Ecology," p. 131.

159. Wang Jiazhu, quoted in "The Three Gorges: The Case for Development," p. 51.

160. A point made by Wolfgang Sachs: "Through the trick of a biological metaphor, a simple economic activity turns into a natural and evolutionary process, as though hidden qualities would be progressively developed to their final state. The metaphor thus says that the real destiny of natural goods is to be found in their economic utilization" (quoted in Livingston, *Rogue,* p. 61).

161. One of Shepard's central arguments, in fact, is that Western history has the character of a "continuing *dedevelopment*" (my emphasis). He speculates, that is, that "the history of Western man has been a progressive peeling back of the psyche," with "mutilations of personal maturity" being "the vehicle of cultural progress and environmental decimation" (*Nature,* p. 16). It is not insignificant, then, when Maria Mies reports of male sex tourists found in Thailand who "demand that the . . . [prostitute] bath and feed them like a baby, and oil and powder their buttocks" (Maria Mies and Vandana Shiva, *Ecofeminism,* p. 136).

162. In his *The Human Cycle,* Colin Turnbull contrasts his own experiences through the various stages of the life cycle to those of the different peoples he has studied around the world as an anthropologist. It was a very moving read for me, and certainly complements well the discussion here. Needless to say, virtually all of Paul Shepard's writings may be sought out for further treatment of the present topic.

163. In his article "The Child's Relations with Others" (in *The Primacy of Perception*), Merleau-Ponty argued, however, that our usual Cartesian view of persons—as self-contained, solitary, rational, and externally related individuals—makes this kind of infantile experiencing a logical impossibility. Descartes began with the experience of dualistically split, isolated, intellectual adults, whereas infants exist in an original being-together with the world and only gradually come to differentiate and enter into relations with others. As Paul Nonnekes puts it, the infant is involved in "a pulsation of growth that is neither an inside nor an outside, but an *intertwining*" ("The Intertwining Wildness of Flesh-Child Becoming," p. 20). For a good discussion of how developmental theorists often start not with the child but with the rational adult word, which is then used as a yardstick against

which "the child is judged to be more or less competent," see Chris Jenks, "Introduction: Constituting the Child." Jenks says that much developmental "theory moves to envelop the child within its own projections," such that the child is "abandoned in theory," or "reimported as an afterthought." See, also, David Levin, *The Listening Self* (pp. 150–166) for a general discussion of mirroring and infancy.

164. The rise and fall of the speech of parents, for example, has been observed to correspond to rises and falls in the trunk movements and gesturings of their infants. At times the boundaries between caregiver and infant may become indefinite, where there exists only an "interpresenced participation in the flesh" (Nonnekes, "The Intertwining," p. 22), a blurring of identities in a nondual and synergistic feeling space. See Zachariah Boukydis, "A Theory of Empathic Relations Between Parents and Infants: Insight from a Client-Centred/Experiential Perspective."

165. As discussed, for instance, in Levin, *The Listening,* p. 152.

166. Dillon, *Merleau-Ponty's,* p. 167.

167. Erik Erikson, quoted in Cobb, *The Ecology,* p. 57.

168. Morris Berman, borrowing from educator John Holt, in *Coming to Our Senses,* p. 42.

169. Eugene Gendlin, "The Primacy of the Body, Not the Primacy of Perception," p. 350.

170. Gill, *Merleau-Ponty,* p. 97.

171. Perls et al, *Gestalt,* p. 270. See, also, Mary Ainsworth, "Attachment as Related to Mother-Infant Interaction" for a discussion of the "pre-adapted . . . system of maternal behaviour."

172. Shepard, *Nature,* pp. 7, 9.

173. Winnicott, *The Maturational,* p. 87.

174. Barrows mentions that some ecofeminists do this as a deliberate ritual ("The Ecopsychology," p. 104).

175. Harold Searles, quoted in Levin, *Listening,* p. 155. Searles remarks are based on "daily-life observations of infants and young children, and from psychoanalytic and psychotherapeutic work with neurotic and psychotic adults."

176. Liedloff, *The Continuum,* p. 34.

177. See Boukydis, "A Theory."

178. Ainsworth, "Attachment," p. 44.

179. As Boyd Eaton, et al., note: "More or less constant carrying of the infant in a sling or pouch at the mother's side or back is characteristic of hunters and gatherers in widely separated geographic regions" (*The Paleolithic Prescription,* p. 207). See, also, Turnbull, *The Human* (especially p. 76), and Liedloff, *The Continuum.*

180. See, for example, Ainsworth, "Attachment" and Winnicott, *The Maturational.* Jean Liedloff's *The Continuum* is a powerful testimony to the wrong-headedness of much conventional Western belief about child raising. On the emotional mistreatment of children in western society, see also Phyllis Bronstein, "Promoting Healthy Emotional Development in Children."

181. Liedloff, *The Continuum,* p. 71. This follows because a basic infantile need is to know that we have a *right to be.* As Winnicott puts it, when well-mirrored the baby can in effect say: "When I look I am seen, so I exist" (*Playing,* p. 114).

182. See, for example James Masterson, *The Search for the Real Self* and chapter fourteen of Gary Yontef, *Awareness, Dialogue and Process.* The existence today of parent-infant psychotherapy suggests, as well, how much trouble our society gets into in raising its infants.

183. See, for example, chapter six of Judith Herman, *Trauma and Recovery* and chapter two of John Briere, *Therapy for Adults Molested as Children.*

184. See Donald Dutton, *The Abusive Personality.*

185. Gary Paul Nabhan and Stephen Trimble, *The Geography of Childhood.*

186. Cobb, "The Ecology," pp. 123–124.

187. Shepard, *Nature,* p. 11. See, also, the chapter "Kids' Stuff" in Livingston, *Rogue,* pp. 119–136.

188. Paul Shepard, "Place in American Culture," p. 32. Emphasis mine. Shepard believed that: "every child under ten has three ecological needs: architecturally complex play space shared with companions; a cumulative and increasingly diverse experience of non-human forms, animate and inanimate, whose taxonomic names and generic relations he must learn; and occasional and progressively more strenuous exertions into the wild world where he may, in a limited way, confront the nonhuman" (*The Tender,* p. 267).

189. Perls et al, *Gestalt,* p. 270.

190. Myers, *Children,* pp. 15, 64. Emphasis mine.

191. Shepard, *Thinking,* p. 59.

192. Myers, *Children,* p. 5.

193. Myers, *Children,* p. 16.

194. Myers, *Children,* pp. 41–42. This again shows a split between the symbolic and experiential in our society.

195. Myers, *Children,* p. 170. Myers suggests, in fact, that the child who is "provided with a human social environment but deprived of nonhuman others," will be unable to develop "her or his full humanity."

196. Jenks writes that for Piaget play "is merely diverting fun or fantasy, it deflects the child from his true logical purpose within the system of rationality; the criteria of play need not equate with the rigorous factual demands of reality" ("Introduction," p. 22). Compare these remarks to those of a Gestaltist, Laura Perls: "A small child, before becoming socialized, lives *on* the [contact] boundary: looks at everything, touches everything, gets into everything. He discovers the world, expands his awareness and means of coping at his own pace: playfully serious or seriously playing, he makes an ongoing creative adjustment to his own potential" ("Comments on the New Directions," p. 223; emphasis mine). On the significance of play in childhood, see also David Levin, *The Body's Recollection of Being,* p. 238–240.

197. Eaton, et al., *The Paleolithic,* pp. 211–212. I have spliced some words into this quote from elsewhere on the same page.

198. As is thoroughly discussed in Turnbull, *The Human;* and Shepard, *Coming,* p. 159.

199. Martin, *In the Spirit,* p. 9.

200. Myers, *Children,* p. 141.

201. Shepard, *The Others,* p. 282.

202. Shepard, *Thinking,* p. 121.

203. Myers, *Children,* p. 10. Emphasis mine. Adding another dimension to this, Shepard notes: "Fantasies of animals wearing clothes and building houses, what may seem a too-close similarity between them and [children], creates an excess of common ground, stored for late adolescence when disjunction almost swamps the ego" (*The Others,* p. 88).

204. Shepard, *The Others,* p. 83. Myers mentions a child (Billy) who after a turtle was introduced to his classroom imagines that he is himself in the water and that a shark is nearby. Playing the turtle, he pulls his arms in tight to his sides, and only when the coast is clear extends them back out. "For Billy, the turtle symbolizes not only safety and coherence but the whole affective experience of surviving an imagined life-threatening situation. Notably, Billy's symbolization took the embodied form first of a tightly closed-off protective posture and them of an expansive, mobile, and agentic one—conveying qualities that would be hard to represent verbally" (*Children,* p. 57). Qualities such as *agency* (animals have their own purposes, confirming the child's own); *coherence* (animals are not contradictory or ambiguous, as are adults; they do not lie, they are whole); *affectivity* (all animals convey feelings in their voices, motions, and manner); and *continuity* (the child experiences the continuity of her or his own self through the maintenance of her relations with animal others) are thereby made available to the child in her or his interaction with animals.

205. Shepard, "The Ark," p. 55.

206. Myers, *Children,* p. 171.

207. Stephen Trimble in Nabhan and Trimble, *The Geography,* pp. 170–171.

208. Turnbull, *The Human,* p. 81. "The consequences of our folly are to be seen all around us in the violence, neurosis, and loneliness of our youth, our adults, and our aged, some of whom never even approach the fullness and richness of life that could have been theirs had their adolescence been handled with more wisdom, understanding, and gentle respect."

209. Peter Breggin writes: "Adolescence, with its struggle to form identity in the face of unleashed passions, easily gets called 'mental illness.' Whether adolescents become mentally ill often depends mostly on the love, patience, and tolerance of the adults who surround them" (*Toxic Psychiatry,* p. 33). Whereas critics like Breggin trace the onset of schizophrenia and other "mental illnesses" among adolescents to the acute psychospiritual and social demands of this stage of life, the biopsychiatric establishment generally does not make such a link, sticking to its biochemical and genetic explanations. See, also, Medard Boss, *Existential,* pp. 235–236.

210. Turnbull, *The Human,* p. 122.

211. Erik Erikson, *Identity: Youth and Crisis,* p. 258. Emphasis mine. Adolescence,

says Erikson, is a time for, "the mutual confirmation of individual and community, in the sense that society recognizes the young individual as a bearer of fresh energy and that the individual so confirmed recognizes society as a living process which inspires loyalty as it receives it, maintains allegiance as it attracts it, honors confidence as it demands it" (p. 241).

212. Erik Erikson, *Identity and the Life Cycle*, p. 95.

213. Carleton Coon, *The Hunting Peoples*, p. 392.

214. Erikson, *Identity and the Life*, p. 97.

215. Says Erikson: the adolescent "would rather act shamelessly in the eyes of his elders, out of free choice, than be forced into activities which would be shameful in his own eyes or in those of his peers" (*Identity: Youth*, p. 130).

216. Erikson, *Identity: Youth*, p. 254.

217. "Sexual and spiritual awareness as modes of experience are just as valid as physical and intellectual awareness; and like those other modes of apprehension they can be turned in any direction, inward or outward, restricted to the individual self or encouraged to expand and encompass the infinitely greater social self" (Turnbull, *The Human*, pp. 122–123).

218. M. C. Dillon, "Toward a Phenomenology of Love and Sexuality: An Inquiry into the Limits of the Humans Situation as They Condition Loving," p. 344.

219. Turnbull, *The Human*, p. 82.

220. Eaton, et al., *The Paleolithic*, p. 215. "For the growing child among the !Kung, as opposed to among ourselves," for example, "sex becomes less taboo, less frightening, and less unknown" (p. 221). Mbuti children also spend much time in imitation of "how the wide diversity of territorial, kinship, age, and sex roles are played" (Turnbull, *The Human*, p. 45).

221. Mircea Eliade, *Rites and Symbols of Initiation: The Mysteries of Birth and Rebirth*, pp. 1, 39.

222. Among tribal societies males and females generally undergo different forms of initiation. Both involve a period of severance or isolation from the community and a ceremonial return. The female rites, however, tend to center on initiation into the sacrality of womanhood, or of the female mode of being, and generally follow the first menstruation. Male rites are generally more elaborate, involving various trials or ordeals, and focusing on mythology, cosmology, and the like. Among those who are today reviving initiatory practices in our own society, the female/male distinction is often maintained, although rites such as vision quests are being offered to both males and females, without distinction. For a broad treatment, see Louise Mahdi et al., ed., *Betwixt and Between: Patterns of Masculine and Feminine Initiation*.

223. See Toni Nelson, "Violence Against Women."

224. See David Gilmore, *Manhood in the Making*. Gilmore is careful to point out that these violent rituals do have a social function. If, for example, a society requires for its continuance that men take great risks in hunting and warfare, then it makes a sort of sense to convert boys into "fearless" men through painful initiation tests. Be that as it may, the

need in our own society to question traditional ideals of masculinity—a need first brought home by the women's movement—puts any violent form of male initiation into question. Rituals and socialization processes that shame males into disowning essential aspects of their humanity—including their vulnerable emotions and relational needs—are not only violent to men, but contribute to the creation of men who are then violent with women.

225. Geertz, *The Interpretation,* p. 125.

226. Shepard, *Nature,* p. 66.

227. Eliade, *Rites,* p. 130.

228. Thus when initiatory rites declined in the middle ages they were replaced by literature containing initiatory motifs, as in the heroic tales of Arthur or Percival. Fairy tales were later to dramatically express initiatory scenarios that "answers a deep need in the human being." In our own time, finally, best sellers continue to be full of mythological figures.

229. In addition to Eliade's work, see: Mahdi et al., ed., *Betwixt;* the works of Stephen Foster and Meredith Little; Joseph Epes Brown, ed., *The Sacred Pipe: Black Elk's Account of the Seven Rites of the Oglala Sioux;* Victor Turner, *The Ritual Process;* Arnold van Gennep, *The Rites of Passage;* and James Wright, *The Bones of Metamorphosis.* The classic account of attaining a vision for one's people is told in John Neihardt's *Black Elk Speaks.*

230. Shepard, *Nature,* p. 10.

231. Shepard, *Coming,* p. 44.

232. Thus for Shepard, "the frame-work of nature as metaphorical foundation for cosmic-at-homeness is as native to the human organism in its adolescent years as any nutritive element in the diet" (*Nature,* p. 71).

233. Shepard, "Place," p. 90.

234. Shepard, *The Others,* p. 89.

235. Erikson, *Childhood,* p. 269.

236. Michael Meade, *Men and the Waters of Life,* p. 19.

237. Mahdi et al., ed., *Betwixt,* p. xi. In introducing Arnold van Gennep's *The Rites of Passage,* Solon Kimball writes that the "situation in psychology is a very curious one. Except in psychoanalysis, there is no indication of knowledge of or interest in rites of passage, or in events of this type, in the individual's life. . . . The critical problems of becoming male or female, of relations within the family, and of passing into old age are directly related to the devices which the society offers the individual to help him achieve the new adjustment. Somehow we seem to have forgotten this. . . . It seems . . . likely that one dimension of mental illness may arise because an increasing number of individuals are forced to accomplish their transitions alone and with private symbols" (pp. xiv, xviii).

238. Meade, "Foreword," to Eliade, *Rites,* p. xx.

239. Meade, "Foreword," p. xxi.

240. Shepard, *Coming,* p. 46.

241. Leidloff, *The Continuum,* p. 149.

242. Friedrich Nietzsche, quoted in Norman O. Brown, *Life Against Death,* p. 107.

Chapter Six

1. Jean Liedloff, *The Continuum Concept*, p. 137.
2. Norman O. Brown, *Life Against Death*, p. 16.
3. David Noble, *Progress Without People*, p. 128.
4. As Jeanette Armstrong remarks: "A serious life principle is being happy at what we do; that is, fulfilled at what we do, internally whole at what we do, doing something because we love to participate in it and feeling that we need to do it or our lives are empty shells" (Interviewed by Derrick Jensen, p. 282).
5. Brown, *Life*, p. 8.
6. David Strong, *Crazy Mountains*, p. 80.
7. Fredric Jameson notes, in this regard, that the capitalist mode of production has engendered three stages of revolution in technology: steam-driven motors; electric and combustion motors; and electronic and nuclear-powered apparatuses. These revolutions correspond to three "fundamental movements in capitalism, each one marking a dialectical expansion over the previous stage": market capitalism, monopoly capitalism, and multinational capitalism ("Postmodernism, or The Cultural Logic of Late Capitalism," p. 78). See, also, Andrew Freenberg's "The Critical Theory of Technology," in which he argues that capitalism is in itself a technical system; that technology has an essentially social character.
8. I draw heavily on Noble in what follows, both because he provides a comprehensive narrative and because he uses some recent scholarship which revises the usual view of Luddites as irrational opponents of technology.
9. Noble, *Progress*, p. 139.
10. Francis Bacon, quoted in William Leiss, *The Limits of Satisfaction*, p. 37.
11. Noble, *Progress*, p. 12. Noble is himself drawing here on Geoffrey Bernstein.
12. Noble, *Progress*, p. 142. See, also, Noble's *The Religion of Technology*.
13. Sigmund Freud, *Civilization and Its Discontents*, p. 24.
14. Sigmund Freud, "The Future of an Illusion," p. 194.
15. Freud, *Civilization*, p. 33. Next quote, p, 24.
16. Freud, "The Future," p. 185. Civilization "presupposes precisely the non-satisfaction . . . of powerful instincts" (Freud, *Civilization*, p. 44).
17. Freud, "The Future," p. 194.
18. Freud, *Civilization*, pp. 30, 81.
19. Max Horkheimer, *Eclipse of Reason*, pp. 94 and 162. See also Herbert Marcuse, *Counterrevolution and Revolt*, chapter two. On the use of the notion of the revolt of nature by the early critical theorists in general, see Robyn Eckersley, "The Failed Promise of Critical Theory"; and Henry Blanke, "Domination and Utopia: Marcuse's Discourse on Nature, Psyche, and Culture."
20. Although Horkheimer was originally referring only to the revolt of human nature, William Leiss writes: "If it is the case that the natural environment cannot tolerate the present level of irrational technological applications without suffering breakdowns in

the mechanisms that govern its cycles of self-renewal, then we would be justified in speaking of a revolt of external nature which accompanies the rebellion of human nature" (*The Domination of Nature*, p. 164).

21. Paul Shepard, *The Others*, p. 265.

22. Leiss, *The Domination*, p. 194.

23. Horkheimer, *The Eclipse*, p. 94.

24. Stanley Diamond, *In Search of the Primitive*, p. 44.

25. Peter Breggin, *Toxic Psychiatry*, p. 275.

26. See Brian Tokar, *Earth for Sale;* and Tom Athanasiou, *Divided Planet*, p. 242. As an example of the power of public relations, Athanasiou notes: "When a scandal-ridden company called Nuclear Engineering, Inc. changes its name to U.S. Ecology, wins the contract to build a hotly contested radioactive waste dump, and distributes slick brochures explaining the dump's displacement of a threatened desert tortoise as 'A New Home for Endangered Friends,' it is obviously the logic of appearances that sets the terms" of our age (p. 232).

27. Joel Kovel, "The Justifiers," p. 1.

28. This term comes from the theoretical work of the Re-evaluation Counselling Communities. See their booklet "What's Wrong with the 'Mental Health' System: And What Can Be Done About It."

29. Brown, *Life*, p. 15. See Freud, *Civilization*, p. 80.

30. Joel Kovel, *The Age of Desire*, p. 174. A "line of self-alienation must be drawn, above which is 'normal capitalist restlessness' and below which is neurosis and frank psychosis. The mental-health professionals have been stationed to patrol this boundary no less than their brethren police exist to hold the line against objective criminality" (p. 122).

31. Hence, the repression of the revolt of nature is enforced by our fear of social censure, of being unloved, of facing the void. Our existential insecurity, in other words, keeps us from questioning our own violation.

32. See Phyllis Bronstein, "Promoting Healthy Emotional Development in Children." As Bronstein notes, some psychologists even support this rule, claiming that mature people have learned to inhibit their strong emotions. My next sentence draws from the work of N. Henley, cited by Bronstein.

33. It is not uncommon even for psychotherapists to be afraid of emotional catharsis. In this case, they are unable to discern those instances when a catharsis is in fact a movement toward healing (see "What's Wrong"). In *The Stormy Search for the Self,* Christina and Stan Grof discuss how a great deal of spiritual experience is also diagnosed as "mental illness."

34. Rogers, *Solving*, p. 86.

35. As Peter Breggin observes: "After passionate people get psychiatrically labeled, they become especially vulnerable to defeat and disaster. Psychiatrists commonly force treatment on them, then claim that they must be 'mentally ill,' because they resent and resist being diagnosed and treated" (*Toxic Psychiatry*, pp. 33–34).

36. Noble, *Progress*, p. 21.

37. Joel Kovel does not mince his words on this point: "a colossal burden of neurotic misery in the population . . . continually and palpably betrays the capitalist ideology, which maintains that commodity civilization promotes human happiness" ("Therapy in Late Capitalism," in *The Radical Spirit,* p. 136).

38. Jules Henry, quoted in David Levin, "Clinical Stories: A Modern Self in the Fury of Being," p. 480.

39. See Rogers, *Solving,* p. 20.

40. This has much in common, for example, with earlier leftist strategies for raising class consciousness. In his Marxist days, for instance, the psychoanalyst Wilhelm Reich argued that to awaken this consciousness "we must begin with the assumption that no social order that requires the frustration of instinct can lead to human happiness. Therefore, a fundamental dissatisfaction will always be present, at least in latent form. Radical politics must kindle this latent dissatisfaction into revolutionary class consciousness. . . . Only people fully in touch with their own needs and interests can be counted on to resist both capitalist exploitation and communist domination" (the words are Roger Gottlieb's, in *Marxism,* pp. 126–127). Whether the kind of strategy I and others propose has an advantages over Reich's, or any greater likelihood of success, remains to be seen.

41. Jameson, "Postmodernism," p. 77.

42. Jameson writes: "distance in general (including 'critical distance' in particular) has very precisely been abolished in the new space of postmodernism. . . . the prodigious new expansion of multilateral capital ends up penetrating and colonizing those very pre-capitalist enclaves (Nature and the Unconscious) which offered extraterritorial and Archimedian footholds for critical effectivity. . . . we all, in one way or another, dimly feel that not only punctual and local countercultural forms of cultural resistance and guerrilla warfare, but also even overtly political interventions like those of *The Clash,* are all somehow secretly disarmed and reabsorbed by a system of which they themselves might well be considered a part, since they can achieve no distance form it" ("Postmodernism," p. 87). On the difficulties of being caught, as a member of our society, within the very meanings we oppose, see also Charles Taylor, "Interpretation and the Sciences of Man," p. 72.

43. Robert Bourassa, quoted in Carol Bigwood, *Earth Muse,* p. 224.

44. Martin Heidegger, *Discourse on Thinking,* p. 50.

45. Martin Heidegger, "The Question Concerning Technology," in *The Question Concerning Technology and Other Essays,* p. 14.

46. Bill McKibben, *The End of Nature,* p. 165. "Eventually, all plants might 'become unnecessary,' replaced by artificial leaves that would 'waste' none of the sunlight they receive on luxuries such as roots but instead use 'all the energy they trap to make things for us to use.'"

47. Paul Shepard, *Nature and Madness,* p. 38.

48. Carol Bigwood, *Earth Muse,* pp. 149, 170. Emphasis mine.

49. Hence, "nature takes orders from man and works under his authority" (quoted in Carolyn Merchant, *The Death of Nature,* p. 171).

50. Martin Heidegger, "The Word of Nietzsche: 'God Is Dead,'" in *The Question Concerning Technology and Other Essays,* p. 100.

51. See George Steiner, *Heidegger,* p. 132.

52. Martin Heidegger, quoted in Bruce Foltz, "On Heidegger and the Interpretation of the Ecological Crisis," p. 334.

53. Noble, *Progress,* p. 4.

54. The commodity is what the device provides, what function it serves, what it is there for, or what gets consumed. Thus television sets provide news and entertainment, cars provide transportation, and so on.

55. Albert Borgmann, *Technology and the Character of Contemporary Life,* p. 192.

56. Albert Borgmann, *Crossing the Postmodern Divide,* p. 137.

57. This is an example used by Borgmann, but which I am presenting in my own way.

58. Borgmann, *Technology,* p. 77.

59. Borgmann, *Technology,* p. 77.

60. Borgmann does make room in his scheme for issues of social justice, saying that the pattern of technology acts to maintain inequalities. He does not, however, give them much detailed treatment. For myself, I would like to have included more class, gender, and race analysis in this chapter, but did not feel adequate to the task. As I mentioned in chapter one, the working out of a more thorough critical perspective remains a future project for me.

61. I believe that Borgmann's linking of a philosophy of technology to the commodification of reality is a very important move, as it opens the door for the kind of economic thinking largely absent in Heidegger, and to a great extent missing even in Borgmann himself. Although my exercise here is a limited one, I hope in what follows to demonstrate some of the potential the device paradigm offers in this respect.

62. Kovel "Therapy," in *The Radical,* p. 135.

63. Medard Boss, *Existential Foundations of Medicine and Psychology.* p. 209. Borgmann adds: "When commodities have reached the final stage of reduction and refinement, leisure outwardly will no longer be distinguished from sleep or unconsciousness" (*Technology,* p. 131). On this general point, see also Sigmund Kvaløy, "Ecophilosophy and Ecopolitics: Thinking and Acting in Response to the Threats of Ecocatastrophe."

64. Noble mentions a deskilled machinist who summarizes his job as follows: "I sweep up robot doo-doo."

65. A point made well by Wendell Berry in *The Unsettling of America.* See also Strong, *Crazy,* p. 166.

66. See Paul Shepard, *Coming Home to the Pleistocene,* p. 125; and Richard Nelson, Interview, "Life-Ways of the Hunter," p. 82.

67. Robert Romanyshyn, "The Human Body as Historical Matter and Cultural Symptom," p. 174.

68. William Leiss suggests that this aspect gives a "more precise image" of commodity fetishism as it appears in an advanced capitalist setting (*The Limits,* p. 87). This entire paragraph draws heavily on Leiss's work.

69. Leiss, *The Limits,* p. 22. See, also, Jerry Mander's discussion of the EPCOT

Center at Disneyworld, where the "'natural environment' has been perfected and packaged to eliminate any of nature's troubling variables" (*In the Absence of the Sacred*, p. 155).

70. Leiss, "The Imperialism." p. 33.

71. Leiss, *The Limits*, p. 18.

72. Leiss, "The Imperialism." p. 33. For a discussion of some South American indigenous societies in which, in the absence of a high-intensity market setting, needs are met more simply, simultaneously, or densely, see Liedloff, *The Continuum*, especially chapter one.

73. Christopher Lasch, *The Minimal Self*, p. 30.

74. Borgmann, *Technology*, p. 52.

75. I don't know of anybody who argues for an outright elimination of market exchanges.

76. Borgmann, *Technology*, p. 51. See, also, Strong, *Crazy*, p. 94.

77. Alan Durning, "Are We Happy Yet?," p. 69.

78. Kovel, *The Age*, p. 82. Kovel also notes how in a capitalist society the "child loses her/his functionality in the household and becomes a pure consumer. . . . With this the child-mind in everyone becomes celebrated, as indeed it should be by the managers of society, who are clever enough to sense in the infantile mental organization a possible way out of the crisis instigated by the glut of commodities" (pp. 121–122).

79. Kovel, *The Age*, pp. 58–59.

80. Leiss, "The Imperialism." p. 31.

81. Leiss, "The Imperialism." p. 32.

82. As David Loy remarks, our economic system "feeds on and is fed by a sense of lack" ("Trying to Become Real: A Buddhist Critique of Some Secular Heresies," p. 419. Kovel also observes: "For the purposes of advanced capital . . . it is increasingly imperative that the commodity lead not to satiety but to restless reconsumption" (*The Age*, p. 82).

83. Joel Kovel, "On the Ontology of Capital," from *The Enemy of Nature*, p. 4 of my version. As Kovel adds: "Ego and capital grow together."

84. Loy, "Trying," p. 408. This is, of course, something the media themselves understand very well. The quest for media fame was personified by the actor Nicole Kidman in the movie *To Die For*.

85. This is certainly not to rule out the possibility of love, per se. It is rather to identify a form of obsessive and fantasy-based love, originating in eleventh-century Europe, which is "effectively a religious experience, in which the deity worshipped is the beloved. Hence, to lose one's love is to lose one's life; is to lose the entire world" (Morris Berman, *Coming to Our Senses*, p. 207).

86. Loy, "Trying," p. 420.

87. Diamond, *In Search*, p. 40.

88. Loy, "Trying," p. 421.

89. This view is exhaustively presented in Jules Henry's classic *Culture Against Man*.

90. Max Horkheimer and Theodor Adorno, *The Dialectic of Enlightenment*, p. 147. Sigmund Kvaløy similarly speaks of the "Disney Land effect," in reference to cultural

diversions that bear not at all on the central or pressing issues of life ("Ecophilosophy and Ecopolitics: Thinking and Acting in Response to the Threats of Ecocatastrophe," p. 19).

91. Kovel, *The Age,* p. 184.

92. Horkheimer and Adorno, *The Dialectic,* p. 167.

93. Borgmann, *Technology,* pp. 52, 130.

94. Borgmann, *Technology,* p. 55.

95. Jean Liedloff, *The Continuum Concept,* p. 113. Liedloff traces our deprivation most forcefully to a relative poverty of physically close, "in-arms" contact in infancy.

96. Borgmann, *Technology,* p. 142.

97. Using 1990 data, Jerry Mander says that "the main activity of life for Americans, aside from work or sleep, has become watching television" (*In the Absence,* p. 76). A research project conducted in 1985 found that: "Eighty percent of leisure is passive consumption; being passive, it is essentially solitary. Television comprises sixty percent of it" (Borgmann, *Crossing,* p. 44). I don't know how accurate these numbers are for today, but the statistics don't ultimately matter for the points I am making. See, also Mander's *Four Arguments for the Elimination of Television.*

98. Fredric Jameson, "Postmodernism, or The Cultural Logic of Late Capitalism," p. 79. Indeed, despite the great amount of time spent in front of the television, it apparently brings little satisfaction to its viewers. In reference to a study performed on leisure, Borgmann notes: "It appears that people enjoy least what they indulge in most. Generally they find activities without personal interaction unsatisfying. And television in particular is thought to have little intrinsic benefit. . . . Commodious privacy [such as TV watching] remains both strong and unloved" (*Crossing,* p. 45). See, also, David Strong's discussion in *Crazy,* pp. 87–91.

99. Berry, *The Unsettling,* p. 130.

100. Thus does the "protective capsule . . . becomes a household of the living dead" (Berry, *The Unsettling,* p. 119).

101. Martin Lewis, quoted in Raymond Rogers, *Nature and the Crisis of Modernity,* p. 145, 151, 156. Emphasis in first quote mine.

102. Richard Nelson writes, in this respect, that the main source of satisfaction among Koyukon Indians lies in their "providing a livelihood from nature." The pleasure of living close to wild nature is, in fact, "probably the most pervasive theme in their existence." A decoupled human being, then, would not even have the possibility of saying, as did old Chief Henry: "I have had a good life. I have camped many times beneath spruce trees, roasting grouse over my campfire. So there is no reason to pray that I might live on much longer" (*Make Prayers to the Raven,* p. 46).

103. Paul Shepard, "On Animal Friends," p. 294.

104. An argument made by John Livingston in *The Fallacy of Wildlife Conservation* (pp. 92–94); and Sigmund Kavaløy, in "Ecophilosophy and Ecopolitics: Thinking and Acting in Response to the Threats of Ecocatastrophe."

105. On this Mary Midgley writes: "The impression of desertion or abandonment which Existentialists have is due, I am sure, not to the removal of God, but to [the]

contemptuous dismissal of almost the whole biosphere—plants, animals, and children. Life shrinks to a few urban rooms; no wonder it becomes absurd" (*Beast and Man,* p. 18).

106. E. O. Wilson, *Biophilia,* p. 118.

107. As discussed in Gary Paul Nabhan and Sara St. Antoine, "The Loss of Floral and Faunal Story: The Extinction of Experience." "Any conditions which reduce such intimate experience, Pyle claims, creates a cycle of disaffection, apathy, and irresponsibility toward natural habitats" (p. 239).

108. Paul Shepard, *Thinking Animals,* p. 251–252. Following Shepard, I suggest that it is cause for grave concern when a survey reports that 50 percent of "high school students polled said that they would prefer to be taught by a machine, and gave as their reason that they wished to be left alone" (cited in Morris Berman, "The Cybernetic Dream of the Twenty-First Century," p. 35). Human social relations, it seems, are becoming too much of a burden. It doesn't help either when the author of a book called *How to Teach Your Child to Be Gifted,* Charles Ling, claims that "Computers are smarter than humans and they are the best tutors at home. . . . If kids can start working on them, they can soon form those thinking patterns like a computer" (quoted in Nicholas Keung, "Can you actually make your child smarter?," p. BE3).

109. Terrence Real, *I Don't Want to Talk About It,* p. 107.

110. William Irwin Thompson. Interview, "Mind Jazz," p. 14.

111. Shepard, *Nature,* p. 129.

112. John Livingston, *The Fallacy of Wildlife Conservation,* p. 94.

113. This is the phrase used by Jason Lanier, the very person who coined the term "virtual reality" (quoted in Noble, *The Religion,* p. 158).

114. See the discussion in Mander, *In the Absence,* pp. 150–152.

115. Borgmann, "Artificial," pp. 195–197.

116. Witness a remark made by Thompson: "I don't feel threatened by technology because I know being a city kid, most of my mystical experiences in my life have come from things like watching *Fantasia,* when I was five, listening to Tchaikovsky on the radio when I was seven" ("Mind," p. 13). If all that matters is having mystical experiences for ourselves (by which it is not clear what Thompson means), then what of our relationships and responsibilities to others, including wild, nonhuman others?

117. Frederick Perls et al., *Gestalt Therapy,* p. 231. Emphasis mine.

118. Plural realism, recall, opposes any wholesale relativizing of reality. If I were to adopt a purely relativistic position, the argument I am making here would fall apart.

119. It was in this vein that Harold Searles wrote that a "fruitful effect of the mature human being's sense of relatedness with his nonhuman environment . . . is the enhancement, the sharpening, the deepening, the strengthening, of the individual's experiencing his own existence, and the existence of the world around him, as being *real*" (*The Nonhuman Environment,* p. 135.) Stanley Diamond also writes that the primitive's direct "engagement with nature and natural physiological functions" engenders a "sense of reality [that] is heightened to the point where it sometimes seems to 'Blaze'" (*In Search of the Primitive,* p. 170). The weakest reality or poorest contact, conversely, is what we have in mind when we

speak of being in a derealized condition, wherein we feel cut off from a world whose immediate presence is only vaguely felt. I think of the example of a person who is driving at high speed toward a wall, but who experiences the situation flatly or unemotionally. She or he sees the oncoming wall, but does not sense the immediacy of the danger.

120. Michael Zimmerman, *Contesting Earth's Future*, p. 371.

121. Charles Taylor, "Interpretation and the Sciences of Man," p. 73.

122. Borgmann, *Technology*, p. 208.

123. See "Part Three, The Reform of Technology," in Borgmann, *Technology*; as well as the growing literature on radical/alternative technology.

124. Noble, *Progress*, pp. 72, 112. This is a theme given much concrete detail by Noble.

125. Martin Heidegger, *Discourse on Thinking*, p. 54.

126. A point repeatedly made by Shepard.

127. Rodman, "The Liberation," p. 113.

128. Joseph Campbell, *Creative Mythology*, p. 6. For the sake of readability I have deleted Campbell's alphabetized "enumeration" of these four cosmic realms, while leaving out the usual ellipses.

129. Loy, "Trying," p. 419. Economic/technological progress is not, however, the only myth we could name. I discuss below, for example, a myth that Richard Slotkin has called "regeneration through violence."

130. Robert Bringhurst, "Myths Create a World of Meaning," p. C1.

131. According to Heidegger, it is only the great, epoch-making thinkers and poets who are capable of revealing those new cultural understandings that change the course of history. Gendlin has criticized this view by saying that Heidegger did not understand how *every* person's experiencing implicitly exceeds or speaks back to her or his culture. Heidegger was thus unable to "further examine the role of individual humans in the coming of new history" ("Thinking Beyond Patterns," p. 32). As I discuss below, then, this is a process in which I believe that all people can be actively engaged. On the possibility of singing new myths, see the Epilogue to Sean Kane, *Wisdom of the Mythtellers*.

132. William Irwin Thompson, quoted in Coates, "Future," p. 75.

133. Russell Jacoby, *Social Amnesia*, p. 64. Jacoby uses his own flood image: "Today the process of reification is a storm tide; and the human subject is locked in the basement. The frantic search for authenticity, experience, emotions, is the pounding on the ceiling as the water rises" (p. 18).

134. Robyn Eckersley, "The Failed Promise of Critical theory," p. 71. Today, Noble likewise laments the fortunes of "an ever-weaker labour movement" (*Progress*, p. 47).

135. James Masterson, *The Search for the Real Self*, p. vii.

136. Although "focal practice" is Borgmann's term, I should note that I am not following him in all respects; I am concentrating on the "focusing" effect of such practice.

137. Gary Snyder, "Buddhism and the Coming Revolution," in *Earth Household*, p. 91.

138. Borgmann, *Technology*, p. 245.

139. I am taking cues here from Borgmann, *Technology,* p. 214.

140. Paul Shepard, *Coming Home to the Pleistocene,* p. 173.

141. Richard Nelson. "Exploring the Near at Hand," p. 41.

142. I have moved out of Toronto since writing these words, but decided to leave them in the present tense.

143. Hans Peter Duerr, *Dreamtime,* p. 92. Thus any genuine wildlife conservation practice will protect natural entities not just in their biodiversity (or whatever), but in their being.

144. Personal communication. The quote in the previous sentence is from David Abram, "To Speak as a (Human) Animal: A Reply to Ted Toadvine."

145. Ursula LeGuin, *Buffalo Gals; And Other Animal Presences,* p. 12. "Coming into Animal Presence" is a poem by Denise Levertov (p. 13).

146. See, for example, Cisco Lassiter, "Relocation and Illness: The Plight of the Navajo."

147. This is the title of a recent book by Joanna Macy and Molly Young Brown, which updates Macy's earlier work, *Despair and Personal Power in the Nuclear Age.* I chose it for the heading here because it fits my own theme, as well as to acknowledge the kind of work that Macy and others are doing.

148. Dorothy Dinnerstein, "Survival on Earth: The Meaning of Feminism," p. 198.

149. Lasch, *The Minimal,* p. 16.

150. Jacoby, *Social,* p. 101.

151. Jacoby, *Social,* p. 116. "Society ineluctably coerces everyone to attend to the remaining fragments of self and subjectivity" (p. 15).

152. Issac Prilleltensky, *The Morals and Politics of Psychology,* p. 82.

153. Christopher Lasch, *The Culture of Narcissism,* p. 29.

154. Lasch, *The Culture,* p. 64.

155. Another factor here is that within the pattern of technology we become less and less engaged in general. Political engagement dwindles, in particular, as the governmental and corporate machinery takes over. See Borgmann, *Technology,* pp. 107–109.

156. This point has been made by people ranging from one of the earliest revisionists of Marx's ideas, Rosa Luxemburg; through the critical theorists; and on to one of my own favourite authors, Joel Kovel (see the last chapter of *The Age of Desire*). The same idea underlies critical education, all sorts of consciousness-raising, and so on. The Buddhist Ken Jones puts the matter very strongly: "Buddhism implies that unless there is some significant personal and individual change in the way we feel and think about ourselves and about others we shall try to go on evolving societies which express and reinforce the futile struggle of each of us to escape from our root fear into varieties of acquisitiveness and aggressive belongingness identity" (*The Social Face of Buddhism,* p. 123).

157. I thus disagree with Murray Bookchin when he remarks that "nearly all ecological problems are social problems" (*Remaking Society,* p. 24). For I believe he is committing the reductive fallacy of "sociologism," in which psyche is not abstracted from society, but society from psyche.

158. Roger Gottlieb, *Marxism,* p. 78. "The task of the genuine revolutionary is therefore to help generate capacities for self-organization and self-expression on the part of the mass of people in society, to foster many independent self-acting, self-conscious centers of power and awareness" (103). The discussion which follows also draws on Gottlieb.

159. Paul Goodman, *Nature Heals,* p. xxii. By a "natural society" I believe Goodman meant one that attends to human nature and experience. Goodman considered himself a "sociotherapist," that is, he applied the principles of Gestalt therapy on a social level so as "to remedy institutions that hinder experience from occurring." Much of Goodman's work in education, for example, argued against curricula that did not meet student "'need, desire, curiosity, or [imagination].' All else was parroting and conditioning, either promptly forgotten after the examination, or worse, introjected as part of self-control and conforming to authority." Insofar as students were interested and excited and growing, the curriculum was a good one. Thus Goodman did not believe in manifestos or received truths, but in the ability of people to create their own solutions through experimenting with their social situations and following their own experience as to what felt most satisfying or life-enhancing. He felt, moreover, that there must be some artistry to solving social problems, for our social life is grounded in the same human nature as is all art. Quotations are from Paul Stoehr, in his "Paul Goodman and the Political Dimensions of Gestalt Therapy."

160. I might have call this the "growth threshold," but given the hurt state of our society I think "healing threshold" is more appropriate. All healing, moreover, is itself a process of growth.

161. Ken Jones, *The Social Face of Buddhism,* p. 200.

162. Eugene Gendlin, *Experiential Psychotherapy,* p. 308. Emphasis removed.

163. I have not taken the space here to elaborate Gendlin's entire political position, which is essentially based on introducing focusing skills widely enough to create a society of people capable of making the kinds of microchanges in their immediate contexts that will add up to structural change on the larger scale. I refer the reader to *Focusing,* "The Politics of Giving Therapy Away," "A Philosophical Critique of the Concept of Narcissism," "Process Ethics and the Political Question," and "Experiential Psychotherapy." Gendlin is aware that "individual development does not usually change the social structure." He therefore suggests that "We need a whole new branch of social science to study the *more rare* conditions under which social change moves *from* the articulation of experience *to* structural change" ("How Philosophy Cannot Appeal to Experience, and How It Can," p. 35).

164. Joanna Macy in the preface to Katrina Shields, *In the Tiger's Mouth,* p. xi. James Hillman likewise speaks of "a psychological activism" that works from aesthetic responses. "The motivation must come from *below* the superego, from the id of desire" ("Aesthetics and Politics," pp. 38, 76).

165. See Thomas Scheff, "Reevaluation Counseling: Social Implications"; Virginia Coover, et al., *Resource Manual for a Living Revolution,* part four; Cherie Brown and George Mazza, "Anti-Racism, Healing, and Community Activism;" and Janet Foner, "Surviving the 'Mental Health' System with Co-Counseling."

166. Philip Lichtenberg, "Shame and the Making of a Social System," p. 284. In

The Mermaid and the Menotaur, Dorothy Dinnerstein speaks of the "rigid forms of symbiosis, of fixed psychological complementarity, which have so far dominated the relationships between men and women." Men and women are both complicit, in other words, in maintaining mutually oppressive sexual arrangements.

167. Audre Lorde, "Poetry Is Not a Luxury,' pp. 126–127.

168. Anne Bell, "Critical Environmental Education/Ecological Critical Education," p. 5.

169. Constance Russel, et al., "Navigating the Waters of Canadian Environmental Education," p. 6.

170. Mike Weilbacher, cited in Bell, "Critical," p. 6.

171. Russell, et al., "Navigating," p. 6.

172. Gary Snyder, *The Practice of the Wild,* p. 68.

173. Stephen Foster and Meredith Little, *Wilderness Vision Questing and the Four Shields of Human Nature,* p. 18.

174. In his book *Creative Mythology,* Joseph Campbell writes: "A mythological canon is an organization of symbols, ineffable in import, by which the energies of aspiration are evoked and gathered toward a focus. . . . For those in whom a local mythology still works, there is an experience both of accord with the social order, and of harmony with the universe. For those, however, in whom the authorized signs no longer work—or, if working, produce deviant effects—there follows inevitably a sense both of dissociation from the local social nexus and of quest, within and without, for life, which the [intellect] will take to be for 'meaning'" (p. 5). Creating new mythologies from one's own experience, versus making sense of one's experience through existing mythologies, is the work of "creative mythologizing."

175. In Buddhist thought, "pain" refers to unpleasant bodily sensations associated with gross physical and mental states, whereas "suffering" is a broader term which refers to our general insecurity or unease in an impermanent, insubstantial world, and which is better rendered as "unsatisfactoriness." In this section, however, the distinction between the two terms is not so important, so I use them synonymously. The word *suffer* itself derives from *suf,* as in "sub-," and *fer,* as in "bear": our suffering is what we "bear under." The Latin and Greek origins of the word *pain* both mean "penalty."

176. Freud, *Civilization,* p. 22.

177. *Agamemnon,* 1. 177, quoted in Paul Ricoeur, "Psychoanalysis and Contemporary Culture," in *The Conflict of Interpretations,* p. 159.

178. Coates, "Future," p. 75. Coates is commenting on the work of William Irwin Thompson.

179. Venerable Myokyo-ni, a western teacher of Zen Buddhism, quoted in Ken Jones, *The Social Face of Buddhism,* p. 366.

180. Donald Goodwin, quoted in Peter Breggin, *Toxic Psychiatry,* p. 219.

181. Slotkin, "Dreams."

182. Luc Sante, quoted in Loy, "Avoiding," p. 152.

183. Freud was committed to an irremediably dualistic universe in which opposing

forces battle it out. In "Beyond the Pleasure Principle" he proposed the existence of a destructive death instinct (Thanatos), which is the first and most conservative instinct of all, namely, to return to the inanimate and pain-free state that preceded the very emergence of life on earth. Thus Life (Eros) is always having to struggle against the basic pull toward Death. In brief, I suggest that the most basic "instinct" is not simply toward death, but toward growth and the completion of life, at the natural end of which is death. Aggression, as I discussed in chapter three, is not a separate instinct from that of life, but is itself an intrinsic aspect of it. As I am suggesting here, we turn our aggression against our own living, we self-destruct, only when the pain of life itself becomes unbearable. To be clear: all creative and appetitive living does of course involve destruction, in the sense of destructuring our food by chewing on it, taking apart and selectively assimilating another person's ideas, or transforming the world in general. This is to be distinguished, however, from annihilation, which is "is a defensive response to pain, bodily invasion or danger." Annihilation is a "cold" response because it does not satisfy a "hot" appetite, but simply aims to eliminate pain and danger (Perls, et al., *Gestalt*, p. 341). Freud put forward his "fateful question" in the last paragraph of *Civilization and Its Discontents*. See, also, Paul Goodman's "Critique of Freud's Thanatos," in Perls et al., *Gestalt*, pp. 349–352.

184. James Kepner, *Healing Tasks*, p. 101.

185. Clifford Geertz, *The Interpretation of Cultures*, p. 104.

186. See, also, Joanna Macy, "Buddhist Resources for Moving Through Nuclear Death" and *World as Lover, World as Self.*

187. Jones, *The Social*, p. 123.

188. Ram Dass, "Compassion: The Delicate Balance," p. 235.

189. Buddhist practice teaches one how to identify less with one's painful Ego dramas, and to concentrate instead on being of service, which is much more satisfying. It also teaches that all feelings pass. Even the biggest experiences of grief or rage just flow right through us if we let them be—a crucial ability to possess in a time such as ours, with its great losses and frustrations. Buddhism teaches, finally, how to stay equanimous in the face of all experience, how to maintain that spontaneous, caring, selfless, and optimally distanced attitude that is called for by nature (dharma).

190. Michael Higgins, speaking on the Canadian Broadcasting Corporation radio programme "This Morning," August 8, 1999. Higgins thus feels that Sartre's "hell is other people" is an entirely wrong sentiment.

191. Joel Kovel, "Schizophrenic Being and Technocratic Society," p. 346. I have reversed the sequence of the text around the ellipses.

192. Kovel, "On the Ontology," p. 5. Stated still otherwise, the "movement of capitalist society is toward *dedifferentiation*," which is marked by, among other things, "an increasing number of *desociated* characters of one kind or another" (Kovel, *The Age*, pp. 248–249. Second emphasis mine).

193. See, for example, Ken Norwood and Kathleen Smith, *Rebuilding Community in America.*

194. According to J. H. van den Berg, medical records indicate that there "has been

an increased sensitivity to pain since the beginning of the nineteenth century," and attributes this to our increasing loss of contact with others (*Divided Existence and Complex
Society,* pp. 215–228).

195. James Hillman, "The Animal Kingdom in the Human Dream," p. 326. Hillman himself gives credit for this insight to Paul Kugler.

196. Paul Shepard and Barry Sanders, *Sacred Paw,* p. xii.

BIBLIOGRAPHY

Abram, David. "Merleau-Ponty and the Voice of the Earth." *Environmental Ethics* 10 (1986): 101–120.

———. "The Mechanical and the Organic: On the Impact of Metaphor in Science." In *Scientists on Gaia*, ed. Stephen H. Schneider and Penelope J. Boston. Cambridge: MIT Press, 1991.

———. *The Spell of the Sensuous: Perception and Language in a More-than-Human World.* New York: Pantheon, 1996.

———. "To Speak as a (Human) Animal: A Reply to Ted Toadvine." In *Interrogating Ethics*, ed. James Hatley. Northwestern University Press, forthcoming.

Ainsworth, Mary D. Salter. "Attachment as Related to Mother-Infant Interaction." In *Advances in the Study of Behavior*, vol. 9, ed. Jay Rosenblatt et al. New York: Academic Press, 1979.

———, et al. *Patterns of Attachment: A Psychological Study of the Strange Situation.* Hillsdale, N.J.: Erlbaum, 1978.

Alderman, Harold. "The Dreamer and the World." *Soundings* 60 (1977): 331–346.

American Psychiatric Association. *Diagnostic and Statistical Manual of Mental Disorders*, 4th ed. Washington, D.C.: American Psychiatric Association, 1994.

Anthony, Carl. "Ecopsychology and the Deconstruction of Whiteness." In *Ecopsychology: Restoring the Earth, Healing the Mind*, ed. Theodore Roszak, Mary E. Gomes, and Allen D. Kanner. San Francisco: Sierra Club, 1995.

———, and Renée Soule. "A Multicultural Approach to Ecopsychology." *The Humanistic Psychologist* 26.1–3 (1998), 155–161.

Armstrong, Jeannette. Interviewed by Derrick Jensen. In *Listening to the Land*, ed. Derrick Jensen. San Francisco: Sierra Club, 1995.

———. "Keepers of the Earth." In *Ecopsychology: Restoring the Earth, Healing the Mind*, ed. Theodore Roszak, Mary E. Gomes, and Allen D. Kanner. San Francisco: Sierra Club, 1995.

Athanasiou, Tom. *Divided Planet: The Ecology of Rich and Poor.* Boston: Little, Brown, 1996.

Avens, Robert S. "Heidegger and Archetypal Psychology." *International Philosophical Quarterly* 22 (1982): 183–202.

Ayto, John. *Bloomsbury Dictionary of Word Origins.* London: Bloomsbury, 1990.

Badiner, Alan Hunt, ed. *Dharma Gaia: A Harvest of Essays in Buddhism and Ecology.* Berkeley, Calif.: Parallax, 1990.

Bakhtin, M. M. *Speech Genres and Other Late Essays.* Austin: University of Texas Press, 1986.

———. *Toward a Philosophy of the Act.* Austin: University of Texas Press, 1993.

Barfield, Owen. "The Meaning of the Word 'Literal.'" In *Metaphor and Symbol,* ed. L. C. Knights and Basil Cottle. London: Butterworth Scientific, 1960.

———. *Poetic Diction: A Study in Meaning,* 3rd ed. Middletown, Conn.: Wesleyan University Press, 1973.

———. "The Rediscovery of Meaning." In *The Rediscovery of Meaning and Other Essays.* Middletown, Conn.: Wesleyan University Press, 1977.

———. *Saving the Appearances: A Study in Idolatry,* 2nd ed. Middletown, Conn.: Wesleyan University Press, 1988.

Barrows, Anita. "The Ecopsychology of Child Development." In *Ecopsychology: Restoring the Earth, Healing the Mind,* ed. Theodore Roszak, Mary E. Gomes, and Allen D. Kanner. San Francisco: Sierra Club, 1995.

———. "Crying for the Manatees: Youth and Our Endangered World." *ReVision* 20.4 (1998): 9–17.

Barton, Anthony. "Humanistic Contributions to the Field of Psychotherapy: Appreciating the Human and Liberating the Therapist." In *The Humanistic Movement: Recovering the Person in Psychology,* ed. Frederick J. Wertz. Lake Worth, Fla.: Gardner, 1994.

Batchelor, Martine, and Kerry Brown, eds. *Buddhism and Ecology.* London: Cassell, 1992.

Bateson, Gregory. *Steps to an Ecology of Mind.* New York: Ballantine, 1972.

———. *Mind and Nature: A Necessary Unity.* Toronto: Bantam, 1979.

Becker, Ernest. *Angel in Armor: A Post-Freudian Perspective on the Nature of Man.* New York: George Braziller, 1969.

Bell, Anne. "Critical Environmental Education/ Ecological Critical Education." Unpublished paper, 1995.

Benton, Ted. "Biology and Social Theory in the Environmental Debate." In *Social Theory and the Global Environment,* ed. Michael Redclift and Ted Benton. New York: Routledge, 1994.

Bergman, Charles. "'The Curious Peach': Nature and the Language of Desire." In *Green Culture: Environmental Rhetoric in Contemporary America,* ed. Carl G Herndl and Stuart C. Brown. Madison, Wis.: University of Wisconsin Press, 1996.

Berman, Morris. *The Reenchantment of the World.* New York: Bantam, 1981.

———. "The Cybernetic Dream of the 21st Century." *Journal of Humanistic Psychology* 26.2 (1986): 24–51.

———. *Coming to Our Senses.* New York: Bantam, 1989.

Bernstein, Richard J. *Beyond Objectivism and Relativism: Science, Hermeneutics, and Praxis.* Philadelphia: University of Pennsylvania Press, 1988.

Berry, Wendell. *The Unsettling of America: Culture and Agriculture.* Second ed. San Francisco: Sierra Club, 1986.

Biehl, Janet. "Ecofeminism and Deep Ecology: Unresolvable Conflict?" *Our Generation* 19.2 (1988): 19–31.

Bigwood, Carol. *Earth Muse: Feminism, Nature and Art.* Philadelphia: Temple University Press, 1993.

Binswanger, Ludwig. Introduced by Jacob Needleman. *Being-in-the-World.* Harper Torchbook ed. New York: Harper & Row, 1968.

Bird, Elizabeth Ann R. "The Social Construction of Nature: Theoretical Approaches to the History of Environmental Problems." *Environmental Review* 11.4 (1987): 255–264.

Birkeland, Janice. "Ecofeminism: Linking Theory and Practice." In *Ecofeminism: Women, Animals, Nature,* ed. Greta Gaard. Philadelphia: Temple University Press, 1993.

Blanke, Henry T. "Domination and Utopia: Marcuse's Discourse on Nature, Psyche, and Culture." In *Minding Nature: The Philosophers of Ecology,* ed. David Macauly. New York: Guilford, 1996.

Bolton, Neil. "The Lived World: Imagination and the Development of Experience." *Journal of Phenomenological Psychology* 13.1 (1982): 1–18.

Bookchin, Murray. *Remaking Society.* Montreal: Black Rose, 1989.

———. *The Ecology of Freedom: The Emergence and Dissolution of Hierarchy.* Revised ed. Montreal: Black Rose, 1991.

Boorstin, Daniel J. *Democracy and Its Discontents: Reflections on Everyday America.* New York: Random House, 1971.

Borgmann, Albert. *Technology and the Character of Contemporary Life.* Chicago: University of Chicago Press, 1984.

———. "Artificial Realities: Centering One's Life in an Advanced Technological Setting." In *The Presence of Feeling in Thought,* ed. B. den Ouden and M. Moen. New York: Peter Lang, 1991.

———. *Crossing the Postmodern Divide.* Chicago: University of Chicago Press, 1992.

———. "The Nature of Reality and the Reality of Nature." In *Reinventing Nature?: Responses to Postmodern Deconstruction,* ed. Michael Soulé and Michael Lease. Washington, D.C.: Island, 1995.

Boss, Medard. *Meaning and Content of Sexual Perversions: A Daseinsanalytic Approach to the Psychopathology of the Phenomenon of Love.* New York: Grune & Stratton, 1949.

———. *The Analysis of Dreams.* London: Rider, 1957.

———. "Anxiety, Guilt and Psychotherapeutic Liberation." *Review of Existential Psychology and Psychiatry* 2 (1962): 173–202.

———. *Psychoanalysis and Daseinsanalysis.* New York: Basic Books, 1963.

———. "Dreaming and the Dreamed in the Daseinsanalytical Way of Seeing." *Soundings* 60.3 (1977): 235–263.

———. *Existential Foundations of Medicine and Psychology.* New York: Jason Aronson, 1979.

Boukydis, Kathleen M. "Changes: Peer-Counseling Supportive Communities as a Model of Community Mental Health." In *Teaching Psychological Skills: Models for Giving Therapy Away,* ed. D. Larson. Monterey, Calif.: Brooks/Cole, 1984.

Boukydis, C. F. Zachariah. "A Theory of Empathic Relations Between Parents and Infants: Insight from a Client-Centred/Experiential Perspective." *The Focusing Folio* 4 (1985): 3–28.

———. "Focusing-Oriented Parent-Infant Play and Psychotherapy." Funding Request. Infant Development Centre, Women and Infants Hospital, St. Providence, R.I., 1999.

Bowlby, John. *A Secure Base: Parent-Child Attachment and Healthy Human Development.* Basic Books, 1988.

Bradford, George. "Toward a Deep Social Ecology." In *Environmental Philosophy: From Animal Rights to Radical Ecology,* ed. Michael E. Zimmerman. Englewood Cliffs, N.J.: Prentice Hall, 1993.

Breggin, Peter R. *Toxic Psychiatry.* New York: St. Martin's, 1991.

———. "Psychotherapy in Emotional Crises Without Resort to Psychiatric Medication." *The Humanistic Psychologist* 25.2 (1997): 2–14.

———, and E. Mark Stern, eds. *Psychosocial Approaches to Deeply Disturbed Persons.* New York: Hawthorn, 1996.

Bridges, William. *Transitions: Making Sense of Life's Changes.* Reading, Mass.: Perseus Books, 1980.

Briere, John. *Child Abuse Trauma.* Newbury Park: Sage, 1992.

———. *Therapy for Adults Molested as Children.* New York: Springer, 1996.

Bringhurst, Robert. "Myth Creates a World of Meaning." *Globe and Mail* May 7, 1988: C1, C18.

Bronstein, Phyllis. "Promoting Healthy Emotional Development in Children." *Journal of Primary Prevention* 5.2 (1984): 92–110.

———. "Re-Evaluation Counselling: A Self-Help Model for Recovery from Emotional Distress." *Women and Therapy* 5.1 (1986): 41–54.

Brown, Cherie R., and George J. Mazza. "Anti-Racism, Healing and Community Activism." *The Humanistic Psychologist* 24.3 (1996): 391–402.

Brown, Joseph Epes. *The Spiritual Legacy of the American Indian.* New York: Crossroads, 1982.

———. "The Bison and the Moth: Lakota Correspondences." *Parabola* 8.2 (1983): 6–13.

———, ed. *The Sacred Pipe: Black Elk's Account of the Seven Rites of the Oglala Sioux.* Norman: University of Oklahoma Press, 1989.

Brown, Judith, et al. "The Implications of Gestalt Therapy for Social Change." *The Gestalt Journal* 16.1 (1993): 7–54.

Brown, Norman O. *Life Against Death: The Psychoanalytic Meaning of History,* 2nd ed. Middletown, Conn.: Wesleyan University Press, 1985.

Bruchac, Joseph. "Understanding the Great Mystery." In *The Soul of Nature,* ed. Michael Tobias. New York: Continuum, 1994.

Bryant, Donald C. "Rhetoric: Its Function and Its Scope." In *Philosophy, Rhetoric and Argumentation,* ed. Maurice Natanson and Henry W. Johnstone, Jr. University Park, Penn.: Pennsylvania State University Press, 1965.

Burke, Kenneth. *Permanence and Change.* New York: Bobbs-Merrill, 1965.
———. *Counter-Statement.* Berkeley, Calif.: University of California Press, 1968.
———. *A Rhetoric of Motives.* Berkeley, Calif.: University of California Press, 1969.
Burstow, Bonnie, and Don Weitz, eds. *Shrink Resistant: The Struggle Against Psychiatry in Canada.* Vancouver: New Star, 1988.
Cahalan, William. "Ecological Groundedness in Gestalt Therapy." In *Ecopsychology: Restoring the Earth, Healing the Mind,* ed. Theodore Roszak, Mary E. Gomes, and Allen D. Kanner. San Francisco: Sierra Club, 1995.
Campbell, Joseph. *Creative Mythology.* New York: Penguin, 1968.
Campbell, Paul N. "Poetic-Rhetorical, Philosophical, and Scientific Discourse." *Philosophy & Rhetoric* 6.1 (1973): 1–29.
———. *Rhetoric-Ritual.* Encino, Calif.: Dickenson Publishing, 1972.
Canter, David V., and Kenneth H. Craik. "Environmental Psychology." *Journal of Environmental Psychology* 1 (1981): 1–11.
Caputo, John D. *Radical Hermeneutics: Repetition, Deconstruction, and the Hermeneutic Project.* Bloomington: Indiana University Press, 1987.
Chen, Ellen. *The Tao Te Ching: A New Translation with Commentary.* New York: Paragon House, 1989.
Cheney, Jim. "Eco-Feminism and Deep Ecology." *Environmental Ethics* 9 (1987): 115–145.
———. "Postmodern Environmental Ethics: Ethics as Bioregional Narrative." *Environmental Ethics* 11 (1989): 117–134.
Chodorow, Nancy. "Gender, Relation, and Difference in Psychoanalytic Perspective." In *The Future of Difference,* ed. Hester Eisenstein and Alice Jardine. New Brunswick: Rutgers, 1980.
———. *Feminism and Psychoanalytic Theory.* New Haven: Yale University Press, 1989.
Clarkson, Petruska. *Gestalt Counselling in Action.* London: Sage, 1989.
Coates, Gary. "Future Images, Present Possibilities: Revisioning Nature, Self, and Society." In *Resettling America,* ed. Gary Coates. Andover, Mass.: Brick House, 1981.
Cobb, Edith. "The Ecology of Imagination in Childhood." In *The Subversive Science,* ed. Paul Shepard and Daniel McKinley. Boston: Houghlan Mifflin, 1969.
———. *The Ecology of Imagination In Childhood.* New York: Columbia University Press, 1977.
Coles, Romand. "Ecotones and Environmental Ethics: Adorno and Lopez." In *In the Nature of Things,* ed. Jane Bennett and William Chaloupka. Minneapolis: University of Minnesota Press, 1993.
Condrau, Gion, and Medard Boss. "Existential Analysis." *Modern Perspectives in World Psychiatry,* ed. John G. Howells. New York: Brunner/Mazel, 1971.
Conn, Sarah. "Protest and Thrive: The Relationship Between Social Responsibility and Personal Empowerment." Cambridge, Mass.: Center for Psychology and Social Change, 1990. Also published in *New England Journal of Social Policy* 6.1 (1990), 163–177.

————. "When the Earth Hurts, Who Responds?" In *Ecopsychology: Restoring the Earth, Healing the Mind,* ed. Theodore Roszak, Mary E. Gomes, and Allen D. Kanner. San Francisco: Sierra Club, 1995.

Connolly, William. "Voices from the Whirlwind." In *In the Nature of Things,* ed. Jane Bennett and William Chaloupka. Minneapolis: University of Minnesota Press, 1993.

Coon, Carleton. *The Hunting Peoples.* New York: Nick Lyons, 1971.

Cooper, Marilyn M. "Environmental Rhetoric in the Age of Hegemonic Politics: Earth First! and the Nature Conservancy." In *Green Culture: Environmental Rhetoric in Contemporary America,* ed. Carl G. Herndl, and Stuart C. Brown. Madison: University of Wisconsin Press, 1996.

Coovers, Virginia, et al. *Resource Manual for a Living Revolution.* Philadelphia: New Society, 1977.

Cornell, Ann Weiser. *The Focusing Student's Manual,* 3rd ed. Berkeley, Cal.: Focusing Resources, 1994. Available from Focusing Resources, 2625 Alcatraz Ave., #202, Berkeley, CA 94705, U.S.A.

————. *The Power of Focusing.* Oakland, Calif.: New Harbinger, 1996.

Cronon, William, ed. *Uncommon Ground: Rethinking the Human Place in Nature.* New York: W. W. Norton, 1996.

Cushman, Philip. "Why the Self Is Empty: Toward a Historically Situated Psychology." *American Psychologist* 45.5 (1990): 599–611.

————. "Ideology Obscured: Political Uses of the Self in Daniel Stern's Infant." *American Psychologist* 46.3 (1991): 206–219.

Davidson, Larry. "Philosophical Foundations of Humanistic Psychology." In *The Humanistic Movement: Recovering the Person in Psychology,* ed. Frederick J. Wertz. Lake Worth, Fla. Gardner, 1994.

Davis-Berman, Jennifer, and Dene Berman. *Wilderness Therapy: Foundations, Theory & Research.* Dubuque, Iowa: Kendal/Hunt, 1994.

Decarvalho, Roy. *Founders of Humanistic Psychology.* New York: Praeger, 1991.

Denzin, Norman K., and Yvonna S. Lincoln. "Introduction: Entering the Field of Qualitative Research." In *Handbook of Qualitative Research,* ed. Norman K. Denzin and Yvonna S. Lincoln. Thousand Oaks, Calif.: Sage, 1994.

De Koning, Andre. "Reflections on the Heart." In *The Changing Reality of Modern Man: Essays in Honour of Jan Hendrik van den Berg,* ed. Dreyer Kruger. Pittsburgh: Duquesne University Press, 1985.

Devall, Bill. *Simple in Means, Rich in Ends: Practicing Deep Ecology.* Salt Lake City: Gibbs Smith, 1988.

————, and George Sessions. *Deep Ecology: Living as if Nature Mattered.* Salt Lake City: Gibbs M. Smith, 1985.

Dewey, John. *Experience and Nature,* 2nd ed. New York: Dover, 1958.

Diamond, Stanley. *In Search of the Primitive: A Critique of Civilization.* New Brunswick, N.J.: Transaction, 1974.

Di Chiro, Giovanna. "Nature as Community: The Convergence of Environment and Social Justice." In *Uncommon Ground: Rethinking the Human Place in Nature*, ed. William Cronon. New York: Norton, 1996.

Dillon, M.C. "A Phenomenological Conception of Truth." *Man and World* 10 (1977): 382–392.

———. "Merleau-Ponty and the Psychogenesis of the Self." *Journal of Phenomenological Psychology* 9.1&2 (1978): 84–98.

———. "'Eye and Mind': The Intertwining of Vision and Thought." *Man and World* 13 (1980): 155–171.

———. "Toward a Phenomenology of Love and Sexuality: An Inquiry into the Limits of the Humans Situation as They Condition Loving." *Soundings* 63 (1980): 341–360.

———. "Merleau-Ponty and the Reversibility Thesis." *Man and World* 16 (1983): 365–388.

———. "Erotic Desire." *Research in Phenomenology* 15 (1985): 145–163.

———. *Merleau-Ponty's Ontology*. Bloomington, Ind.: Indiana University Press, 1988.

———. "Merleau-Ponty and Postmodernity." In *Merleau-Ponty Vivant*, ed. M.C. Dillon. Albany: SUNY Press, 1991.

Dinnerstein, Dorothy. "Survival on Earth: The Meaning of Feminism." In *Healing the Wounds: The Promise of Ecofeminism*, ed. Judith Plant. Toronto: Between the Lines, 1989.

Downing, Christine. "Poetically Dwells Man on This Earth." *Soundings* 60.3 (1977): 313–330.

Draper, Patricia. "Social and Economic Constraints on Child Life among the !Kung.' In *Kalahari Hunter-Gatherers*, ed. Richard Lee and Irene DeVore. Cambridge, Mass.: Harvard University Press, 1976.

Dreyfus, Hubert L. "Holism and Hermeneutics." *Review of Metaphysics* 34 (1980): 3–23.

———. "Beyond Hermeneutics: Interpretation in Late Heidegger and Recent Foucault." In *Hermeneutics: Questions and Prospects*, ed. Gary Shapiro and Alan Sica. Amherst: University of Massachusetts Press, 1984.

———. *Being-in-the-World: A Commentary on Heidegger's Being and Time, Division I*. Cambridge, Mass.: MIT Press, 1991.

———, and Charles Spinosa. "Highway Bridges and Feasts: Heidegger and Borgmann on How to Affirm Technology." *Man and World* 30.159–177 (1997).

Duerr, Hans Peter. *Dreamtime: Concerning the Boundary Between Wilderness and Civilization*. New York: Basil Blackwell, 1985.

Durning, Alan Thein. "Are We Happy Yet?" In *Ecopsychology*, ed. Theodore Roszak, Mary E. Gomes, and Allen D. Kanner. San Francisco: Sierra Club, 1995.

Dutton, Donald G. *The Abusive Personality: Violence and Control in Intimate Relationships*. New York: Guilford, 1998.

Eaton, Boyd, Marjorie Shostak, and Melvin Konner. *The Paleolithic Prescription: A Program of Diet and Exercise and a Design for Living*. New York: Harper & Row, 1988.

Eckersley, Robyn. "The Failed Promise of Critical Theory." In *Ecology*, ed. Carolyn Merchant. Atlantic Highlands, N.J.: Humanities Press, 1994.

Ehrenfeld, David. *The Arrogance of Humanism*. New York: Oxford, 1978.

Ehrlich, Anne, and Paul Ehrlich. *Healing the Planet: Strategies for Resolving the Environmental Crisis*. Reading, Mass.: Addison-Wesley, 1991.

Eliade, Mircea. *Rites and Symbols of Initiation: The Mysteries of Birth and Rebirth*. Woodstock, Conn.: Spring, 1995.

Erikson, Erik. *Childhood and Society*, rev. and enlarged ed. New York: W. W. Norton, 1963.

———. *Identity: Youth and Crisis*. New York: W. W. Norton, 1968.

———. *Identity and the Life Cycle*. New York: W. W. Norton, 1980.

Evernden, Neil. "The Environmentalists' Dilemma." In *The Paradox of Environmentalism*, ed. Neil Evernden. Downsview: York University, 1984.

———. "Ecology in Conservation and Conversation." In *After Earth Day: Continuing the Conservation Effort*, ed. Max Oelschlaeger. Denton, Tex.: University of North Texas Press, 1992.

———. *The Social Creation of Nature*. Baltimore: Johns Hopkins University Press, 1992.

———. *The Natural Alien: Humankind and Environment*, 2nd ed. Toronto: University of Toronto Press, 1993.

———. Interviewed by Derrick Jensen. In *Listening to the Land: Conversations About Nature, Culture, and Eros*, ed. Derrick Jensen. San Francisco: Sierra Club, 1995.

Fischer, William F. "On the Phenomenological Approach to Psychopathology." *Journal of Phenomenological Psychology* 17.1 (1986): 65–76.

Fisher, Andy. "Toward a More Radical Ecopsychology." *Alternatives* 22.3 (1996): 20–26.

Fleischner, Thomas L. "Revitalizing Natural History." *Wild Earth* (Summer 1999): 81–89.

Flynn, Bernard Charles. "Descartes and the Ontology of Subjectivity." *Man and World* 16 (1983): 3–23.

Fodor, Iris E. "A Woman and Her Body: The Cycles of Pride and Shame." In *The Voice of Shame: Silence and Connection in Psychotherapy*, ed. Robert G. Lee and Gordon Wheeler. San Francisco: Jossey-Bass, 1996.

Foltz, Bruce V. "On Heidegger and the Interpretation of the Environmental Crisis." *Environmental Ethics* 6 (1984): 323–338.

———. *Inhabiting the Earth: Heidegger, Environmental Ethics, and the Metaphysics of Nature*. Atlantic Highlands, N.J.: Humanities Press, 1995.

Foner, Janet. "Surviving the 'Mental Health' System with Co-Counseling." In *Psychosocial Approaches to Deeply Disturbed Persons*, ed. Peter R. Breggin and E. Mark Stern. New York: Haworth, 1996.

Foster, Mary LeCron. "Body Process in the Evolution of Language." In *Giving the Body Its Due*, ed. Maxine Sheets-Johnstone. Albany: State University of New York Press, 1992.

Foster, Steven, and Meredith Little. *The Book of the Vision Quest: Personal Transformation in the Wilderness*. Revised and Expanded ed. New York: Prentice Hall, 1988.

————. *The Roaring of the Sacred River: The Wilderness Quest for Vision and Self-Healing.* New York: Prentice Hall, 1989.

————. *Wilderness Vision Questing and the Four Shields of Human Nature.* Moscow, Id.: University of Idaho Wilderness Research Center, 1996.

Foster, Steven, with Meredith Little. *The Four Shields: The Initiatory Seasons of Human Nature.* P.O. Box 55, Big Pine, Calif., 93513: Lost Borders Press, 1998.

Four Worlds International Institute for Human and Community Development. *The Sacred Tree: Reflections on Native American Spirituality.* Twin Lakes, Wis.: Lotus Light, 1985.

Foti, Véronique. "Alterity and the Dynamics of Metaphor." In *Language Beyond Postmodernism: Saying and Thinking in Gendlin's Philosophy,* ed. David Micheal Levin. Evanston, Ill.: Northwestern University Press, 1997.

Foucault, Michel. *Madness and Civilization: A History of Insanity in the Age of Reason.* New York: Random House, 1965.

Fox, Warwick. "The Deep Ecology-Ecofeminism Debate and Its Parallels." *Environmental Ethics* 11.1 (1989): 5–25.

————. *Toward a Transpersonal Ecology.* Boston: Shambhala, 1990.

Frankl, Victor. *Man's Search for Meaning.* New York: Pocket Books, 1963.

Freenberg, Andrew. "The Critical Theory of Technology." *Capitalism Nature Socialism* 1:2 (1990), 17–31.

Freud, Sigmund. *An Outline of Psychoanalysis.* New York: Norton, 1949.

————. *The Ego and the Id.* New York: Norton, 1960.

————. *Civilization and Its Discontents.* New York: Norton, 1961.

————. *Introductory Lectures on Psychoanalysis.* Harmondsworth, England: Pelican, 1973.

————. "Beyond the Pleasure Principle." In *On Metapsychology.* London: Penguin, 1991.

————. *New Introductory Lectures on Psychoanalysis.* London: Penguin, 1991.

————. "The Future of an Illusion." In *Civilization, Society and Religion.* London: Penguin, 1991.

Fromm, Erich. *The Sane Society.* New York: Fawcett World Library, 1955.

————. *The Art of Loving.* New York: Bantam, 1956.

Gadamer, Hans-Georg. *Philosophical Hermeneutics.* Berkeley, Calif.: University of California Press, 1976.

————. "Practical Philosophy as a Model of the Human Sciences." *Research in Phenomenology* 9 (1979): 74–85.

————. "The Hermeneutics of Suspicion." In *Hermeneutics: Questions and Prospects,* ed. Gary Shapiro and Alan Sica. Amherst: University of Massachusetts Press, 1984.

————. "The Problem of Historical Consciousness." In *Interpretive Social Science: A Second Look,* ed. Paul Rabinow and William M. Sullivan. Berkeley, Calif.: University of California Press, 1987.

————. *Truth and Method.* Second Revised ed. New York: Crossroads, 1989.

Gare, Arran. *Nihilism Incorporated: European Civilization and Environmental Destruction.* Bungendore, NSW, Australia: Eco-Logical Press, 1993.

Gardner, Michael. *The Dialogics of Critique: M.M. Bakhtin and the Theory of Ideology.* London: Routledge, 1992.

Gallagher, Shaun. "Lived Body and Environment." *Research in Phenomenology* 16 (1986): 139–170.

Geertz, Clifford. *The Interpretation of Cultures.* New York: Basic Books, 1973.

———. *Local Knowledge: Further Essays in Interpretive Anthropology.* New York: Basic Books, 1983.

Geller, E. Scott. "Solving Environmental Problems: A Behavior Change Perspective." In *Psychology and Social Responsibility: Facing Global Challenges,* ed. Sylvia Staub and Paula Green. New York: New York University Press, 1992.

Gendlin, Eugene T. *Experiencing and the Creation of Meaning.* New York: Free Press of Glencoe, 1962.

———. "A Theory of Personality Change." In *Personality Change,* ed. Philip Worchell and Donn Byrne. New York: John Wiley & Sons, 1964.

———. "Existentialism and Experiential Psychotherapy." In *Existential Child Therapy: The Child's Discovery of Himself,* ed. Clark Moustakas. New York: Basic Books, 1966.

———. "Neurosis and Human Nature in the Experiential Method of Thought and Therapy." *Humanitas* 3.2 (1967): 139–152.

———. "Experiential Explication and Truth." In *The Sources of Existentialism as Philosophy,* ed. Fernando R. Molina. Englewood Cliffs, N.J.: Prentice Hall, 1969.

———, with Carol Tavis. "A Small, Still Voice." *Psychology Today* (June 1970): 57–59.

———. "A Phenomenology of Emotions: Anger." In *Explorations in Phenomenology,* ed. David Carr and Edward S. Casey. The Hague: Martinus Nijhoff, 1973.

———. "Experiential Phenomenology." In *Phenomenology and the Social Sciences, Vol. 1,* ed. Maurice Natanson. Evanston, Ill.: Northwestern University Press, 1973.

———. "The Role of Knowledge in Practice." In *The Counselor as a Person,* ed. Gail F. Farwell, Neal R. Gamsky and Philippa Mathieu-Coughlan. New York: Intext Educational, 1974.

———. "*Befindlichkeit:* Heidegger and the Philosophy of Psychology." *Review of Existential Psychology and Psychiatry* 16.1–3 (1978–1979): 43–71.

———. "Experiential Psychotherapy." In *Current Psychotherapies,* ed. Raymond J. Corsini. 2nd ed. Itasca, Ill.: F. E. Peacock Publishers, 1979.

———. *Focusing.* New York: Bantam, 1981.

———. "The Client's Client: The Edge of Awareness." In *Client-Centered Therapy and the Person-Centered Approach,* ed. Ronald F. Levant and John M. Schlien. New York: Praeger, 1984.

———. "The Politics of Giving Therapy Away: Listening and Focusing." In *Teaching Psychological Skills: Models for Giving Therapy Away,* ed. D. Larson. Monterey, Calif.: Brooks/Cole, 1984.

———, with Doralee Grindler, and Mary McGuire. "Imagery, Body, and Space in Focus-

ing." In *Imagination and Healing,* ed. Anees A. Sheikh. Farmingdale, N.Y.: Bay-
wood, 1984.

———. "Nonlogical Moves and Nature Metaphors." In *Analecta Husserliana,* ed. A-T
Tymieniecka. Boston: D. Reidel, 1985. Vol. XIX.

———. *Experiential Psychotherapy (Draft).* Chicago: The Focusing Institute, 1986.

———. *Let Your Body Interpret Your Dreams.* Wilmette, Ill.: Chiron, 1986.

———. "Process Ethics and the Political Question." In *Analecta Husserliana,* ed. A-T.
Tymieniecka. Boston: D. Reidel Publishing Company, 1986. Vol. XX.

———. "A Philosophical Critique of the Concept of Narcissism: The Significance of the
Awareness Movement." In *Pathologies of the Modern Self: Postmodern Studies on
Narcissism, Schizophrenia, and Depression,* ed. David Michael Levin. New York: New
York University Press, 1987.

———. "Dwelling." In *The Horizons of Continental Philosophy,* ed. Hugh J. Silverman, et
al. Dordrecht: Kluwer Academic, 1988.

———. "Schizophrenia: Problems and Methods of Psychotherapy." *Review of Existential
Psychology and Psychiatry* 20.1–3 (1990): 181–191.

———. "The Small Steps of the Therapy Process: How They Come and How to Help
Them Come." In *Client-Centred and Experiential Psychotherapy in the Nineties,* ed.
G. Lietaer, J. Rombants and R. Van Balen. Leuven/Louvain, Belgium: Leuven
University Press, 1990.

———. "On Emotion in Therapy." In *Emotion, Psychotherapy and Change,* ed. J. D. Safran
and L. S. Greenberg. New York: Guilford, 1991.

———. "Meaning Prior to the Separation of the Five Senses." In *Current Issues in Linguistic
Meaning, 73: Current Advances in Semantic Theory,* ed. Max Stamenov. Amsterdam/
Philadelphia: John Benjamins, 1992.

———. "The Primacy of the Body, Not the Primacy of Perception." *Man and World* 00
(1992): 341–353.

———. "The Wider Role of Bodily Sense in Thought and Language." In *Giving the Body
Its Due,* ed. Maxine Sheets-Johnstone. Albany: SUNY Press, 1992.

———. "Thinking Beyond Patterns." In *The Presence of Feeling in Thought,* ed. B. den
Ouden and M. Moen. New York: Peter Lang, 1992.

———. "Human Nature and Concepts." In *Psychological Aspects of Modernity,* ed. Jerome
Braun. Westport, Conn.: Praeger, 1993.

———. "Celebrations and Problems of Humanistic Psychology." In *The Humanistic Movement: Recovering the Person in Psychology,* ed. Frederick J. Wertz. Lake Worth, Fla.:
Gardner, 1994.

———. "Crossing and Dipping: Some Terms for Approaching the Interface between
Natural Understanding and Logical Formulation." From the world wide web site:
www.focusing.org. Also in *Mind and Machines* 5.4 (1995): 547–560.

———. *Focusing-Oriented Psychotherapy.* New York: Guilford, 1996.

———. "Philosophy—Beyond Post-Modernism." New York: The Focusing Institute,
1996. From the world wide web site: www.focusing.org.

———. *A Process Model.* New York: The Focusing Institute, 1997.

———. "How Philosophy Cannot Appeal to Experience, and How It Can." In *Language Beyond Postmodernism: Saying and Thinking in Gendlin's Philosophy,* ed. David Michael Levin. Evanston, Ill.: Northwestern University Press, 1997.

Gergen, Kenneth J. "Emerging Challenges for Theory and Psychology." *Theory and Psychology* 1.1 (1991): 13–35.

Gill, Jerry H. *Merleau-Ponty and Metaphor.* Atlantic Highlands, N.J.: Humanities Press, 1991.

Gilligan, Carol. *In a Different Voice: Psychological Theory and Women's Development.* Cambridge, Mass.: Harvard University Press, 1982.

Gilmore, David D. *Manhood in the Making: Cultural Concepts of Masculinity.* New Haven: Yale University Press, 1990.

Giorgi, Amedeo. "Whither Humanistic Psychology?" In *The Humanistic Movement: Recovering the Person in Psychology,* ed. Frederick J. Wertz. Lake Worth, Fla.: Gardner Press, 1994.

Glendinning, Chellis. *My Name Is Chellis and I'm in Recovery from Western Civilization.* Boston: Shambhala, 1994.

———. "Yours Truly From Indian Country." *Yoga Journal* January/February (1995): 79–85.

Goldfarb, Mica "Making the Unknown Known: Art as the Speech of the Body." In *Giving the Body Its Due,* ed. Maxine Sheets-Johnstone. Albany: State University of New York Press, 1992.

Gomes, Mary E., and Allen D. Kanner. "The Rape of the Well-Maidens: Feminist Psychology and the Environmental Crisis." In *Ecopsychology: Restoring the Earth, Healing the Mind,* ed. Theodore Roszak, Mary E. Gomes, and Allen D. Kanner. San Francisco: Sierra Club, 1995.

Gomes, Mary E. "Personal Transformation and Social Change: Conversations with Ecopsychologists in Action." *The Humanistic Psychologist* 26. 1–3 (1998), 217–241.

Goodman, Paul. *New Reformation.* New York: Random House, 1970.

———. *Nature Heals.* New York: Free Life Editions, 1977.

Gottlieb, Roger S. *Marxism 1844–1990: Origins, Betrayal, Rebirth.* New York: Routledge, 1992.

Grange, Joseph. "Being, Feeling, and Environment." *Environmental Ethics* 7 (1985): 351–364.

Leslie Gray, "Shamanic Counseling and Ecopsychology." In *Ecopsychology: Restoring the Earth, Healing the Mind,* ed. Theodore Roszak, Mary E. Gomes, and Allen D. Kanner. San Francisco: Sierra Club, 1995.

Greenberg, Jay, and Stephen Mitchell. *Object Relations in Psychoanalytic Theory.* Cambridge, Mass.: Harvard University Press, 1983.

Greenway, Robert. "Notes in Search of an Ecopsychology," Unpublished paper presented at the first Esalen Institute Ecopsychology Conference. Big Sur, California, July, 1993.

———. "Psychoecology as a Search for Language." Unpublished draft, 1994.

———. "The Wilderness Effect and Ecopsychology." In *Ecopsychology: Restoring the Earth, Healing the Mind,* ed. Theodore Roszak, Mary E. Gomes, and Allen D. Kanner. San Francisco: Sierra Club, 1995.

Grene, Marjorie. "The Paradoxes of Historicity." *Review of Metaphysics* 32 (1978): 15–36.

Griffin, Susan. *A Chorus of Stones.* New York: Doubleday, 1992.

Grof, Christina, and Stanislav Grof. *The Stormy Search for the Self.* Los Angeles: Jeremy P. Tarcher, 1990.

Grof, Stanislav. *The Adventure of Self-Discovery: Dimensions of Consciousness and New Perspectives in Psychotherapy and Inner Exploration.* Albany: SUNY Press, 1985.

Haraway, Donna J. *Primate Visions: Gender, Race, and Nature in the World of Modern Science.* New York: Routledge, 1989.

Harris, Ian. "How Environmentalist Is Buddhism?" *Religion* 21 (1991): 101–114.

———. "Buddhist Environmental Ethics and Detraditionalization: The Case of EcoBuddhism." *Religion* 25 (1995): 199–211.

Harvey, Irene E. "Schizophrenia and Metaphysics: Analyzing the DSM-III." In *Pathologies of the Modern Self: Postmodern Studies on Narcissism, Schizophrenia, and Depression,* ed. David Michael Levin. New York: New York University Press, 1987.

Hatab, Lawrence J. *Myth and Philosophy.* La Salle, Ill.: Open Court, 1990.

Hauser, Gerard A., and Donald P. Cushman. "McKeon's Philosophy of Communication: The Architectonic and Interdisciplinary Arts." *Philosophy & Rhetoric* 6.4 (1973): 211–234.

Heelan, Patrick A. "Why a Hermeneutical Philosophy of the Natural Sciences?" *Man and World* 30 (1997): 271–298.

Heidegger, Martin. *An Introduction to Metaphysics.* New Haven: Yale University Press, 1959.

———. *Being and Time.* New York: Harper & Row, 1962.

———. *Discourse on Thinking.* New York: Harper & Row, 1966.

———. *On the Way to Language.* New York: Harper & Row, 1971.

———. *Poetry, Language, Thought.* New York: Harper & Row, 1971.

———. *Basic Writings.* New York: Harper & Row, 1977.

———. *The Question Concerning Technology and Other Essays.* New York: Harper & Row, 1977.

———. "The Fieldpath." *Journal of Chinese Philosophy* 13 (1986): 455–458.

Hendricks, M. Excerpts from "Focusing Oriented/Experiential Psychotherapy." In *Humanistic Psychotherapies: Handbook of Research and Practice,* ed. D. Cain and J. Seeman. Washington, D.C.: American Psychological Association, 2001.

Henry, Jules. *Culture Against Man.* New York: Vintage, 1963.

Herman, Judith. *Trauma and Recovery.* New York: Basic Books, 1997.

Herndl, Carl G., and Stuart C. Brown, eds. *Green Culture: Environmental Rhetoric in Contemporary America.* Madison: University of Wisconsin Press, 1996.

Hillman, James. *The Dream and the Underworld.* New York: Harper & Row, 1979.

———. "Anima Mundi: The Return of the Soul to the World." *Spring* (1982): 71–93.

——. "Let the Creatures Be: An Interview with James Hillman." *Parabola* 8.2 (1983): 49–53.

——. "The Animal Kingdom in the Human Dream." In *Eranos Jabruch*, ed. Rudolf Ritsema. Frankfurt a/M: Insel Verlag, 1983. Vol. 51.

——. "Going Bugs." *Spring* (1988): 40–72.

——. *Re-Visioning Psychology*. New York: Harper Perennial, 1992.

——. "Animal Presence." (Interview by Jonathon White.) In *Talking on the Water*, ed. Jonathon White. San Francisco: Sierra Club, 1994.

——. "Notes on Opportunism." In *Puer Papers*, ed. James Hillman. Dallas: Spring, 1994.

——. "A Psyche the Size of the Earth." In *Ecopsychology: Restoring the Earth, Healing the Mind*, ed. Theodore Roszak, Mary E. Gomes, and Allen D. Kanner. San Francisco: Sierra Club, 1995.

——. "Aesthetics and Politics." *Tikkun* 11.6 (1996): 38–40, 75–76.

——, and Michael Ventura. *We've Had a Hundred Years of Psychotherapy and the World's Getting Worse*. New York: HarperCollins, 1992.

Hood, Robert. "Recovering Green Identity: Paul Shepard's Archeology of Self." In *The Company of Others: Essays in Celebration of Paul Shepard*, ed. Max Oelschlaeger. Durago, Colo.: Kivakí, 1995.

Horkheimer, Max. *Eclipse of Reason*. New York: Continuum, 1947.

——, and Theodor W. Adorno. *Dialectic of Enlightenment*. New York: Herder and Herder, 1972.

Hull, Fritz. *Earth and Spirit: The Spiritual Dimension of the Ecological Crisis*. New York: Continuum, 1993.

The Humanistic Psychologist 26.1–3 (1998). Special issue on Humanistic Psychology and Ecopsychology.

Hynes, Mary Ellen. "Walking in a World of Wounds: The Work of Donna Meadows." *CenterPiece* (1994): 10–11, 15.

Ingleby, David. "Understanding 'Mental Illness.'" In *Critical Psychiatry*, ed. David Ingleby. New York: Pantheon, 1980.

Ingold, Tim. *The Appropriation of Nature: Essays on Human Ecology and Social Relations*. Iowa City: University of Iowa Press, 1987.

Ingram, Catherine. *In the Footsteps of Gandhi: Conversations with Spiritual Social Activists*. Berkeley, Calif.: Parallax, 1990.

Jackins, Harvey. *How "Re-evaluation Counseling" Began*. Seattle: Rational Island, 1994.

——. *The List: Everything I Know About Re-Evaluation Counselling (and the World) Until Now*, 2nd ed. Seattle: Rational Island, 1997.

Jacoby, Russell. *Social Amnesia: A Critique of Conformist Psychology from Adler to Laing*. Boston: Beacon, 1975.

Jaffe, Aniela. "Symbolism in the Visual Arts." In *Man and His Symbols*, ed. Carl Jung. New York: Dell, 1964.

Jameson, Fredric. "Postmodernism, or The Cultural Logic of Late Capitalism." *New Left Review* 146 (1984): 53–92.

Jenks, Chris. "Introduction: Constituting the Child." In *The Sociology of Childhood: Essential Readings*, ed. Chris Jenks. London: Batsford Academic and Educational Ltd., 1982.

Johnson, Will. *The Posture of Meditation.* Boston: Shambhala, 1996.

Jonas, Hans. *The Phenomenon of Life.* New York: Delta, 1966.

Jones, Ken. *The Social Face of Buddhism: An Approach to Political and Social Activism.* London: Wisdom, 1989.

Jung, C. G. "Approaching the Unconscious." In *Man and His Symbols*, ed. C.G. Jung. New York: Dell, 1964.

Jung, C. G. *Memories, Dreams, Reflections.* New York: Vintage, 1965.

———. *The Portable Jung*, ed. Joseph Campbell. New York: Penguin, 1971.

———. *C. G. Jung: Letters*, ed. G. Adler. Princeton, N.J.: Princeton University Press, 1973 (Vol. 1.), 1975 (Vol. 2).

Jung, Hwa Yol. "The Ecological Crisis: A Philosophical Perspective, East and West." *Bucknell Review* 20.3 (1972): 25–44.

Kane, Sean. *Wisdom of the Mythtellers.* Peterborough: Broadview Press, 1994.

Kanner, Allen D. "The Voice of the Earth: A Review." *The Trumpeter* 9.4 (1992): 169–170.

———. "Mount Rushmore Syndrome: When Narcissism Rules the Earth." *The Humanistic Psychologist* 26.1–3 (1998), 101–122.

Kanner, Allen D., and Mary E. Gomes. "The All-Consuming Self." In *Ecopsychology: Restoring the Earth, Healing the Mind*, ed. Theodore Roszak, Mary E. Gomes, and Allen D. Kanner. San Francisco: Sierra Club, 1995.

Kaplan, Rachel, and Stephen Kaplan. *The Experience of Nature.* Cambridge: Cambridge University Press, 1989.

Karon, Bertram P., and Leighton C. Whitaker. "Psychotherapy and the Fear of Understanding Schizophrenia." In *Psychosocial Approaches to Deeply Disturbed Persons*, ed. Peter R. Breggin and E. Mark Stern. New York: Haworth, 1996.

Kaza, Stephanie. *The Attentive Heart: Conversations with Trees.* New York: Fawcett Columbine, 1993.

Kearney, Richard. *Poetics of Modernity: Toward a Hermeneutic Imagination.* New Jersey: Humanities, 1995.

Keller, Evelyn Fox. *Reflections on Gender and Science.* New Haven: Yale University Press, 1985.

Kepner, James I. *Body Process: Working with the Body in Psychotherapy.* San Francisco: Jossey-Bass, 1993.

———. *Healing Tasks: Psychotherapy with Adult Survivors of Childhood Abuse.* San Francisco: Jossey-Bass, 1995.

Kerényi, Karl. *Hermes: Guide of Souls.* Dallas: Spring, 1976.

Keung, Nicholas. "Can you actually make your child smarter?" *The Toronto Star* June 13, 1999: BE3.

Kheel, Marti. "Ecofeminism and Deep Ecology: Reflections on Identity and Difference." In *Reweaving the World: The Emergence of Ecofeminism,* ed. Irene Diamond and Gloria Feman Orenstein. San Francisco: Sierra Club, 1990.

Kidner, David W. "Why Psychology Is Mute About the Ecological Crisis." *Environmental Ethics* 16 (1994): 359–378.

Kincheloe, Joe L., and Peter L. McLaren. "Rethinking Critical Theory and Qualitative Research." In *Handbook of Qualitative Research,* ed. Norman K. Denzin and Yvonna S. Lincoln. Thousand Oaks, Calif.: Sage, 1994.

King, Ynestra. "The Ecology of Feminism and the Feminism of Ecology." In *Healing the Wounds: The Promise of Ecofeminism,* ed. Judith Plant. Toronto: Between the Lines, 1989.

———. "Healing the Wounds: Feminism, Ecology, and the Nature/Culture Dualism." In *Reweaving the World: The Emergence of Ecofeminism,* ed. Irene Diamond and Gloria Feman Orenstein. San Francisco: Sierra Club, 1990.

Kirsner, Douglas. *The Schizoid World of Jean-Paul Sartre and R. D. Laing.* Atlantic Highlands, N.J.: Humanities, 1977.

Kleinman, Arthur. *Rethinking Psychiatry: From Cultural Category to Personal Experience.* New York: Free Press, 1988.

Kleese, Deborah A. "Toward an Ecological Epistemology for Psychology." *The Trumpeter* 6.4 (1989): 137–143.

Kline, Stephen, and William Leiss. "Advertising, Needs, and 'Commodity Fetishism.'" *Canadian Journal of Political and Social Theory* 2.1 (1978): 5–30.

Kockelmans, Joseph J. "On the Hermeneutical Nature of Modern Natural Science." *Man and World* 30 (1997): 299–313.

Koenig, Thomas R. "Ricoeur's Interpretation of the Relation between Phenomenological Philosophy and Psychoanalysis." *Journal of Phenomenological Psychology* 13.2 (1982), 115–142.

Kohák, Erazim. *The Embers and the Stars.* Chicago: University of Chicago Press, 1984.

Konner, Melvin J. "Maternal Care, Infant Behavior and Development Among the !Kung." In *Kalahari Hunter-Gatherers,* ed. Richard B. Lee and Irene DeVore. Cambridge, Mass.: Harvard University Press, 1976.

Kornfield, Jack. *A Path With Heart: A Guide Through the Perils and Promises of Spiritual Life.* New York: Bantam, 1993.

Kovel, Joel. "Things and Words: Metapsychology and the Historical Point of View." *Psychoanalysis and Contemporary Thought* 1.1 (1978): 21–88.

———. "The American Mental Health Industry." In *Critical Psychiatry,* ed. David Ingleby. New York: Pantheon, 1980.

———. *The Age of Desire: Case Histories of a Radical Psychoanalyst.* New York: Pantheon, 1981.

———. *White Racism: A Psychohistory.* New York: Columbia University Press, 1984.

———. "Schizophrenic Being and Technological Society." In *Pathologies of the Modern Self: Postmodern Studies in Narcissism, Schizophrenia, and Depression,* ed. David Michael Levin. New York: New York University Press, 1987.

———. "Freud's Ontology—Agency and Desire: Commentary on Hubert L. Dreyfus and Jerome Wakefield." In *Hermeneutics and Psychological Theory: Interpretive Perspectives on Personality, Psychotherapy, and Psychopathology,* ed. Stanley B. Messer, Louis A. Sass and Robert L. Woolfolk. New Brunswick: Rutgers University Press, 1988.

———. "On the Notion of Human Nature: A Contribution Toward a Philosophical Anthropology" and "Rejoinder to Kenneth J. Gergen." In *Hermeneutics and Psychological Theory: Interpretive Perspectives on Personality, Psychotherapy, and Psychopathology,* ed. Stanley B. Messer, Louis A. Sass and Robert L. Woolfolk. New Brunswick: Rutgers University Press, 1988.

———. *The Radical Spirit: Essays on Psychoanalysis and Society.* London: Free Association, 1988.

———. "A Critique of DSM-III." *Research in Law, Deviance and Social Control* 9 (1988): 127–146.

———. *History and Spirit.* Boston: Beacon, 1991.

———. "The Marriage of Radical Ecologies." In *Environmental Philosophy: From Animal Rights to Radical Ecology,* ed. Michael E. Zimmerman. Englewood Cliffs, N.J.: Prentice Hall, 1993.

———. *The Enemy of Nature.* Chapters 1 and 2, and an excerpt entitled "On the Ontology of Capital." Unpublished manuscript.

———. "The Justifiers: A Critique of Julian Simon, Stephen Schmidheiny, and Paul Hawken on Capitalism and Nature." *Capitalism Nature Socialism* 10.3 (September 1999): 3–36.

Kruger, Dreyer, ed. *The Changing Reality of Modern Man: Essays in Honour of Jan Hendrik van den Berg.* Pittsburgh: Duquesne University Press, 1985.

Kvaløy, Sigmund. "Ecophilosophy and Ecopolitics: Thinking and Acting in Response to the Threats of Ecocatastrophe." *The North American Review* 260 (1974): 17–28.

———. "Touristic Life Styles Versus Work in Nature." In *The Search for Absolute Value in a Changing World.* New York: International Cultural Foundation, 1978. Vol. 1.

Laduke, Winona. "From Resistance to Regeneration." In *Ecology,* ed. Carolyn Merchant. Atlantic Highlands, N.J.: Humanities, 1994.

Laing, R. D. *The Politics of Experience; and the Bird of Paradise.* New York: Ballantine, 1967.

Lame Deer, John (Fire), and Richard Erdoes. *Lame Deer: Seeker of Visions.* New York: Pocket Books, 1972.

Lasch, Christopher. *The Culture of Narcissism: American Life in an Age of Diminishing Expectations.* New York: W. W. Norton, 1979.

———. *The Minimal Self: Psychic Survival in Troubled Times.* London: Pan, 1984.

Lassiter, Cisco. "Relocation and Illness: The Plight of the Navajo." In *Pathologies of the Modern Self: Postmodern Studies on Narcissism, Schizophrenia, and Depression,* ed. David Michael Levin. New York: New York University Press, 1987.

Latner, Joel. "The Theory of Gestalt Therapy." In *Gestalt Therapy: Perspectives and Applications,* ed. Edwin Nevis. New York: Gardner, 1992.

Leary, David E. "Psyche's Muse: The Role of Metaphor in the History of Psychology." In *Metaphors in the History of Psychology,* David E. Leary. Cambridge: Cambridge University Press, 1990.

Lee, Richard B., and Irene DeVore, eds. *Kalahari Hunter-Gatherers.* Cambridge, Mass.: Harvard University Press, 1976.

Lee, Robert G. "Shame and the Gestalt Model." In *The Voice of Shame: Silence and Connection in Psychotherapy,* ed. Robert G. Lee and Gordon Wheeler. San Francisco: Jossey-Bass, 1996.

LeGuin, Ursula K. *Buffalo Gals; And Other Animal Presences.* New York: ROC (Penguin), 1987.

Leiss, William. *The Domination of Nature.* Boston: Beacon, 1974.

———. "The Imperialism of Human Needs." *The North American Review* 259 (1974): 27–34.

———. *The Limits to Satisfaction: An Essay on the Problem of Needs and Commodities.* Toronto: University of Toronto Press, 1976.

Leopold, Aldo. *A Sand County Almanac; And Sketches Here and There.* New York: Oxford University Press, 1949.

Levin, David Michael. "Sanity and Myth in Affective Space: A Discussion of Merleau-Ponty." *The Philosophical Forum* 14.2 (1982–83): 157–189.

———. "Eros and Psyche: A Reading of Merleau-Ponty." *Review of Existential Psychology and Psychiatry* 18.1–3 (1982–83): 219–239.

———. "Logos and Psyche: A Hermeneutics of Breathing." *Research in Phenomenology* 14 (1984): 121–147.

———. *The Body's Recollection of Being: Phenomenological Psychology and the Deconstruction of Nihilism.* London: Routledge & Kegan Paul, 1985.

———. "Clinical Stories: A Modern Self in the Fury of Being." In *Pathologies of the Modern Self: Postmodern Studies on Narcissism, Schizophrenia, and Depression,* ed. David Michael Levin. New York: New York University Press, 1987.

———. "Introduction." In *Pathologies of the Modern Self: Postmodern Studies on Narcissism, Schizophrenia, and Depression,* ed. Dvaid Michael Levin. New York: New York University Press, 1987.

———. "Psychopathology in the Epoch of Nihilism." In *Pathologies of the Modern Self: Postmodern Studies on Narcissism, Schizophrenia, and Depression,* ed. David Michael Levin. New York: New York University Press, 1987.

———. *The Opening of Vision: Nihilism and the Postmodern Condition.* New York: Routledge, 1988.

———. *The Listening Self: Personal Growth, Social Change and the Closure of Metaphysics.* London: Routledge, 1989.

———. "Phenomenology in America." Chicago: Unpublished Manuscript, 1991. Published as "Phenomenology in America," *Philosophy and Social Criticism* 17.2 (1991): 103–119.

———. "Visions of Narcissism: Intersubjectivity and the Reversals of Reflection." In *Merleau-Ponty Vivant*, ed. M. C. Dillon. Albany: SUNY Press, 1991.

———. "Transpersonal Phenomenology." In *Psychological Aspects of Modernity*, ed. Jerome Braun. Westport, Conn.: Praeger, 1993.

———. "Gendlin's Use of Language: Historical Connections, Contemporary Implications." In *Language Beyond Postmodernism: Saying and Thinking in Gendlin's Philosophy*, ed. David Michael Levin. Evanston, Ill.: Northwestern University Press, 1997.

———, ed. *Language Beyond Postmodernism: Saying and Thinking in Gendlin's Philosophy.* Evanston, Ill.: Northwestern University Press, 1997.

Levin, Roger. "Multiple Personality, Transpersonal Guides, and Malevolent Possessions: Discriminating Kinds of Alterity in a Psychotherapy Case by Means of Bodily Felt Sensing." *The Folio* 17.1 (1999): 35–41.

Levine, Stephen. *Poiesis: The Language of Psychology and the Speech of the Soul.* Toronto: Palmerston, 1992.

Lewis, C. S. *The Abolition of Man.* London: Fount, 1943.

Lichtenberg, Philip. "Shame and the Making of a Social Class System." In *The Voice of Shame: Silence and Connection in Psychotherapy*, ed. Robert G. Lee and Gordon Wheeler. San Francisco: Jossey-Bass, 1996.

Liedloff, Jean. *The Continuum Concept: Allowing Human Nature to Work.* Reading, Mass.: Addison-Wesley Publishing, 1975.

Linge, David E. "Editor's Introduction" to Hans-Georg Gadamer, *Philosophical Hermeneutics.* Berkeley: University of California Press, 1976.

Lipsey, Richard, Douglas Purvis, and Peter Steiner. *Economics.* 6th ed. New York: Harper & Row.

Livingston, John. *The Fallacy of Wildlife Conservation.* Toronto: McClelland & Stewart, 1981.

———. "The Dilemma of the Deep Ecologist." In *The Paradox of Environmentalism*, ed. Neil Evernden. Downsview: York University, 1984.

———. "Ethics as Prosthetics." In *Environmental Ethics: Philosophical and Policy Perspectives*, ed. Philip P. Hanson. Burnaby, B.C.: Institute for Humanities/SFU Publications, 1986. Vol. 1.

———. *Rogue Primate.* Toronto: Key Porter, 1994.

Lopez, Barry. *Of Wolves and Men.* New York: Charles Scribner's Sons, 1978.

———. "Renegotiating the Contracts." *Parabola* 8.2 (1983): 14–19.

Lorde, Audre. "Poetry Is Not a Luxury." In *The Future of Difference*, ed. Hester Eisenstein and Alice Jardine. New Brunswick, N.J.: Rutgers, 1980.

Lowe, Walter James. "On Using Heidegger." *Soundings* 60.3 (1977): 264–284.

Lowen, Alexander. *Bioenergetics.* New York: Penguin, 1975.

———. *Narcissism: Denial of the True Self.* New York: Macmillan, 1985.

Loy, David. "The Nonduality of Life and Death: A Buddhist View of Repression." *Philosophy East and West* 40.2 (1990): 151–174.

―――. "Trying to Become Real: A Buddhist Critique of Some Secular Heresies." *International Philosophical Quarterly* 32.4 (1992): 403–425.

―――. "Avoiding the Void: The *Lack* of Self in Psychotherapy and Buddhism." *Journal of Transpersonal Psychology* 24.2 (1992): 151–179.

Macy, Joanna Rogers. *Despair and Personal Power in the Nuclear Age.* Philadelphia: New Society, 1983.

―――. "Buddhist Resources for Moving Through Nuclear Death." In *Heal or Die: Psychotherapists Confront Nuclear Annihilation,* ed. Keneth Porter, Deborah Rinzler and Paul Olsen. New York: Psychohistory, 1987.

―――. *World as Lover, World as Self.* Berkeley, Cal.: Parallax, 1991.

―――, and Molly Young Brown. *Coming Back to Life.* Gabriola Island, B.C.: New Society, 1998.

Madison, Gary Brent. *Hermeneutics of Postmodernity.* Bloomington: Indiana University Press, 1988.

Mahdi, Louise Carus, Steven Foster, and Meredith Little, eds. *Betwixt and Between: Patterns of Masculine and Feminine Initiation.* La Salle, Ill.: Open Court, 1987.

Mahler, Margaret, Fred Pine, and Anni Bergmann. *The Psychological Birth of the Human Infant.* New York: Basic Books, 1975.

Mander, Jerry. *Four Arguments for the Elimination of Television.* New York: William Morrow, 1978.

―――. *In the Absence of the Sacred: The Failure of Technology and the Survival of the Indian Nations.* San Francisco: Sierra Club, 1991.

Mann, Charles. "How Many Is Too Many?" *The Atlantic Monthly* (February 1993): 47–50, 52–53, 56, 59, 62–64, 66–67.

Marcuse, Herbert. *Counterrevolution and Revolt.* Boston: Beacon, 1972.

―――. "Ecology and Revolution." In *Ecology,* ed. Carolyn Merchant. Atlantic Highlands, N.J.: Humanities, 1994.

Martin, Calvin Luther. *In the Spirit of the Earth: Rethinking History and Time.* Baltimore: The Johns Hopkins University Press, 1992.

Masterson, James. *The Search for the Real Self: Unmasking the Personality Disorders of Our Age.* New York: The Free Press, 1988.

Matthiessen, Peter. "Native Earth." *Parabola* 6 (1981): 6–17.

―――. *Nine-Headed Dragon River.* Boston: Shambhala, 1985.

May, Rollo. *Power and Innocence: A Search for the Sources of Violence.* New York: Dell, 1972.

―――. "The Roots of Our Being." *Storytelling* (1991): 16–19.

Mayeroff, Milton. *On Caring.* New York: Harper & Row, 1971.

McGuire, Kathleen. *Building Supportive Community: Mutual Self-Help Through Peer-Counselling.* Cambridge, Mass.: Center for Supportive Community, 1981. Available from Focusing Northwest, 3440 Onyx Street, Eugene, OR 97405, U.S.A.

———. *The Experiential Dimension in Psychotherapy.* Eugene, Oreg.: Unpublished Working Draft, 1984.

McKeon, Richard. "Philosophy of Communication and the Arts." In *Perspectives in Education, Religion and the Arts,* ed. Howard E. Kiefer and Milton K. Munitz. Albany: SUNY Press, 1970.

———. "The Uses of Rhetoric in a Technological Age: Architectonic Productive Arts." In *The Prospect of Rhetoric,* ed. Lloyd F. Bitzer and Edwin Black. Englewood Cliffs, N.J.: Prentice-Hall, 1971.

McKibben, Bill. *The End of Nature.* New York: Random House, 1989.

McLaughlin, Andrew. *Regarding Nature: Industrialism and Deep Ecology.* Albany: SUNY Press, 1993.

Meade, Michael. *Men and the Water of Life: Initiation and the Tempering of Men.* New York: HarperCollins, 1993.

———. "Foreword" to Mircea Eliade, *Rites and Symbols of Initiation: The Mysteries of Birth and Rebirth.* Woodstock, Conn.: Spring, 1995.

Meeker, Joseph. "Talking with Paul." In *The Company of Others: Essays in Celebration of Paul Shepard,* ed. Max Oelschlaeger. Durango, Colo.: Kivakí, 1995.

Melamed, Melissa. "Reclaiming the Power to Act." *Therapy Now* (1984).

Merchant, Carolyn. *The Death of Nature: Women, Ecology and the Scientific Revolution.* San Francisco: Harper & Row, 1980.

———. *Radical Ecology: The Search for a Livable World.* New York: Routledge, 1992.

———, ed. *Ecology.* Atlantic Highlands, N.J.: Humanities Press, 1994.

Merleau-Ponty, Maurice. *Phenomenology of Perception.* London: Routledge & Kegan Paul, 1962.

———. *The Primacy of Perception.* Evanston, Ill.: Northwestern University Press, 1964.

———. *The Visible and the Invisible.* Evanston, Ill.: Northwestern University Press, 1968.

———. "The Concept of Nature, I." In *Themes from the Lectures at the College de France 1952–1960.* Evanston, Ill.: Northwestern University Press, 1970.

Messer, Stanley B., Louis A. Sass, and Robert L. Woolfolk, eds. *Hermeneutics and Psychological Theory: Interpretive Perspectives on Personality, Psychotherapy, and Psychopathology.* New Brunswick: Rutgers University Press, 1988.

Mezey, Matthew. *Deep Ecology and Transpersonal Psychology: An Enlightening Confrontation.* London: Open Eye, n.d.

Midgley, Mary. *Beast and Man: The Roots of Human Nature.* New York: New American Library, 1978.

Mies, Maria, and Vandana Shiva. *Ecofeminism.* Halifax: Fernwood, 1993.

Miller, Alice. *The Drama of the Gifted Child.* New York: Basic Books, 1981.

———. *For Your Own Good: Hidden Cruelty in Child-Rearing and the Roots of Violence.* New York: Noonday, 1983.

———. *Breaking Down the Wall of Silence.* New York: Meridian, 1991.

Moen, Marcia. "Feeling, Body, Thought." In *The Presence of Feeling in Thought*, ed. B. den Ouden and M. Moen. New York: Peter Lang, 1991.

Mosher, Loren R. "Soteria: A Therapeutic Community for Psychotic Persons." In *Psychosocial Approaches to Deeply Disturbed Persons*, ed. Peter R. Breggin and E. Mark Stern. New York: Hawthorn, 1996.

Mugerauer, Robert. *Interpreting Environments: Tradition, Deconstruction, Hermeneutics.* Austin: University of Texas Press, 1995.

Muir, Star A., and Veenendall. Thomas L., eds. *Earthtalk: Communication Empowerment for Environmental Action.* Westport, Conn.: Praeger, 1996.

Myers, Gene. *Children and Animals: Social Development and Our Connection to Other Species.* Boulder, Colo.: Westview, 1998.

Nabhan, Gary Paul, and Sara St. Antoine. "The Loss of Floral and Faunal Story: The Extinction of Experience." In *The Biophilia Hypothesis,* ed. Stephen Kellert and Edward Wilson. Washington, D.C.: Island, 1993.

Nabhan, Gary Paul, and Stephen Trimble. *The Geography of Childhood: Why Children Need Wild Places.* Boston: Beacon, 1994.

Naess, Arne. "The Shallow and the Deep, Long-Range Ecology Movement. A Summary." *Inquiry* 16 (1973): 95–100.

———. "Identification as a Source of Deep Ecological Attitudes." In *Deep Ecology,* ed. Michael Tobias. San Diego: Avant, 1985.

———. "*Self* Realization: An Ecological Approach to Being in the World." In *Thinking Like a Mountain: Towards a Council of All Beings,* ed. John Seed, et al. Philadelphia: New Society, 1988.

Nanamoli (Bhikkhu). *The Life of the Buddha.* Kandy, Sri Lanka: Buddhist Publication Society, 1992.

Naranjo, Claudio. *The Techniques of Gestalt Therapy.* Highland, N.Y.: Gestalt Journal Press, 1980.

Natanson, Maurice. "The Limits of Rhetoric." In *Philosophy, Rhetoric and Argumentation,* ed. Maurice Natanson and Henry W. Johnstone. University Park, Penn.: Pennsylvania State University Press, 1965.

———. "Rhetoric and Philosophical Argumentation." In *Philosophy, Rhetoric and Argumentation,* ed. Maurice Natanson and Henry W. Johnstone. University Park, Penn.: Pennsylvania State University Press, 1965.

Neihardt, John G. *Black Elk Speaks.* Lincoln: University of Nebraska Press, 1979.

Nelson, Richard K. *Make Prayers to the Raven: A Koyukon View of the Northern Forest.* Chicago: University of Chicago Press, 1983.

———. *The Island Within.* Vancouver: Douglas & McIntyre, 1989.

———. "Exploring the Near at Hand: An Interview with Richard Nelson." *Parabola* 16.2 (1991): 35–43.

———. "Searching for the Lost Arrow: Physical and Spiritual Ecology in the Hunter's World." In *The Biophilia Hypothesis,* ed. Stephen Kellert and E. O. Wilson. Washington, D.C.: Island, 1993.

———. "Life-Ways of the Hunter." (Interview by Jonathon White.) In *Talk on the Water: Conversations About Nature and Creativity,* ed. Jonathon White. San Francisco: Sierra Club, 1994.

Nelson, Toni. "Violence Against Women." *World Watch* (July/August, 1996): 33–38.

Nhat Hanh, Thich. *Interbeing: Fourteen Guidelines for Engaged Buddhism.* Rev. ed. Berkeley: Parallax, 1993.

———. "Love in Action." In *The Soul of Nature,* ed. Michael Tobias. New York: Continuum, 1994.

Nietzsche, Friedrich. *The Will to Power.* New York: Random House, 1967.

Noble, David F. *Progress Without People: New Technology, Unemployment, and the Message of Resistance.* Toronto: Between the Lines, 1995.

———. *The Religion of Technology: The Divinity of Man and the Spirit of Invention.* New York: Alfred A. Knopf, 1998.

Nonnekes, Paul. "The Intertwining Wildness of Flesh-Child Becoming." *Undercurrents* 2 (1990): 20–27.

Norris, Christopher. *Deconstruction: Theory and Practice.* Revised ed. London: Routledge, 1991.

Norwood, Ken, and Kathleen Smith. *Rebuilding Community in America: Housing for Ecological Living, Personal Power, and the New Extended Family.* Berkeley, Calif.: Shared Living Resource Center (2375 Shattuck Ave., Berkeley, CA, 94704, U.S.A.), 1995.

Nyantiloka. *Buddhist Dictionary: Manual of Buddhist Terms and Doctrines.* Kandy, Sri Lanka: Buddhist Publication Society, 1980.

O'Connor, James. "Socialism and Ecology." In *Ecology,* ed. Carolyn Merchant. Atlantic Highlands, N.J.: Humanities Press, 1994.

———. *Natural Causes: Essays in Ecological Marxism.* New York: Guilford, 1998.

Oelschlaeger, Max. *The Idea of Wilderness.* New Haven: Yale University Press, 1991.

Ong, Walter J. *Orality and Literacy: The Technologizing of the Word.* London: Routledge, 1982.

Onions, T. C., ed. *The Oxford Dictionary of English Etymology.* London: Oxford University Press, 1966.

Packer, Martin J. "Hermeneutic Inquiry in the Study of Human Conduct." *American Psychologist* 40.10 (1985): 1081–1093.

Packer, Martin J., and Richard B. Addison. "Introduction." In *Entering the Circle: Hermeneutic Investigation in Psychology,* ed. Martin J. Packer and Richard B. Addison. Albany: State University of New York Press, 1989.

Palmer, Richard E. *Hermeneutics.* Evanston, Ill.: Northwestern University Press, 1969.

———. "On the Transcendability of Hermeneutics (A Response to Dreyfus)." In *Hermeneutics: Questions and Prospects,* ed. Gary Shapiro and Alan Sica. Amherst: University of Massachusetts Press, 1984.

Panikkar, R. *Myth, Faith and Hermeneutics.* New York: Paulist, 1979.

Parkes, Graham. "Human/Nature in Nietzsche and Taoism." In *Nature in Asian Traditions of Thought,* ed. J. Baird Callicott and Roger T. Ames. Albany: SUNY Press, 1989.

Perls, Frederick. *Gestalt Therapy Verbatim.* New York: Bantam, 1969.

———. *The Gestalt Approach and Eye Witness to Therapy.* Palo Alto, Calif.: Science and Behavior, 1973.

———. *Ego, Hunger and Aggression.* Highland, N.Y.: Gestalt Journal Press, 1992.

———, Ralph F. Hefferline, and Paul Goodman. *Gestalt Therapy.* New York: Dell, 1951.

Perls, Laura. "Comments on the New Directions." In *The Growing Edge of Gestalt Therapy,* ed. E. Smith. New York: Brunner/Mazel, 1976.

———. *Living at the Boundary.* Highland, N.Y.: Gestalt Journal Press, 1992.

Plumwood, Val. "Ecosocial Feminism as a General Theory of Oppression." In *Ecology,* ed. Carolyn Merchant. Atlantic Highlands, N.J.: Humanities, 1994.

Polster, Erving, and Miriam Polster. *Gestalt Therapy Integrated.* New York: Vintage, 1973.

Prilleltensky, Isaac. *The Morals and Politics of Psychology: Psychological Discourse and the Status Quo.* Albany: SUNY Press, 1994.

Rabinow, Paul, and William M. Sullivan. "The Interpretive Turn: A Second Look." In *Interpretive Social Science: A Second Look,* ed. Paul Rabinow and William M. Sullivan. Berkeley, Calif.: University of California Press, 1987.

Ram Dass. "Compassion: The Delicate Balance." In *Paths Beyond Ego: The Transpersonal Vision,* ed. Roger Walsh and Frances Vaughan. Los Angeles: Jeremy P. Tarcher, 1993.

Rapaport, Amos. "Australian Aborigines and the Definition of Place." In *Environmental Design: Research and Practice. Proceedings of the EDRA 3/AR 8 Conference, University of California at Los Angeles,* ed. William J. Mitchell, 1972.

Rappaport, Roy. *Ecology, Meaning, and Religion.* Richmond, Calif.: North Atlantic Books, 1979.

Real, Terrence. *I Don't Want to Talk About It: Overcoming the Secret Legacy of Male Depression.* New York: Scribner, 1997.

Rice, L. N., and L. S Greenberg. "Humanistic Approaches to Psychotherapy." In *History of Psychotherapy: A Century of Change,* ed. D. Freedheim. Washington, D.C.: American Psychological Association, 1992.

Richards, Barry, ed. *Capitalism and Infancy: Essays on Psychoanalysis and Politics.* Atlantic Highlands, N.J.: Humanities, 1984.

Richardson, William J. "Heidegger's Critique of Science." *The New Scholasticism* 42.4 (1968): 511–536.

Ricoeur, Paul. *Freud and Philosophy: An Essay on Interpretation.* New Haven: Yale University Press, 1970.

———. "The Model of the Text: Meaningful Action Considered as Text." *Social Research* 38.3 (1971): 529–562.

———. *The Conflict of Interpretations.* Evanston, Ill.: Northwestern University Press, 1974.

———. "The Metaphorical Process as Cognition, Imagination, and Feeling." In *On Metaphor,* ed. Sheldon Sacks. Chicago: University of Chicago Press, 1978.

Rifkin, Jeremy. *The End of Work: The Decline of the Global Labor Force and the Dawn of the Post-Market Era.* New York: G. P. Putnam's Sons, 1995.

Rinzler, Deborah. "Human Disconnection and the Murder of the Earth." In *Heal or Die:*

Psychotherapists Confront Nuclear Annihilation, ed. Kenneth Porter, Deborah Rinzler and Paul Olsen. New York: Psychohistory, 1987.

Rodman, John. "The Liberation of Nature?" *Inquiry* 20 (1977): 83–145.

———. "Theory and Practice in the Environmental Movement: Notes Toward an Ecology of Experience." In *The Search for Absolute Value in a Changing World*. New York: International Cultural Foundation, 1978. Vol. 1.

Rogers, Carl. "A Theory of Therapy, Personality, and Interpersonal Relationships, as Developed in the Client-Centred Framework." In *Psychology: A Study of a Science, Volume 3: Formulations of the Person and the Social Context*, ed. S. Koch. New York: McGraw Hill, 1959.

———. "A Therapist's View of the Good Life: The Fully Functioning Person." In *On Becoming a Person*. Boston: Houghton Mifflin Company, 1961.

———. "Ellen West—And Loneliness." In *A Way of Being*. Boston: Houghton Mifflin, 1980.

Rogers, Raymond A. *Nature and the Crisis of Modernity: A Critique of Contemporary Discourse on Managing the Earth*. Montreal: Black Rose, 1994.

———. *The Oceans are Emptying: Fish Wars and Sustainability*. Montreal: Black Rose, 1995.

———. *Solving History: The Challenge of Environmental Activism*. Montreal: Black Rose, 1998.

Romanyshyn, Robert D. "Dreams and the Anthropological Conditions of Dreaming." *Soundings* 60.3 (1977): 301–312.

———. "Science and Reality: Metaphors of Experience and Experience as Metaphorical." In *Metaphors of Consciousness*, ed. Ronald S. Valle and Rolf von Eckartsberg. New York: Plenum, 1981.

———. "Unconsciousness: Reflection and the Primacy of Perception." In *Phenomenology: Dialogues and Bridges*, ed. Ronald Bruzina and Bruce Wilshire. Albany: SUNY Press, 1982.

———. "The Despotic Eye: An Illustration of Metabletic Phenomenology and Its Implications." In *The Changing Reality of Modern Man: Essays in Honour of Jan Hendrik van den Berg*, ed. Dreyer Kruger. Pittsburgh: Duquesne University Press, 1985.

———. "The Human Body as Historical Matter and Cultural Symptom." In *Giving the Body Its Due*, ed. Maxine Sheets-Johnstone. Albany: SUNY Press, 1992.

Rorty, Richard. *Philosophy and the Mirror of Nature*. Princeton: Princeton University Press, 1979.

Rosen, Ruth. "Who Gets Polluted?: The Movement for Environmental Justice." *Dissent* (Spring 1994): 223–230.

Rosenfield, Lawrence W. "An Autopsy of the Rhetorical Tradition." In *The Prospect of Rhetoric*, ed. Lloyd F. Bitzer and Edwin Black. Englewood Cliffs, N.J.: Prentice-Hall, 1971.

Roszak, Theodore. *The Voice of the Earth: An Exploration of Ecopsychology*. New York: Simon & Schuster, 1992.

————. "The Greening of Psychology." *The Ecopsychology Newsletter* 1 (1994): 1.

————. "The Greening of Psychology: Exploring the Ecological Unconscious." *The Gestalt Journal* 18.1 (1995): 9–46.

————. "Where Psyche Meets Gaia." In *Ecopsychology: Restoring the Earth, Healing the Mind,* ed. Theodore Roszak, Mary E. Gomes, and Allen D. Kanner. San Francisco: Sierra Club, 1995.

Rothberg, Donald. "Buddhist Responses to Violence and War: Resources for Socially Engaged Spirituality." *Journal of Humanistic Psychology* 32.4 (1992): 41–75.

Rowe, Stan. *Home Place.* Edmonton: NeWest, 1990.

————. "The Mechanical and the Organic: Virtual Reality and Nature." *Trumpeter* 14.3 (1997): 154–158.

Royce, Joseph, and Leendert Mos. *Humanistic Psychology: Concepts and Criticisms.* New York: Plenum, 1981.

Russell, Constance L., Anne C. Bell, and Leesa K. Fawcett. "Navigating the Waters of Canadian Environmental Education." In *Progressive Educations in Canada,* ed. Tara Goldstein and David Selby. Toronto, Second Story, 1999. Pagination from draft manuscript.

Salleh, Ariel. "The Ecofeminism/Deep Ecology Debate: A Reply to Patriarchal Reason." *Environmental Ethics* 14 (1992): 195–216.

————. "Class, Race, and Gender Discourse in the Ecofeminism/Deep Ecology Debate." *Environmental Ethics* 15 (1993): 225–244.

Sampson, Edward E. "Cognitive Psychology as Ideology." *American Psychologist* 36.7 (1981): 730–743.

————. "The Debate on Individualism: Indigenous Psychologies of the Individual and Their Role in Personal and Societal Functioning." *American Psychologist* 43.1 (1988): 15–22.

————. "The Challenge of Social Change for Psychology." *American Psychologist* 44.6 (1989): 914–921.

Sanua, Victor D. "The Myth of Organicity of Mental Disorders." *The Humanistic Psychologist* 24 (1996): 55–78.

Sardello, Robert. *Love and the Soul: Creating a Future for Earth.* New York: HarperCollins, 1995.

Sass, Louis A. "Humanism, Hermeneutics, and the Concept of the Human Subject." In *Hermeneutics and Psychological Theory: Interpretive Perspectives on Personality, Psychotherapy, and Psychopathology,* ed. Stanley B. Messer, Louis A. Sass and Robert L. Woolfolk. New Brunswick: Rutgers University Press, 1988.

Scheff, T. J. "Reevaluation Counseling: Social Implications." *Journal of Humanistic Psychology* 12.1 (1972): 58–71.

————. *Catharsis in Healing, Ritual, and Drama.* Berkeley, Calif.: University of California Press, 1979.

————. "Toward Integration in the Social Psychology of Emotions." *Annual Review of Sociology* 9 (1983): 333–354.

Seamon, David. "The Phenomenological Contribution to Environmental Psychology." *Journal of Environmental Psychology* 2 (1982): 119–140.

———, and Robert Mugerauer, eds. *Dwelling, Place and Environment: Towards a Phenomenology of Person and World.* Dordrecht: Martinus Nijhoff, 1985.

Searles, Harold F. *The Nonhuman Environment: In Normal Development and in Schizophrenia.* New York: International Universities Press, 1960.

———. "The Role of the Nonhuman Environment." *Landscape* 11 (1961–62): 31–34.

———. "Unconscious Processes in Relation to the Environmental Crisis." *Psychoanalytic Review* 59 (1972): 361–374.

Seed, John, et al., eds. *Thinking Like a Mountain: Towards a Council of All Beings.* Philadelphia: New Society, 1988.

Sessions, George. "Paul Shepard: Ecological Elder." In *The Company of Others: Essays in Celebration of Paul Shepard,* ed. Max Oelschlaeger. Durago, Colo.: Kivakí, 1995.

Shagbark Hickory. "Environmental Etiquette/Environmental Practice: American Indian Challenges to Mainstream Environmental Ethics." In *The Company of Others: Essays in Celebration of Paul Shepard,* ed. Max Oelschlaeger. Durago, Colo.: Kivakí, 1995.

Shapiro, Elan. "Restoring Habitats, Communities, and Souls." In *Ecopsychology: Restoring the Earth, Healing the Mind,* ed. Theodore Roszak, Mary E. Gomes, and Allen D. Kanner. San Francisco: Sierra Club, 1995.

Sheehan, Thomas. "Reading a Life: Heidegger and Hard Times." In *The Cambridge Companion to Heidegger,* ed. Charles Guignon. Cambridge: Cambridge University Press, 1993.

Shepard, Paul. "Introduction: Ecology and Man—a Viewpoint." In *The Subversive Science: Essays Toward an Ecology of Man,* ed. Paul Shepard and Daniel McKinley. Boston: Houghton Mifflin, 1969.

———. *The Tender Carnivore and the Sacred Game.* New York: Charles Scribner's Sons, 1973.

———. "Place in American Culture." *The North American Review* 262 (1977): 22–32.

———. "The Conflict of Ideology and Ecology." In *The Search for Absolute Value in a Changing World.* New York: International Cultural Foundation, 1978. Vol. 1.

———. *Thinking Animals.* New York: Viking, 1978.

———. *Nature and Madness.* San Francisco: Sierra Club, 1982.

———. "The Ark of the Mind." *Parabola* 8.2 (1983): 54–59.

———. "Searching Out Kindred Spirits." *Parabola* 16.2 (1991), 26–27.

———. "A Post-Historic Primitivism." In *The Wilderness Condition,* ed. Max Oelschlaeger. Washington, D.C.: Island, 1992.

———. "On Animal Friends." In *The Biophilia Hypothesis,* ed. Stephen R. Kellert and Edward O. Wilson. Washington, D.C.: Island, 1993.

———. "The Unreturning Arrow." (Interviewed by Jonathon White.) In *Talking on the Water: Conversations About Nature and Creativity,* ed. Jonathon White. San Francisco: Sierra Club, 1994.

———. "Nature and Madness." In *Ecopsychology: Restoring the Earth, Healing the Mind,* ed.

Theodore Roszak, Mary E. Gomes, and Allen D. Kanner. San Francisco: Sierra Club, 1995.

———. Interviewed by Derrick Jensen. In *Listening to the Land: Conversations About Nature, Culture, and Eros,* ed. Derrick Jensen. San Francisco: Sierra Club, 1995.

———. "Virtual Hunting Reality in the Forests of Simulacra." In *Reinventing Nature?: Responses to Postmodern Deconstruction,* ed. Michael E. Soulé and Gary Lease. Washington, D.C.: Island, 1995.

———. *The Only World We've Got.* San Francisco: Sierra Club, 1996.

———. *The Others: How Animals Made Us Human.* Washington, D.C.: Island, 1996.

———. *Traces of an Omnivore.* Washington, D.C.: Island, 1996.

———. *Coming Home to the Pleistocene.* Washington, D.C.: Island, 1998.

———, and Barry Sanders. *The Sacred Paw: The Bear in Nature, Myth, and Literature.* New York: Viking, 1985.

Shields, Katrina. *In the Tiger's Mouth: An Empowerment Guide for Social Action.* Philadelphia: New Society, 1994.

Simms, Eva-Maria. "The Infant's Experience of the World: Stern, Merleau-Ponty and the Phenomenology of the Preverbal Self." *Humanistic Psychologist* 21 (1993): 26–40.

———. "Phenomenology of Child Development and the Postmodern Self: Continuing the Dialogue with Johnson." *The Humanistic Psychologist* 22 (1994): 228–235.

Slotkin, Richard. "Dreams and Genocide: The American Myth of Regeneration Through Violence." *Journal of Popular Culture* 5.1 (1971): 38–59.

Slovic, Scott. "Epistemology and Politics in American Nature Writing: Embedded Rhetoric and Discrete Rhetoric." In *Green Culture: Environmental Rhetoric in Contemporary America,* ed. Carl G. Herndl and Stuart C. Brown. Madison: University of Wisconsin Press, 1996.

Smith, Laurence D. "Metaphors of Knowledge and Behavior in the Behaviorist Tradition." In *Metaphors in the History of Psychology,* ed. David E. Leary. Cambridge: Cambridge University Press, 1990.

Snyder, Gary. *Earth Household.* New York: New Directions, 1957.

———. *Turtle Island.* New York: New Directions, 1974.

———. *The Real Work: Interviews & Talks, 1964–1979.* New York: New Directions, 1980.

———. Interviewed by Catherine Ingram. In *In the Footsteps of Gandhi: Conversations with Spiritual Activists,* ed. Catherine Ingram. Berkeley, Calif.: Parallax, 1990.

———. *The Practice of the Wild.* San Francisco: North Point, 1990.

———. *No Nature.* New York: Pantheon, 1992.

———. "Hanging Out With Raven." (Interviewed by Jonathon White.) In *Talking on the Water: Conversations About Nature and Creativity,* ed. Jonathon White. San Francisco: Sierra Club, 1994.

———. *A Place in Space: Ethics, Aesthetics, and Watersheds.* Washington, D.C.: Counterpoint, 1995.

Sperling, Micheal B, and William H. Berman, eds. *Attachment in Adults: Clinical and Developmental Perspectives.* New York: Guilford, 1994.

Spiegelberg, Herbert. *The Phenomenological Movement,* 3rd ed. The Hague: Martinus Nijhoff, 1984.

Steiner, George. *Heidegger.* London: Fontana, 1978.

Steed, Judy. *Our Little Secret: Confronting Child Sexual Abuse in Canada.* Toronto: Vintage, 1995.

Stern, Paul C. "Psychological Dimensions of Global Environmental Change." *Annual Review of Psychology* 43 (1992): 269–302.

Stettbacher, J. Konrad. *Making Sense of Suffering.* New York: Meridian, 1990.

Stewart, David, and Algis Mickunus. *Exploring Phenomenology.* 2nd ed. Athens: Ohio University Press, 1990.

Stoehr, Taylor. "Paul Goodman and the Political Dimensions of Gestalt Therapy." *The Gestalt Journal* 16.1 (1993): 55–90.

Stokols, Daniel, and Irwin Altman, eds. *Handbook of Environmental Psychology.* Malabar, Fla.: Krieger, 1991.

Storr, Anthony. "Man's Relationship with the Natural World." *The North American Review* 259 (1974): 18–26.

Strong, David. "Wilderness' Call for Openness." *Trumpeter* 9.1 (1992): 10–14.

———. *Crazy Mountains: Learning from Wilderness to Weigh Technology.* Albany: SUNY Press, 1995.

Suzuki, D. T. "The Role of Nature in Zen Buddhism." In *Zen Buddhism: Selected Writings of D. T. Suzuki,* ed. William Barrett. Garden City, N.Y.: Doubleday Anchor, 1956.

Tandon, S. N. "Dharma—Its Definition and Universal Application." In *Dharma—Its True Nature.* An International Seminar (May 6–7, 1995), Dhamma Giri, Igatpuri, India: Vipassana Research Institute, 1995.

Taylor, Charles. "Understanding in Human Science." *Review of Metaphysics* 34 (1980): 25–38.

———. "Interpretation and the Sciences of Man." In *Interpretive Social Science: A Second Look,* ed. Paul Rabinow and William M. Sullivan. Berkeley, Calif.: University of California Press, 1987.

———. "The Moral Topography of the Self." In *Hermeneutics and Psychological Theory: Interpretive Perspectives on Personality, Psychotherapy, and Psychopathology,* ed. Stanley B. Messer, Louis A. Sass and Robert L. Woolfolk. New Brunswick: Rutgers University Press, 1988.

———. *Sources of the Self: The Making of the Modern Identity.* Cambridge, Mass.: Harvard University Press, 1989.

———. *The Malaise of Modernity.* Concord, Ont.: House of Anansi, 1991.

———. "Heidegger, Language, and Ecology." In *Heidegger: A Critical Reader,* ed. Hubert L. Dreyfus and Harrison Hall. Cambridge, Mass.: Blackwell, 1992.

"The School of Lost Borders." Pamphlet. P.O. Box 55, Big Pine, Calif., 93513, U.S.A.

"The Three Gorges: The Case for Development." *Time* (April 19, 1991): 51.

Thévenaz, Pierre. *What Is Phenomenology? And Other Essays.* Chicago: Quadrangle, 1962.

Thomas, Keith. *Man and the Natural World.* London: Penguin, 1983.

Thomashow, Mitchell. *Ecological Identity: Becoming a Reflective Environmentalist.* Cambridge, Mass.: MIT Press, 1995.

Thomson, William Irwin. "Mind Jazz." (Interviewed by David Cayley, et al.) *Journal of Wild Culture* 2.4 (1990): 10–18.

Thorne, F. C. "Critique of Recent Developments in Personality Counselling Therapy." *Journal of Clinical Psychology* 13 (1957): 234–244.

Thornton, James. "The State of Environmentalists: A Report to the Nathan Cummings Foundation and the Natural Resources Defence Council." 1993.

Tokar, Brian. *Earth for Sale: Reclaiming Ecology in the Age of Corporate Greenwash.* Boston: South End, 1997.

The Trumpeter 12:3 (1995). Issue on "Culture, Bioregionalism, Economics & the Deep Ecology Movement."

Trungpa, Chogyam. *Shambhala: The Sacred Path of the Warrior.* New York: Bantam, 1984.

Turnbull, Colin M. *The Human Cycle.* New York: Simon and Schuster, 1983.

Turner, Victor. *The Ritual Process: Structure and Anti-Structure.* Hawthorne, N.Y.: Aldine de Gruyter, 1995.

Valle, Ronald S., and Rolf von Eckartsberg, eds. *The Metaphors of Consciousness.* New York: Plenum, 1981.

Van den Berg, J. H. *The Changing Nature of Man.* New York: Plenum, 1961.

———. *Things: Four Metabletic Reflections.* Pittsburgh: Duquesne University Press, 1970.

———. "What Is Psychotherapy." *Humanitas* 7.3 (1971): 321–370.

———. *A Different Existence: Principles of Phenomenological Psychology.* Pittsburgh: Duquesne University Press, 1972.

Van der Kolk, Bessel A., Alexander C. McFarlane, and Lars Weisaeth, eds. *Traumatic Stress: The Effects of Overwhelming Experience on Mind, Body, and Society.* New York: Guilford, 1996.

Van Gennep, Arnold. *The Rites of Passage.* London: Routledge and Kegan Paul, 1960.

Veitch, Russell, and Daniel Arkkelin. *Environmental Psychology: An Interdisciplinary Perspective.* Englewood Cliffs, N.J.: Prentice Hall, 1995.

Von Franz, Marie-Louise. "The Process of Individuation." In *Man and His Symbols,* ed. C. G. Jung. New York: Dell, 1964.

Vycinas, Vincent. *Earth and Gods: An Introduction to the Philosophy of Martin Heidegger.* The Hague: Martinus Nijhoff, 1961.

Wallace, Karl R. "The Fundamentals of Rhetoric." In *The Prospect of Rhetoric,* ed. Lloyd F. Bitzer and Edwin Black. Englewood Cliffs, N.J.: Prentice-Hall, 1971.

Wallulis, Jerald. "Carrying Forward: Gadamer and Gendlin on History, Language, and the Body." In *Language Beyond Postmodernism: Saying and Thinking in Gendlin's Philosophy,* ed. David Micheal Levin. Evanston, Ill.: Northwestern University Press, 1997.

Warren, Karen J. "The Power and Promise of Ecological Feminism." In *Environmental Philosophy: From Animal Rights to Radical Ecology,* ed. Michael E. Zimmerman. Englewood Cliffs: Prentice Hall, 1993.

Watts, Alan. *Psychotherapy East and West.* New York: Vintage, 1961.

Webster's Unabridged Dictionary of the English Language. New York: Portland House, 1989.

Weekley, Ernest. *An Etymology Dictionary of Modern English.* London: John Murray, 1921.

Welwood, John. "Meditation and the Unconscious: A New Perspective." *The Journal of Transpersonal Psychology* 9.1 (1977): 1–26.

Wertz, Frederick J., ed. *The Humanistic Movement: Recovering the Person in Psychology.* Lake Worth, Fla.: Gardner Press, 1994.

"What's Wrong with the 'Mental Health' System: And What Can Be Done About It." A Draft Policy Prepared for the Re-evaluation Counseling Communities. P.O. Box 2081, Main Office Station, Seattle, Wash., 98111, U.S.A.: Rational Island Publishers, 1991.

Wheeler, Gordon. *Gestalt Reconsidered: A New Approach to Contact and Resistance.* New York: Gardner Press, 1991.

———. "Self and Shame: A New Paradigm for Psychotherapy." In *The Voice of Shame: Silence and Connection in Psychotherapy,* ed. Robert G. Lee and Gordon Wheeler. San Francisco: Jossey-Bass, 1996.

———, and Daniel Jones. "Finding Our Sons: A Male-Male Gestalt." In *The Voice of Shame: Silence and Connection in Psychotherapy,* ed. Robert G. Lee and Gordon Wheeler. San Francisco: Jossey-Bass, 1996.

Williams, Raymond. "Ideas of Nature." In *Ecology, The Shaping Enquiry,* ed. Jonathan Benthall. London: Longman, 1972.

———. *Keywords.* London: Fontana Press, 1983.

Williams, Terry Tempest. Interviewed by Derrick Jensen. In *Listening to the Land: Conversations About Nature, Culture, and Eros,* ed. Derrick Jensen. San Francisco: Sierra Club, 1995.

Wilson, E. O. *Biophilia.* Cambridge, Mass.: Harvard University Press, 1984.

Winner, Langdon. "Living in Electronic Space." In *Lifeworld and Technology,* ed. Timothy Casey and Lester Embree. Washington, D.C.: The Center for Advanced Research in Phenomenology and University Press of America, 1989.

Winnicott, D. W. *Playing and Reality.* London: Routledge, 1971.

———. *The Maturational Processes and the Facilitating Environment.* London: Karnac, 1990.

Worster, Donald. *Nature's Economy: A History of Ecological Ideas.* Cambridge: Cambridge University Press, 1977.

———. "The Ecology of Order and Chaos." *Environmental History Review* 14.1–2 (1990): 1–18.

———. "Seeing beyond Culture." *The Journal of American History* 76.4 (1990): 1142–47.

———. "Nature and the Disorder of History." In *Reinventing Nature?: Responses to Postmodern Deconstruction,* ed. Michael E. Soulé and Gary Lease. Washington, D.C.: Island, 1995.

Wright, James M. "Cauldron-Born: Speculations on an Old Welsh Vision Quest." Unpublished manuscript, an edited version of which was published as "A Cauldron-

Born Quest: Speculations on European Vision Quest Rituals." *Shaman's Drum* 46 (1997): 51–59.

―――. *The Bones of Metamorphosis: A Quest for the Old Visionary Rituals of Europe.* Rockport, Mass.: Unpublished manuscript, 1998.

Yalom, Irvin D. *Existential Psychotherapy.* New York: Basic Books, 1980.

Yontef, Gary M. *Awareness, Dialogue & Process: Essays on Gestalt Therapy.* Highland, N.Y.: Gestalt Journal Press, 1993.

Young, David E., and Jean-Guy Goulet, eds. *Being Changed: The Anthropology of Extraordinary Experience.* Peterborough, Ont.: Broadview, 1994.

Zimmerman, Michael E. "Marx and Heidegger on the Technological Domination of Nature." *Philosophy Today* 23 (1979): 99–112.

―――, ed. *Environmental Philosophy: From Animal Rights to Radical Ecology.* Englewood Cliffs, N.J.: Prentice Hall, 1993.

―――. *Contesting Earth's Future: Radical Ecology and Postmodernity.* Berkeley, Calif.: University of California Press, 1994.

INDEX